Delicious IN DUNGEON

RYOKO KUI

10

Delicious IN DUNGEON

10

Contents

Chapter 63 **CONFIT** ———————————————— 005

Chapter 64 **RABBITS -1-** ———————————————— 035

Chapter 65 **RABBITS -2-** ———————————————— 059

Chapter 66 **CURRY -1-** ———————————————— 095

Chapter 67 **CURRY -2-** ———————————————— 123

Chapter 68 **SISSEL -1-** ———————————————— 155

Chapter 69 **SISSEL -2-** ———————————————— 191

Bonus   **MISCELLANEOUS MONSTER TALES -10-** — 222

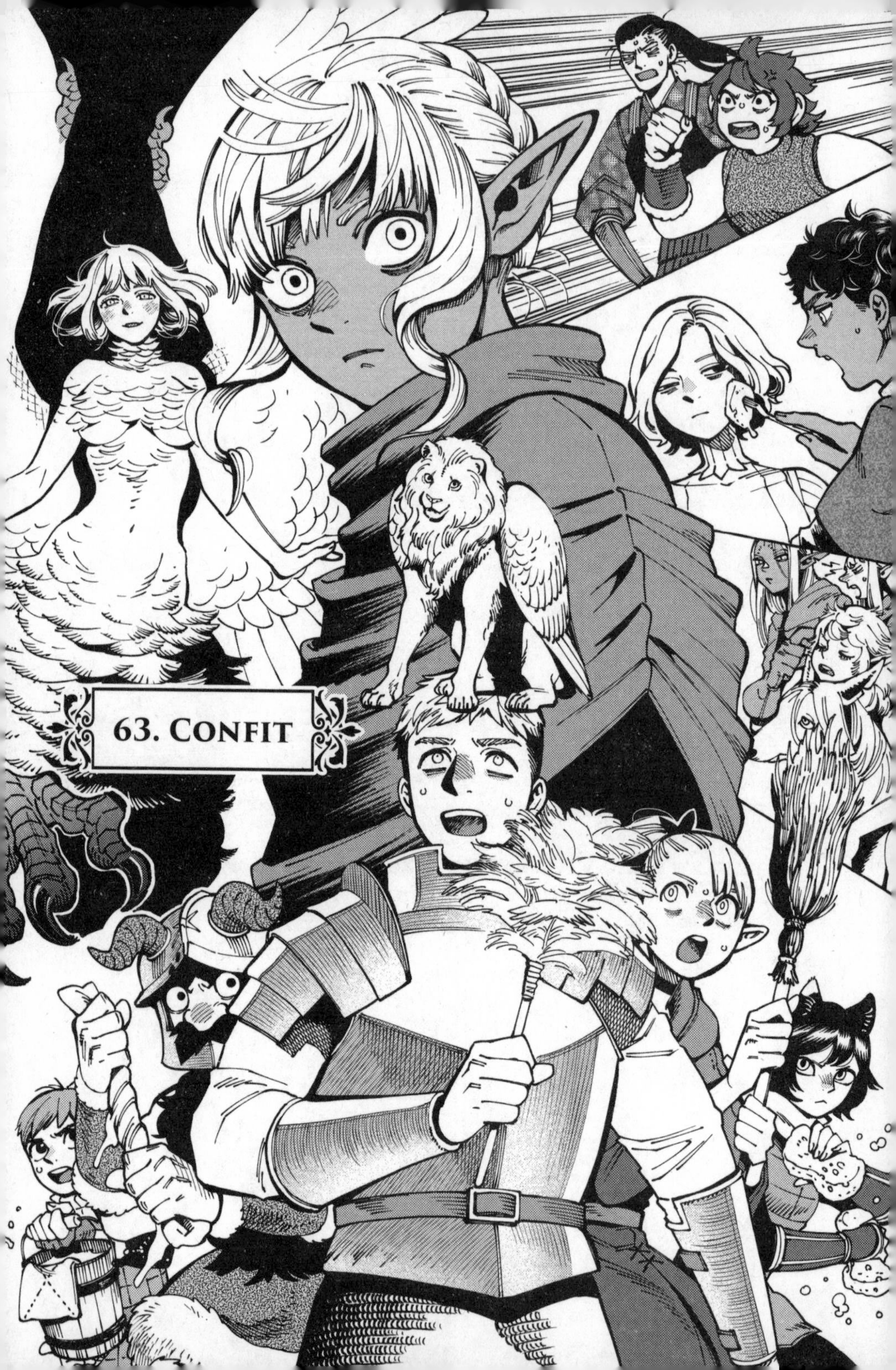
63. CONFIT

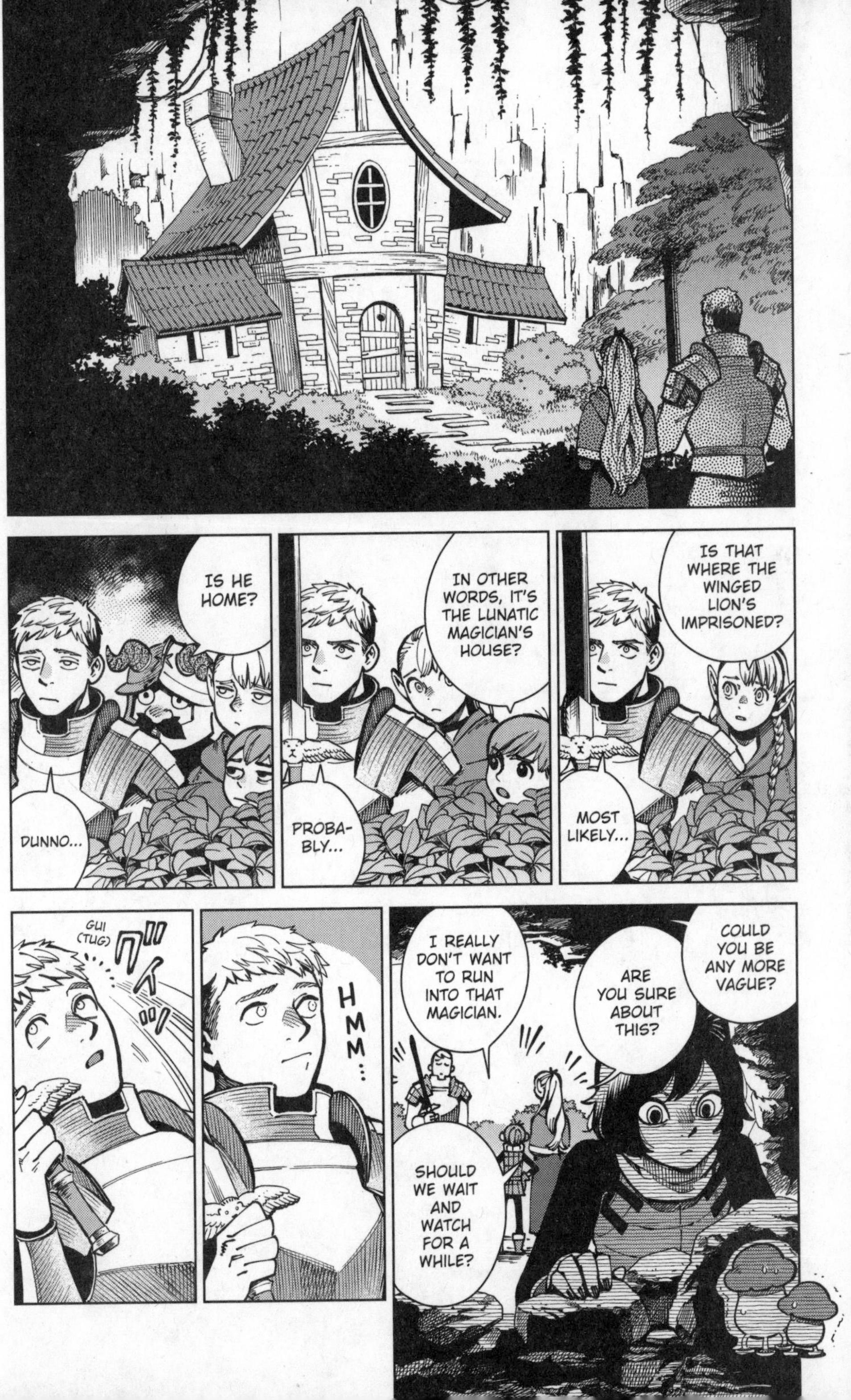
IS THAT WHERE THE WINGED LION'S IMPRISONED?
MOST LIKELY...
IN OTHER WORDS, IT'S THE LUNATIC MAGICIAN'S HOUSE?
PROBA-BLY...
IS HE HOME?
DUNNO...
COULD YOU BE ANY MORE VAGUE?
ARE YOU SURE ABOUT THIS?
I REALLY DON'T WANT TO RUN INTO THAT MAGICIAN.
SHOULD WE WAIT AND WATCH FOR A WHILE?
HMM...
GUI (TUG)

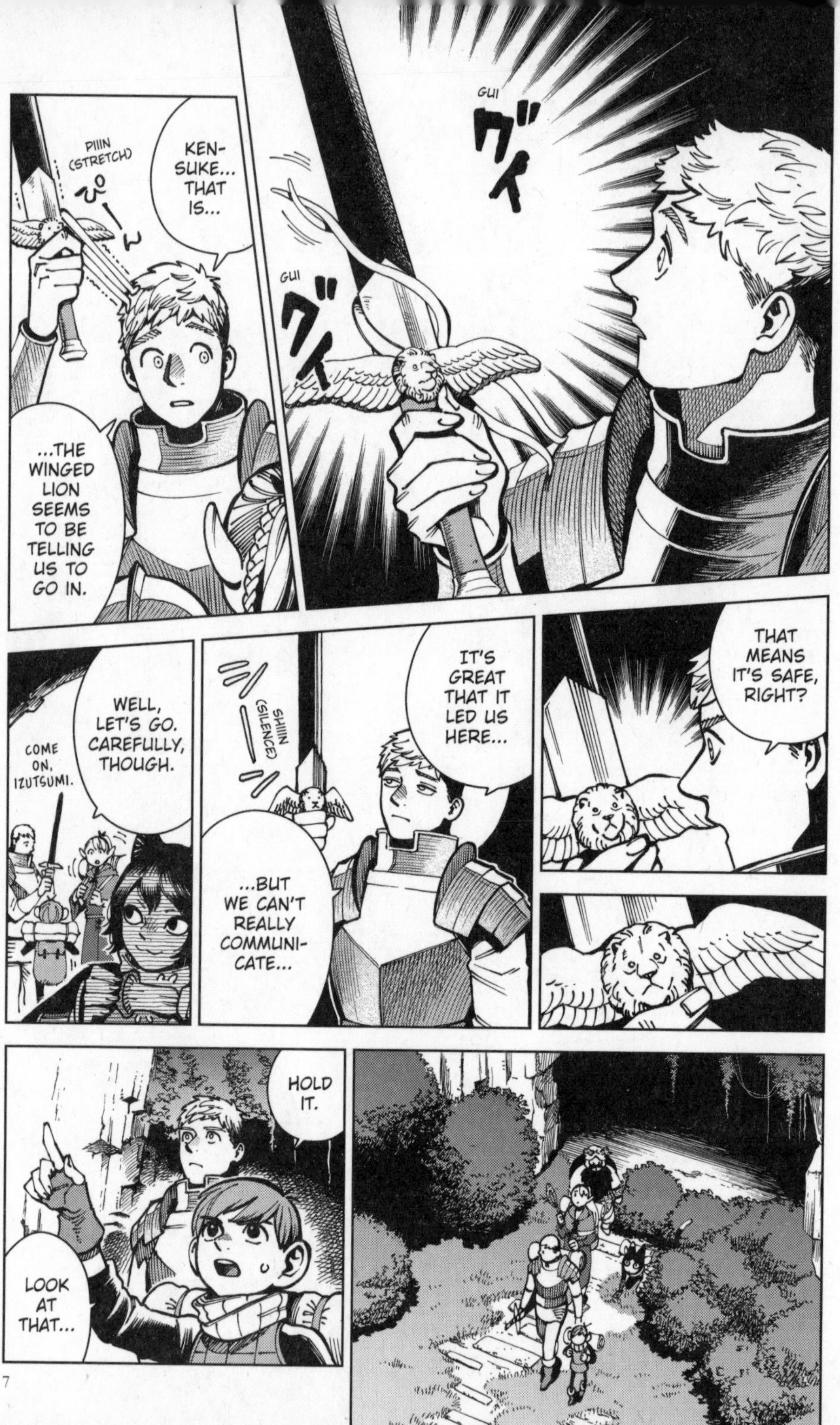
GUI
グイ
GUI
グイ
KEN-SUKE... THAT IS...
PIIIN (STRETCH)
ぴーん
...THE WINGED LION SEEMS TO BE TELLING US TO GO IN.
THAT MEANS IT'S SAFE, RIGHT?
IT'S GREAT THAT IT LED US HERE...
SHIIIN (SILENCE)
...BUT WE CAN'T REALLY COMMUNICATE...
WELL, LET'S GO. CAREFULLY, THOUGH.
COME ON, IZUTSUMI.
HOLD IT.
LOOK AT THAT...

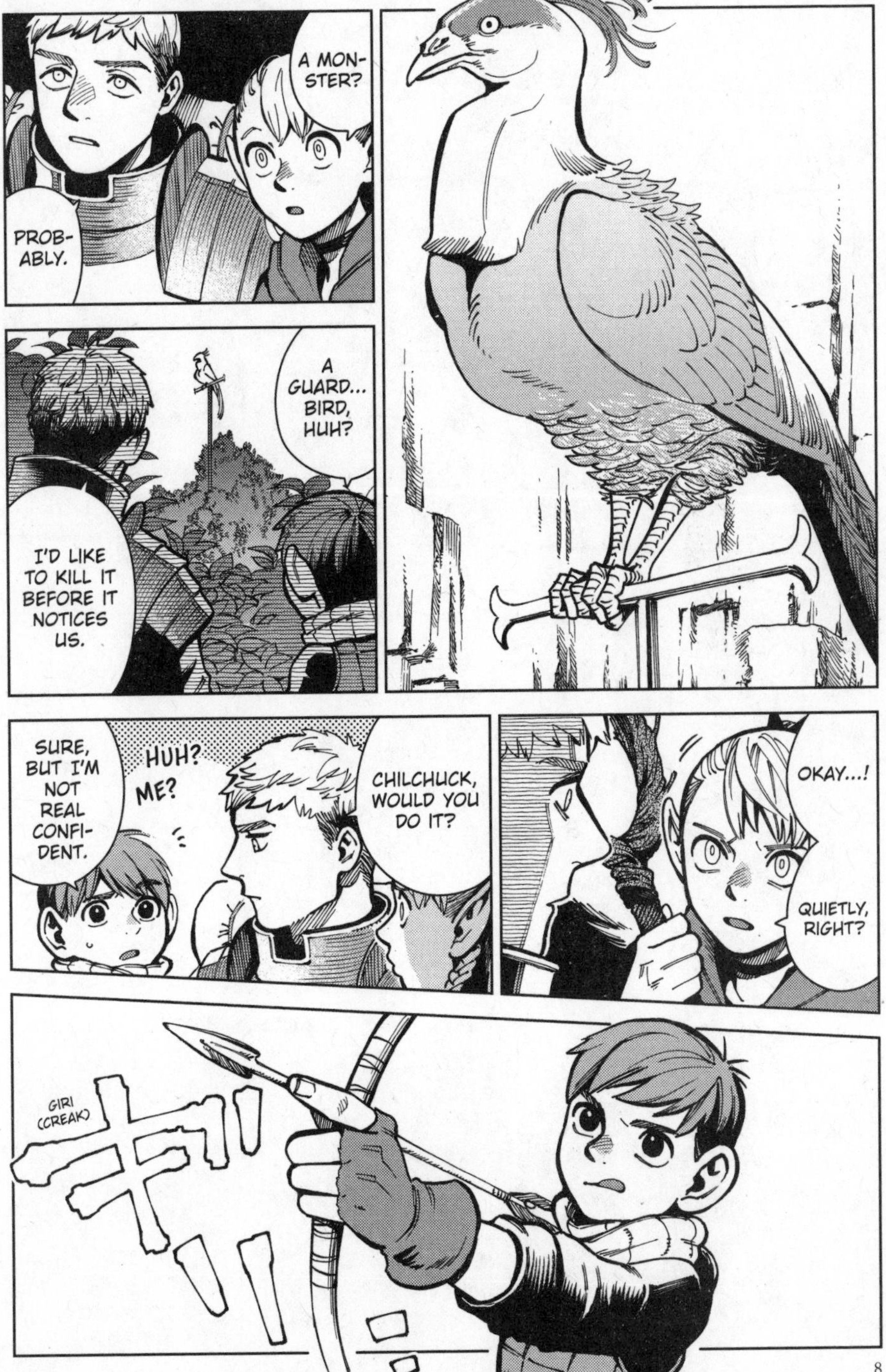
A MON-STER?
PROB-ABLY.
A GUARD... BIRD, HUH?
I'D LIKE TO KILL IT BEFORE IT NOTICES US.
OKAY...!
QUIETLY, RIGHT?
CHILCHUCK, WOULD YOU DO IT?
HUH? ME?
SURE, BUT I'M NOT REAL CONFI-DENT.
GIRI (CREAK)

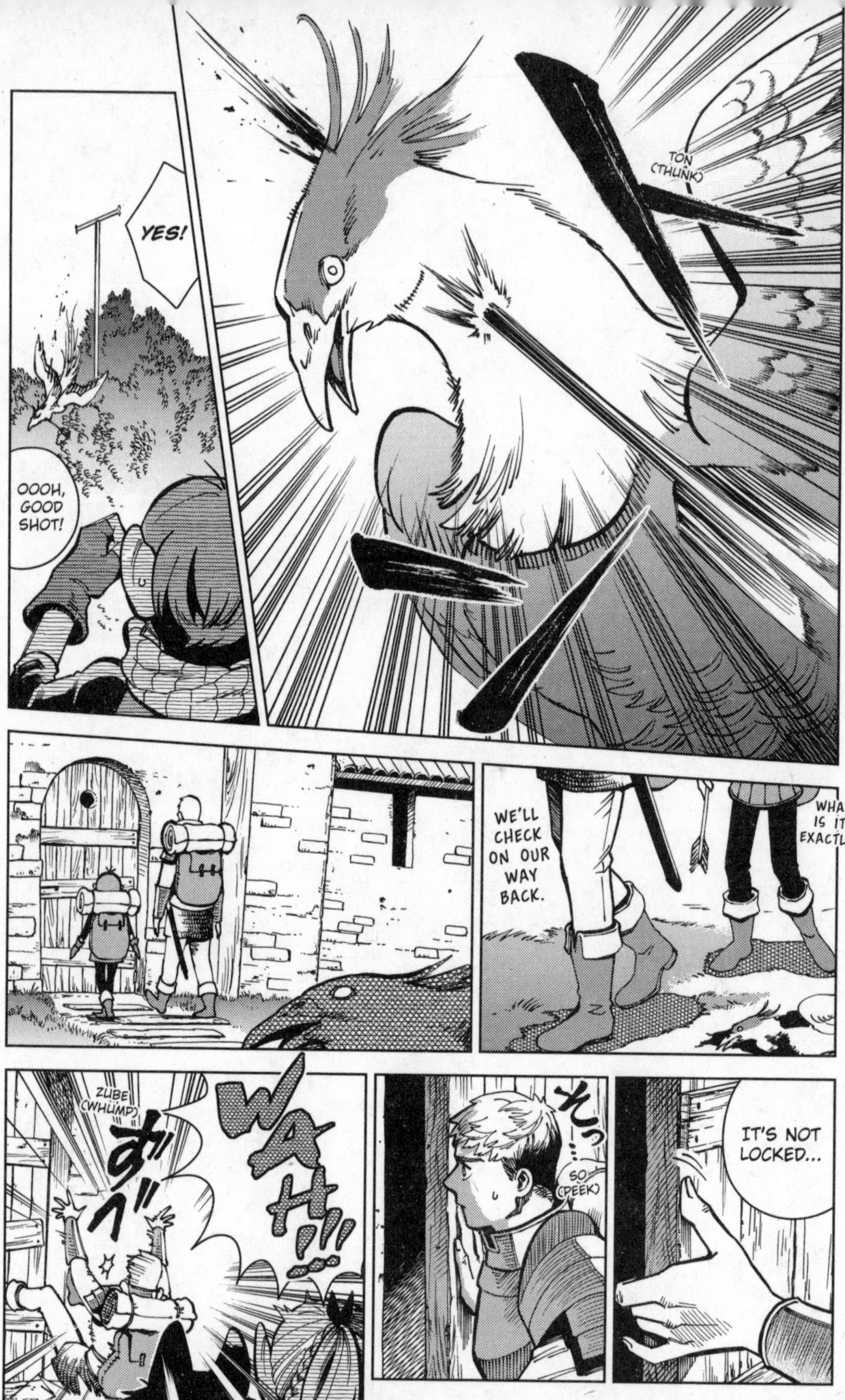
TON (THUNK)
YES!
OOOH, GOOD SHOT!
WHAT IS IT, EXACTLY?
WE'LL CHECK ON OUR WAY BACK.
IT'S NOT LOCKED...
そっ
SO (PEEK)
WAAH!!
ZUBE (WHÜMP)

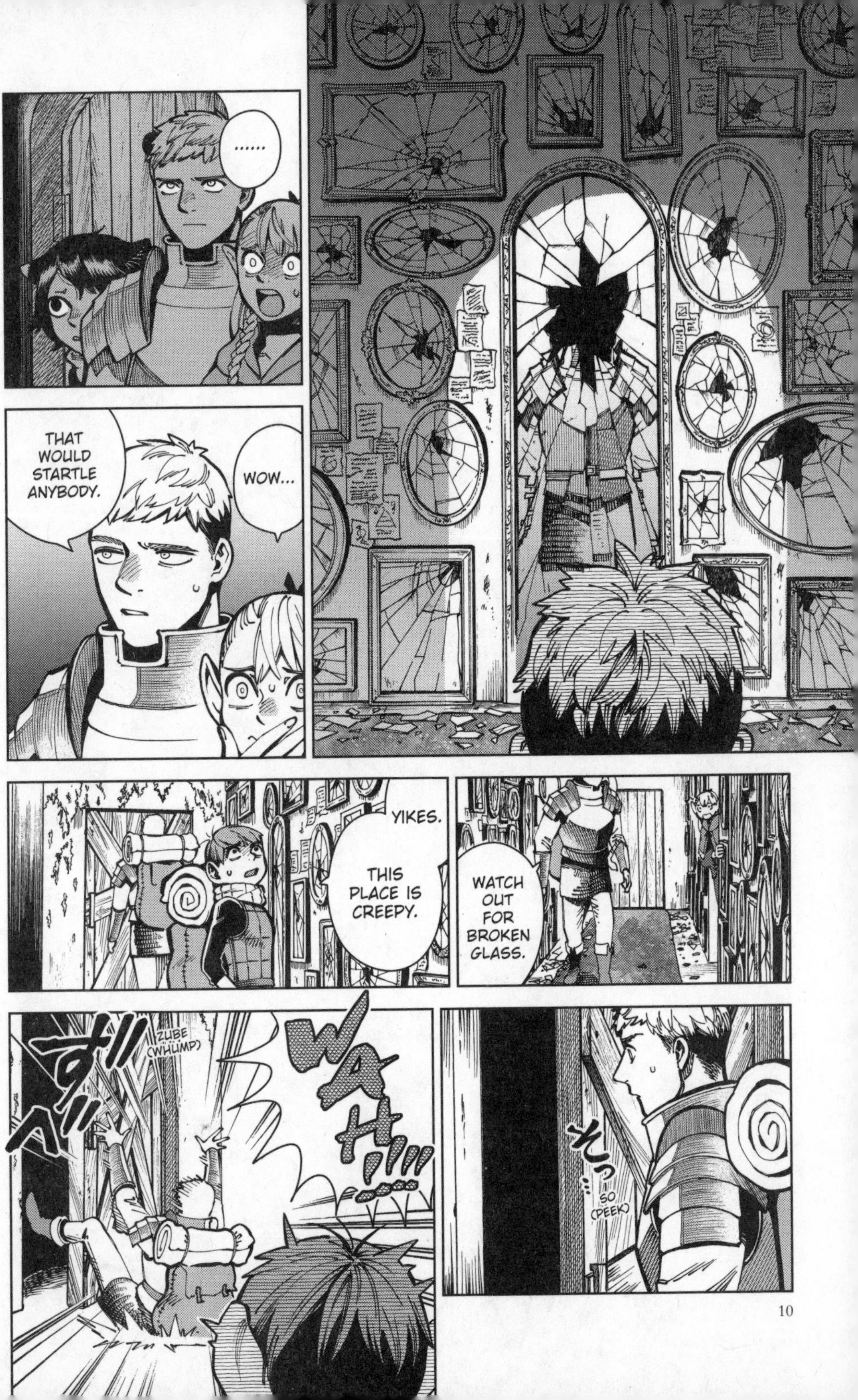
......
WOW...
THAT WOULD STARTLE ANYBODY.
WATCH OUT FOR BROKEN GLASS.
YIKES.
THIS PLACE IS CREEPY.
そっ
SO (PEEK)
WAH!!!!
ずべ
ZUBE (WHUMP)

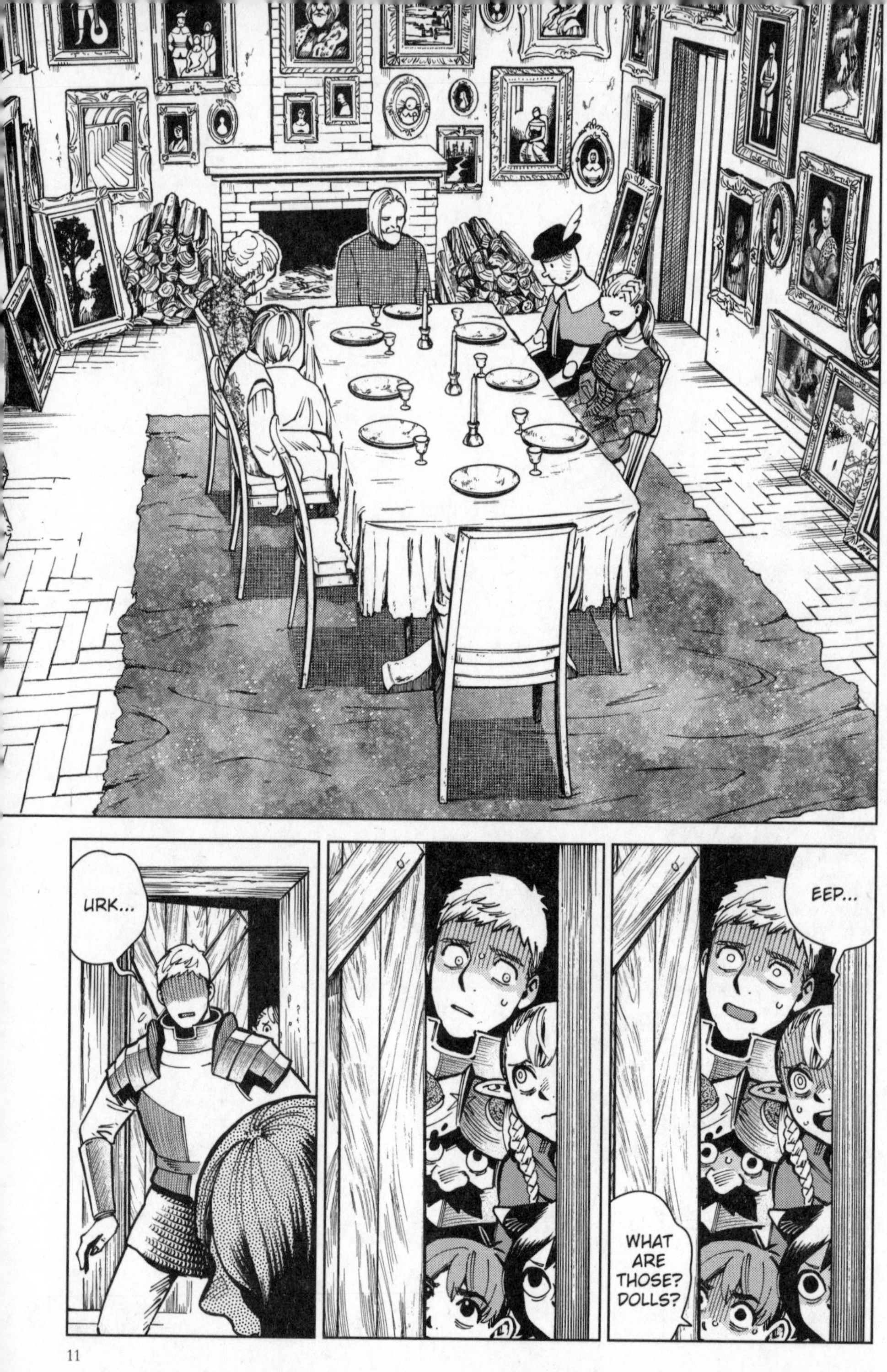
EEP...
WHAT ARE THOSE? DOLLS?
URK...

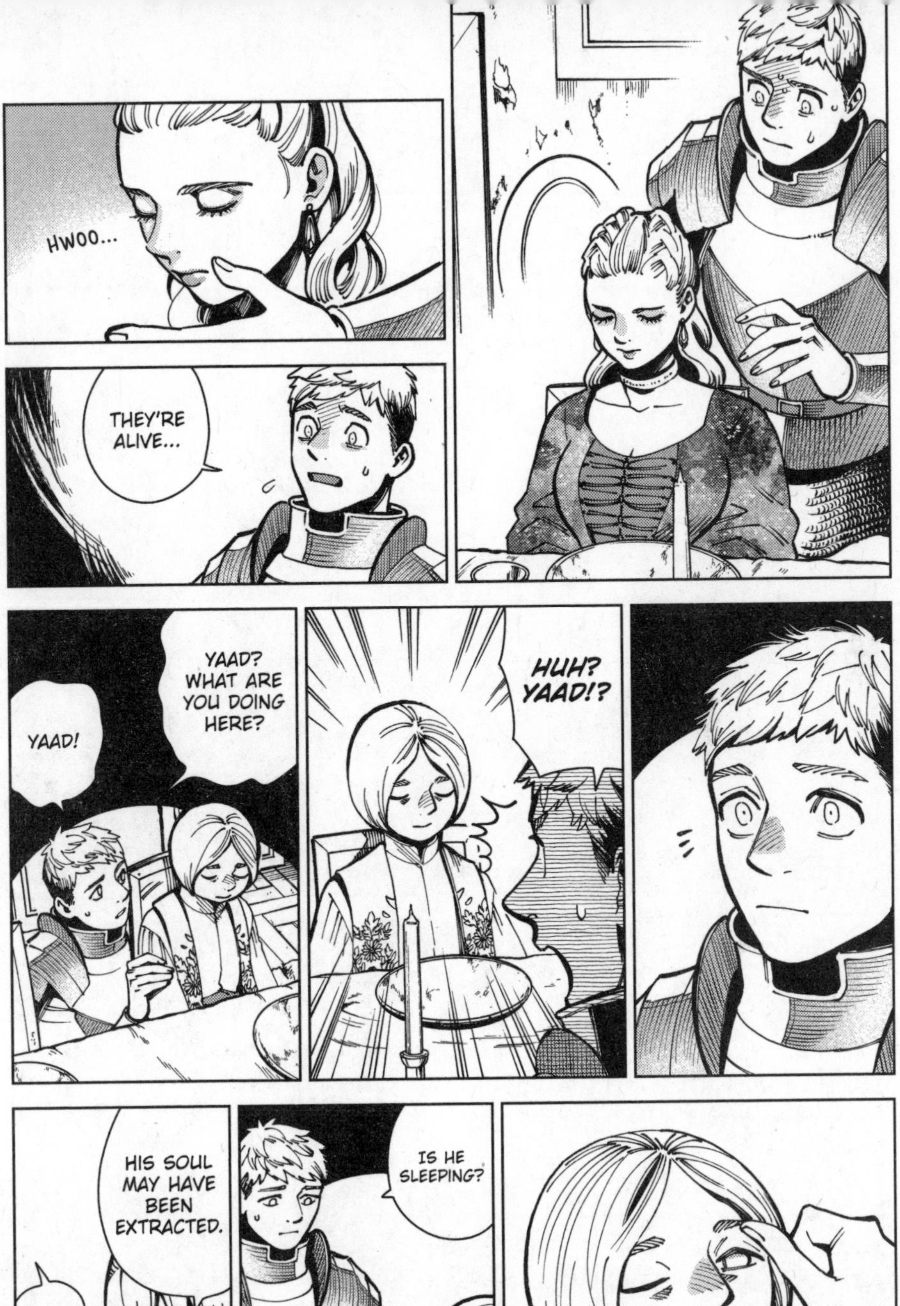
HWOO...
THEY'RE ALIVE...
HUH? YAAD!?
YAAD? WHAT ARE YOU DOING HERE?
YAAD!
IS HE SLEEPING?
HE'S...
HIS SOUL MAY HAVE BEEN EXTRACTED.
HIS SOUL !?

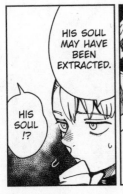

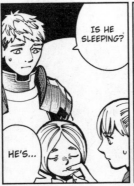

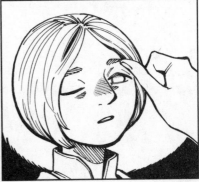

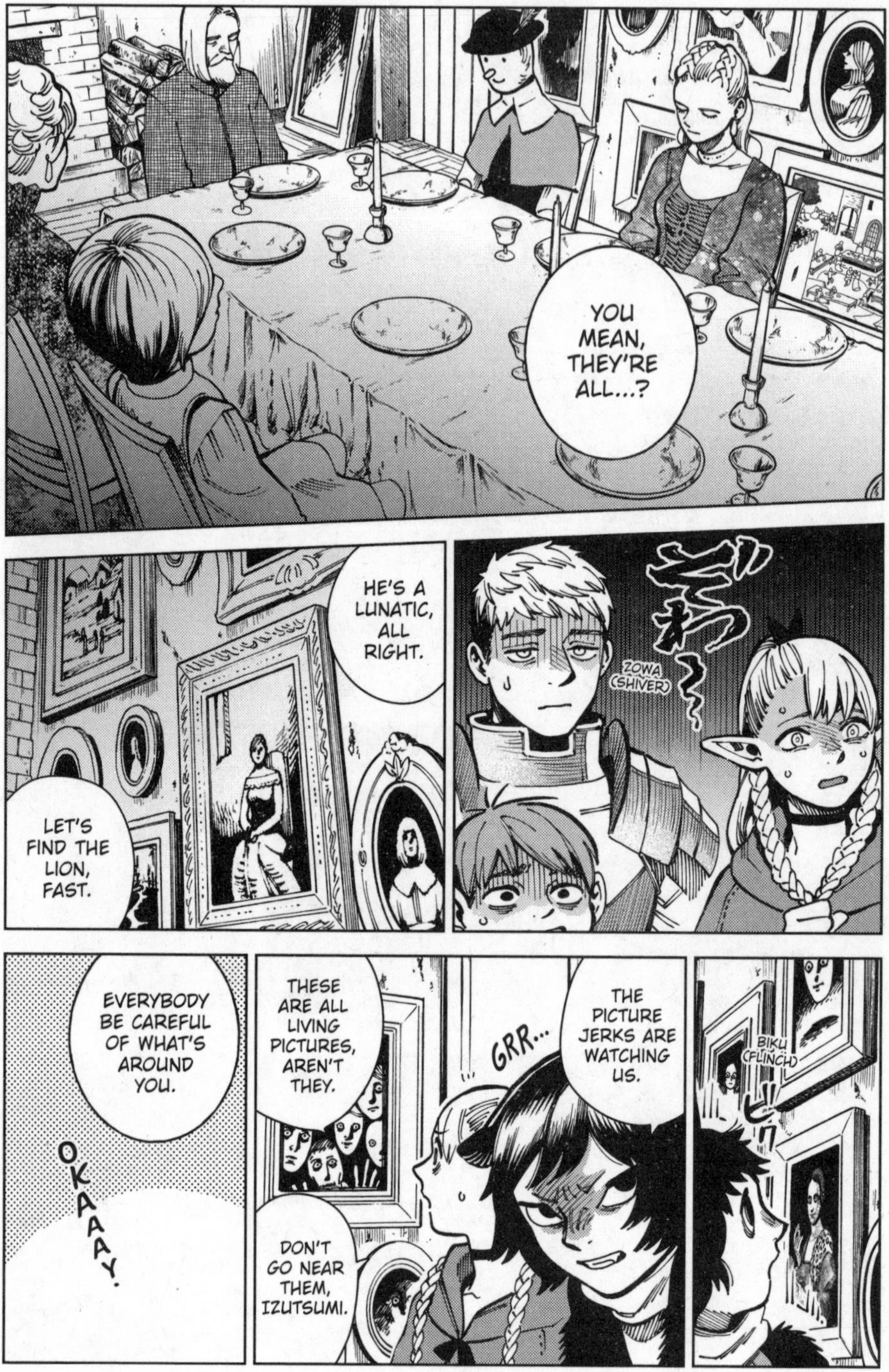
YOU MEAN, THEY'RE ALL...?
ZOWA (SHIVER)
HE'S A LUNATIC, ALL RIGHT.
LET'S FIND THE LION, FAST.
BIKU (FLINCH)
THE PICTURE JERKS ARE WATCHING US.
GRR...
THESE ARE ALL LIVING PICTURES, AREN'T THEY.
DON'T GO NEAR THEM, IZUTSUMI.
EVERYBODY BE CAREFUL OF WHAT'S AROUND YOU.
OKAAAY.

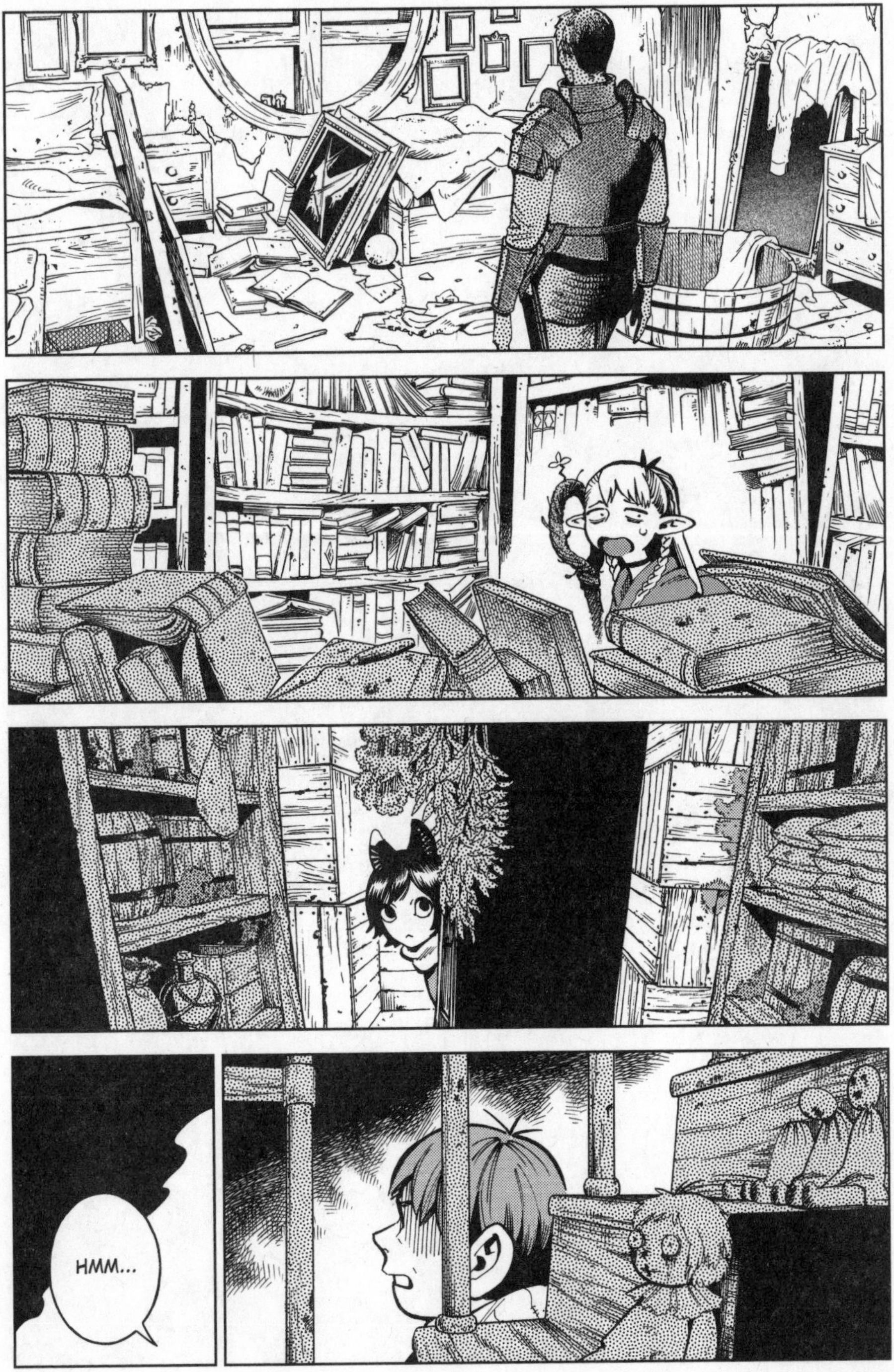
HMM...

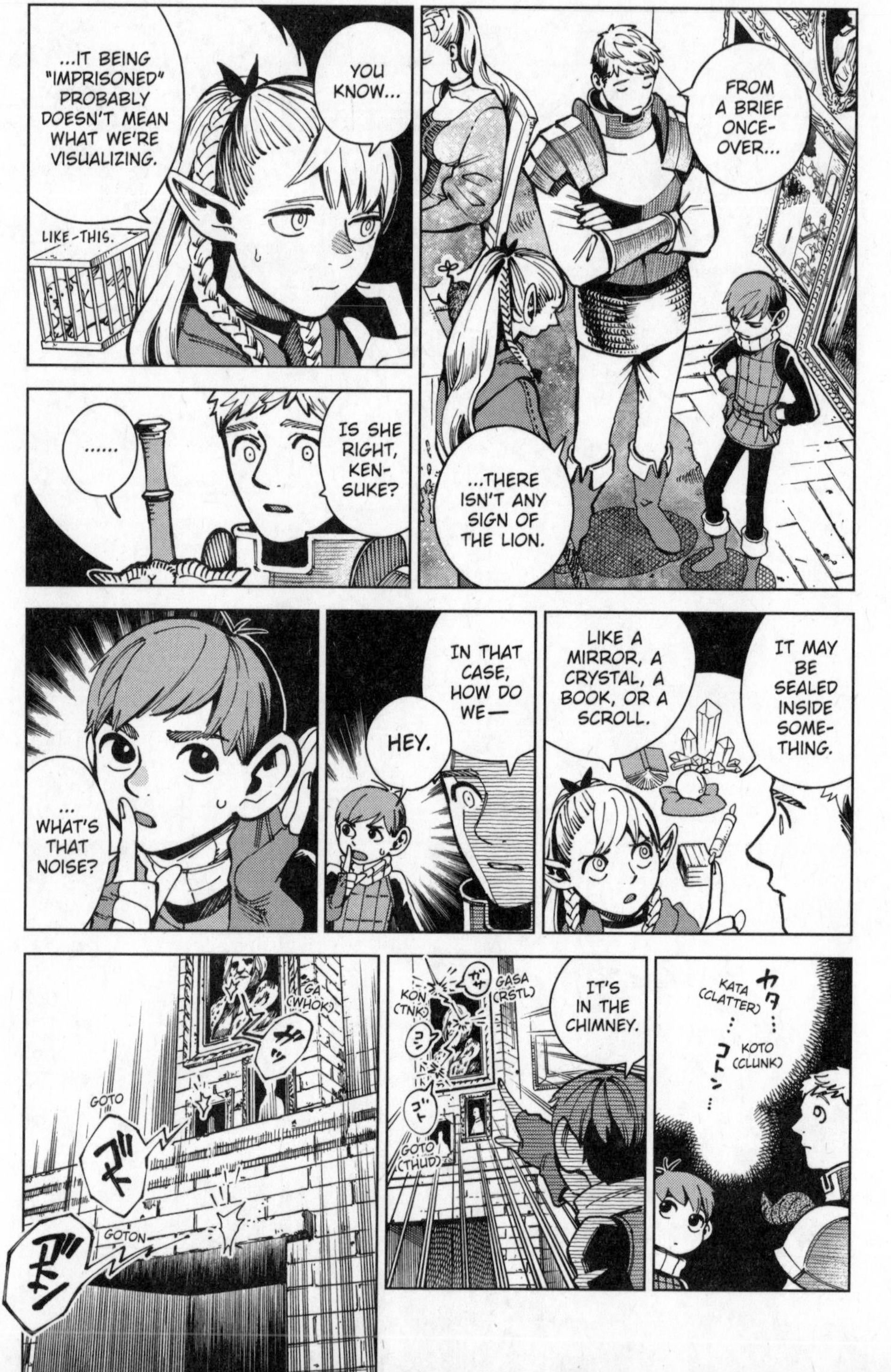
FROM A BRIEF ONCE-OVER...
...THERE ISN'T ANY SIGN OF THE LION.
YOU KNOW...
...IT BEING "IMPRISONED" PROBABLY DOESN'T MEAN WHAT WE'RE VISUALIZING.
LIKE-THIS.
IS SHE RIGHT, KENSUKE?
......
IT MAY BE SEALED INSIDE SOMETHING.
LIKE A MIRROR, A CRYSTAL, A BOOK, OR A SCROLL.
IN THAT CASE, HOW DO WE—
HEY.
...WHAT'S THAT NOISE?
KATA (CLATTER)
KOTO (CLUNK)
IT'S IN THE CHIMNEY.
GASA (RSTL)
KON (TNK)
GOTO (THUD)
GA (WHOK)
GOTO
GOTON

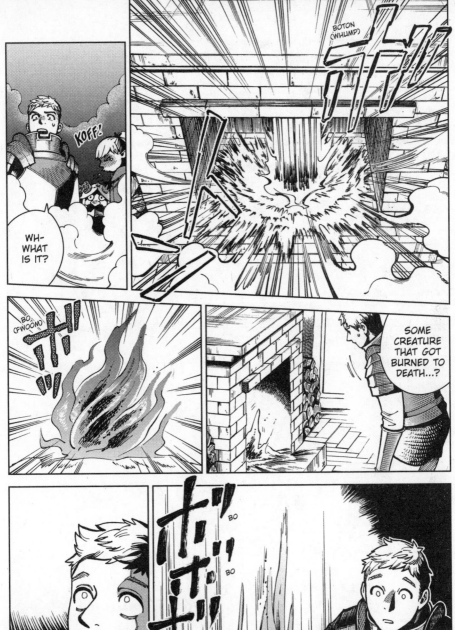

KOFF?!

WH-WHAT IS IT?

BOTON
(WHUMP)

BO
(FWOOM)

SOME CREATURE THAT GOT BURNED TO DEATH...?

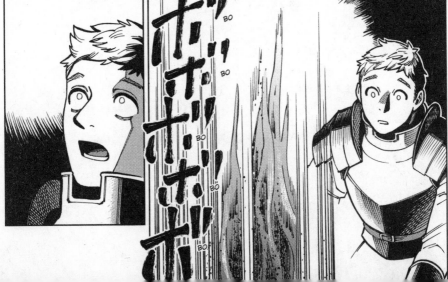

BO

BO

BO

BO

BÖ

BO

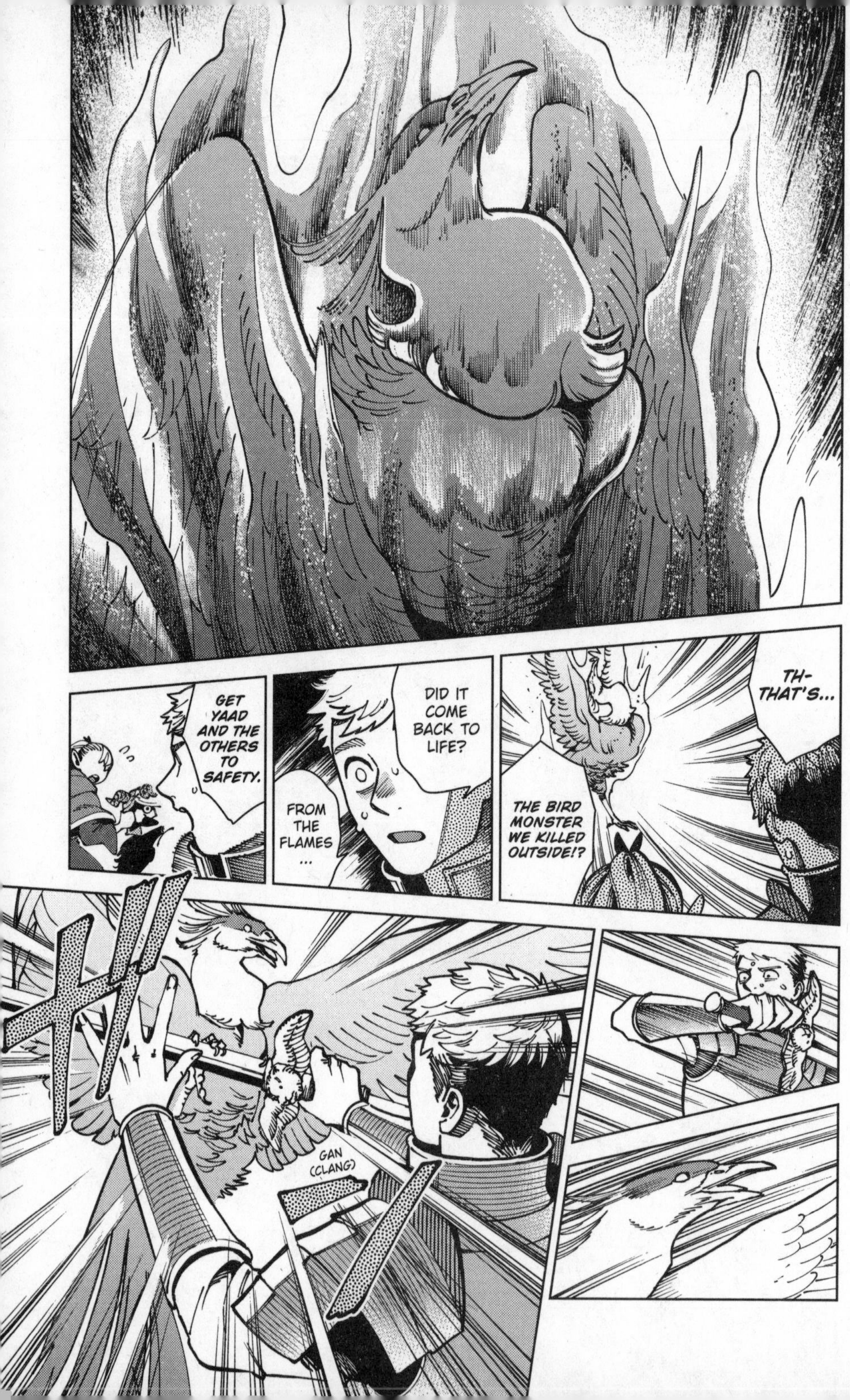
TH-THAT'S...
THE BIRD MONSTER WE KILLED OUTSIDE!?
DID IT COME BACK TO LIFE?
FROM THE FLAMES ...
GET YAAD AND THE OTHERS TO SAFETY.
GAN (CLANG)

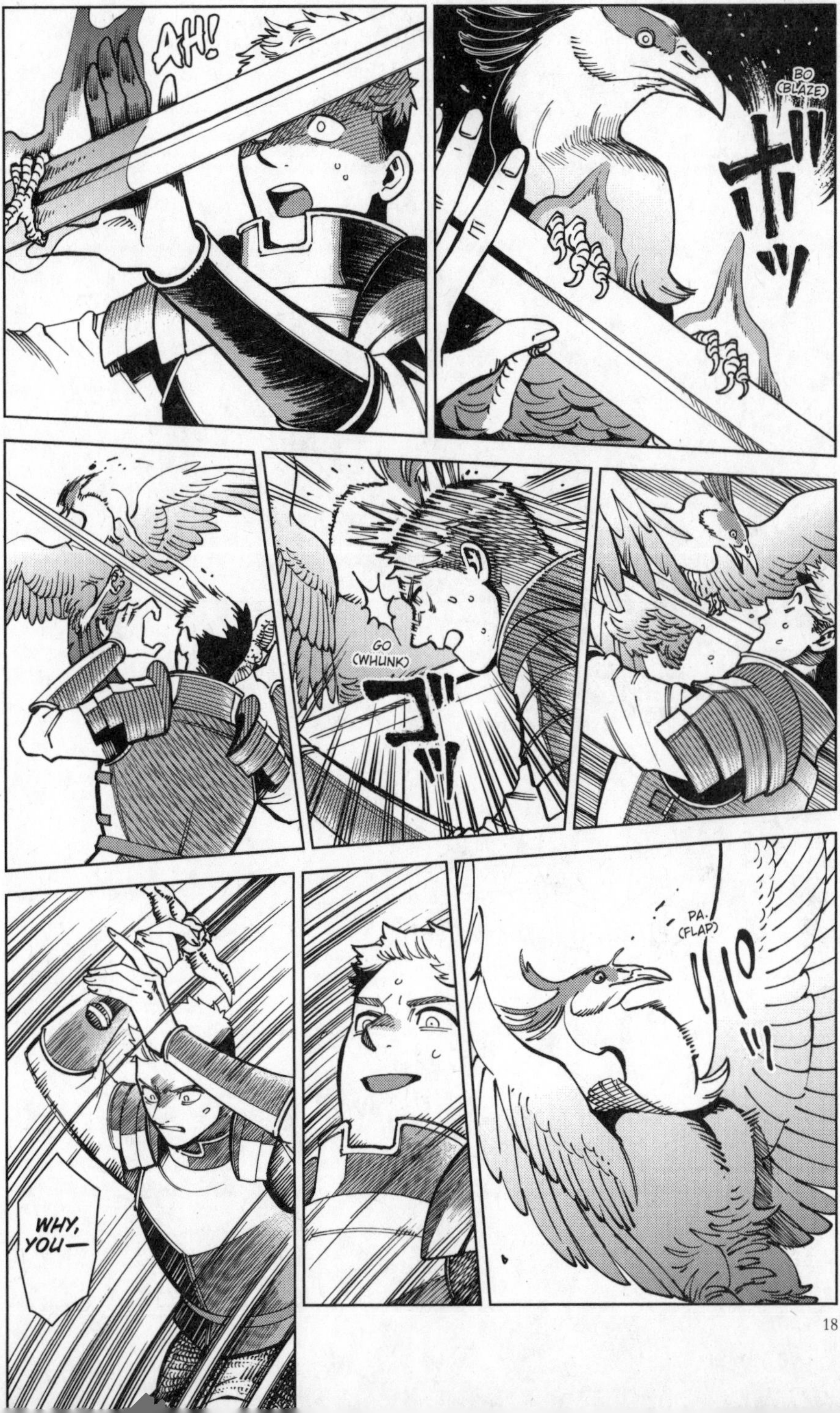
BO
(BLAZE)
AH!
GO
(WHUNK)
PA
(FLAP)
WHY, YOU—

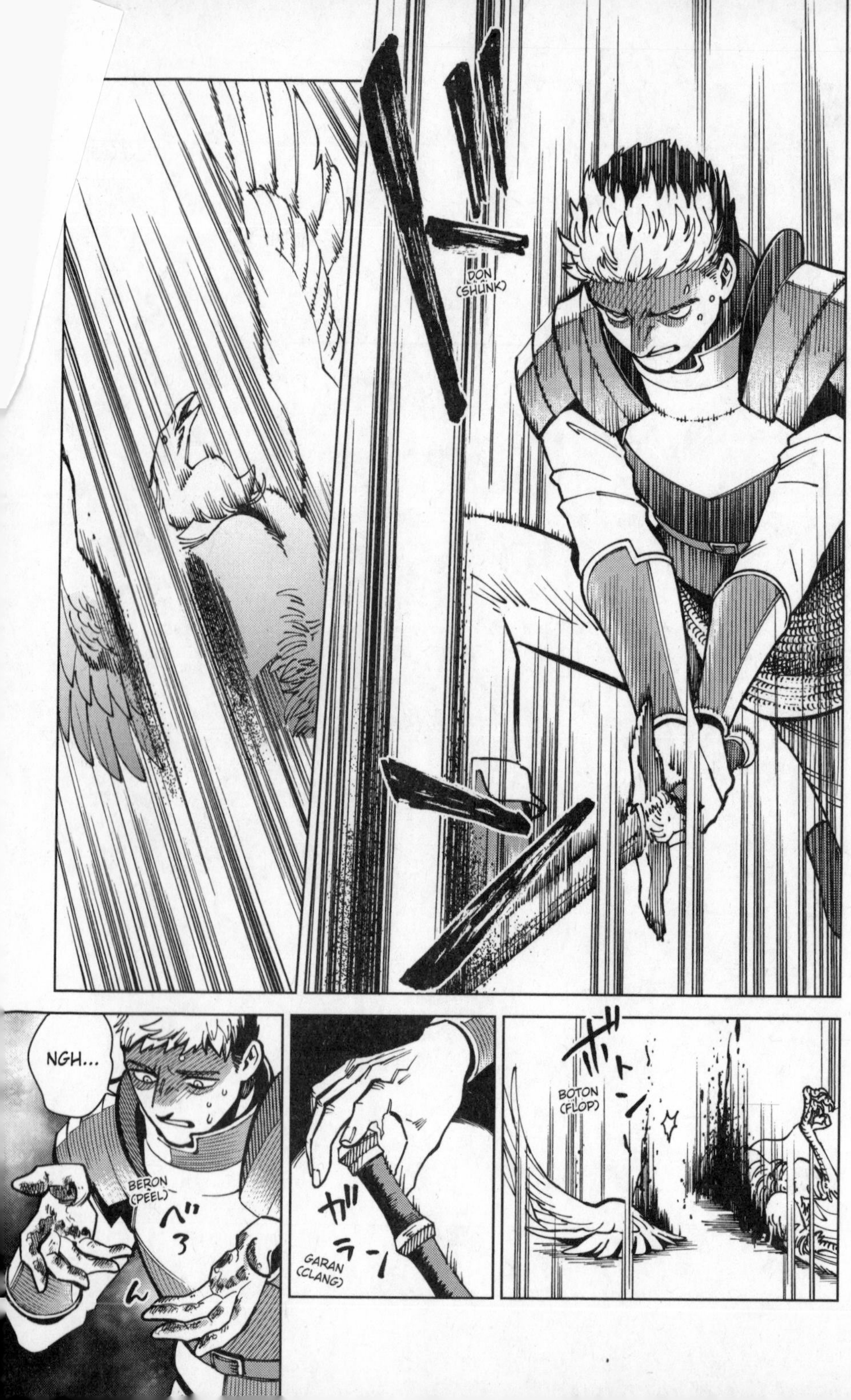
DON
(SHLINK)
ボトン
BOTON
(FLOP)
ガラーン
GARAN
(CLANG)
NGH...
べろん
BERON
(PEEL)

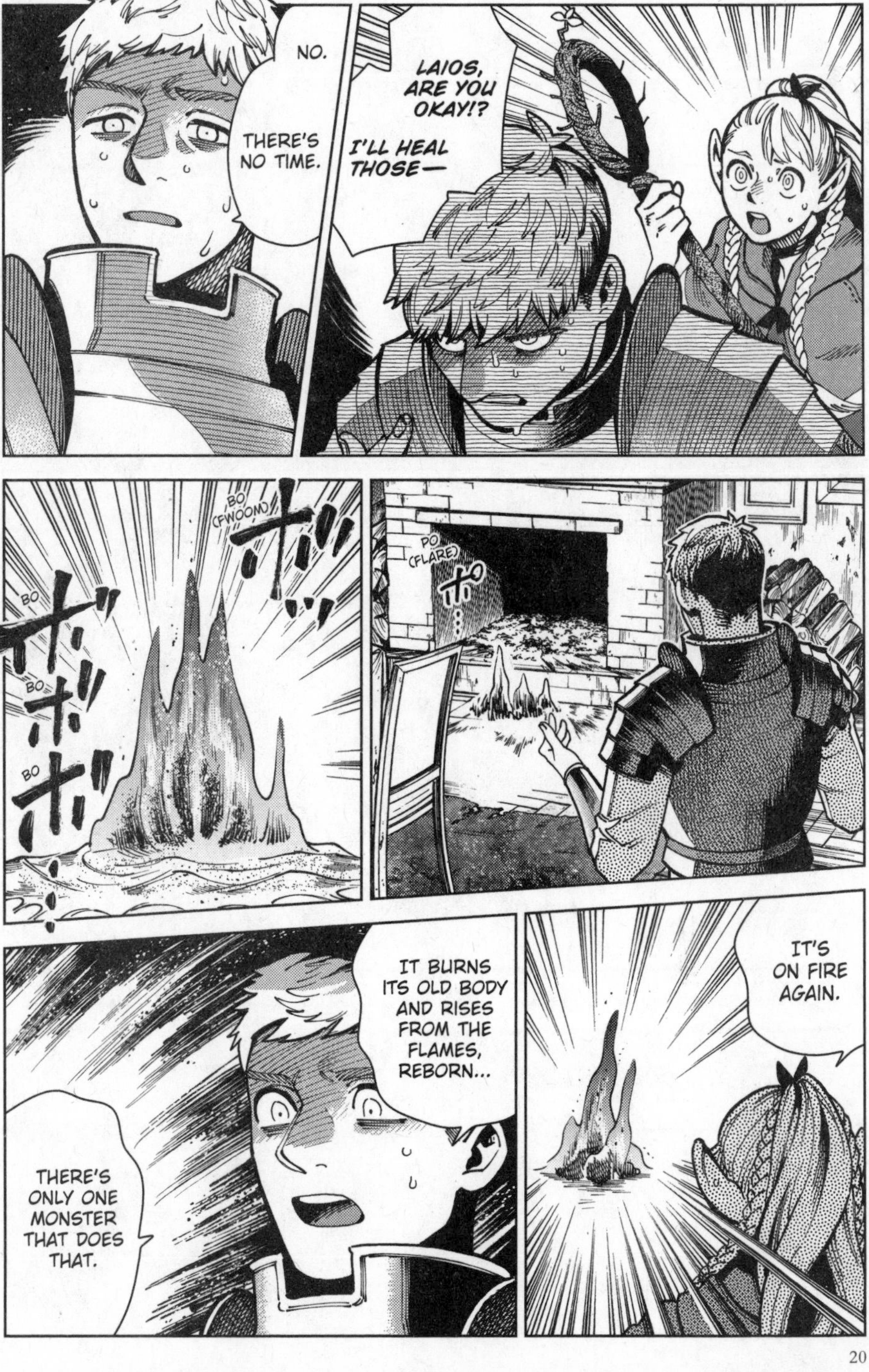
LAIOS, ARE YOU OKAY!?
I'LL HEAL THOSE—
NO.
THERE'S NO TIME.
PO (FLARE)
BO (FWOOM)
BO
BO
BO
IT'S ON FIRE AGAIN.
IT BURNS ITS OLD BODY AND RISES FROM THE FLAMES, REBORN...
THERE'S ONLY ONE MONSTER THAT DOES THAT.

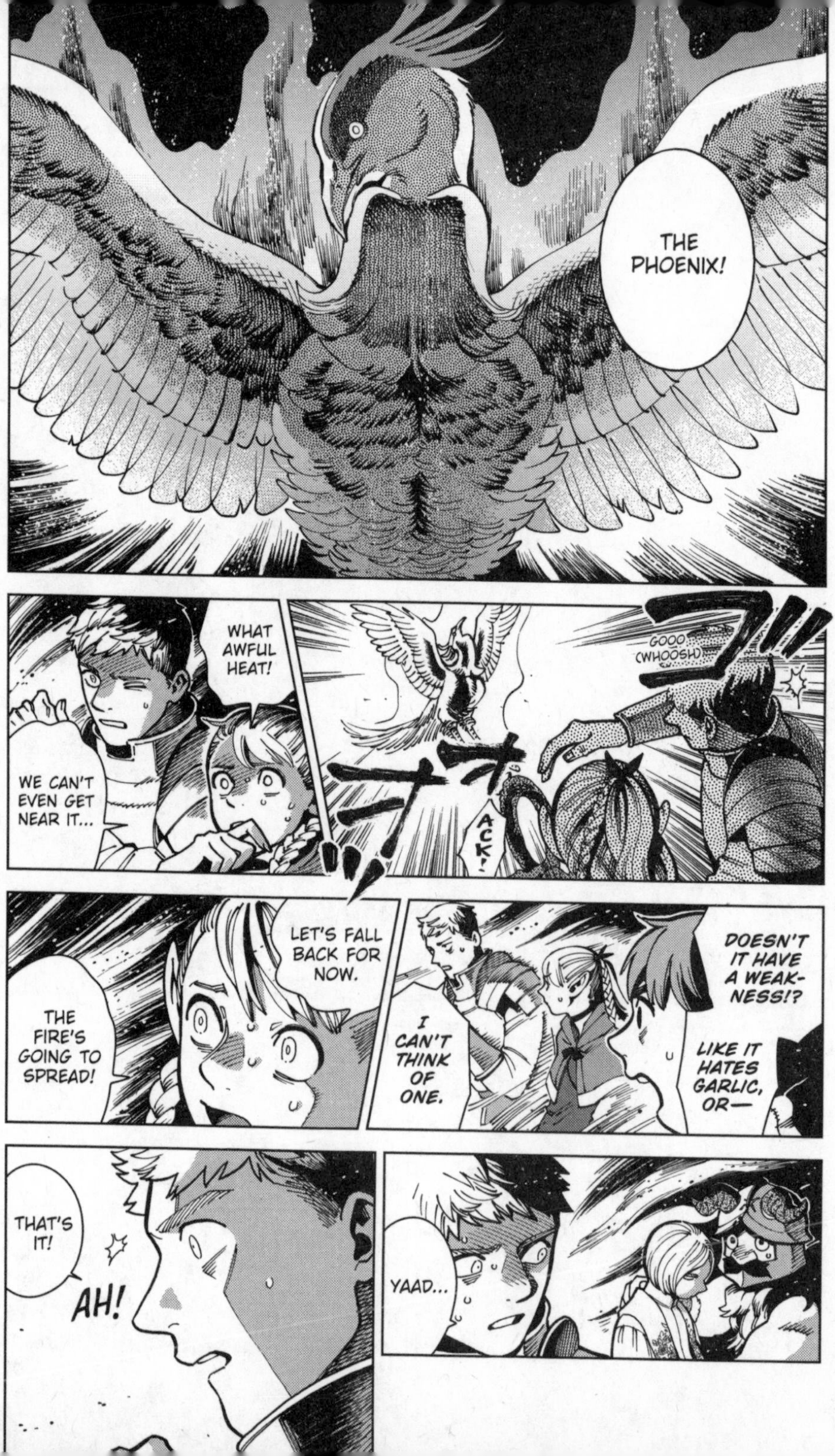
THE PHOENIX!
GOOO (WHOOSH)
ACK!
WHAT AWFUL HEAT!
WE CAN'T EVEN GET NEAR IT...
DOESN'T IT HAVE A WEAKNESS!?
LIKE IT HATES GARLIC, OR—
I CAN'T THINK OF ONE.
LET'S FALL BACK FOR NOW.
THE FIRE'S GOING TO SPREAD!
YAAD...
THAT'S IT!
AH!

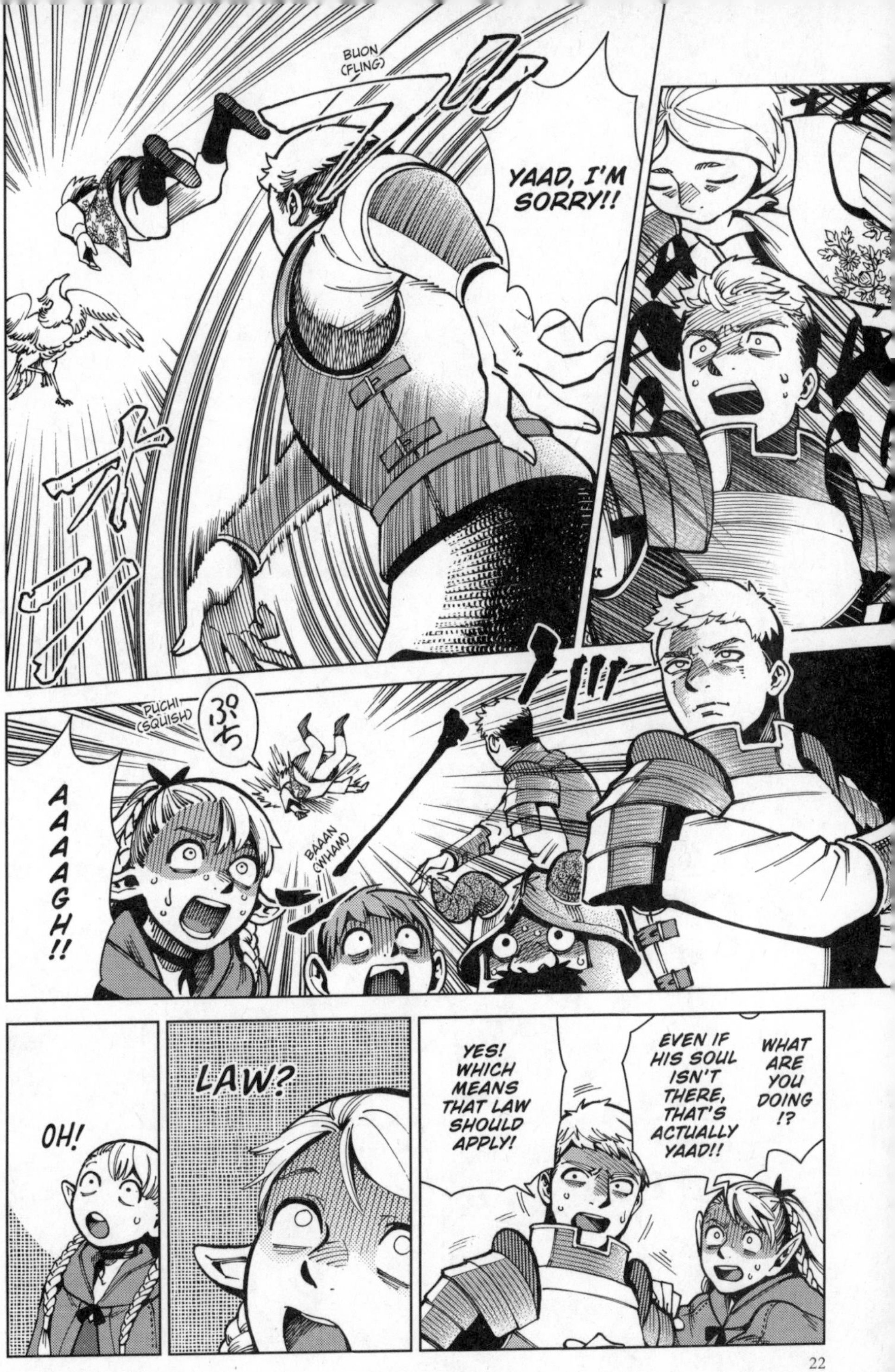
BUON (FLING)
YAAD, I'M SORRY!!
PUCHI (SQUISH)
ぷち
BAAAN (WHAM)
AAAAAGH!!
WHAT ARE YOU DOING!?
EVEN IF HIS SOUL ISN'T THERE, THAT'S ACTUALLY YAAD!!
YES! WHICH MEANS THAT LAW SHOULD APPLY!
LAW?
OH!

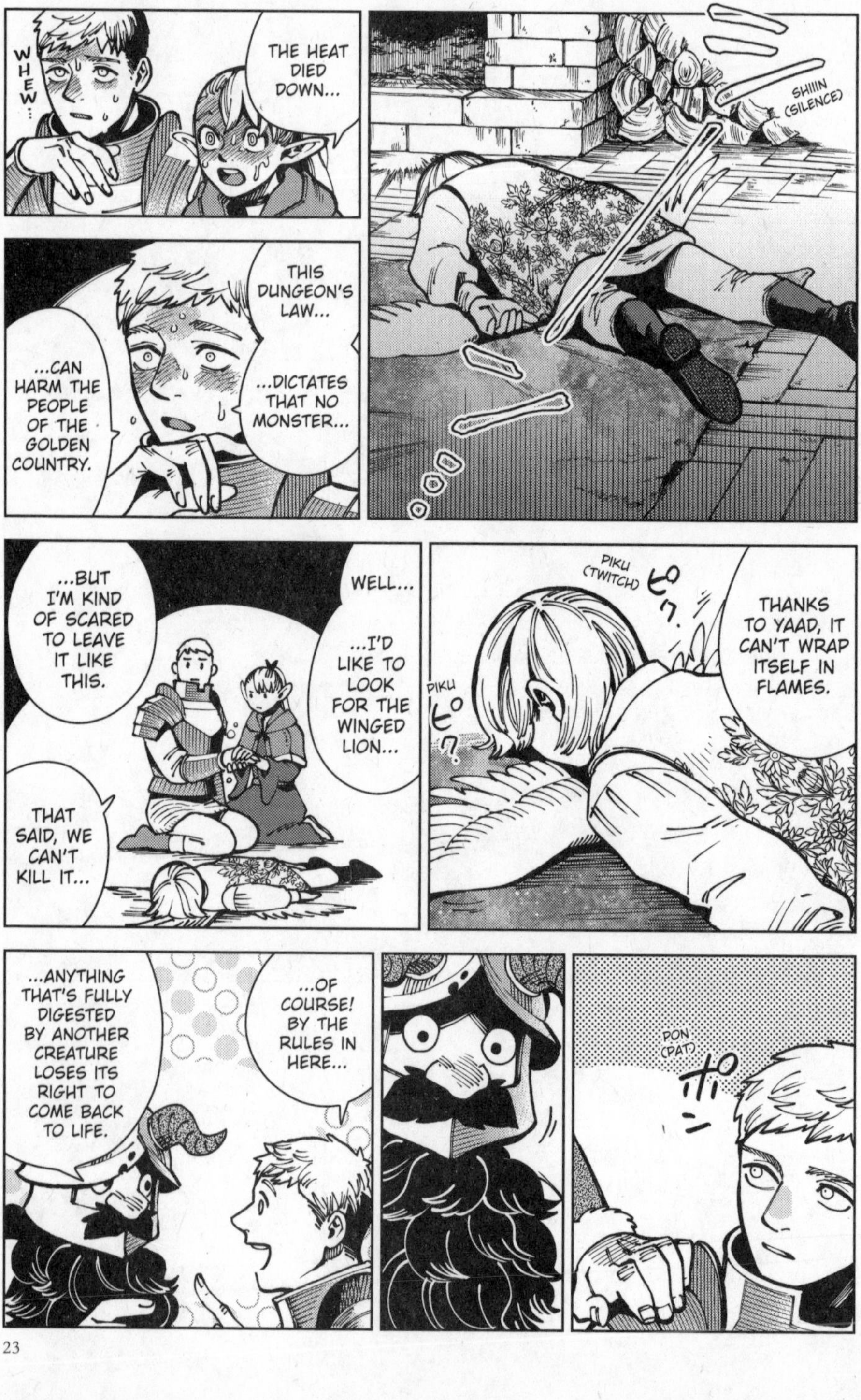
SHIIIN (SILENCE)
THE HEAT DIED DOWN...
WHEW...
THIS DUNGEON'S LAW...
...DICTATES THAT NO MONSTER...
...CAN HARM THE PEOPLE OF THE GOLDEN COUNTRY.
THANKS TO YAAD, IT CAN'T WRAP ITSELF IN FLAMES.
PIKU (TWITCH)
PIKU
WELL...
...I'D LIKE TO LOOK FOR THE WINGED LION...
...BUT I'M KIND OF SCARED TO LEAVE IT LIKE THIS.
THAT SAID, WE CAN'T KILL IT...
PON (PAT)
...OF COURSE! BY THE RULES IN HERE...
...ANYTHING THAT'S FULLY DIGESTED BY ANOTHER CREATURE LOSES ITS RIGHT TO COME BACK TO LIFE.

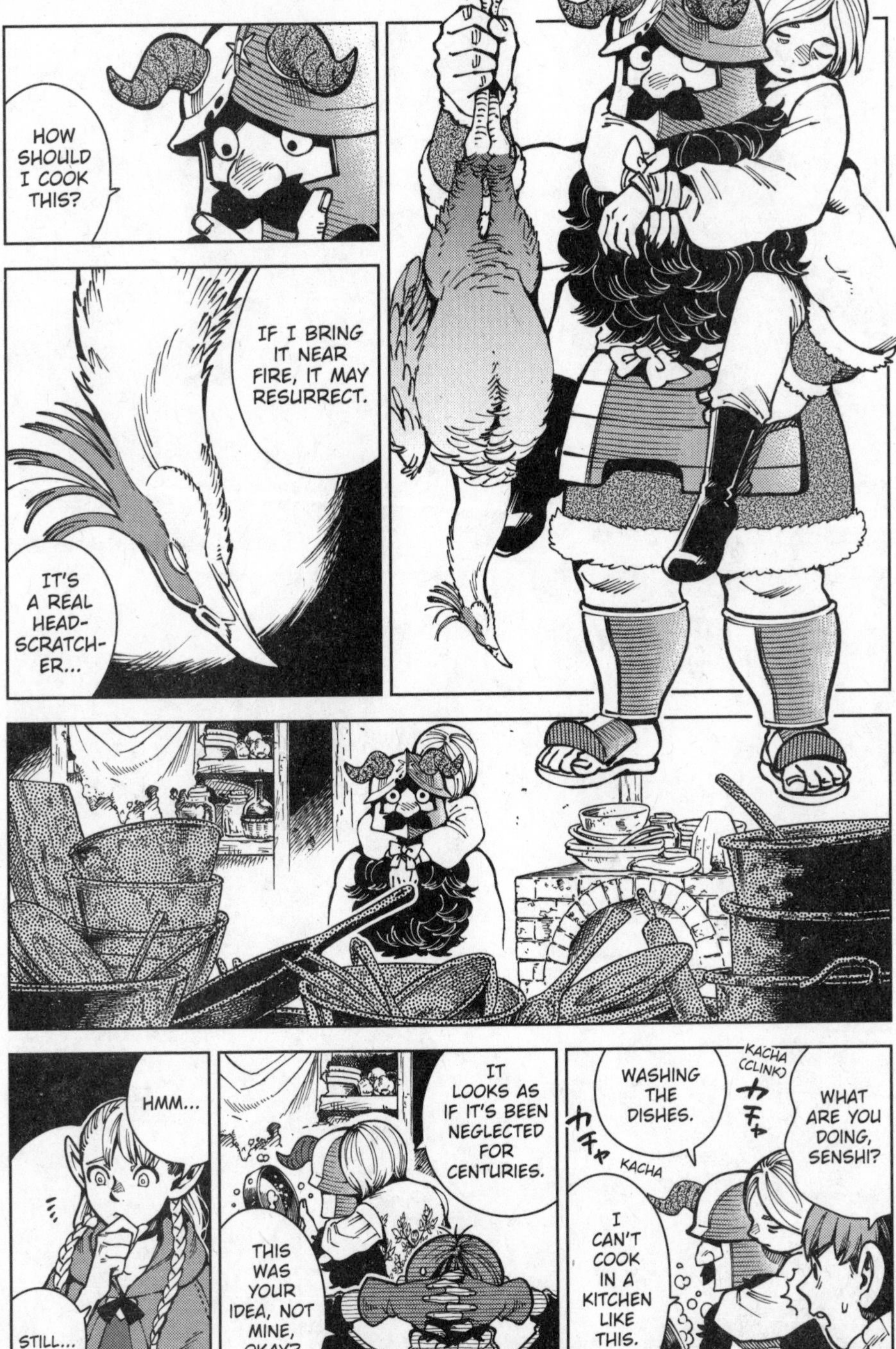
HOW SHOULD I COOK THIS?
IF I BRING IT NEAR FIRE, IT MAY RESURRECT.
IT'S A REAL HEAD-SCRATCHER...
WHAT ARE YOU DOING, SENSHI?
KACHA (CLINK)
カチャ
WASHING THE DISHES.
カチャ
KACHA
I CAN'T COOK IN A KITCHEN LIKE THIS.
IT LOOKS AS IF IT'S BEEN NEGLECTED FOR CENTURIES.
THIS WAS YOUR IDEA, NOT MINE, OKAY?
HMM...
STILL...

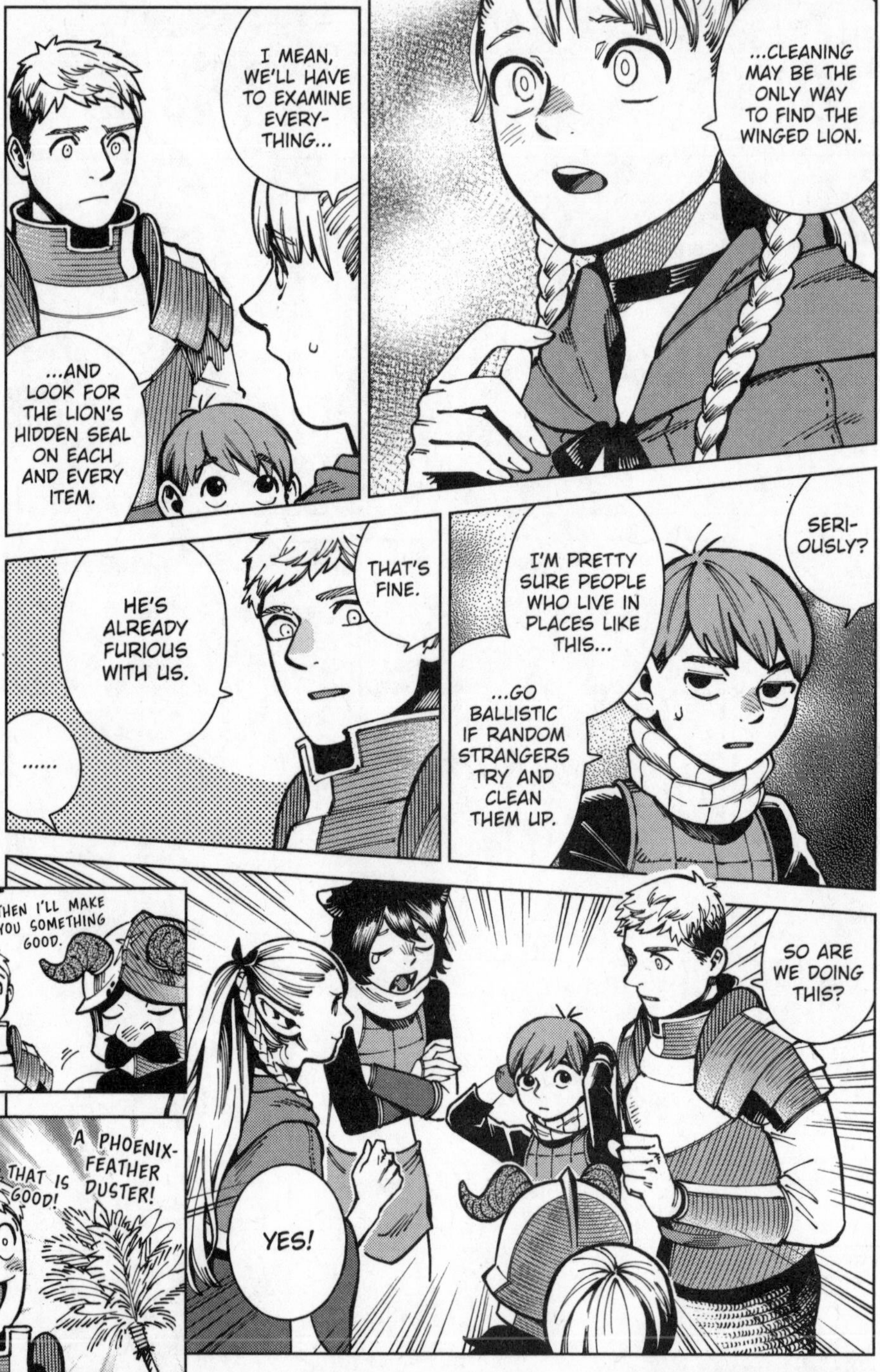
...CLEANING MAY BE THE ONLY WAY TO FIND THE WINGED LION.
I MEAN, WE'LL HAVE TO EXAMINE EVERY-THING...
...AND LOOK FOR THE LION'S HIDDEN SEAL ON EACH AND EVERY ITEM.
SERI-OUSLY?
I'M PRETTY SURE PEOPLE WHO LIVE IN PLACES LIKE THIS...
...GO BALLISTIC IF RANDOM STRANGERS TRY AND CLEAN THEM UP.
THAT'S FINE.
HE'S ALREADY FURIOUS WITH US.
......
SO ARE WE DOING THIS?
YES!
THEN I'LL MAKE YOU SOMETHING GOOD.
A PHOENIX-FEATHER DUSTER!
THAT IS GOOD!

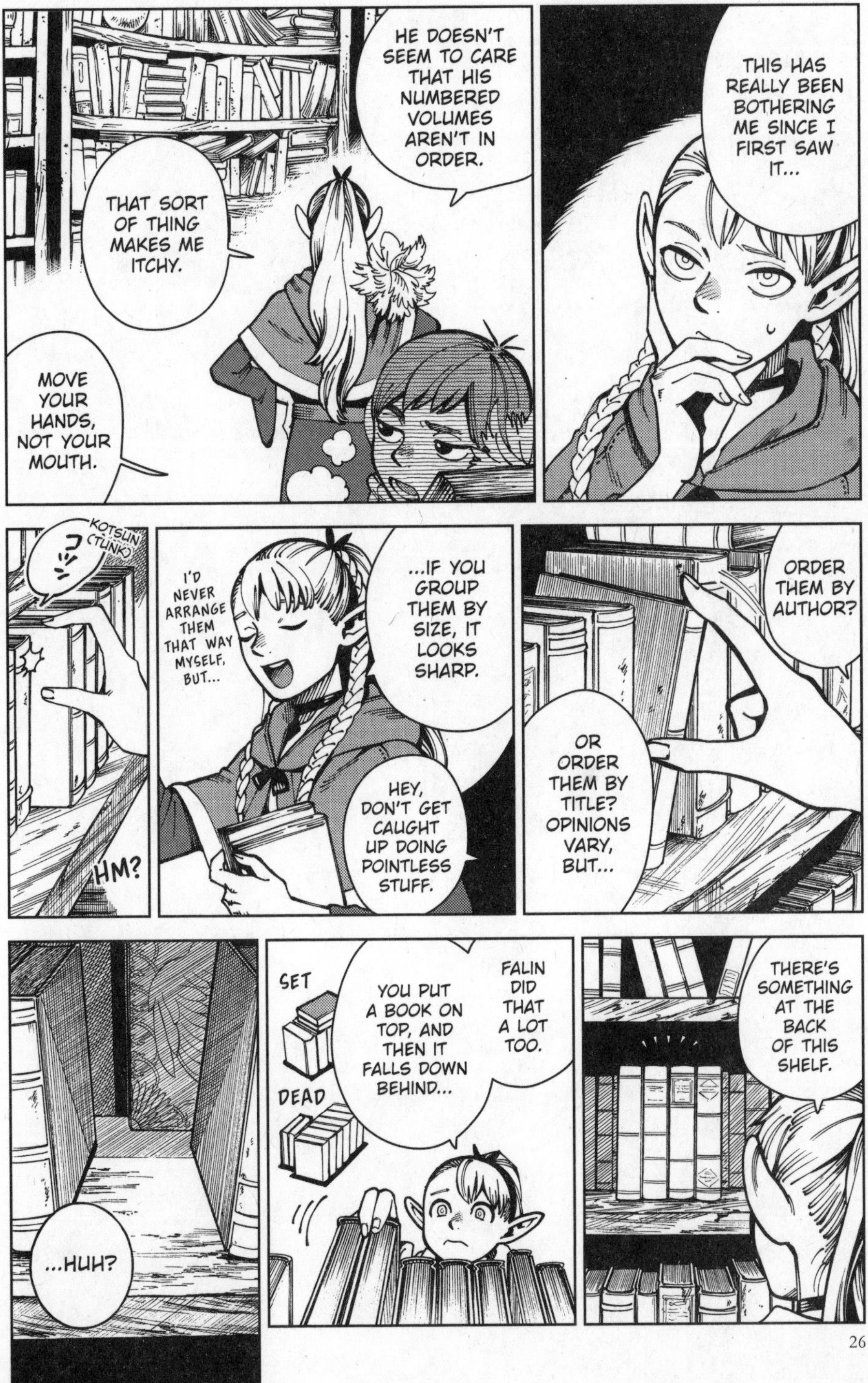
THIS HAS REALLY BEEN BOTHERING ME SINCE I FIRST SAW IT...
HE DOESN'T SEEM TO CARE THAT HIS NUMBERED VOLUMES AREN'T IN ORDER.
THAT SORT OF THING MAKES ME ITCHY.
MOVE YOUR HANDS, NOT YOUR MOUTH.
ORDER THEM BY AUTHOR?
OR ORDER THEM BY TITLE? OPINIONS VARY, BUT...
...IF YOU GROUP THEM BY SIZE, IT LOOKS SHARP.
I'D NEVER ARRANGE THEM THAT WAY MYSELF, BUT...
HEY, DON'T GET CAUGHT UP DOING POINTLESS STUFF.
KOTSUN (TUNK)
HM?
THERE'S SOMETHING AT THE BACK OF THIS SHELF.
FALIN DID THAT A LOT TOO.
YOU PUT A BOOK ON TOP, AND THEN IT FALLS DOWN BEHIND...
SET
DEAD
...HUH?

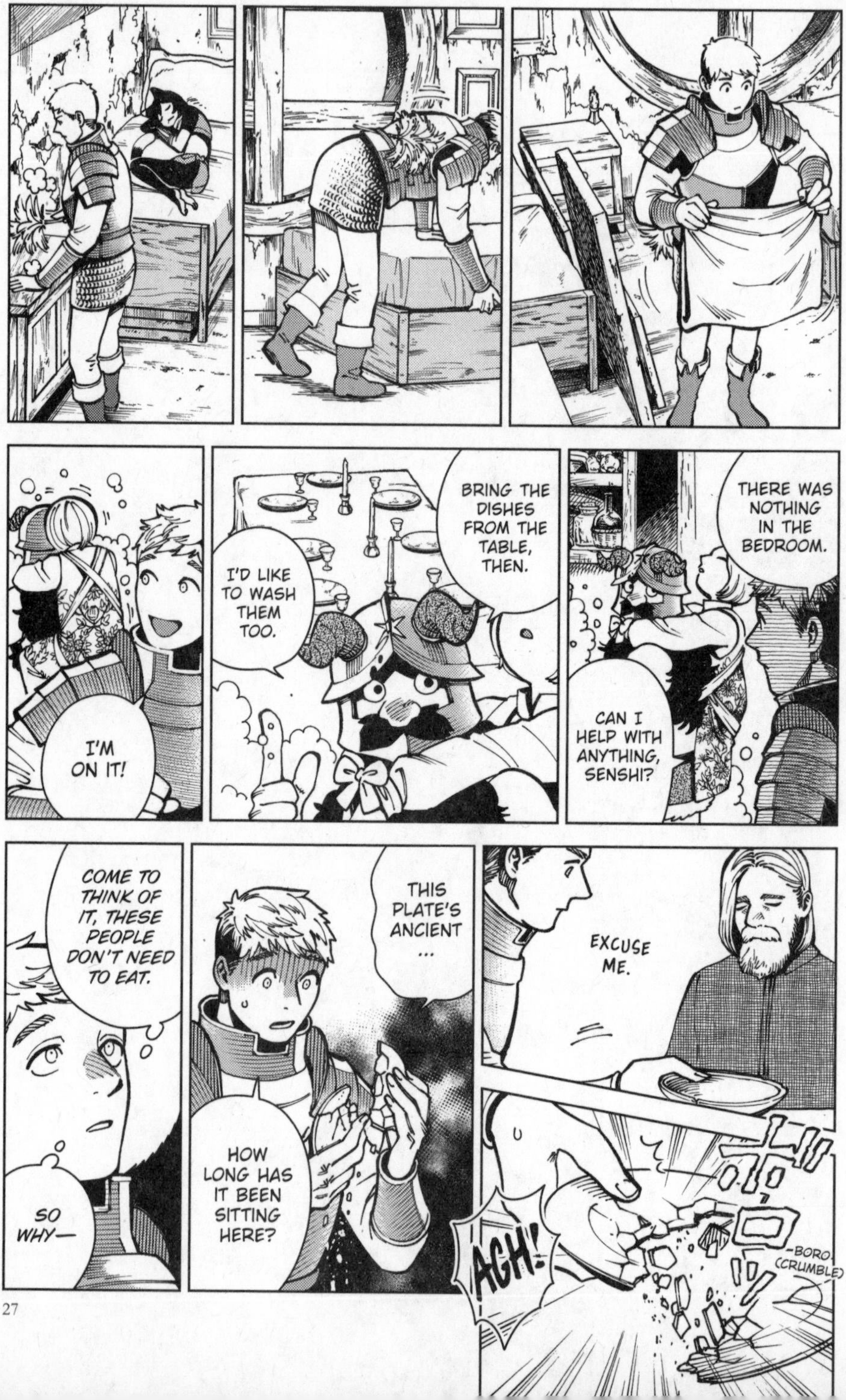
THERE WAS NOTHING IN THE BEDROOM.
CAN I HELP WITH ANYTHING, SENSHI?
BRING THE DISHES FROM THE TABLE, THEN.
I'D LIKE TO WASH THEM TOO.
I'M ON IT!
EXCUSE ME.
AGH!
-BORO (CRUMBLE)
THIS PLATE'S ANCIENT ...
HOW LONG HAS IT BEEN SITTING HERE?
COME TO THINK OF IT, THESE PEOPLE DON'T NEED TO EAT.
SO WHY—

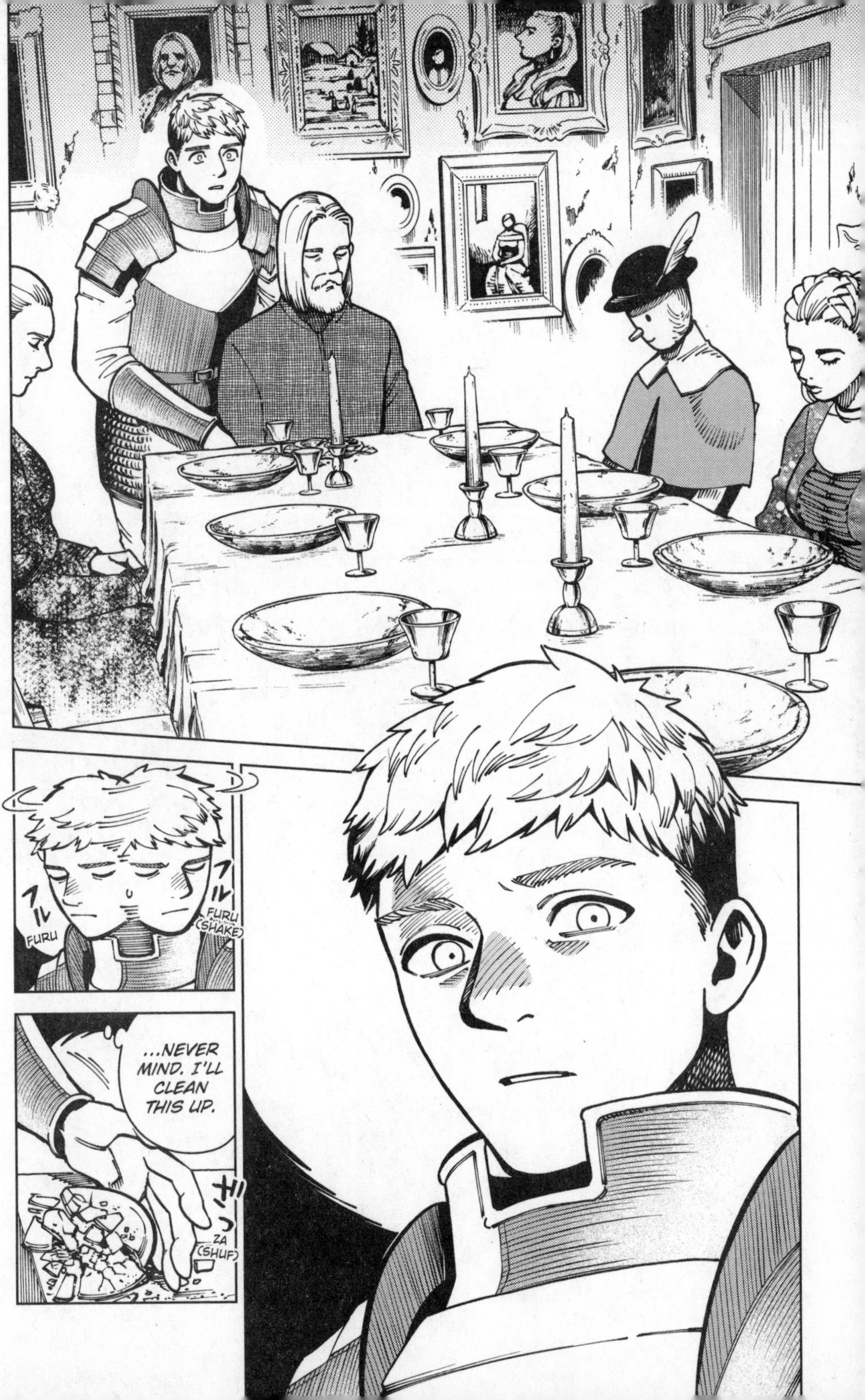
フル
FURU (SHAKE)
フル
FURU
...NEVER MIND. I'LL CLEAN THIS UP.
ザっ
ZA (SHUF)

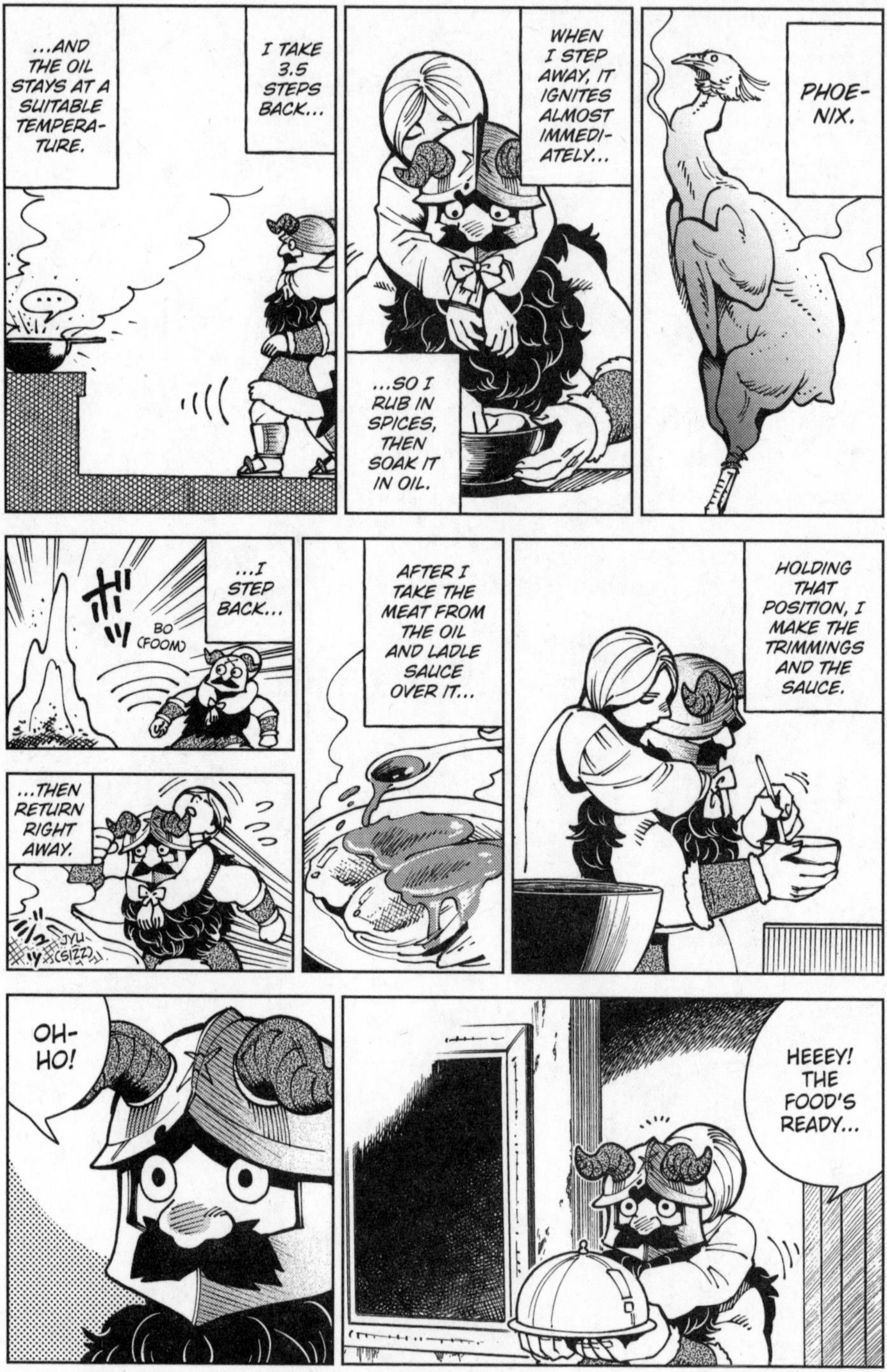
PHOE-NIX.
WHEN I STEP AWAY, IT IGNITES ALMOST IMMEDIATELY...
...SO I RUB IN SPICES, THEN SOAK IT IN OIL.
I TAKE 3.5 STEPS BACK...
...AND THE OIL STAYS AT A SUITABLE TEMPERATURE.
...
HOLDING THAT POSITION, I MAKE THE TRIMMINGS AND THE SAUCE.
AFTER I TAKE THE MEAT FROM THE OIL AND LADLE SAUCE OVER IT...
...I STEP BACK...
BO (FOOM)
...THEN RETURN RIGHT AWAY.
JYU (SIZZ)
HEEEY! THE FOOD'S READY...
OH-HO!

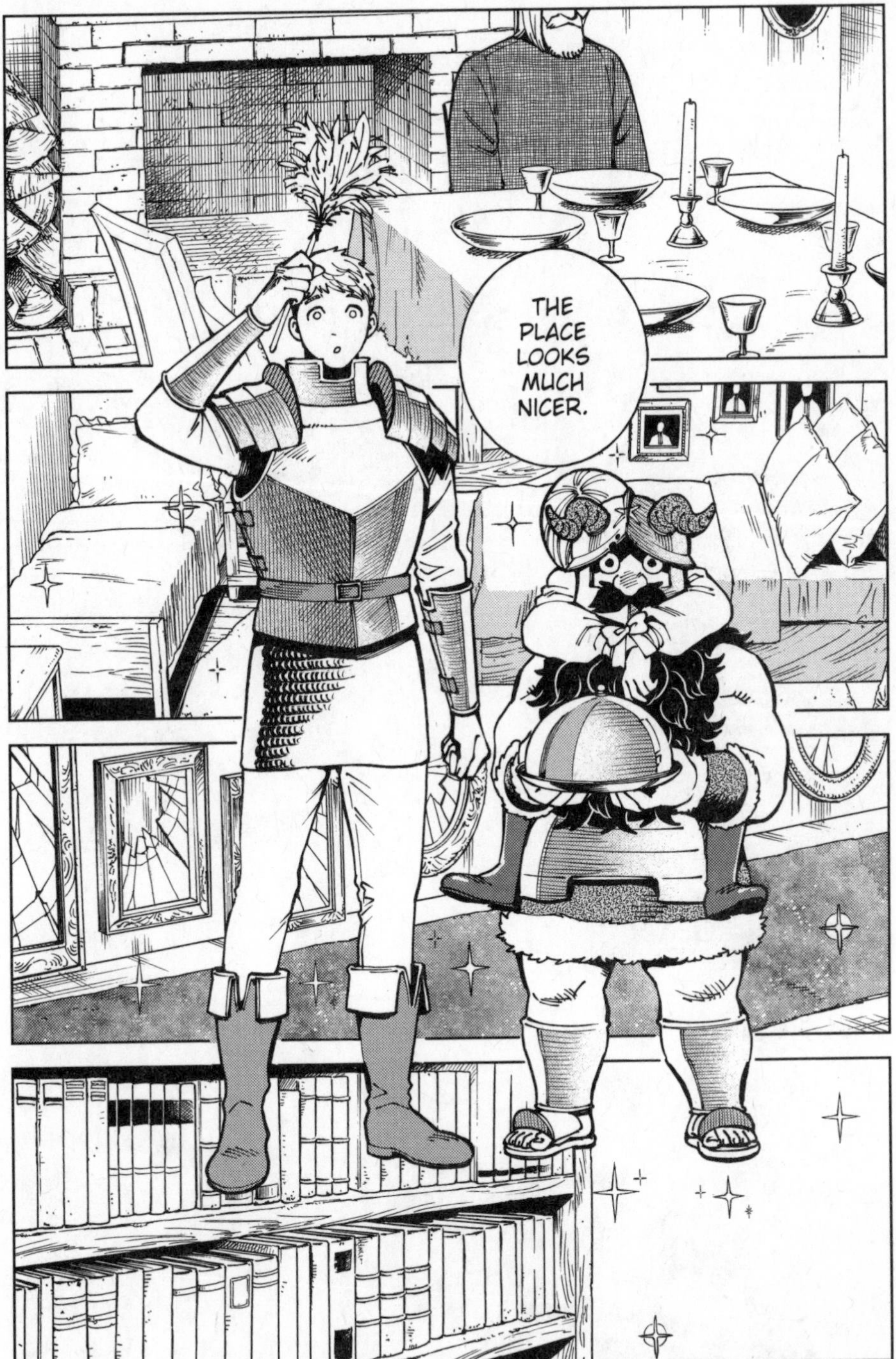
THE PLACE LOOKS MUCH NICER.

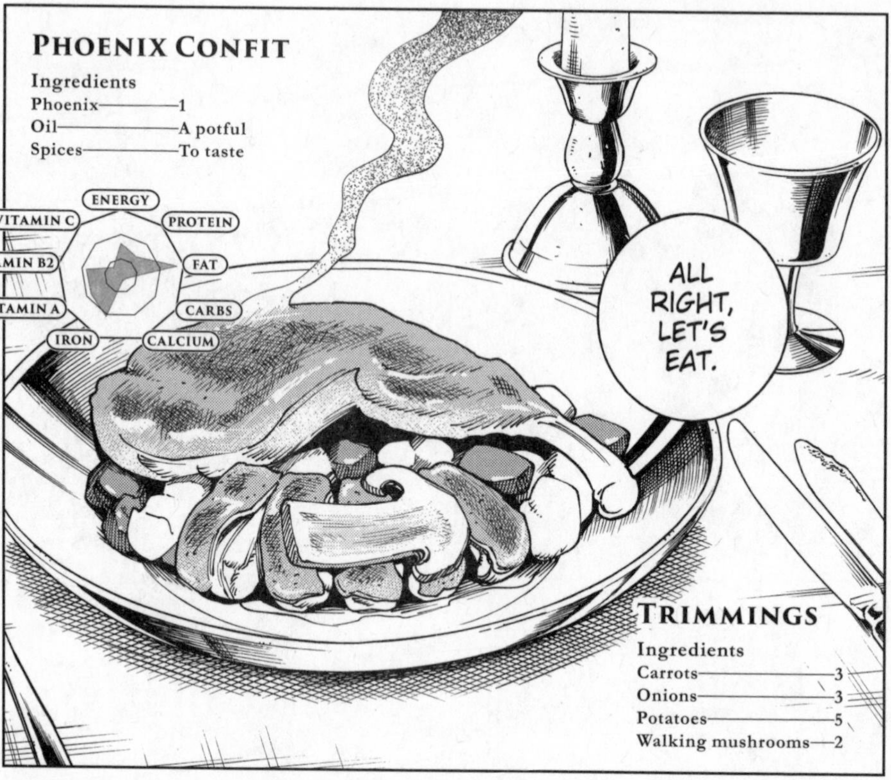
PHOENIX CONFIT
Ingredients
Phoenix—1
Oil—A potful
Spices—To taste
ENERGY
PROTEIN
FAT
CARBS
CALCIUM
IRON
VITAMIN A
VITAMIN B2
VITAMIN C
ALL RIGHT, LET'S EAT.
TRIMMINGS
Ingredients
Carrots—3
Onions—3
Potatoes—5
Walking mushrooms—2

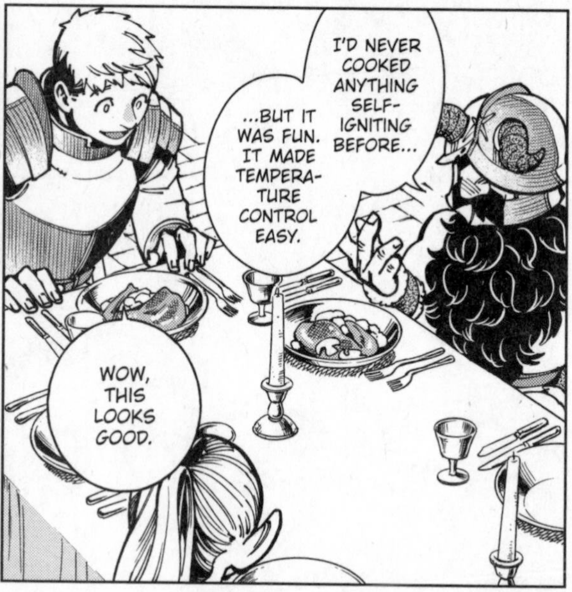
I'D NEVER COOKED ANYTHING SELF-IGNITING BEFORE...
...BUT IT WAS FUN. IT MADE TEMPERATURE CONTROL EASY.
WOW, THIS LOOKS GOOD.

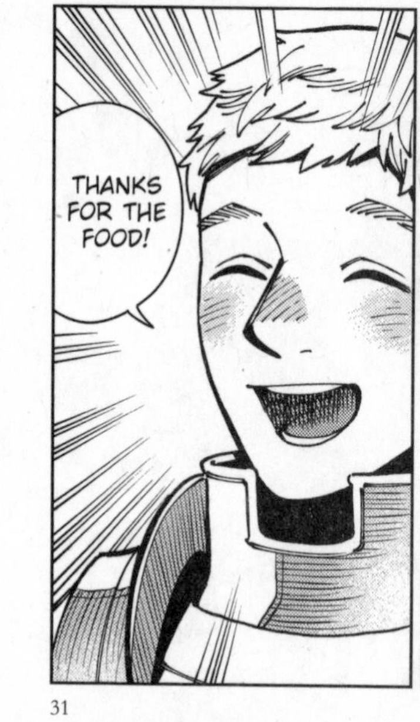
THANKS FOR THE FOOD!

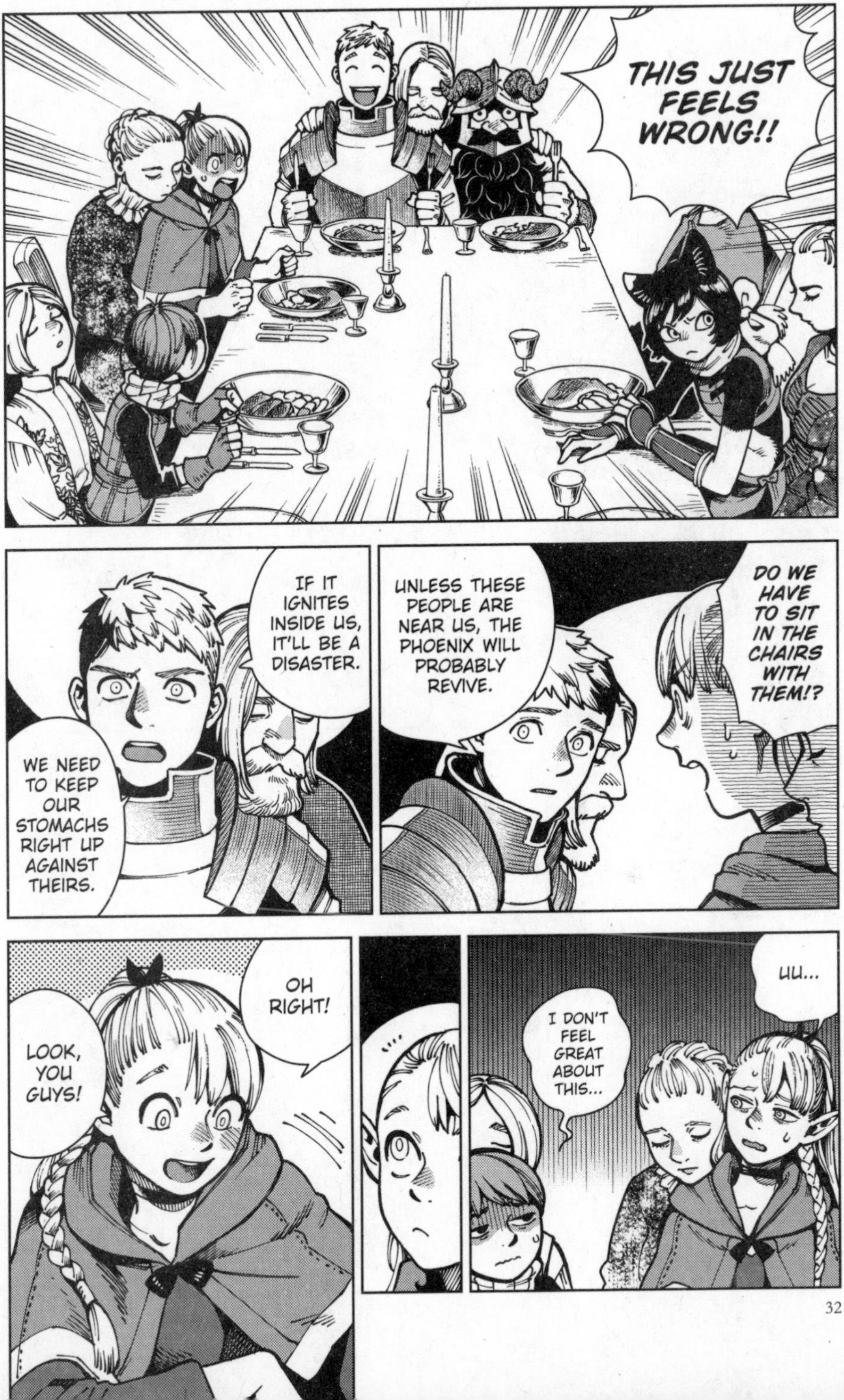
THIS JUST FEELS WRONG!!
DO WE HAVE TO SIT IN THE CHAIRS WITH THEM!?
UNLESS THESE PEOPLE ARE NEAR US, THE PHOENIX WILL PROBABLY REVIVE.
IF IT IGNITES INSIDE US, IT'LL BE A DISASTER.
WE NEED TO KEEP OUR STOMACHS RIGHT UP AGAINST THEIRS.
UU...
I DON'T FEEL GREAT ABOUT THIS...
...
OH RIGHT!
LOOK, YOU GUYS!

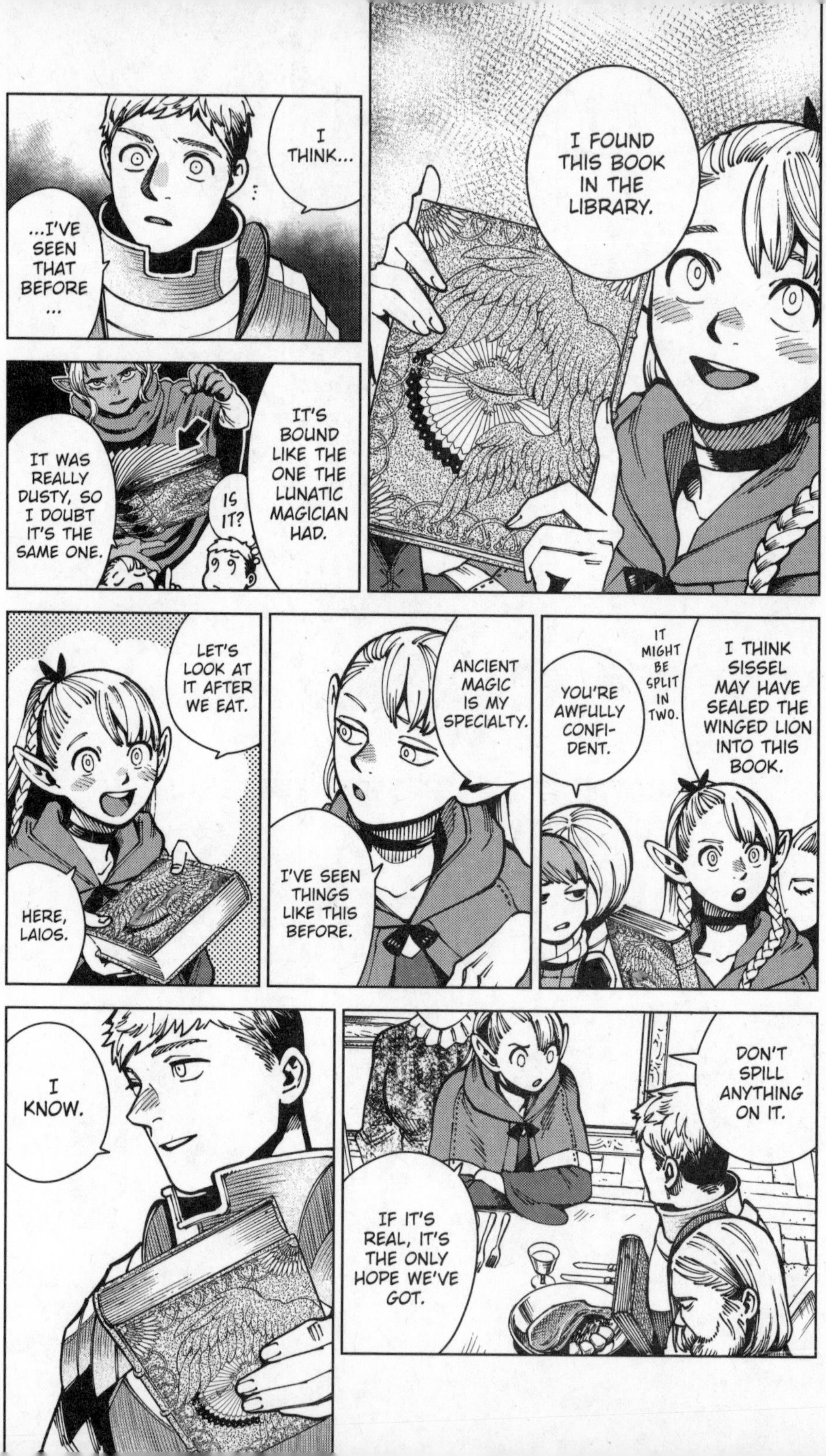
I FOUND THIS BOOK IN THE LIBRARY.
I THINK...
...I'VE SEEN THAT BEFORE ...
IT'S BOUND LIKE THE ONE THE LUNATIC MAGICIAN HAD.
IS IT?
IT WAS REALLY DUSTY, SO I DOUBT IT'S THE SAME ONE.
I THINK SISSEL MAY HAVE SEALED THE WINGED LION INTO THIS BOOK.
IT MIGHT BE SPLIT IN TWO.
YOU'RE AWFULLY CONFI-DENT.
ANCIENT MAGIC IS MY SPECIALTY.
I'VE SEEN THINGS LIKE THIS BEFORE.
LET'S LOOK AT IT AFTER WE EAT.
HERE, LAIOS.
DON'T SPILL ANYTHING ON IT.
IF IT'S REAL, IT'S THE ONLY HOPE WE'VE GOT.
I KNOW.

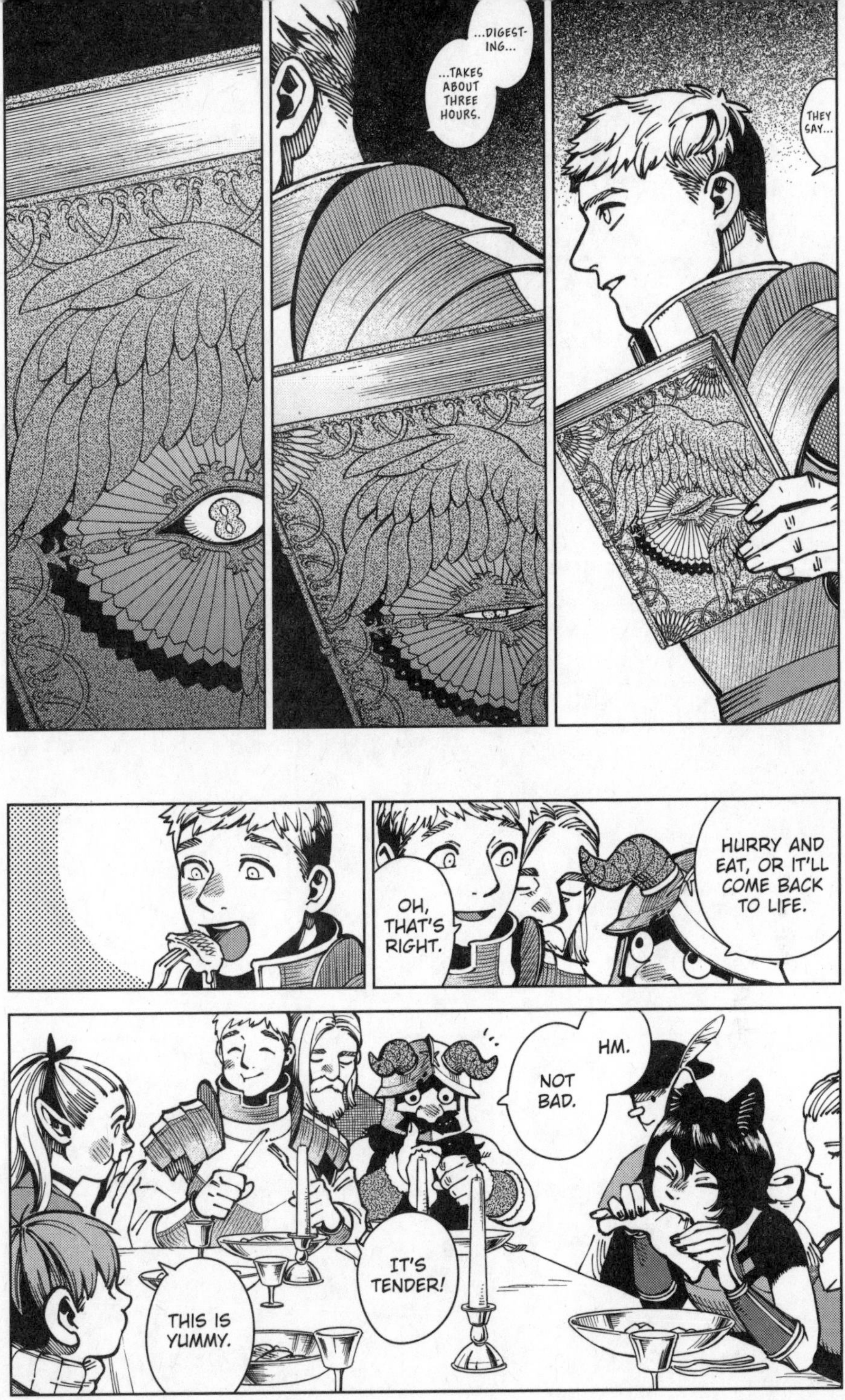
THEY SAY...
...DIGEST-ING...
...TAKES ABOUT THREE HOURS.
HURRY AND EAT, OR IT'LL COME BACK TO LIFE.
OH, THAT'S RIGHT.
HM.
NOT BAD.
IT'S TENDER!
THIS IS YUMMY.

Chapter 63: The End

64. Rabbits -1-

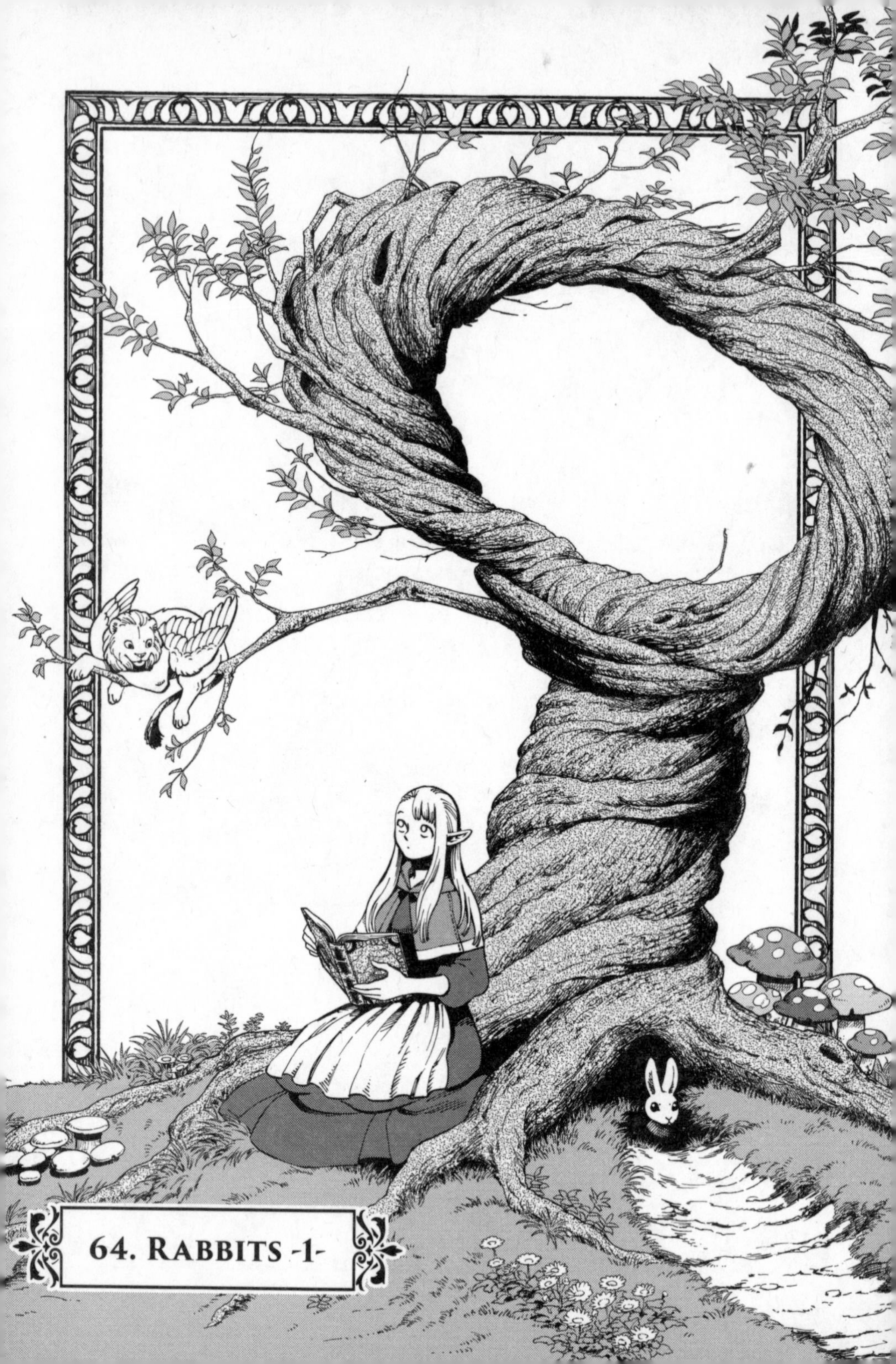

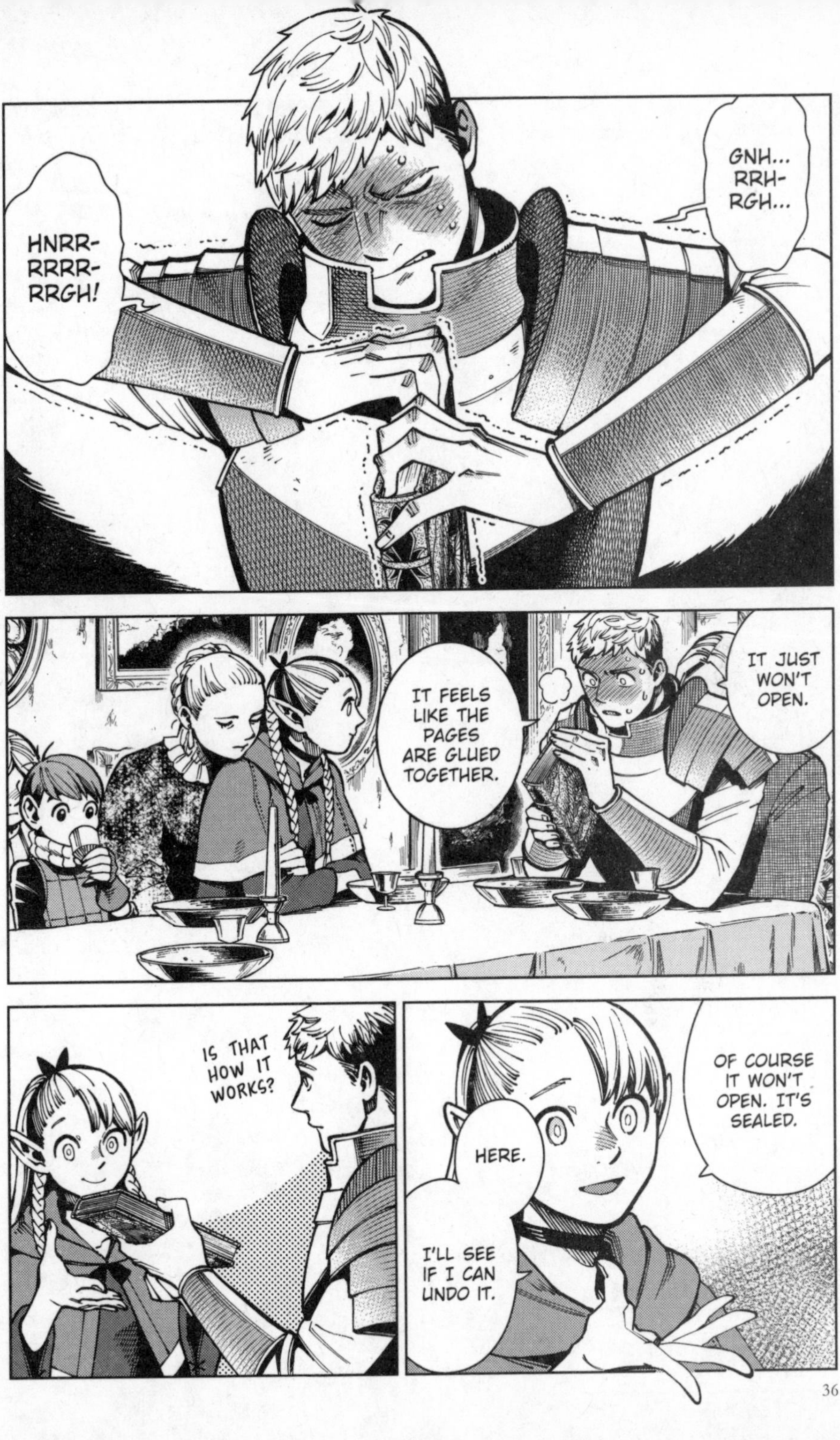
GNH... RRH-RGH...
HNRR-RRRR-RRGH!
IT JUST WON'T OPEN.
IT FEELS LIKE THE PAGES ARE GLUED TOGETHER.
OF COURSE IT WON'T OPEN. IT'S SEALED.
HERE.
I'LL SEE IF I CAN UNDO IT.
IS THAT HOW IT WORKS?

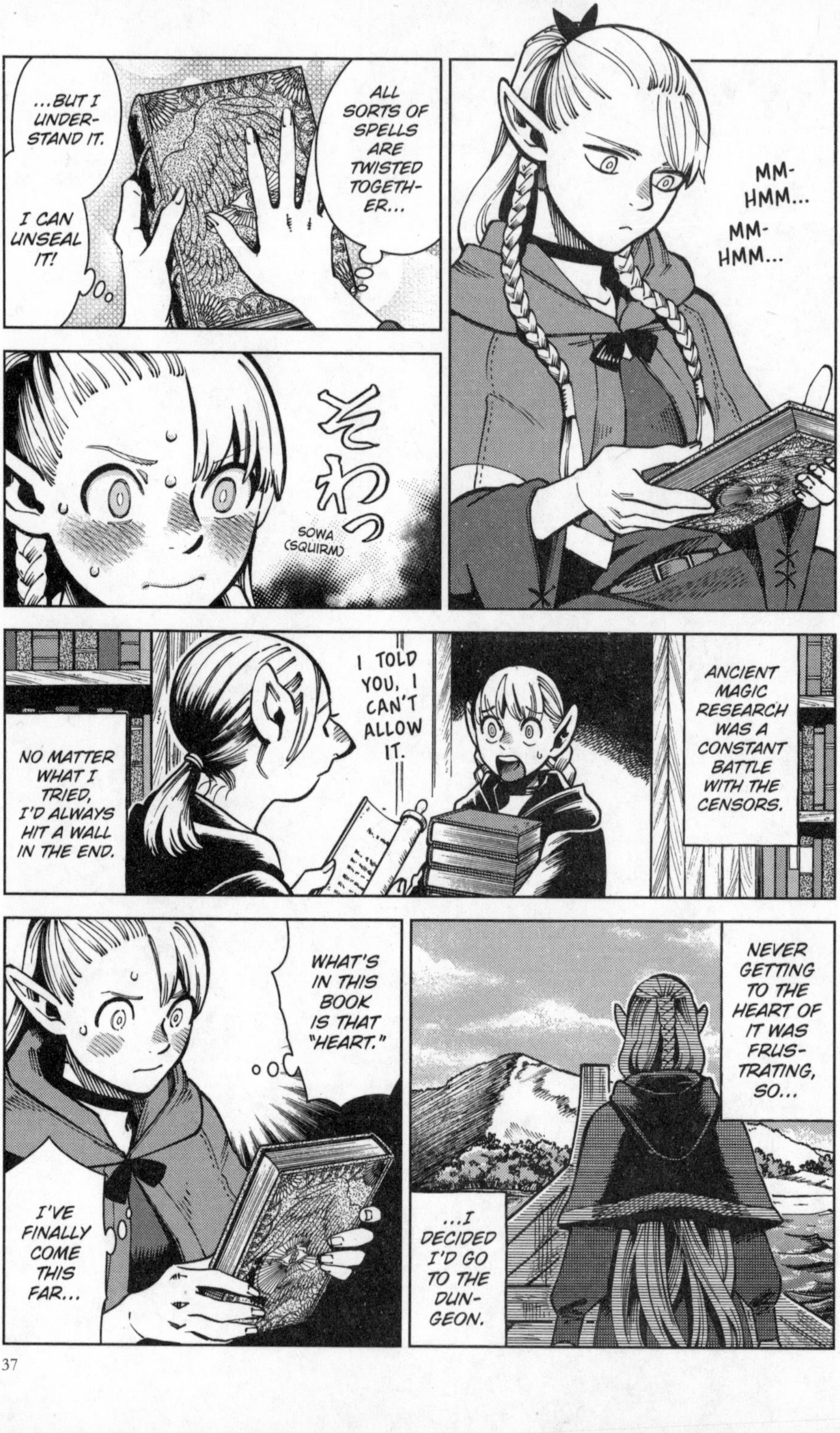
MM-HMM...
MM-HMM...
ALL SORTS OF SPELLS ARE TWISTED TOGETHER...
...BUT I UNDERSTAND IT.
I CAN UNSEAL IT!
そわっ
SOWA (SQUIRM)
ANCIENT MAGIC RESEARCH WAS A CONSTANT BATTLE WITH THE CENSORS.
I TOLD YOU, I CAN'T ALLOW IT.
NO MATTER WHAT I TRIED, I'D ALWAYS HIT A WALL IN THE END.
NEVER GETTING TO THE HEART OF IT WAS FRUSTRATING, SO...
...I DECIDED I'D GO TO THE DUNGEON.
WHAT'S IN THIS BOOK IS THAT "HEART."
I'VE FINALLY COME THIS FAR...

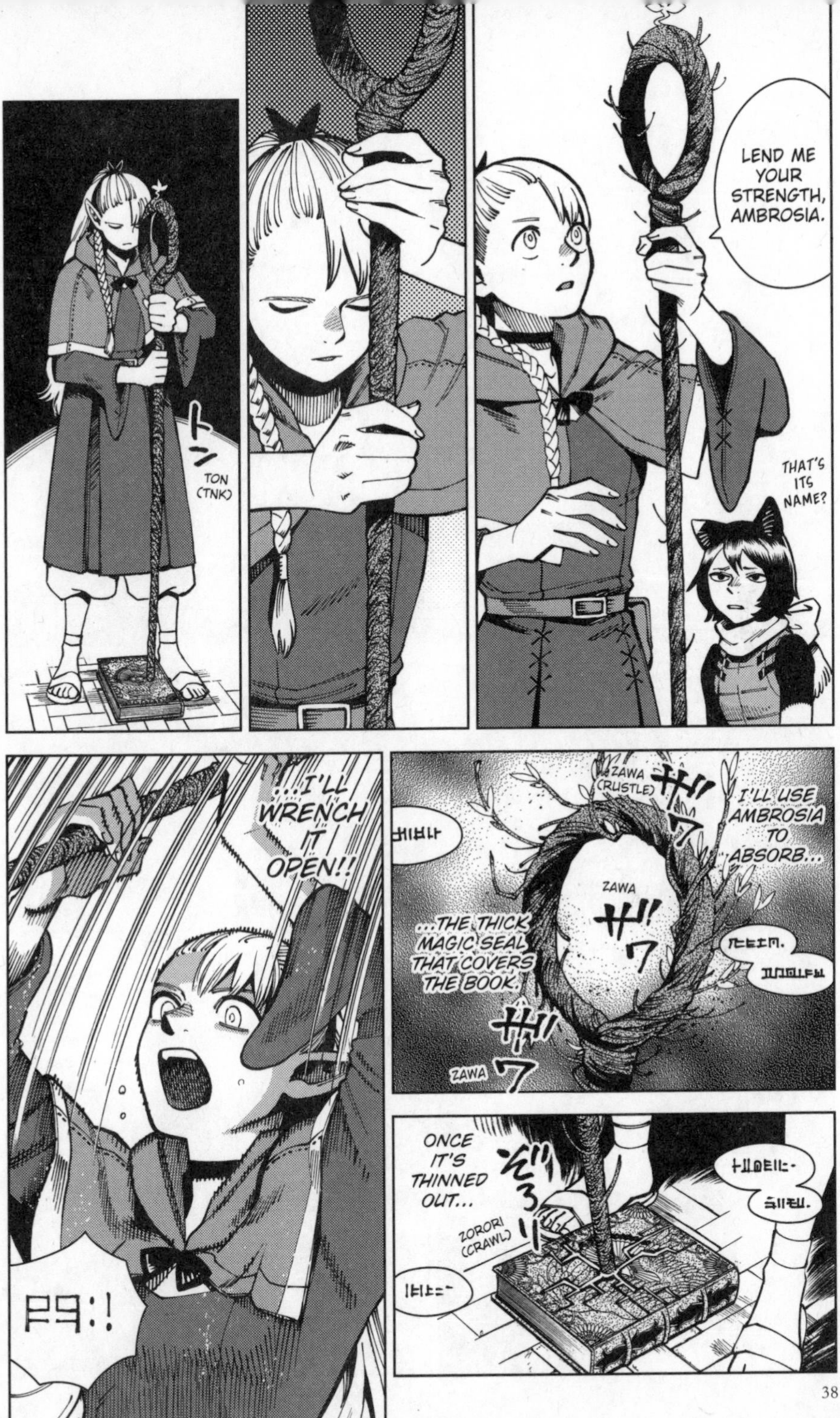
LEND ME YOUR STRENGTH, AMBROSIA.
THAT'S ITS NAME?
TON (TNK)
ZAWA (RUSTLE)
I'LL USE AMBROSIA TO ABSORB...
ZAWA
...THE THICK MAGIC SEAL THAT COVERS THE BOOK.
ZAWA
ONCE IT'S THINNED OUT...
ZORORI (CRAWL)
...I'LL WRENCH IT OPEN!!

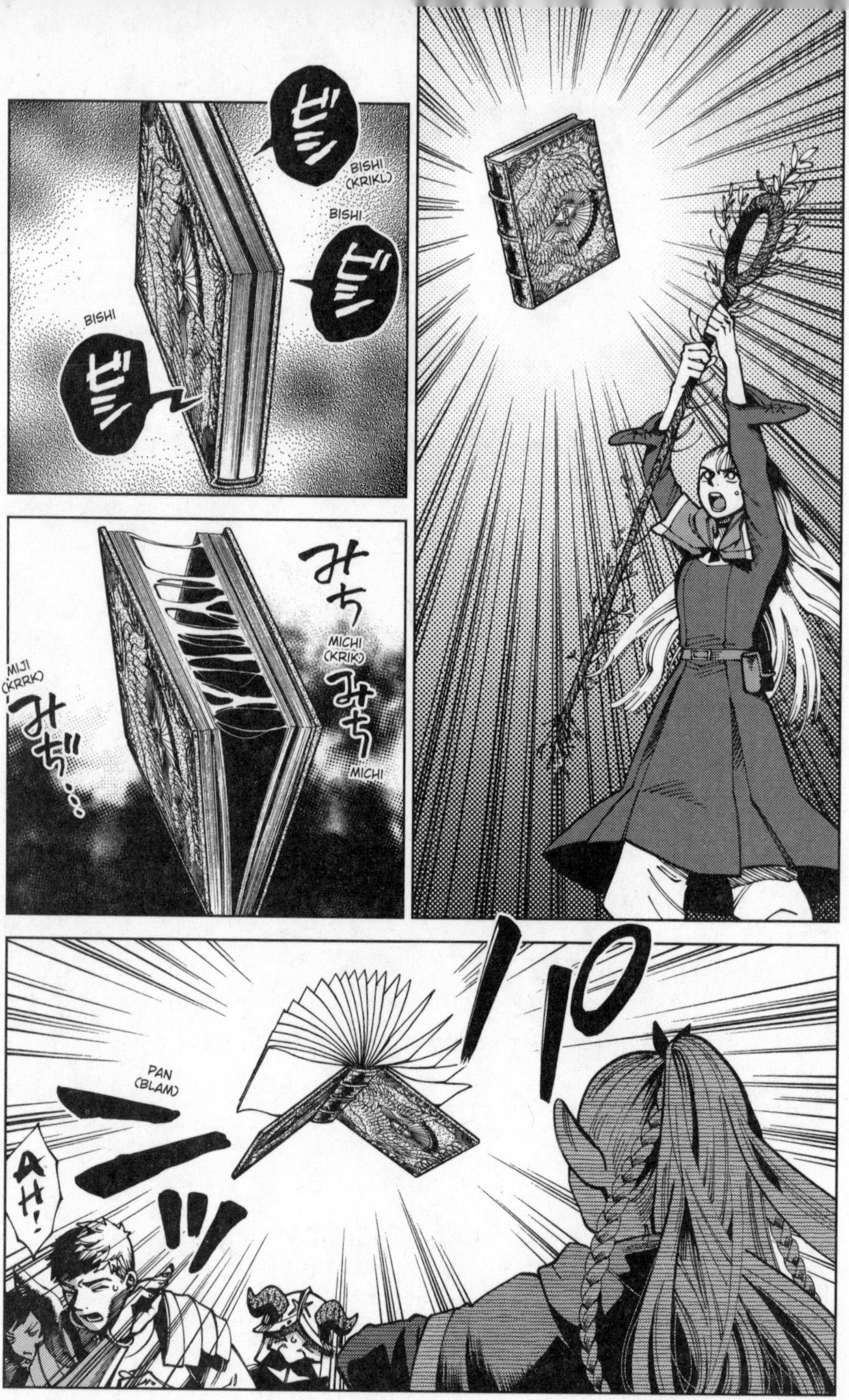

ビシ
BISHI (KRIKL)
ビシ
BISHI
ビシ
BISHI
みち
MICHI (KRIK)
みち
MICHI
みぢ…
MIJI (KRRK)
パーン
PAN (BLAM)
AH!

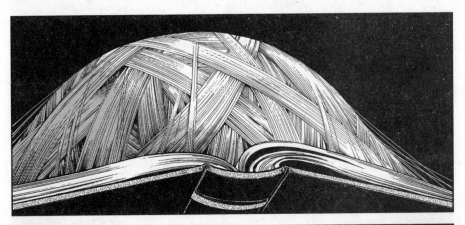

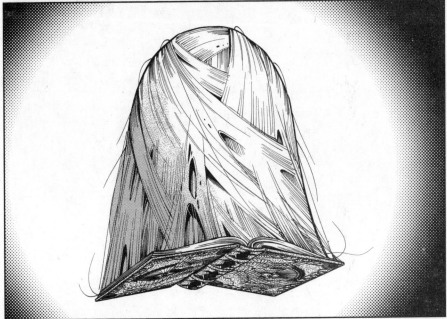

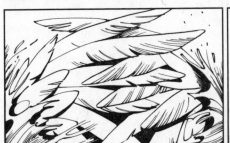
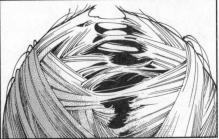

40

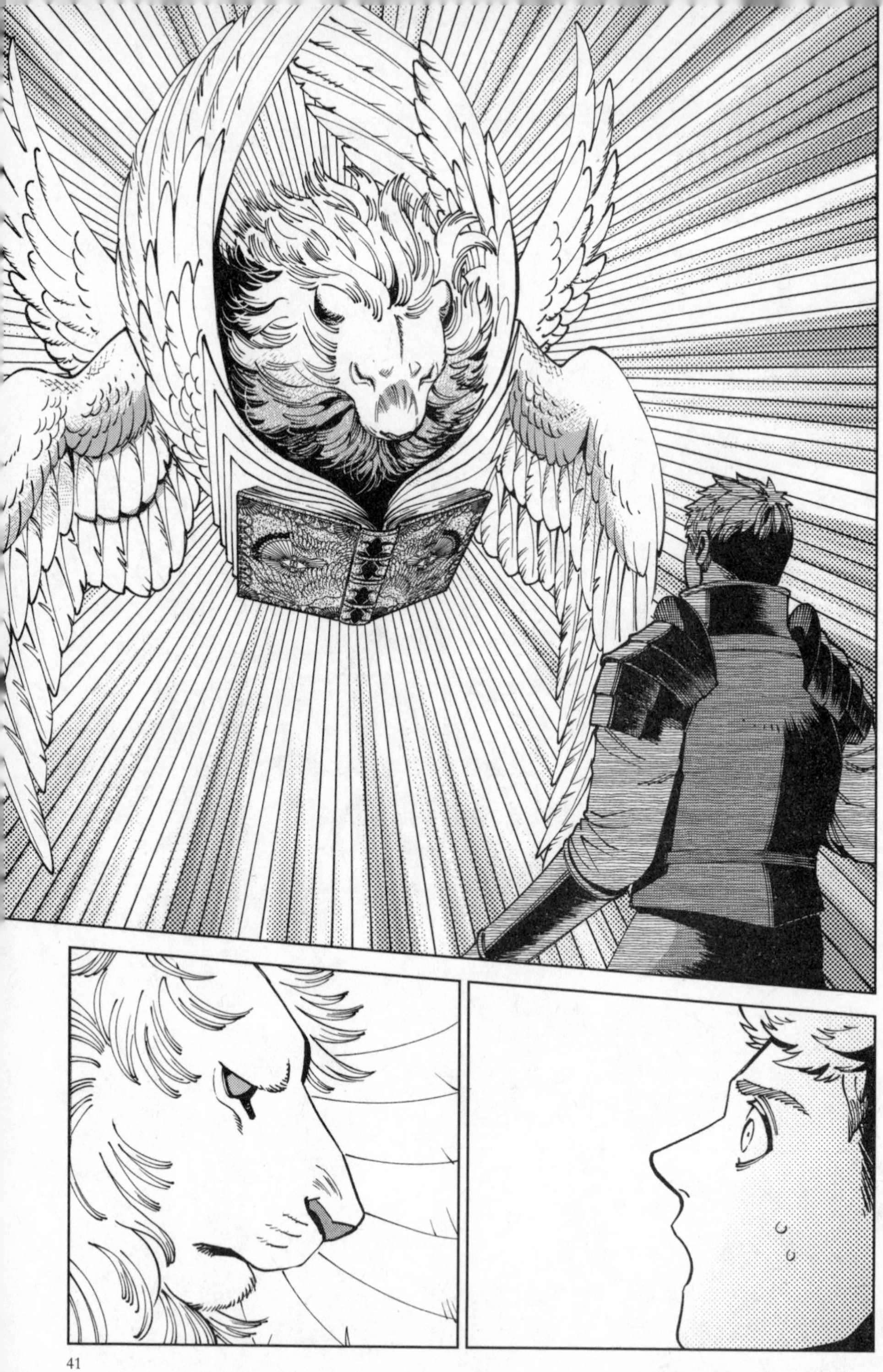

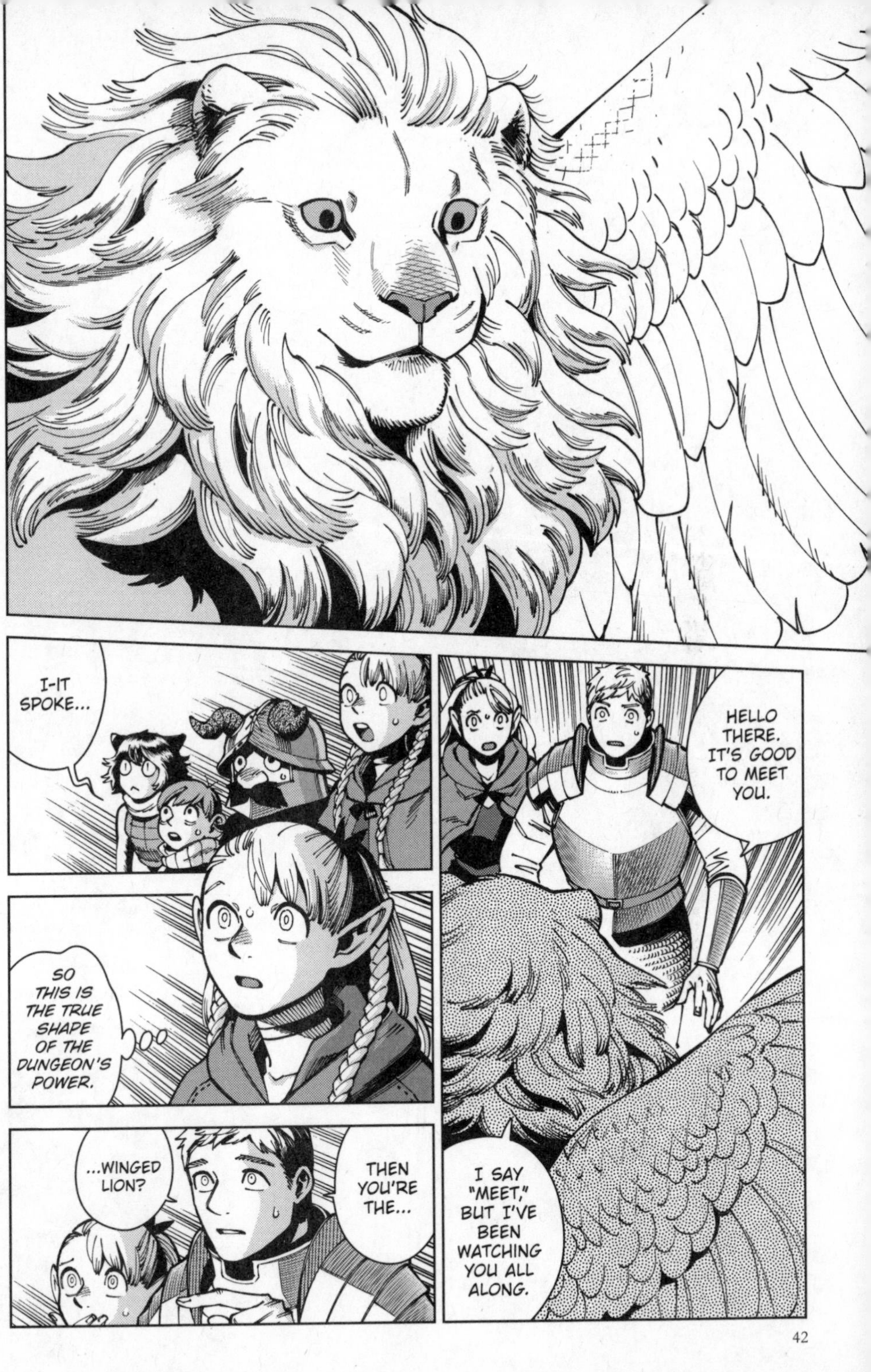
HELLO THERE. IT'S GOOD TO MEET YOU.
I SAY "MEET," BUT I'VE BEEN WATCHING YOU ALL ALONG.
I-IT SPOKE...
SO THIS IS THE TRUE SHAPE OF THE DUNGEON'S POWER.
THEN YOU'RE THE...
...WINGED LION?

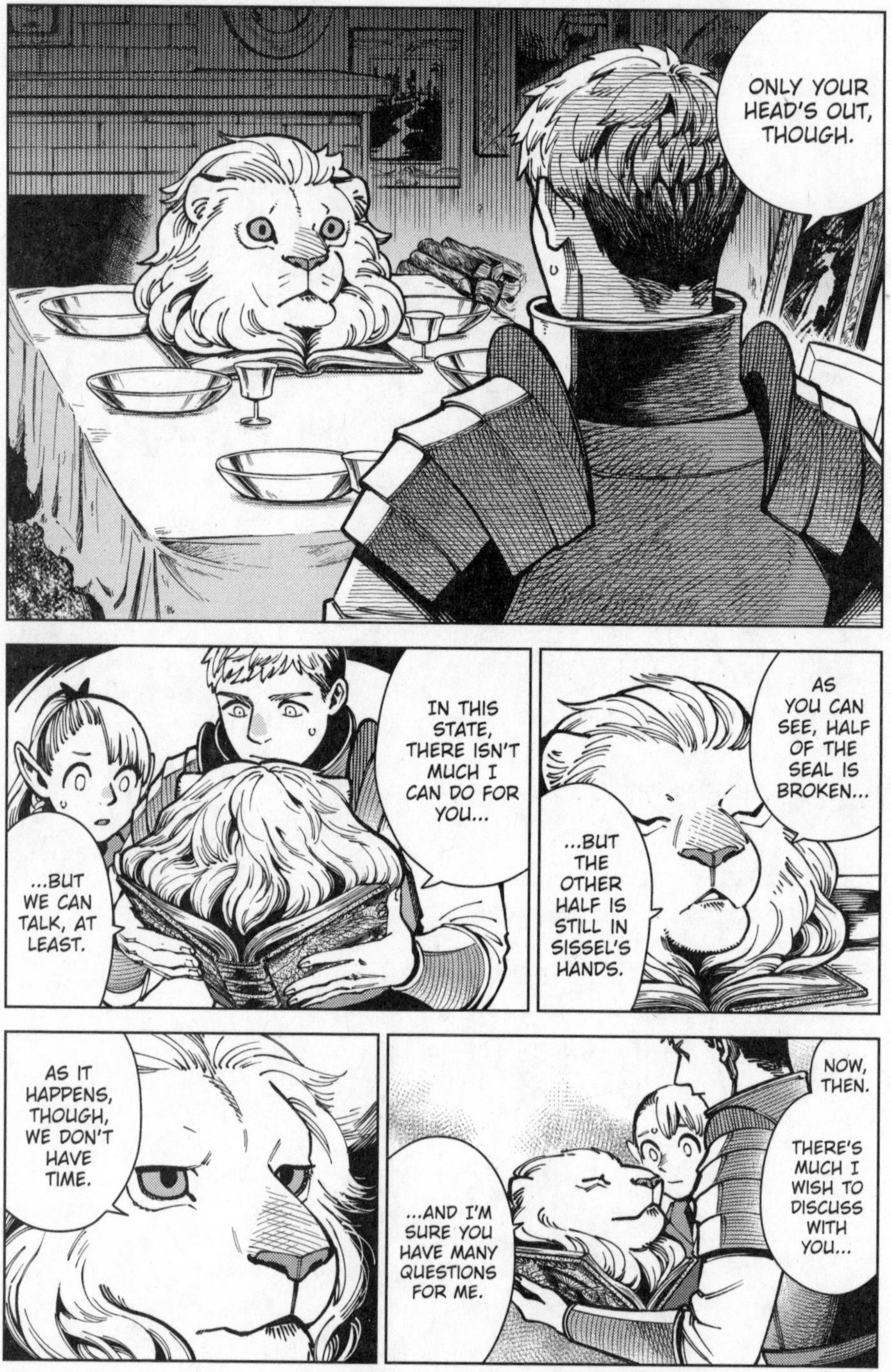
ONLY YOUR HEAD'S OUT, THOUGH.
AS YOU CAN SEE, HALF OF THE SEAL IS BROKEN...
...BUT THE OTHER HALF IS STILL IN SISSEL'S HANDS.
IN THIS STATE, THERE ISN'T MUCH I CAN DO FOR YOU...
...BUT WE CAN TALK, AT LEAST.
NOW, THEN.
THERE'S MUCH I WISH TO DISCUSS WITH YOU...
...AND I'M SURE YOU HAVE MANY QUESTIONS FOR ME.
AS IT HAPPENS, THOUGH, WE DON'T HAVE TIME.

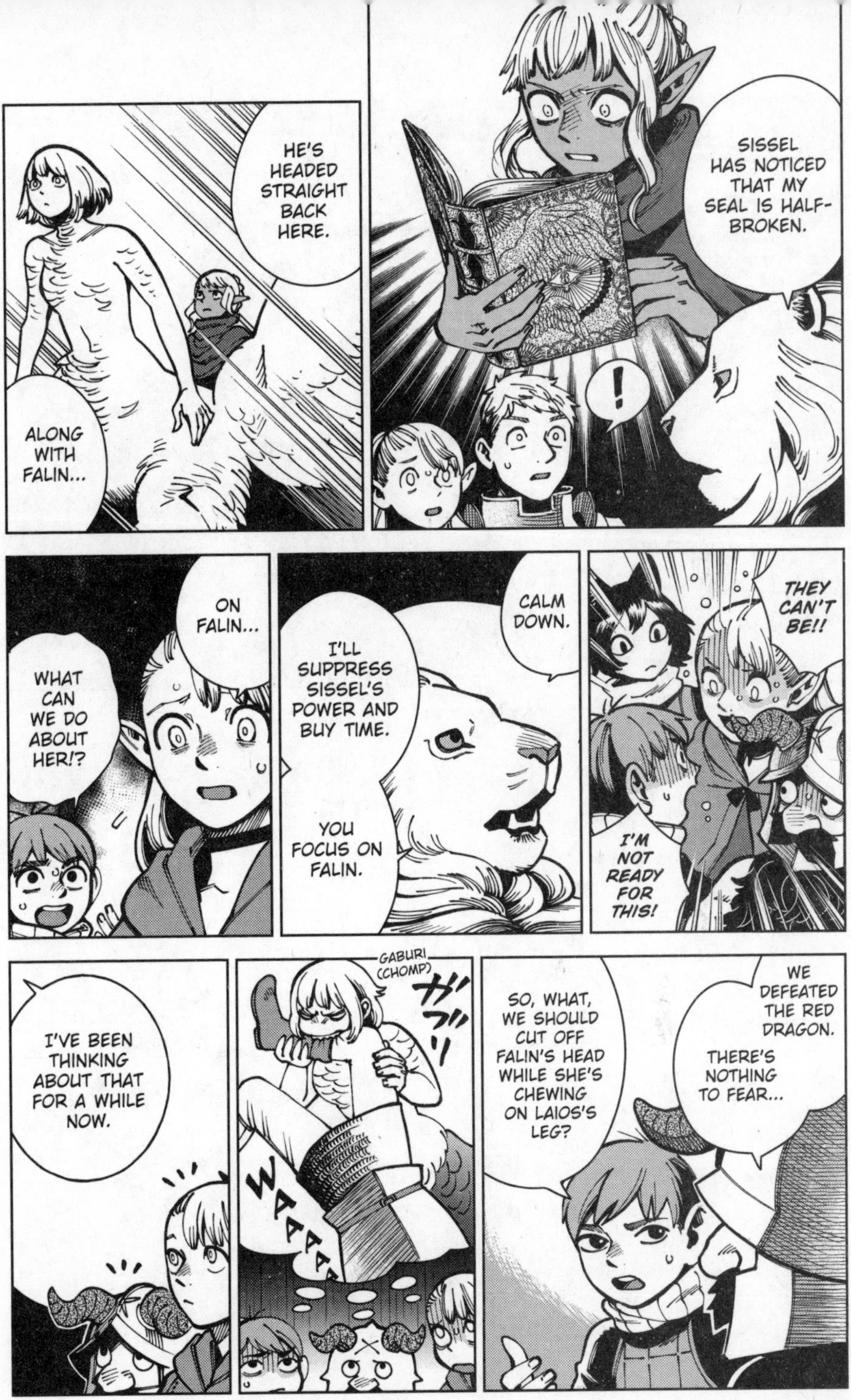
SISSEL HAS NOTICED THAT MY SEAL IS HALF-BROKEN.
!
HE'S HEADED STRAIGHT BACK HERE.
ALONG WITH FALIN...
THEY CAN'T BE!!
I'M NOT READY FOR THIS!
CALM DOWN.
I'LL SUPPRESS SISSEL'S POWER AND BUY TIME.
YOU FOCUS ON FALIN.
ON FALIN...
WHAT CAN WE DO ABOUT HER!?
WE DEFEATED THE RED DRAGON.
THERE'S NOTHING TO FEAR...
SO, WHAT, WE SHOULD CUT OFF FALIN'S HEAD WHILE SHE'S CHEWING ON LAIOS'S LEG?
GABURI (CHOMP)
I'VE BEEN THINKING ABOUT THAT FOR A WHILE NOW.

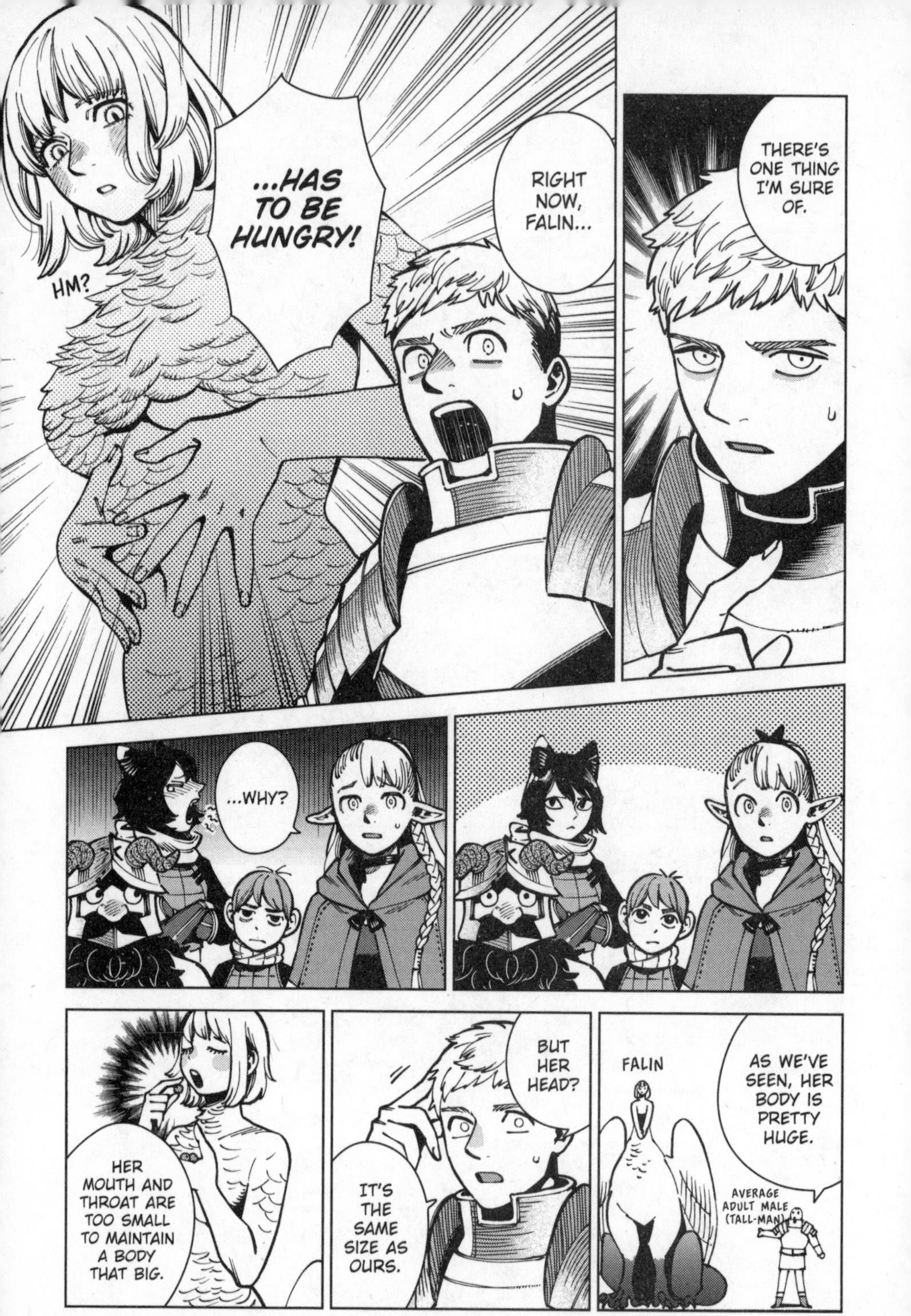
THERE'S ONE THING I'M SURE OF.
RIGHT NOW, FALIN...
...HAS TO BE HUNGRY!
HM?
...WHY?
AS WE'VE SEEN, HER BODY IS PRETTY HUGE.
FALIN
AVERAGE ADULT MALE (TALL-MAN)
BUT HER HEAD?
IT'S THE SAME SIZE AS OURS.
HER MOUTH AND THROAT ARE TOO SMALL TO MAINTAIN A BODY THAT BIG.

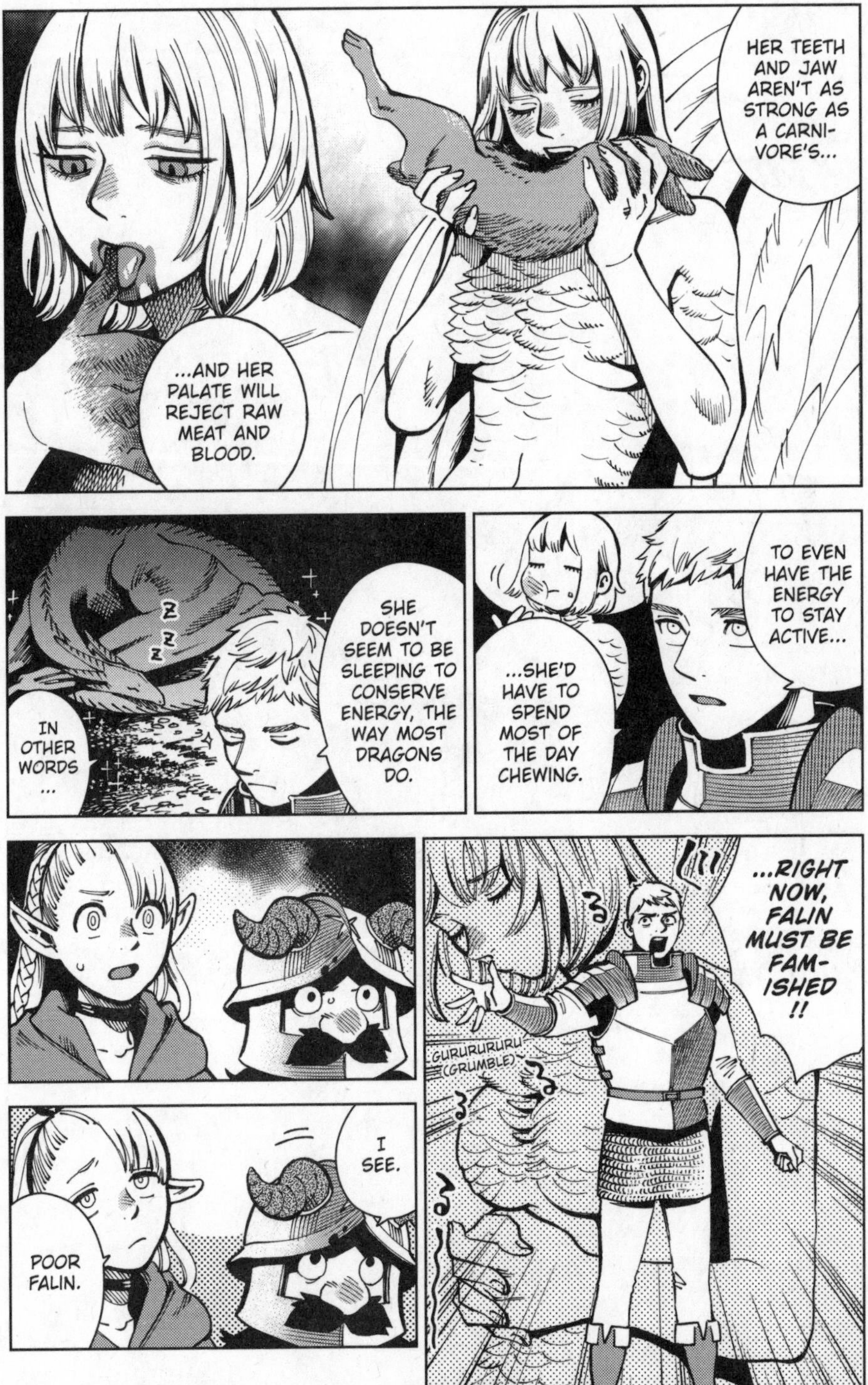
HER TEETH AND JAW AREN'T AS STRONG AS A CARNI-VORE'S...
...AND HER PALATE WILL REJECT RAW MEAT AND BLOOD.
TO EVEN HAVE THE ENERGY TO STAY ACTIVE...
...SHE'D HAVE TO SPEND MOST OF THE DAY CHEWING.
SHE DOESN'T SEEM TO BE SLEEPING TO CONSERVE ENERGY, THE WAY MOST DRAGONS DO.
IN OTHER WORDS ...
...RIGHT NOW, FALIN MUST BE FAM-ISHED !!
GURURURURU (GRUMBLE)
I SEE.
POOR FALIN.

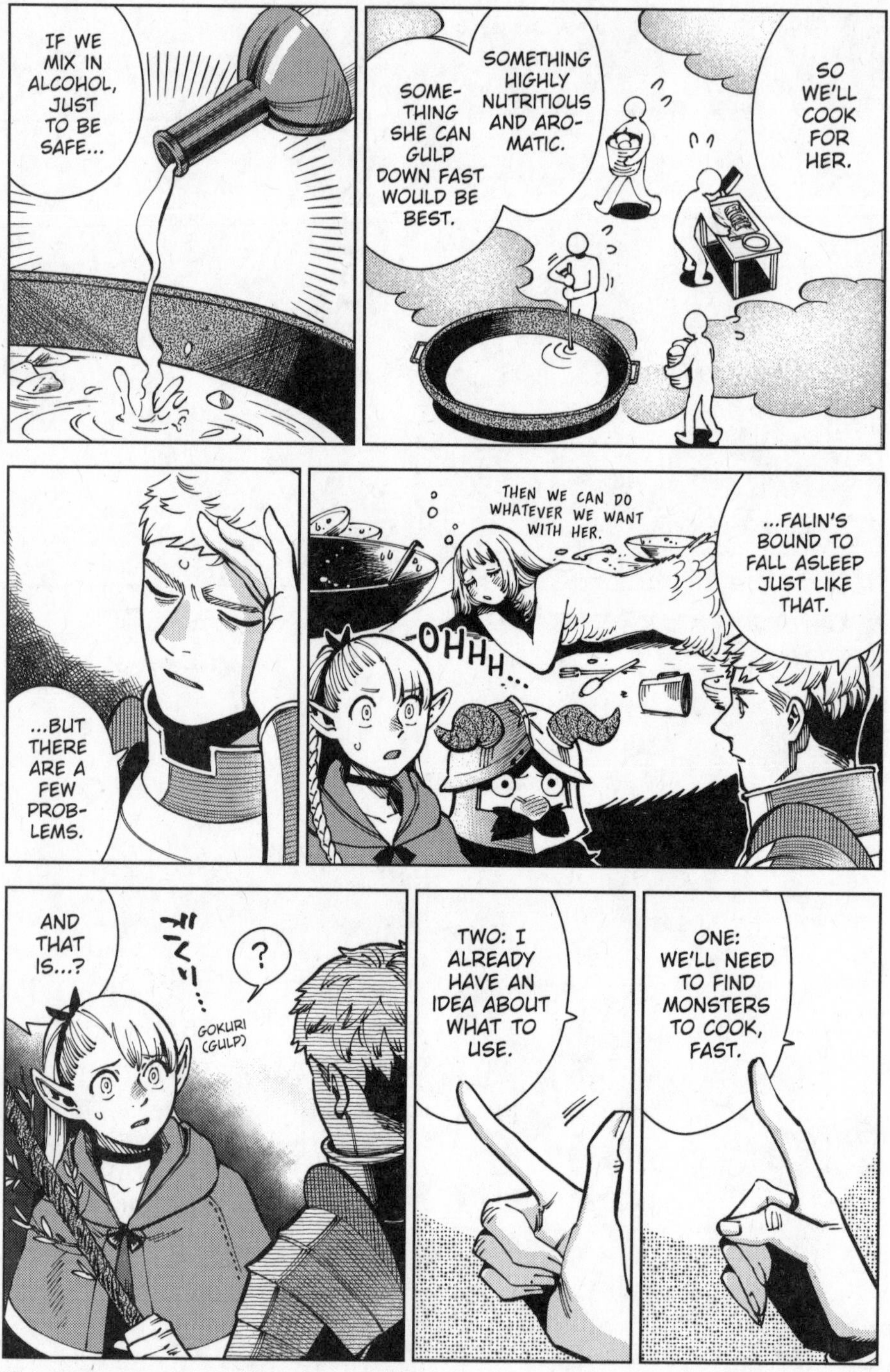
SO WE'LL COOK FOR HER.
SOMETHING HIGHLY NUTRITIOUS AND ARO-MATIC.
SOME-THING SHE CAN GULP DOWN FAST WOULD BE BEST.
IF WE MIX IN ALCOHOL, JUST TO BE SAFE...
...FALIN'S BOUND TO FALL ASLEEP JUST LIKE THAT.
THEN WE CAN DO WHATEVER WE WANT WITH HER.
OHHHH...
...BUT THERE ARE A FEW PROB-LEMS.
ONE: WE'LL NEED TO FIND MONSTERS TO COOK, FAST.
TWO: I ALREADY HAVE AN IDEA ABOUT WHAT TO USE.
AND THAT IS...?
?
GOKURI (GULP)

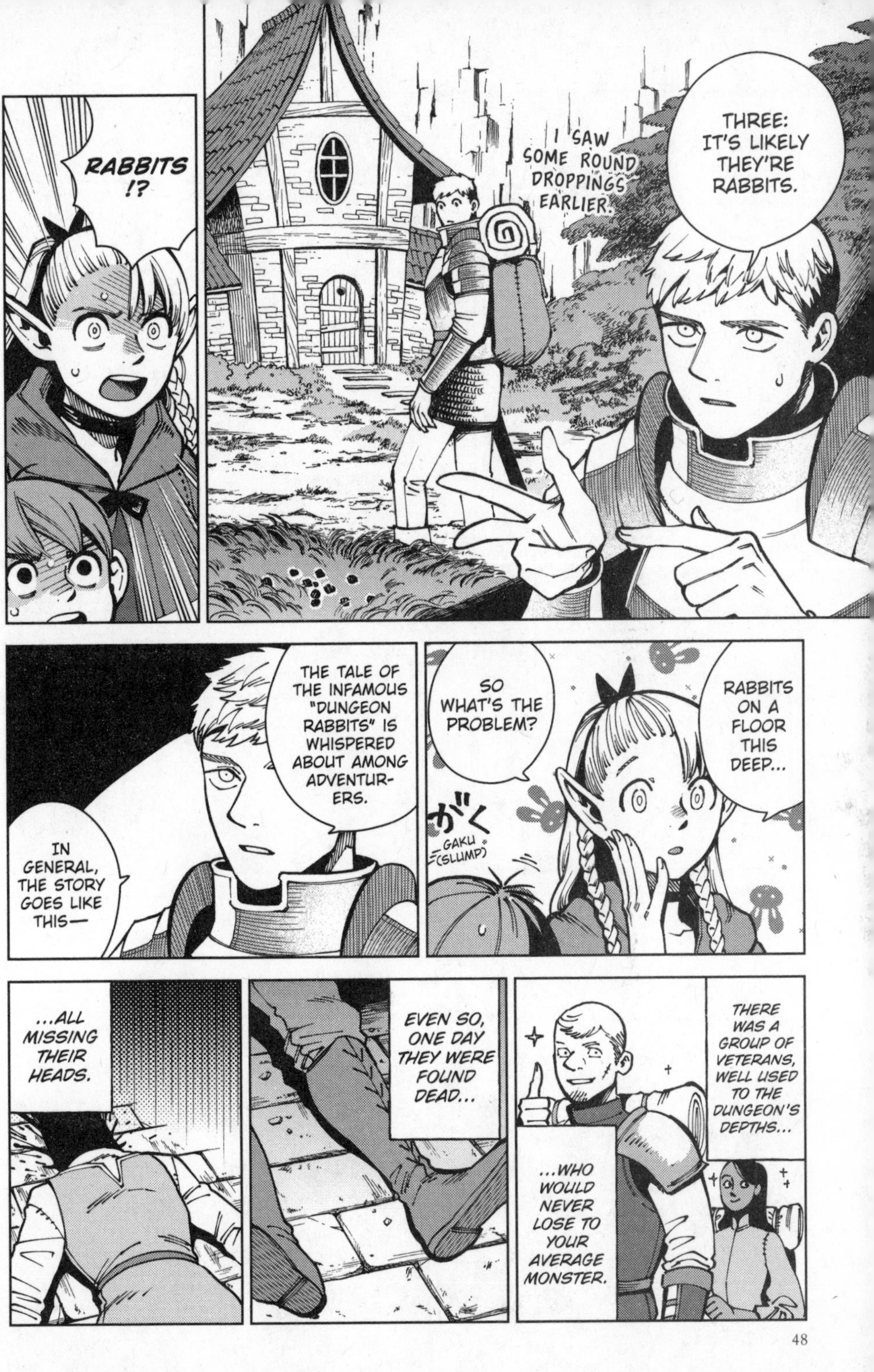
THREE: IT'S LIKELY THEY'RE RABBITS.
I SAW SOME ROUND DROPPINGS EARLIER.
RABBITS !?
RABBITS ON A FLOOR THIS DEEP...
SO WHAT'S THE PROBLEM?
がく
GAKU (SLUMP)
THE TALE OF THE INFAMOUS "DUNGEON RABBITS" IS WHISPERED ABOUT AMONG ADVENTURERS.
IN GENERAL, THE STORY GOES LIKE THIS—
THERE WAS A GROUP OF VETERANS, WELL USED TO THE DUNGEON'S DEPTHS...
...WHO WOULD NEVER LOSE TO YOUR AVERAGE MONSTER.
EVEN SO, ONE DAY THEY WERE FOUND DEAD...
...ALL MISSING THEIR HEADS.

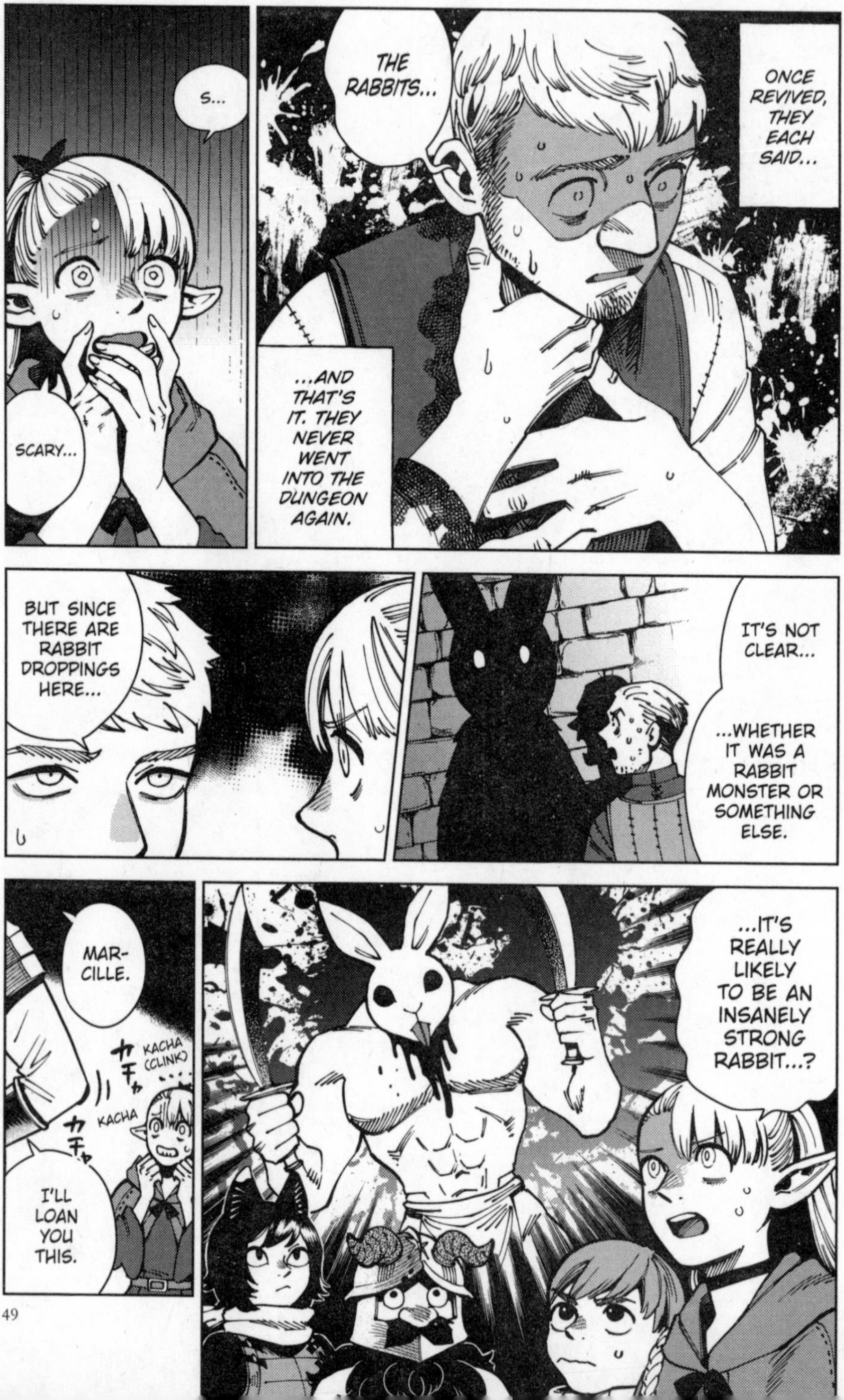
ONCE REVIVED, THEY EACH SAID...
THE RABBITS...
...AND THAT'S IT. THEY NEVER WENT INTO THE DUNGEON AGAIN.
S...
SCARY...
IT'S NOT CLEAR...
...WHETHER IT WAS A RABBIT MONSTER OR SOMETHING ELSE.
BUT SINCE THERE ARE RABBIT DROPPINGS HERE...
...IT'S REALLY LIKELY TO BE AN INSANELY STRONG RABBIT...?
MARCILLE.
カチャ KACHA (CLINK)
カチャ KACHA
I'LL LOAN YOU THIS.

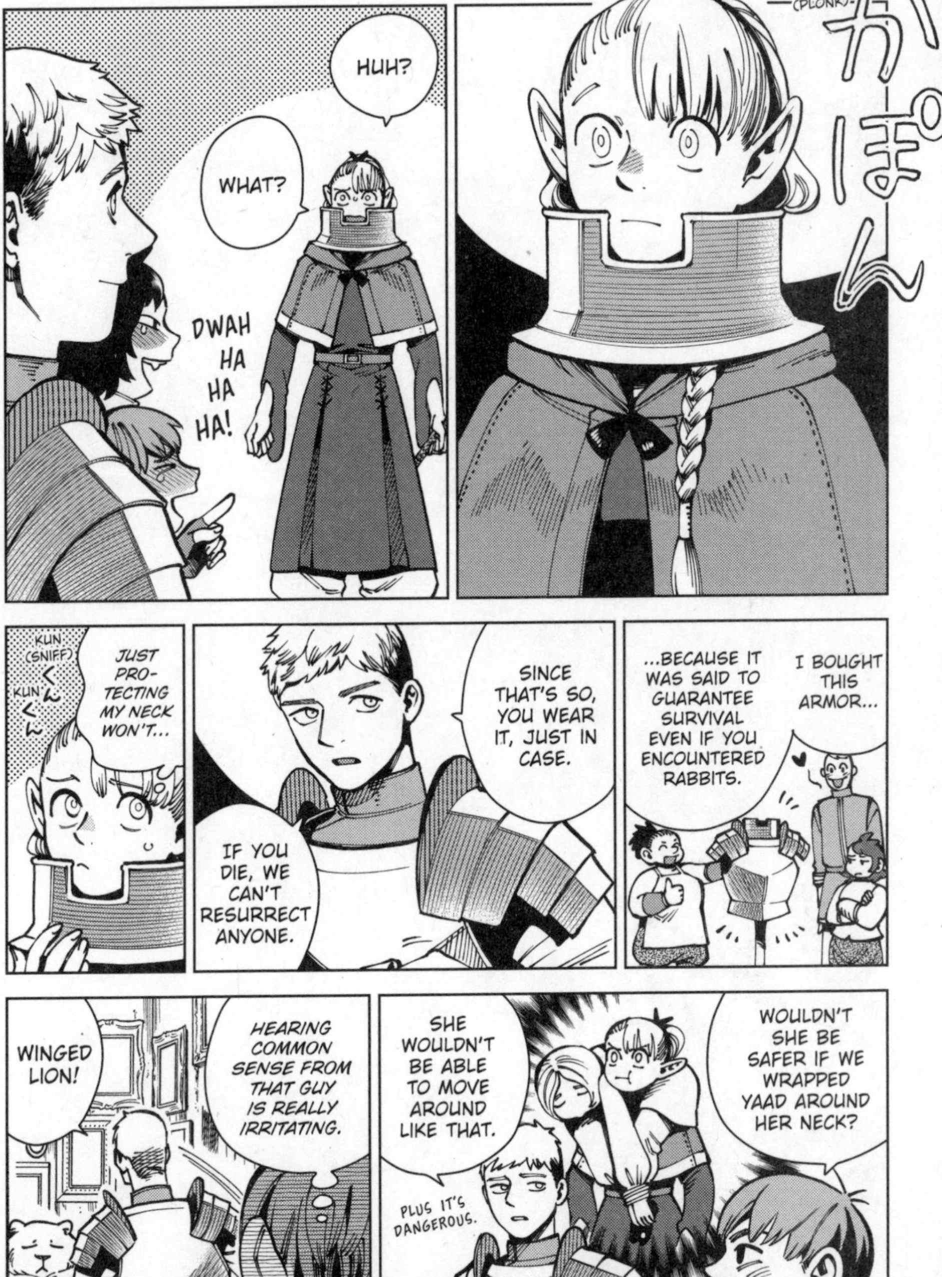
KAPON (PLONK)
かぽん
HUH?
WHAT?
DWAH HA HA HA!
I BOUGHT THIS ARMOR...
...BECAUSE IT WAS SAID TO GUARANTEE SURVIVAL EVEN IF YOU ENCOUNTERED RABBITS.
SINCE THAT'S SO, YOU WEAR IT, JUST IN CASE.
IF YOU DIE, WE CAN'T RESURRECT ANYONE.
KUN (SNIFF)
くん
KUN
くん
JUST PRO-TECTING MY NECK WON'T...
WOULDN'T SHE BE SAFER IF WE WRAPPED YAAD AROUND HER NECK?
SHE WOULDN'T BE ABLE TO MOVE AROUND LIKE THAT.
PLUS IT'S DANGEROUS.
HEARING COMMON SENSE FROM THAT GUY IS REALLY IRRITATING.
WINGED LION!

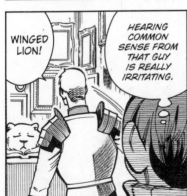

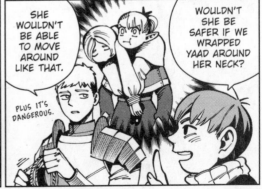

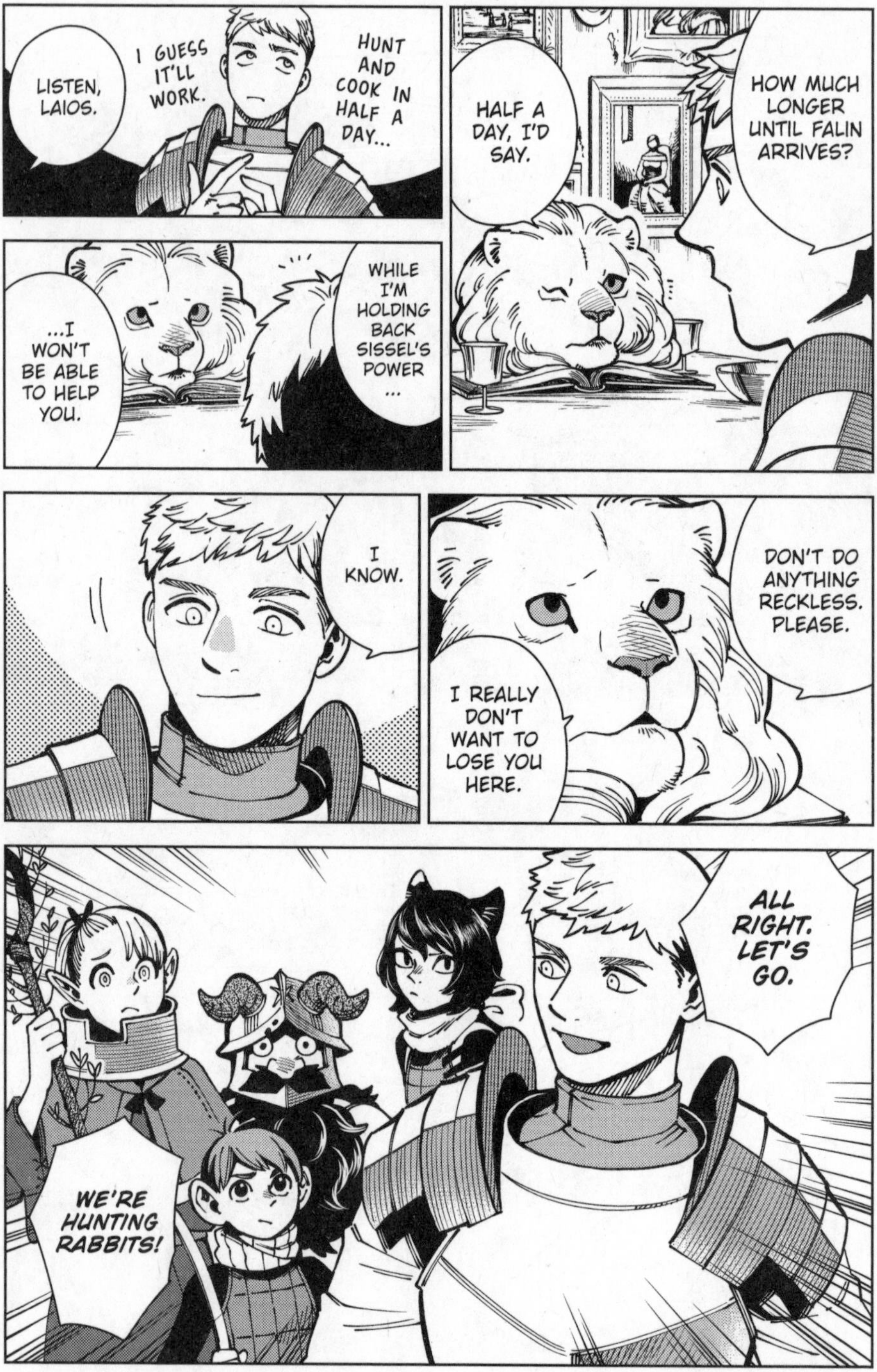
HOW MUCH LONGER UNTIL FALIN ARRIVES?
HALF A DAY, I'D SAY.
HUNT AND COOK IN HALF A DAY...
I GUESS IT'LL WORK.
LISTEN, LAIOS.
WHILE I'M HOLDING BACK SISSEL'S POWER ...
...I WON'T BE ABLE TO HELP YOU.
DON'T DO ANYTHING RECKLESS. PLEASE.
I REALLY DON'T WANT TO LOSE YOU HERE.
I KNOW.
ALL RIGHT. LET'S GO.
WE'RE HUNTING RABBITS!

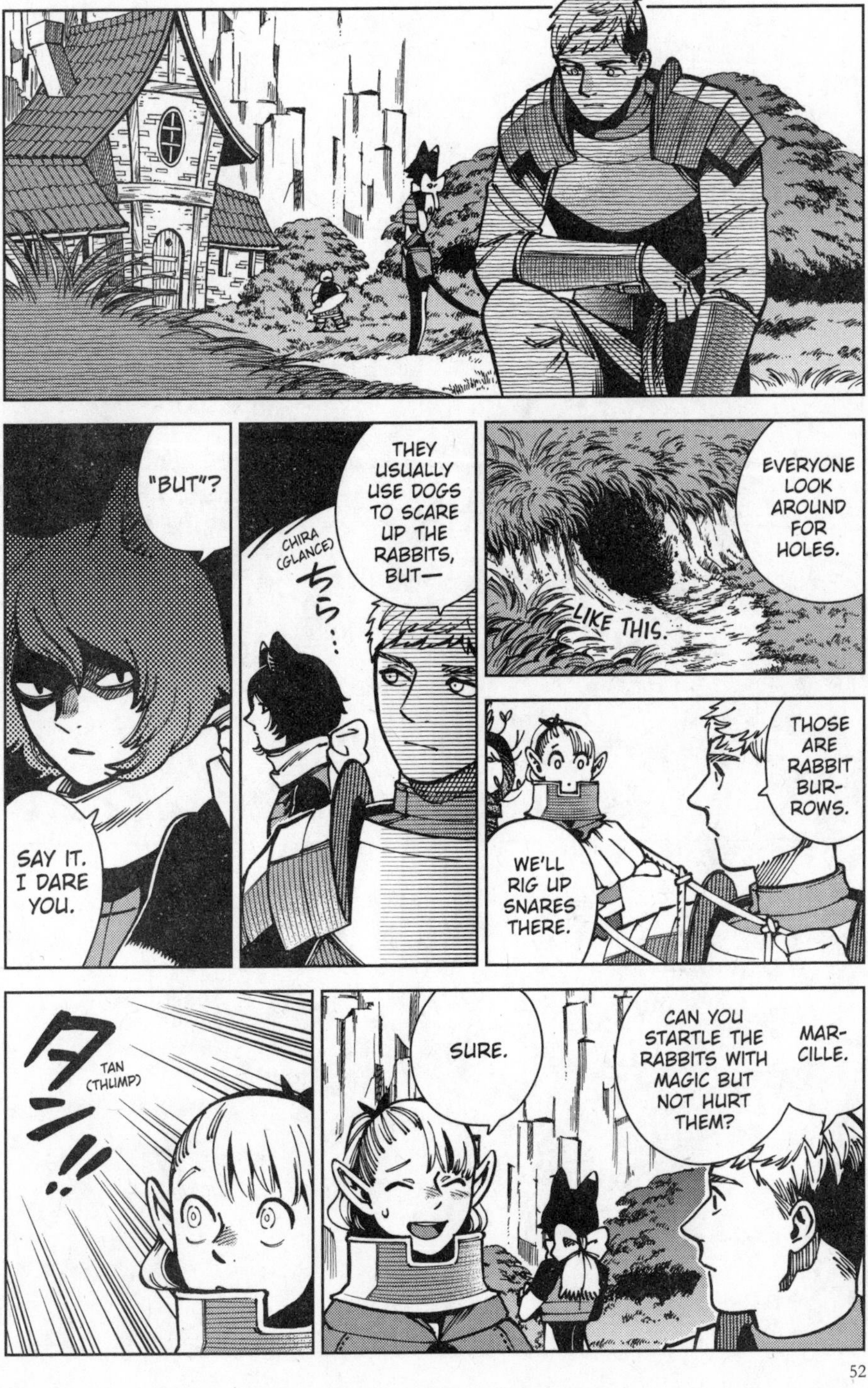
EVERYONE LOOK AROUND FOR HOLES.
LIKE THIS.
THOSE ARE RABBIT BURROWS.
WE'LL RIG UP SNARES THERE.
THEY USUALLY USE DOGS TO SCARE UP THE RABBITS, BUT—
ちら…
CHIRA (GLANCE)
"BUT"?
SAY IT. I DARE YOU.
MARCILLE.
CAN YOU STARTLE THE RABBITS WITH MAGIC BUT NOT HURT THEM?
SURE.
タン!!
TAN (THUMP)

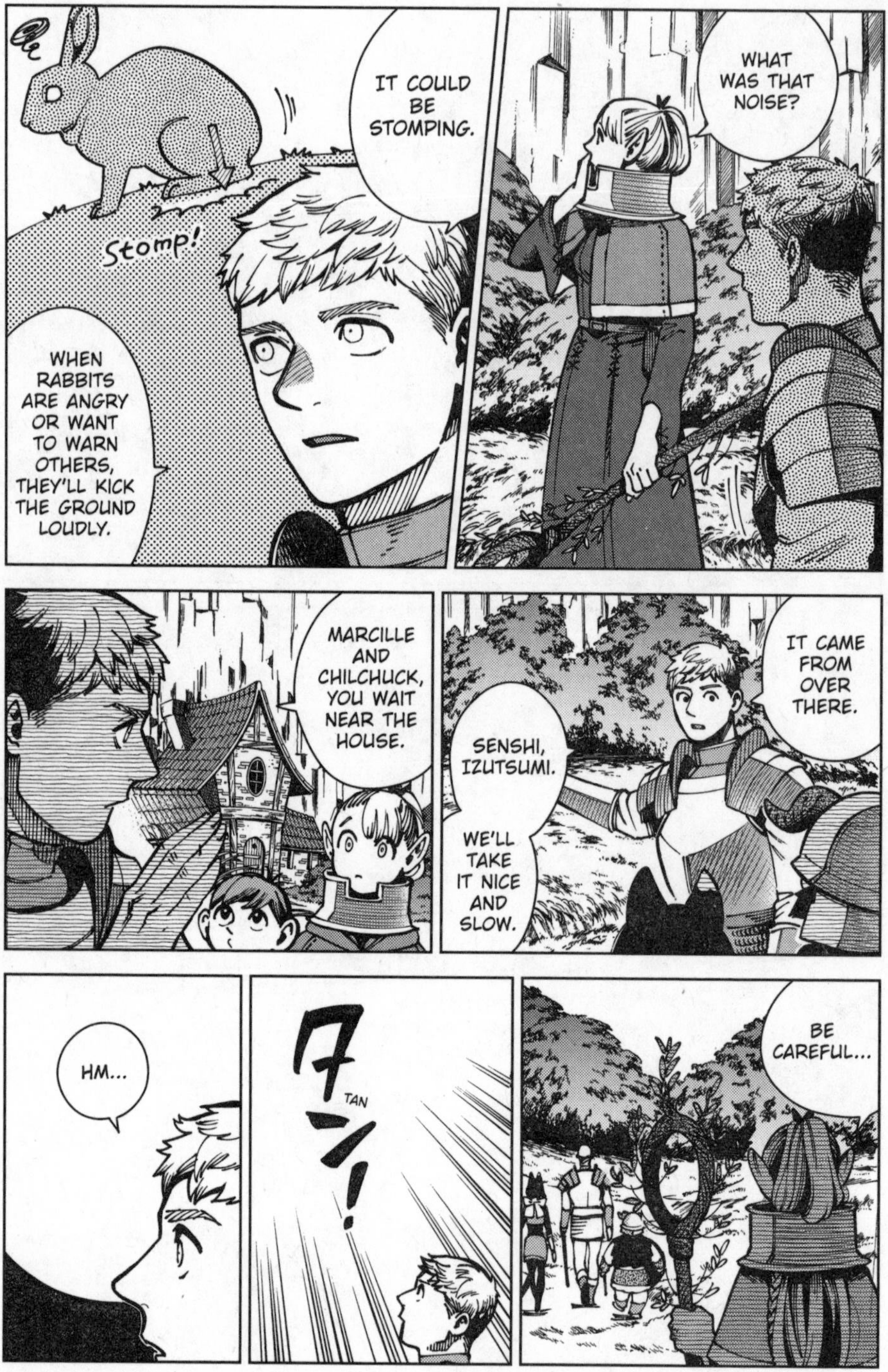
WHAT WAS THAT NOISE?
IT COULD BE STOMPING.
Stomp!
WHEN RABBITS ARE ANGRY OR WANT TO WARN OTHERS, THEY'LL KICK THE GROUND LOUDLY.
IT CAME FROM OVER THERE.
SENSHI, IZUTSUMI.
WE'LL TAKE IT NICE AND SLOW.
MARCILLE AND CHILCHUCK, YOU WAIT NEAR THE HOUSE.
BE CAREFUL...
タン!
TAN
HM...

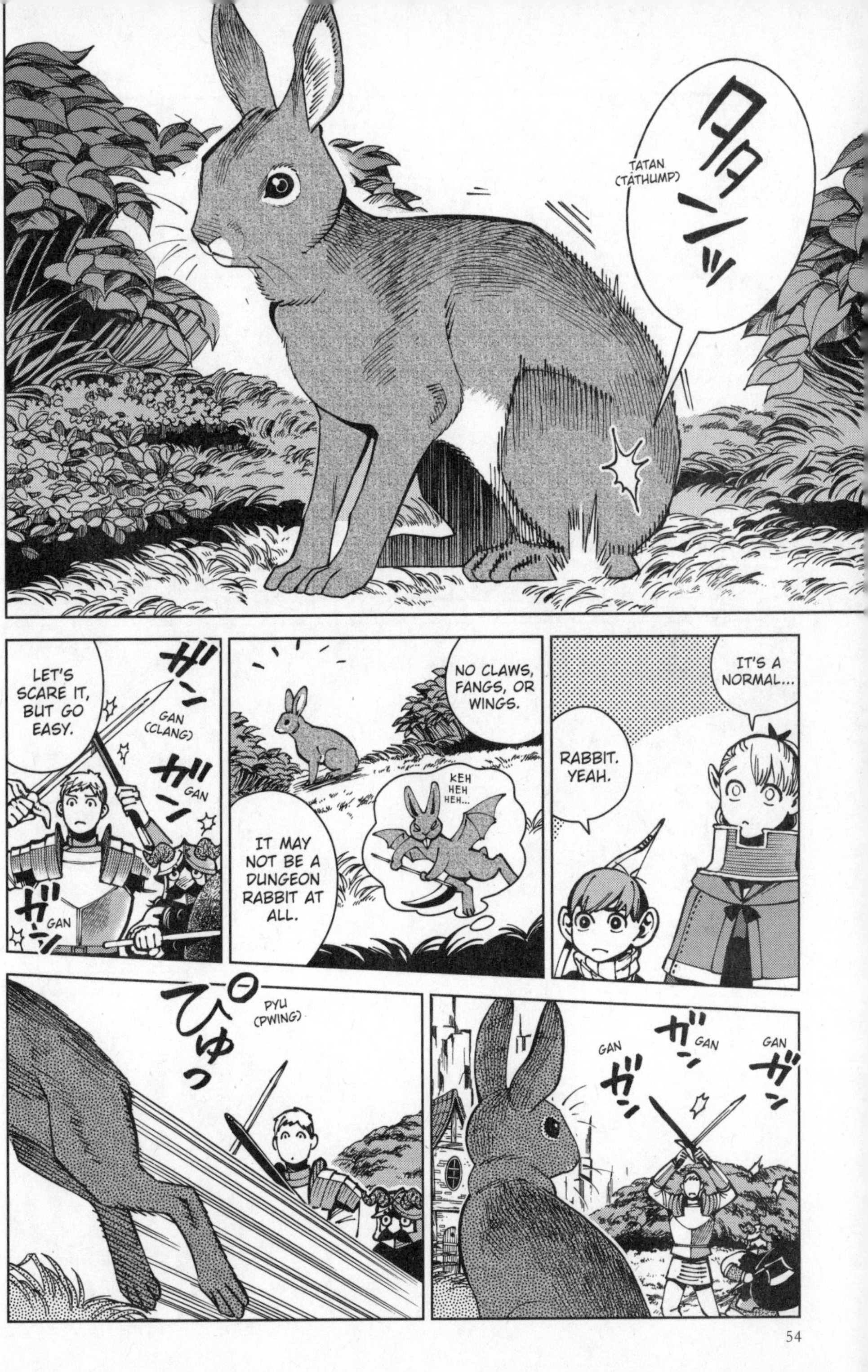
タタンッ
TATAN (TATHUMP)
IT'S A NORMAL...
RABBIT. YEAH.
NO CLAWS, FANGS, OR WINGS.
KEH HEH HEH...
IT MAY NOT BE A DUNGEON RABBIT AT ALL.
LET'S SCARE IT, BUT GO EASY.
ガン
GAN (CLANG)
ガン
GAN
ガン
GAN
ガン
GAN
ガン
GAN
ガン
GAN
ぴゅっ
PYU (PWING)

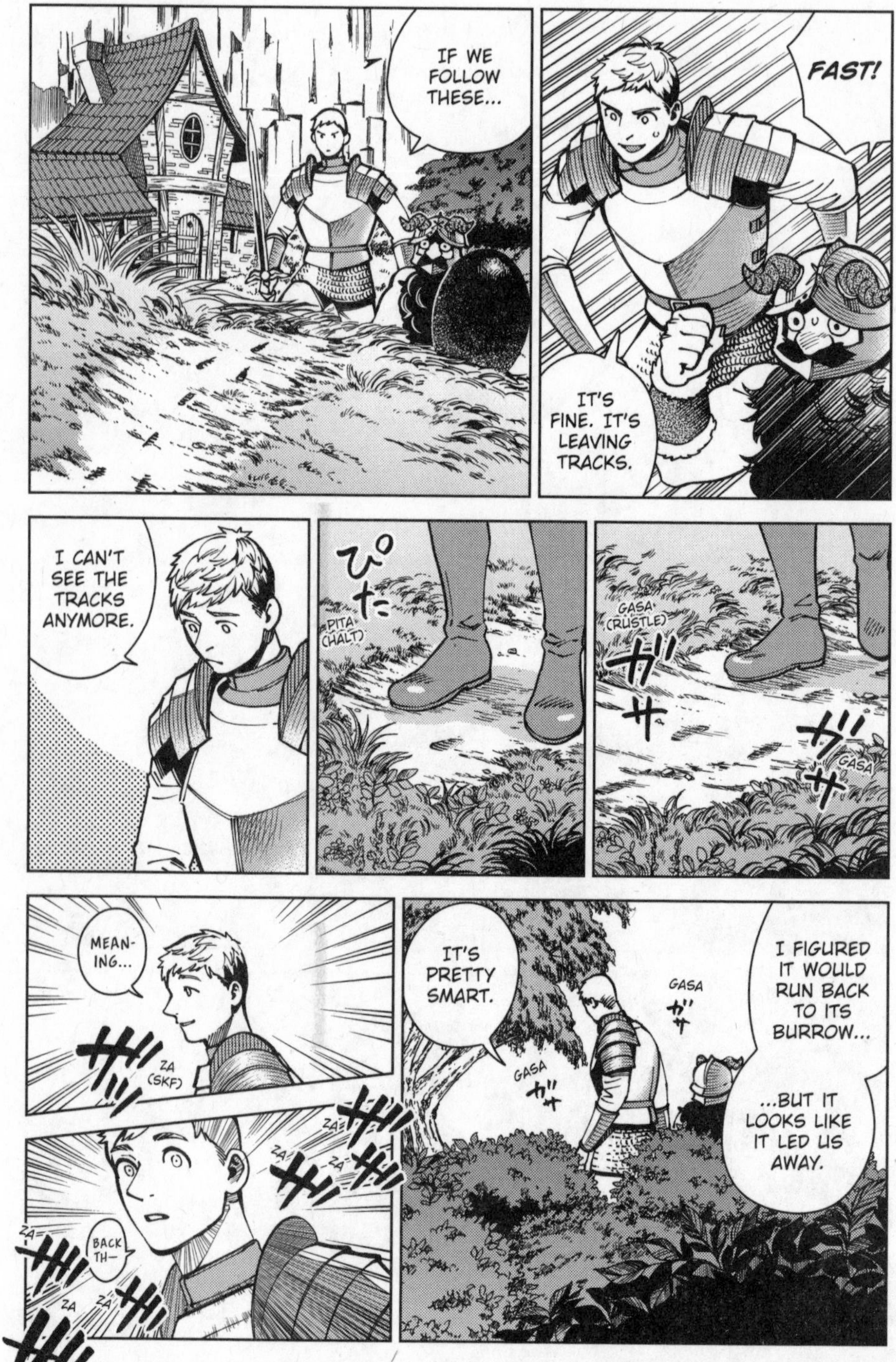
FAST!
IT'S FINE. IT'S LEAVING TRACKS.
IF WE FOLLOW THESE...
ガサ
GASA (RUSTLE)
ガサ
GASA
ぴた
PITA (HALT)
I CAN'T SEE THE TRACKS ANYMORE.
I FIGURED IT WOULD RUN BACK TO ITS BURROW...
...BUT IT LOOKS LIKE IT LED US AWAY.
GASA
ガサ
IT'S PRETTY SMART.
GASA
ガサ
MEAN-ING...
ZA (SKF)
ZA
ZA
ZA
BACK TH—
ZA
ZA
ZA

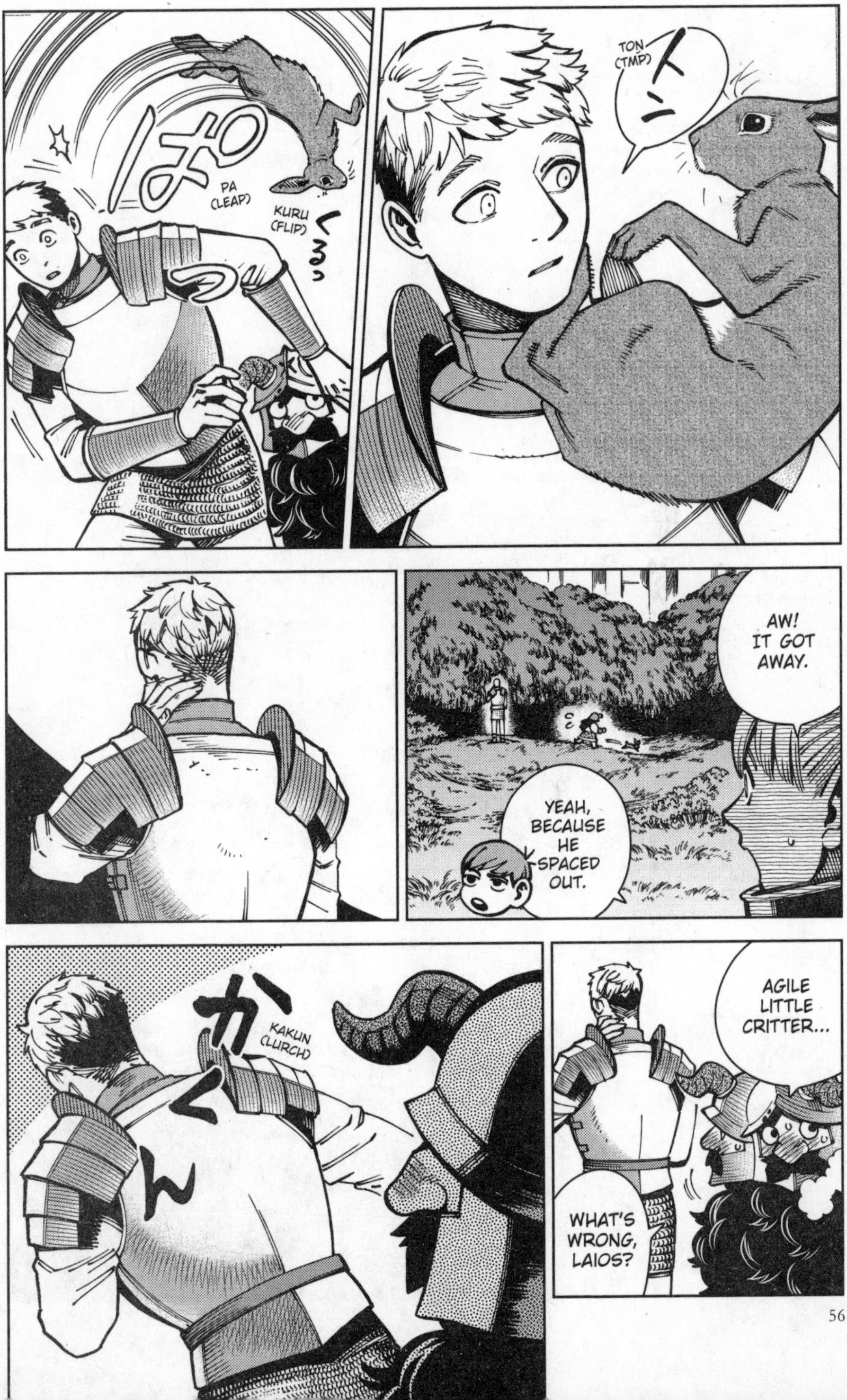
トン
TON (TMP)
ぱっ
PA (LEAP)
くるっ
KURU (FLIP)
AW! IT GOT AWAY.
YEAH, BECAUSE HE SPACED OUT.
AGILE LITTLE CRITTER...
WHAT'S WRONG, LAIOS?
かくん
KAKUN (LURCH)

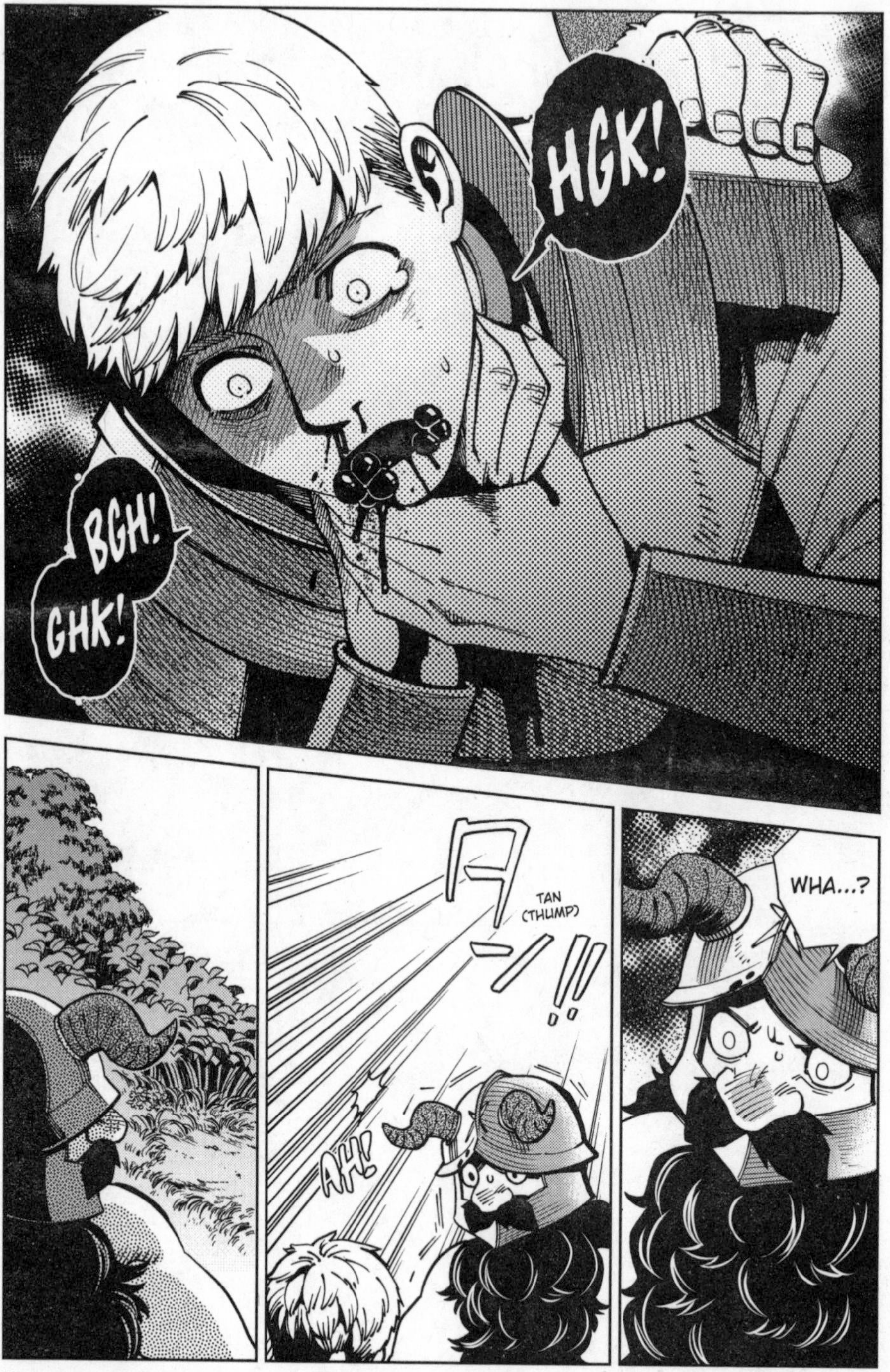
HGK!
BGH!
GHK!
WHA...?
TAN (THUMP)
AH!

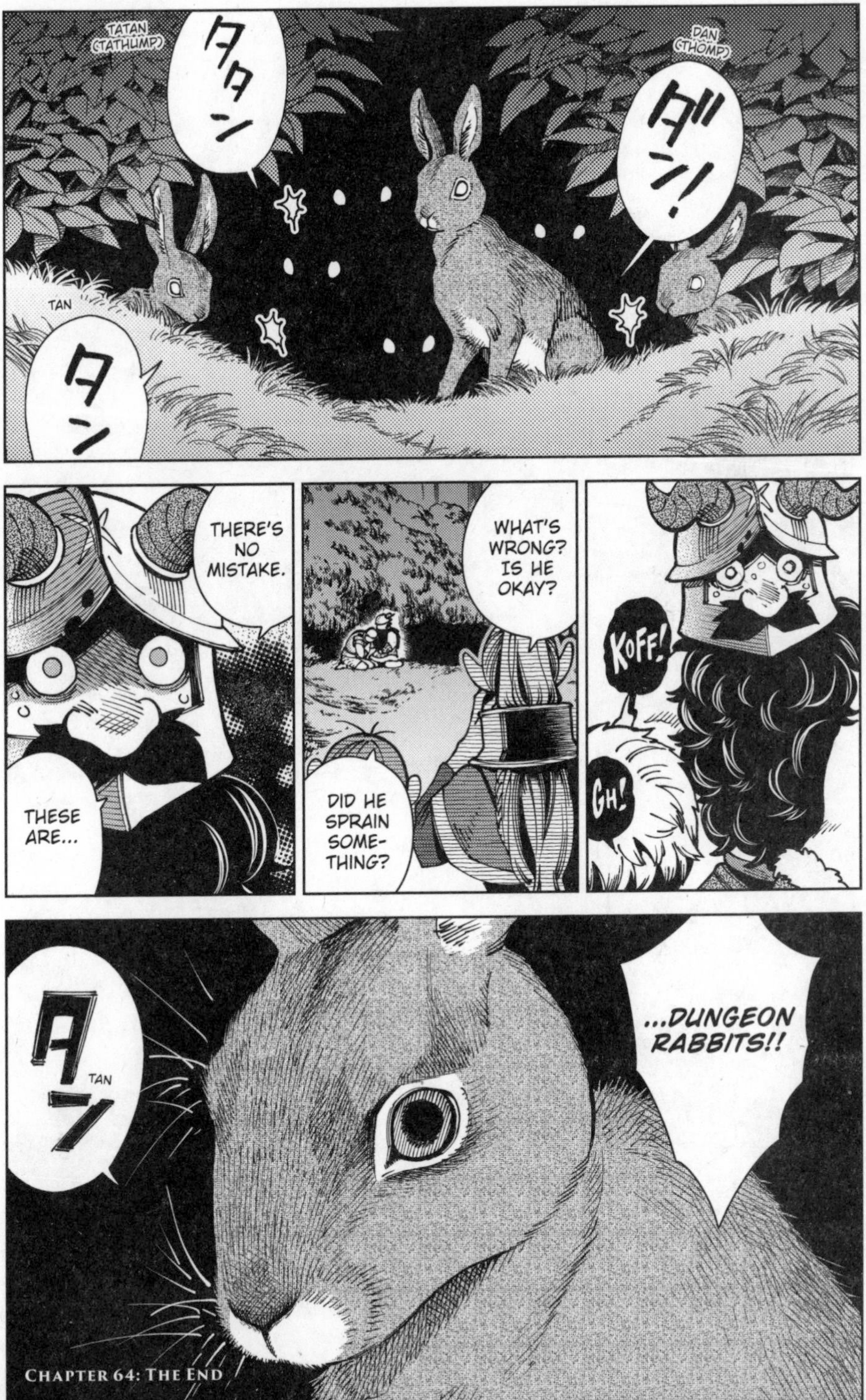
DAN (THOMP)
ダン!
TATAN (TATHUMP)
タタン
TAN
タン
KOFF!
GH!
WHAT'S WRONG? IS HE OKAY?
DID HE SPRAIN SOME-THING?
THERE'S NO MISTAKE.
THESE ARE...
...DUNGEON RABBITS!!
タン
TAN

Chapter 64: The End

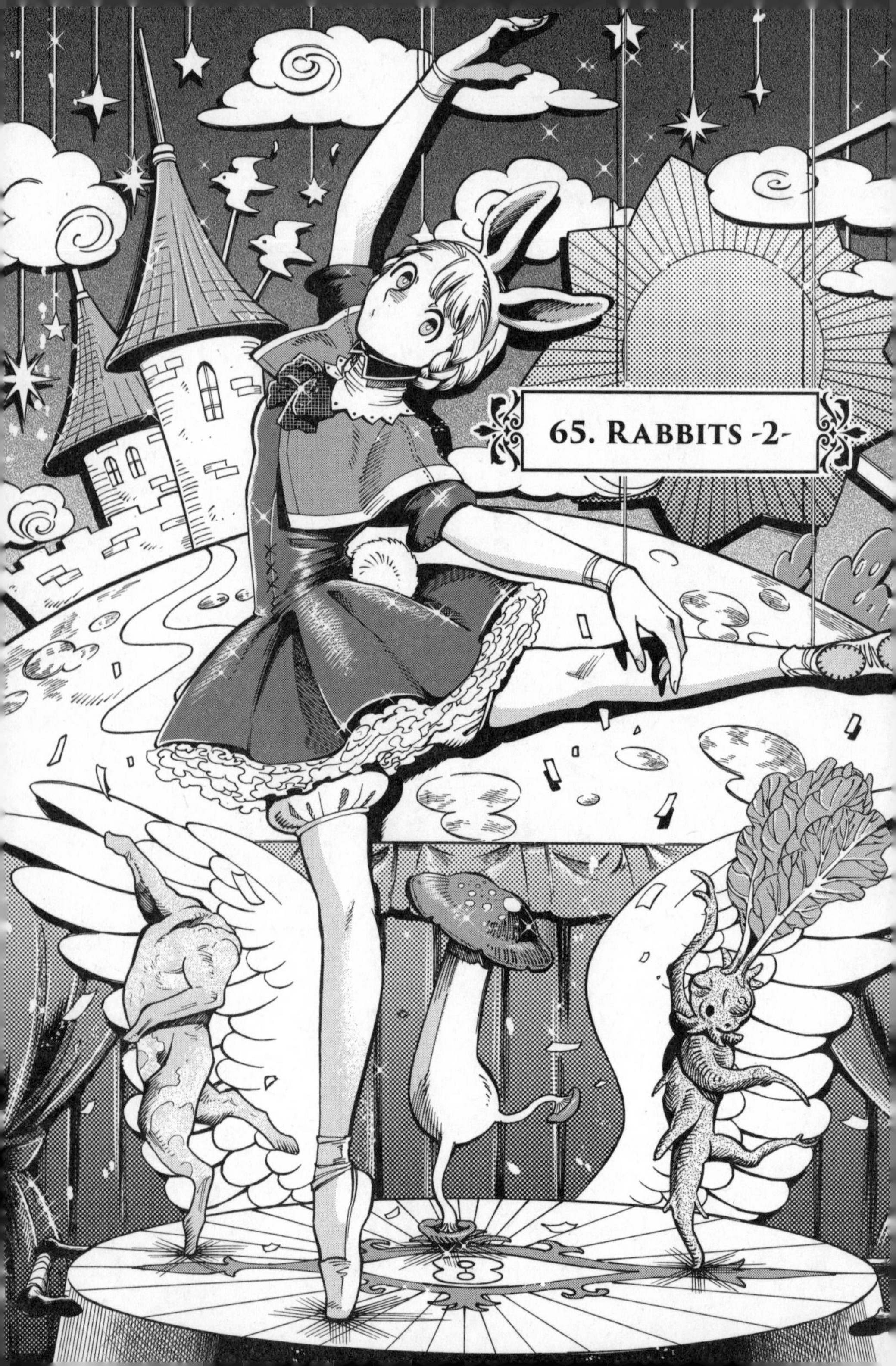
65. RABBITS -2-

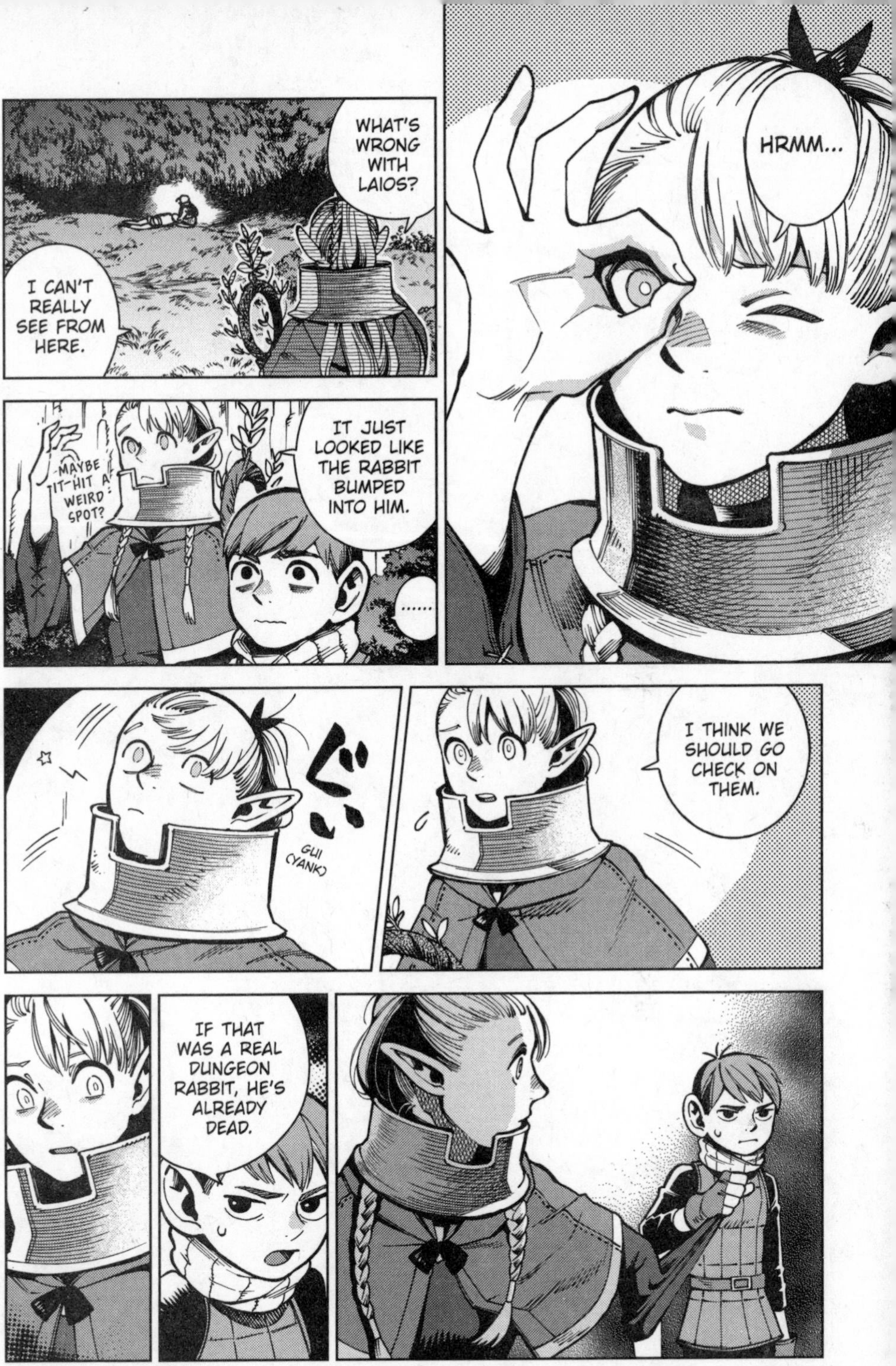
HRMM...
WHAT'S WRONG WITH LAIOS?
I CAN'T REALLY SEE FROM HERE.
IT JUST LOOKED LIKE THE RABBIT BUMPED INTO HIM.
MAYBE IT HIT A WEIRD SPOT?
......
I THINK WE SHOULD GO CHECK ON THEM.
GUI (YANK)
IF THAT WAS A REAL DUNGEON RABBIT, HE'S ALREADY DEAD.

LAIOS.

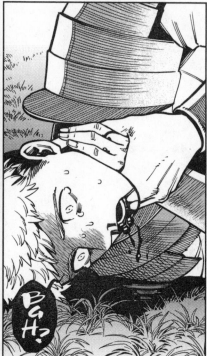

BGH?

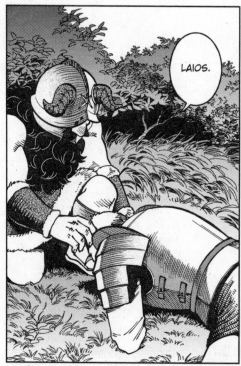

TAN

TATAN
TATHUMP

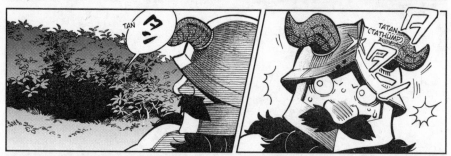

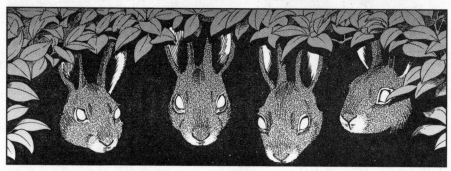

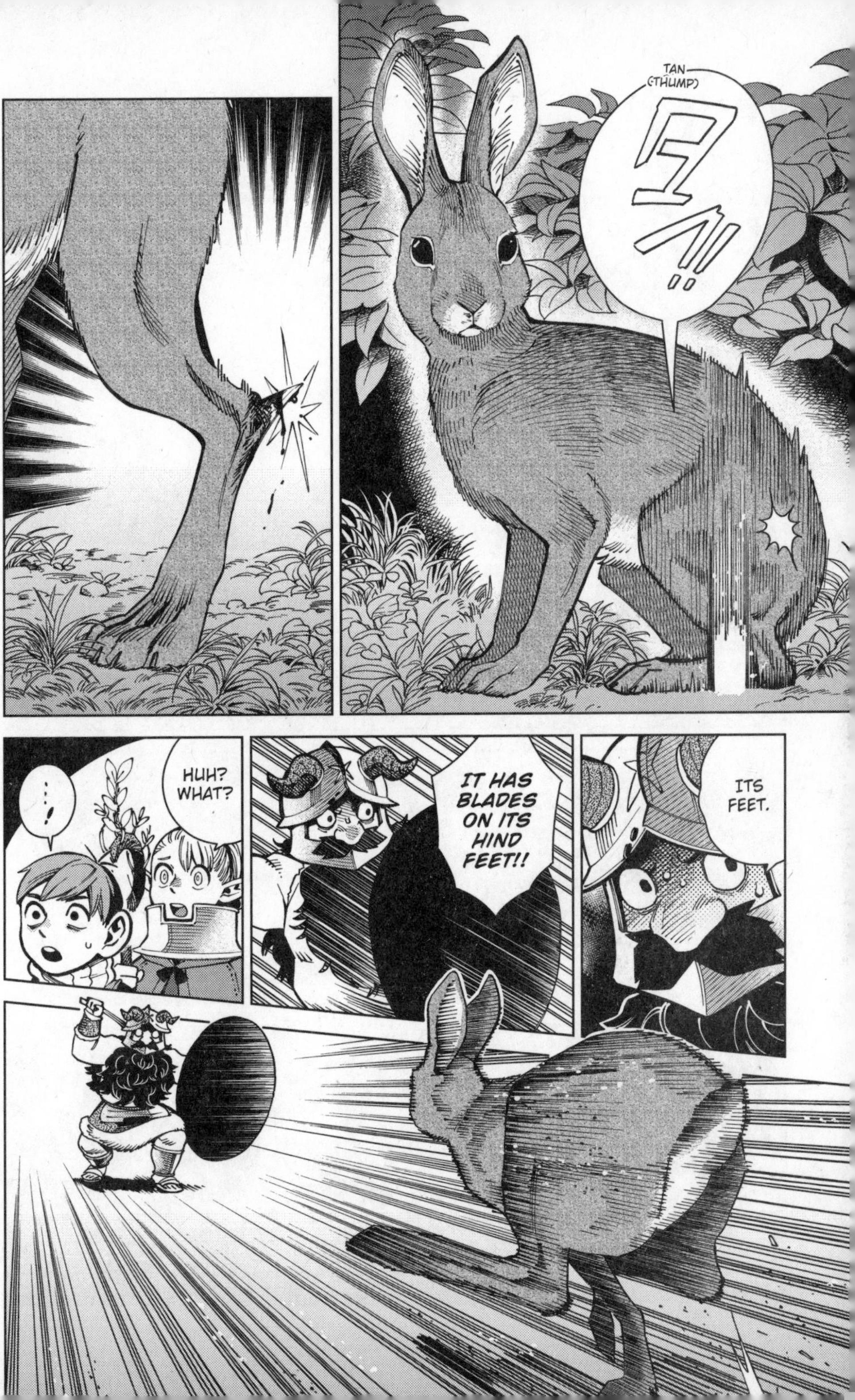
TAN (THUMP)
タン!!
ITS FEET.
IT HAS BLADES ON ITS HIND FEET!!
HUH? WHAT?
...!

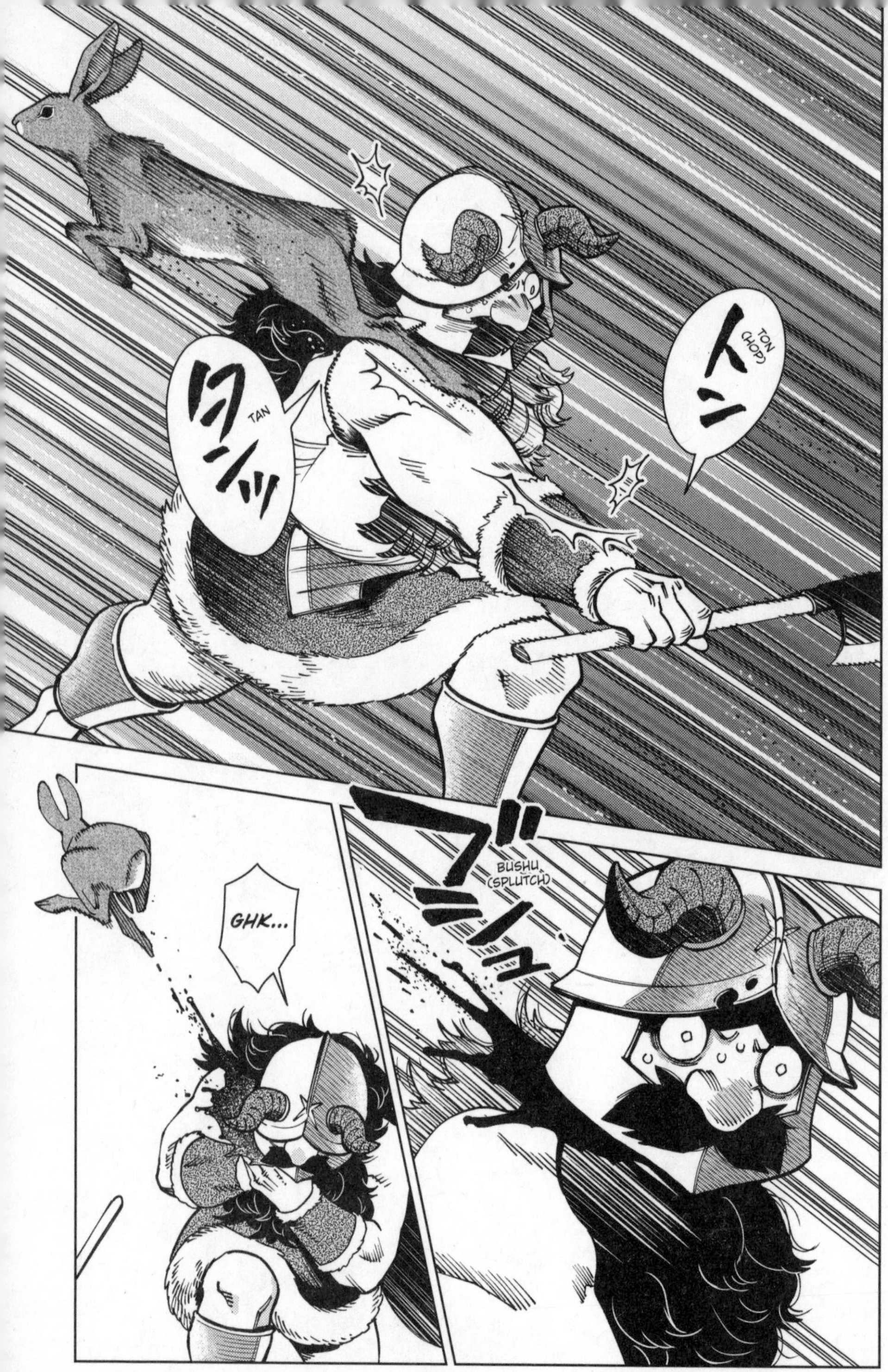
トン
TON (CHOP)
タンッ
TAN
ブシュッ
BUSHU (SPLUTCH)
GHK...

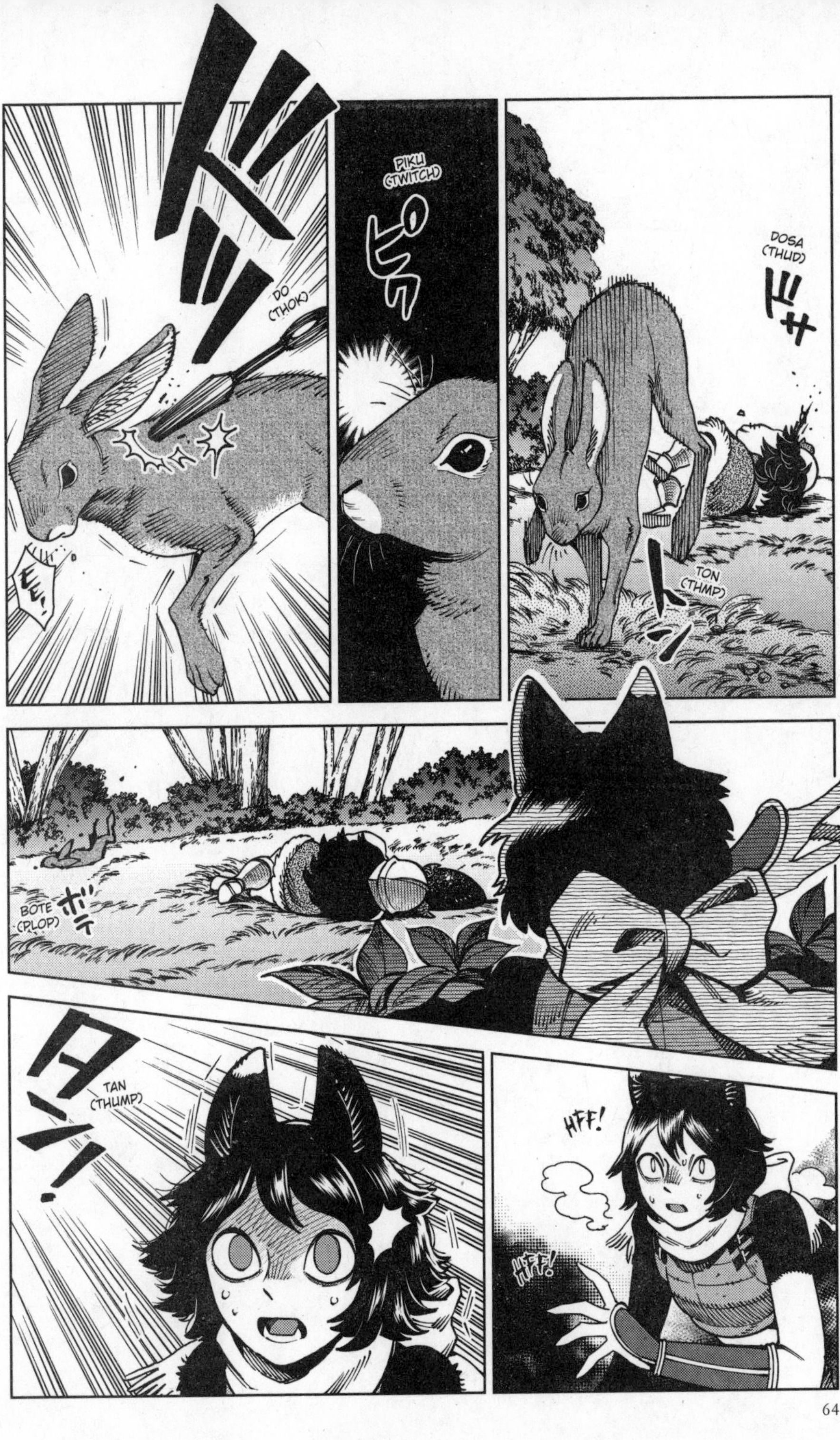
DOSA (THUD)
ドサッ
TON (THMP)
トン
PIKU (TWITCH)
ピク
ドッ
DO (THOK)
EE!
BOTE (PLOP)
ボテ
HFF!
HFF!
TAN (THUMP)
タンッ!

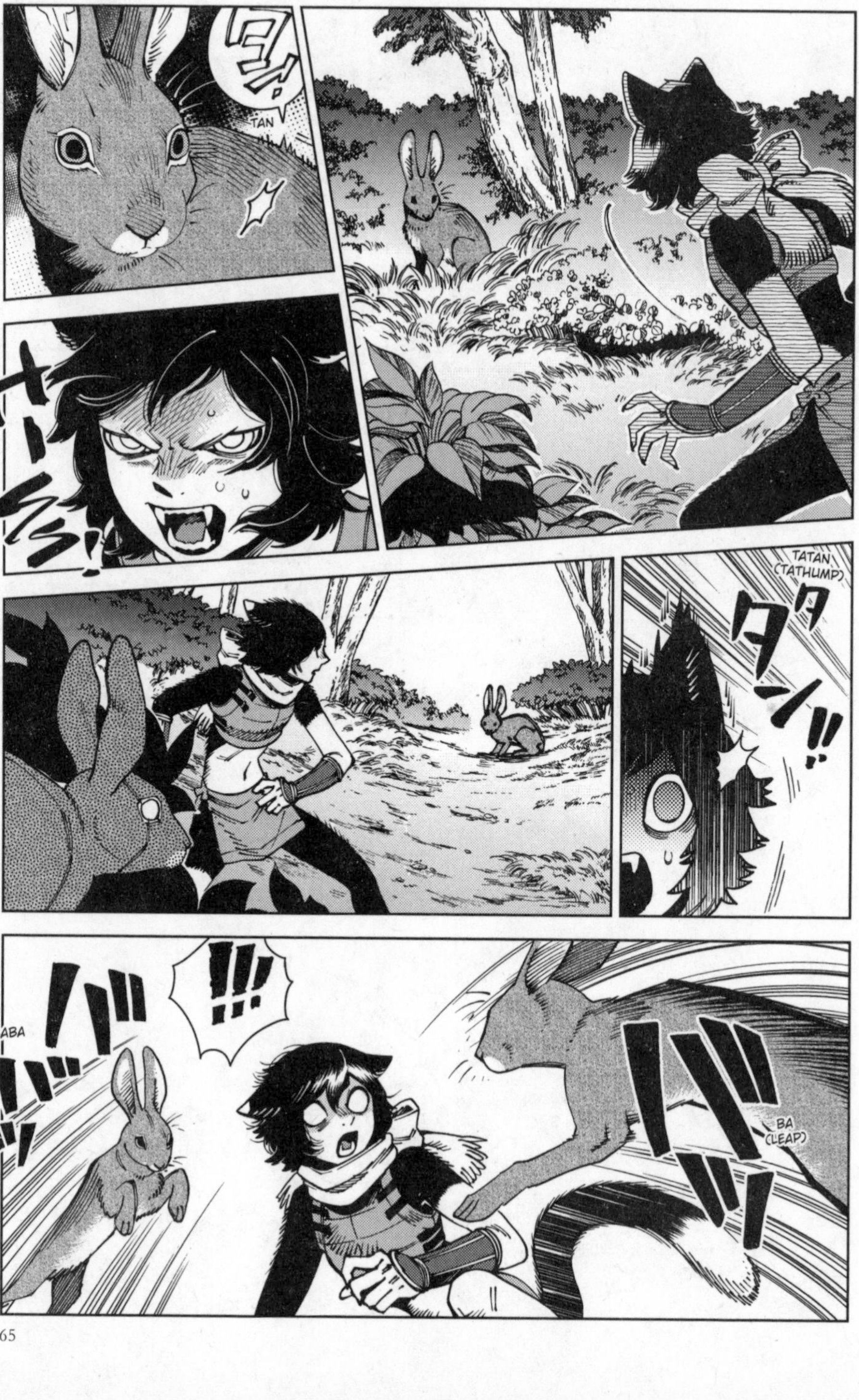
TAN
TATAN (TATHUMP)
BA (LEAP)
!!!
BABA

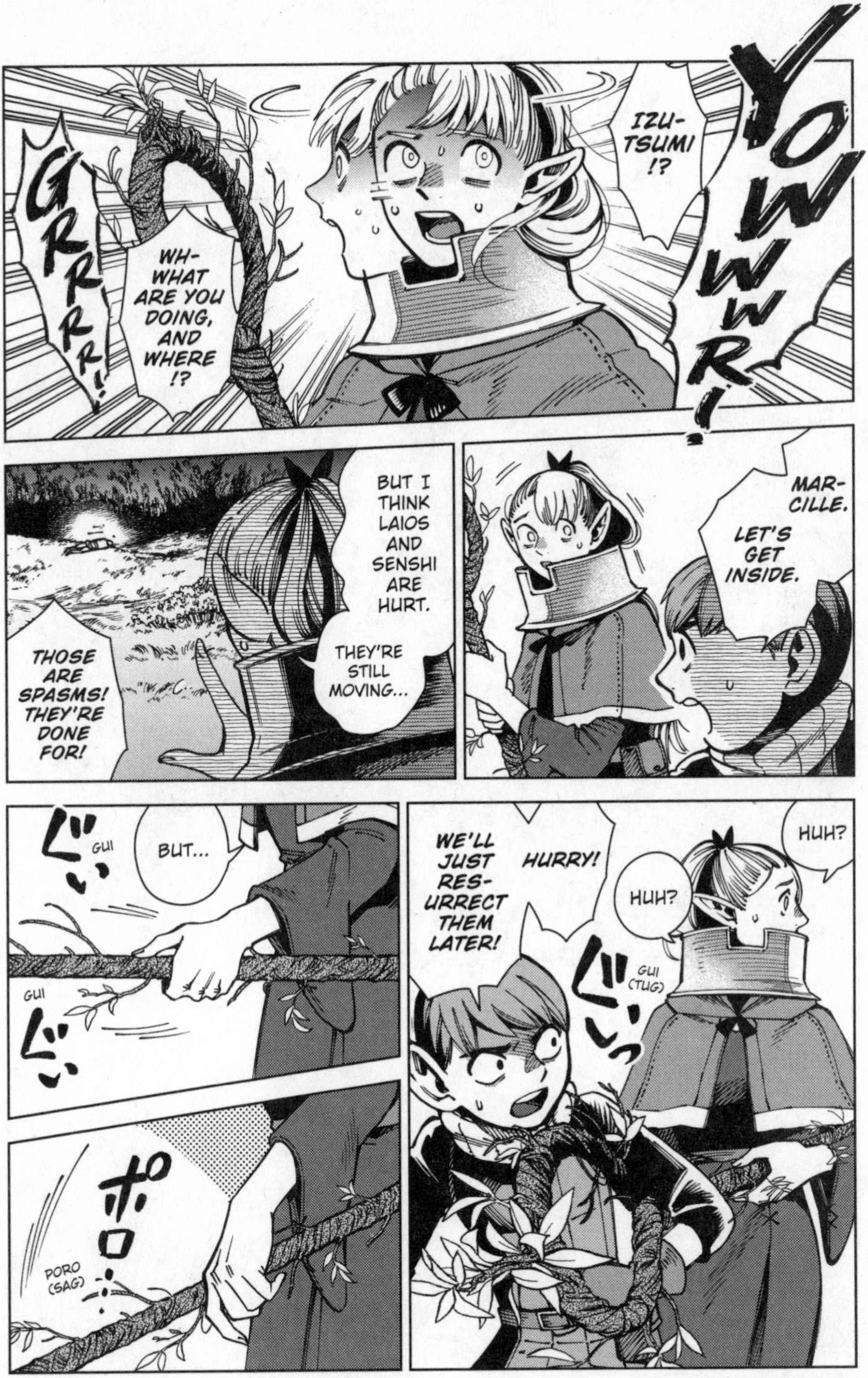
YOWWWRI!
IZU-TSUMI!?
WH-WHAT ARE YOU DOING, AND WHERE!?
GRRRR!
MAR-CILLE.
LET'S GET INSIDE.
BUT I THINK LAIOS AND SENSHI ARE HURT.
THEY'RE STILL MOVING...
THOSE ARE SPASMS! THEY'RE DONE FOR!
HUH?
HURRY!
HUH?
WE'LL JUST RES-URRECT THEM LATER!
ぐいっ
GUI (TUG)
BUT...
ぐい
GUI
ぐい
GUI
ポロ…
PORO (SAG)

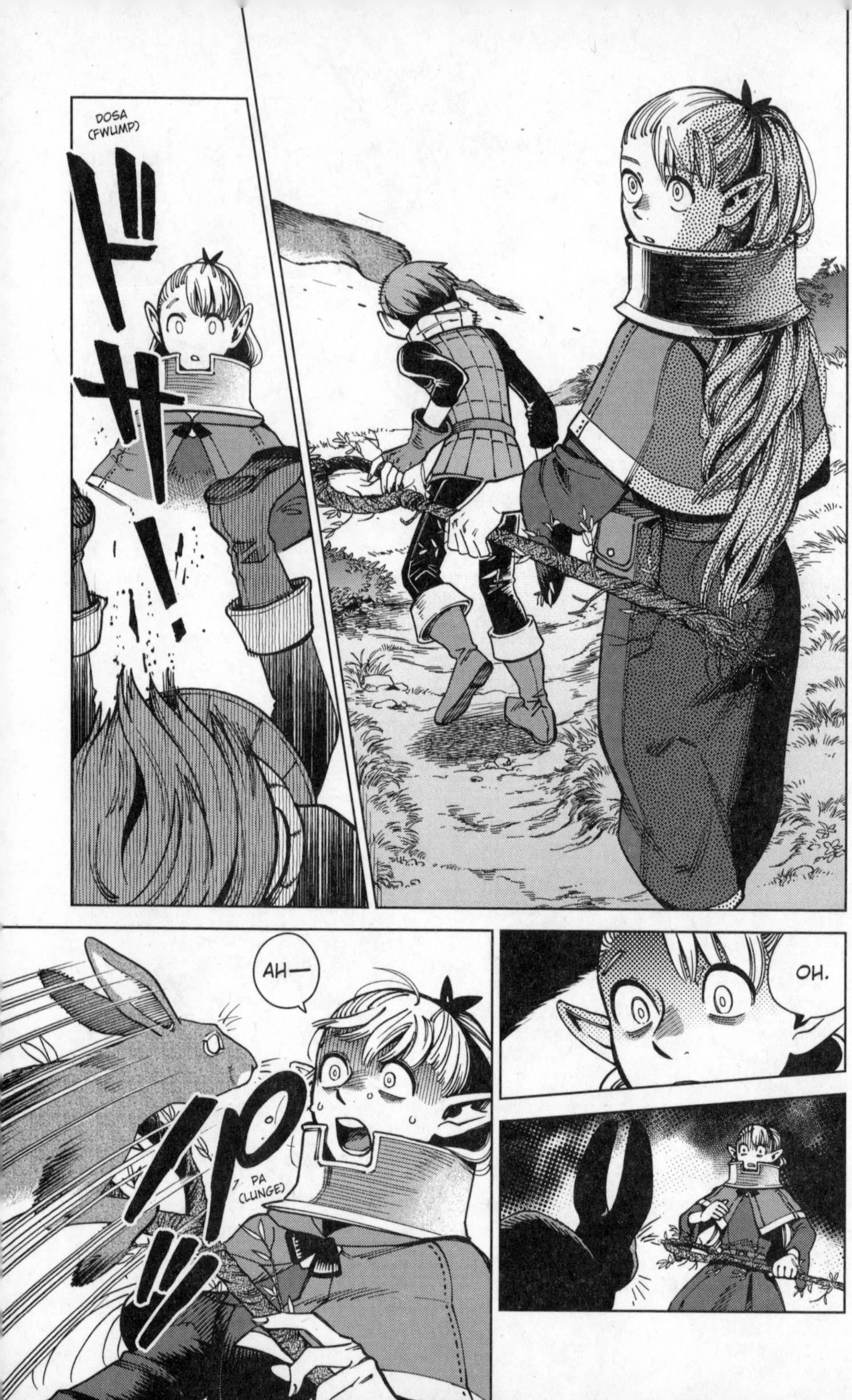
DOSA
(FWUMP)
OH.
AH—
PA
(LUNGE)

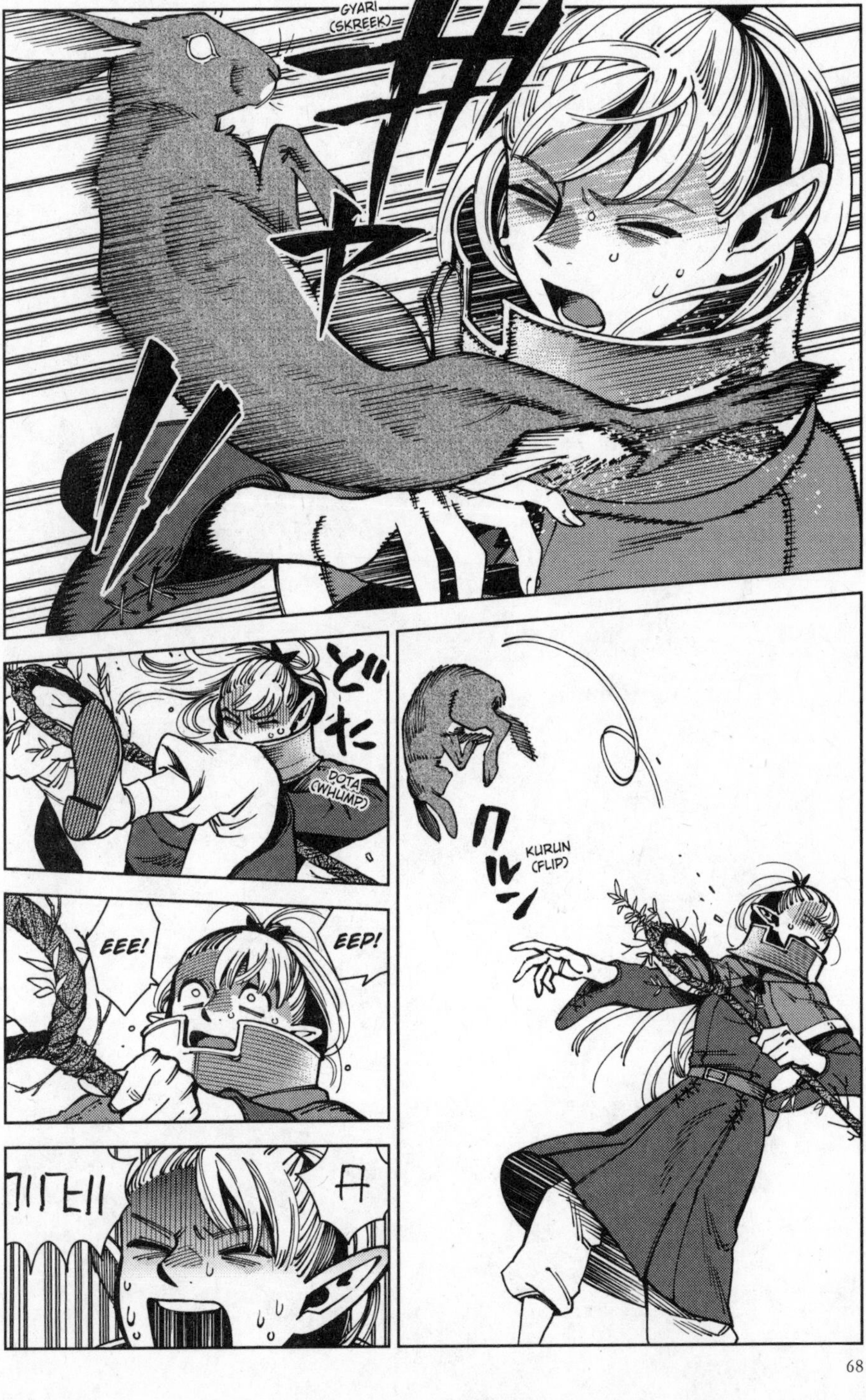
ギャ
GYARI
(SKREEK)
クルン
KURUN
(FLIP)
どた
DOTA
(WHUMP)
EEP!
EEE!

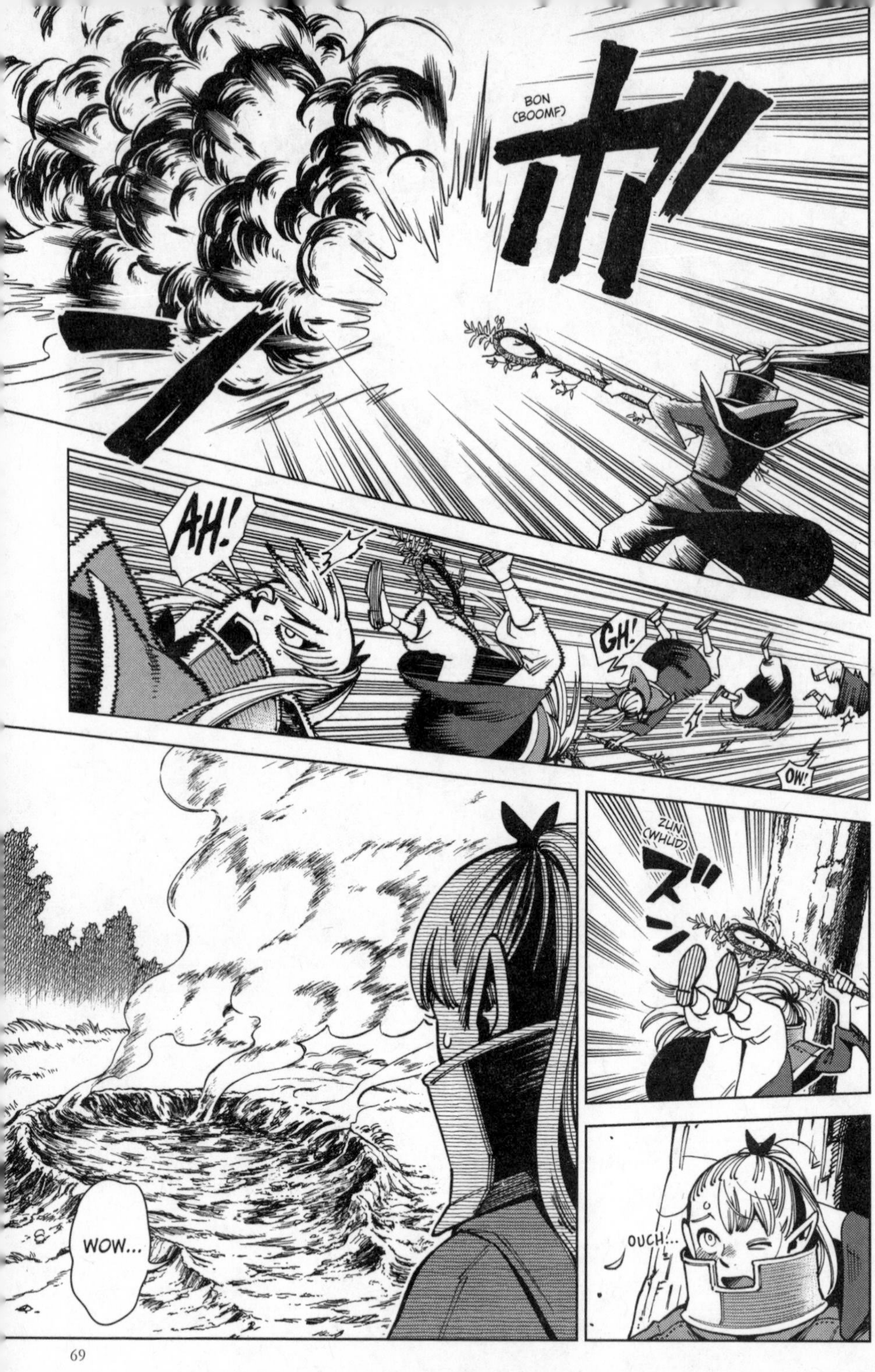
BON (BOOMF)
AH!
GH!
OW!
ZUN (WHUD)
OUCH!...
WOW...

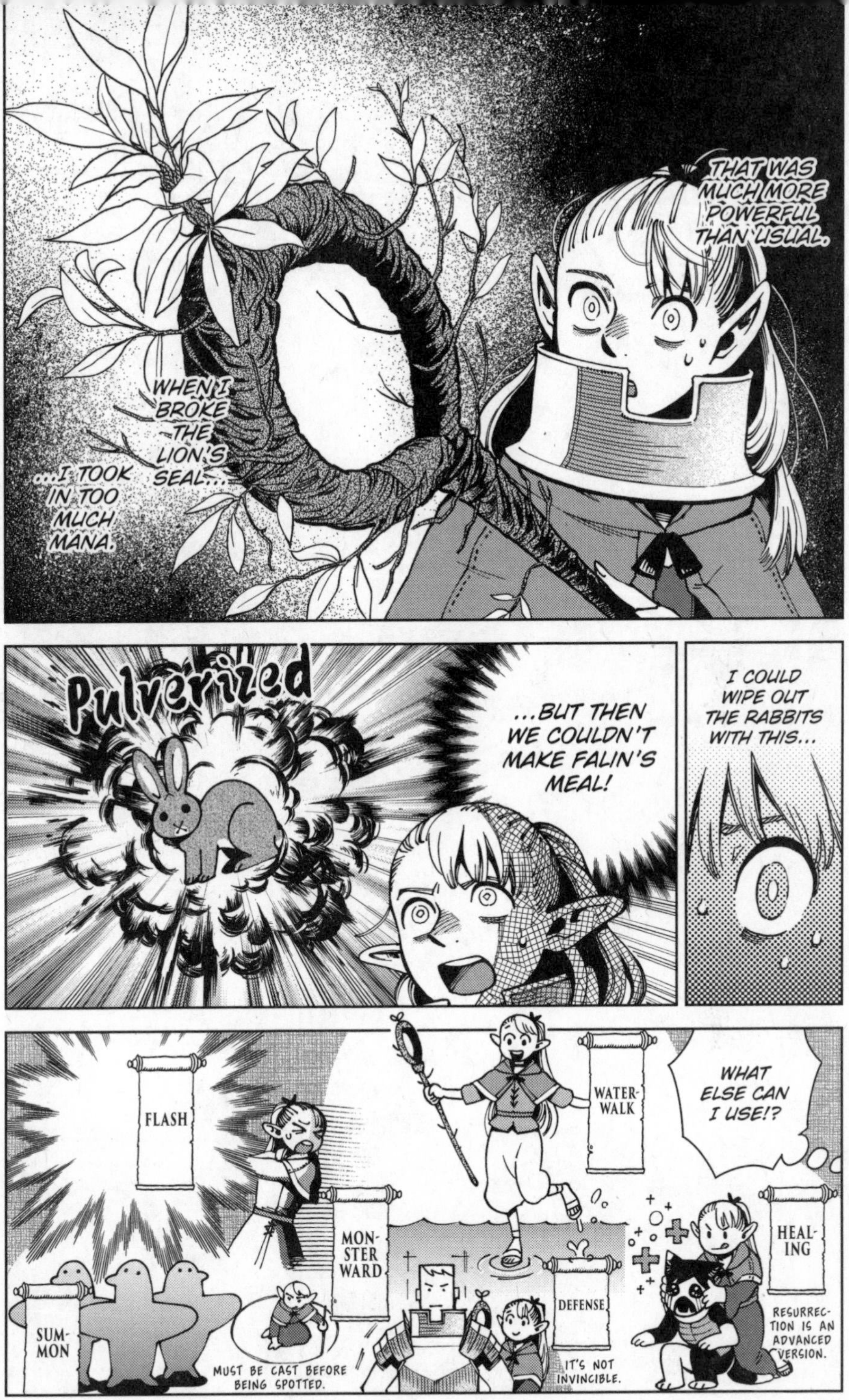
THAT WAS MUCH MORE POWERFUL THAN USUAL.
WHEN I BROKE THE LION'S SEAL...
...I TOOK IN TOO MUCH MANA.
I COULD WIPE OUT THE RABBITS WITH THIS...
...BUT THEN WE COULDN'T MAKE FALIN'S MEAL!
Pulverized
WHAT ELSE CAN I USE!?
HEAL-ING
RESURREC-TION IS AN ADVANCED VERSION.
WATER-WALK
DEFENSE
IT'S NOT INVINCIBLE.
MON-STER WARD
MUST BE CAST BEFORE BEING SPOTTED.
FLASH
SUM-MON

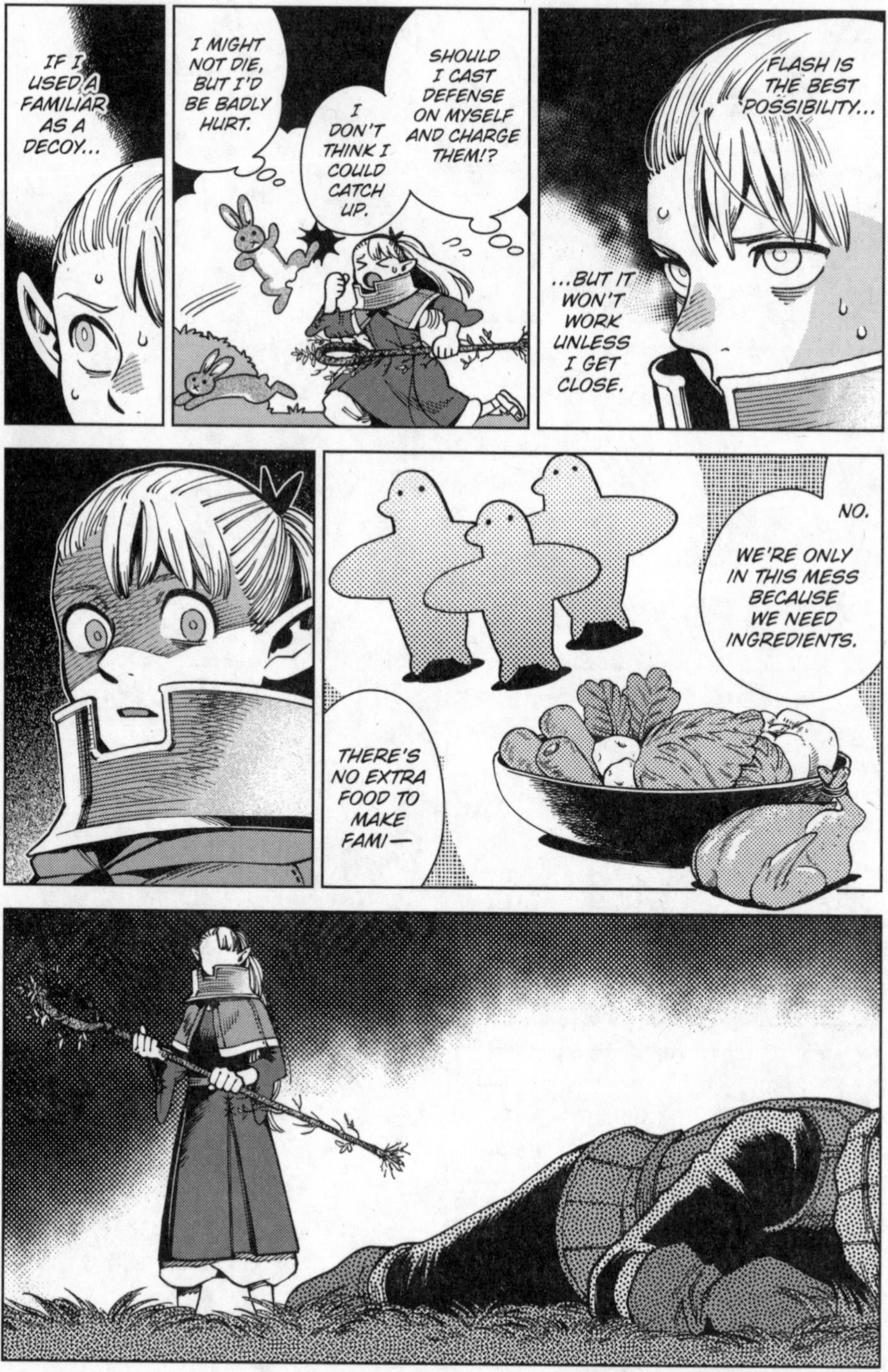
FLASH IS THE BEST POSSIBILITY...
...BUT IT WON'T WORK UNLESS I GET CLOSE.
SHOULD I CAST DEFENSE ON MYSELF AND CHARGE THEM!?
I DON'T THINK I COULD CATCH UP.
I MIGHT NOT DIE, BUT I'D BE BADLY HURT.
IF I USED A FAMILIAR AS A DECOY...
NO.
WE'RE ONLY IN THIS MESS BECAUSE WE NEED INGREDIENTS.
THERE'S NO EXTRA FOOD TO MAKE FAMI—

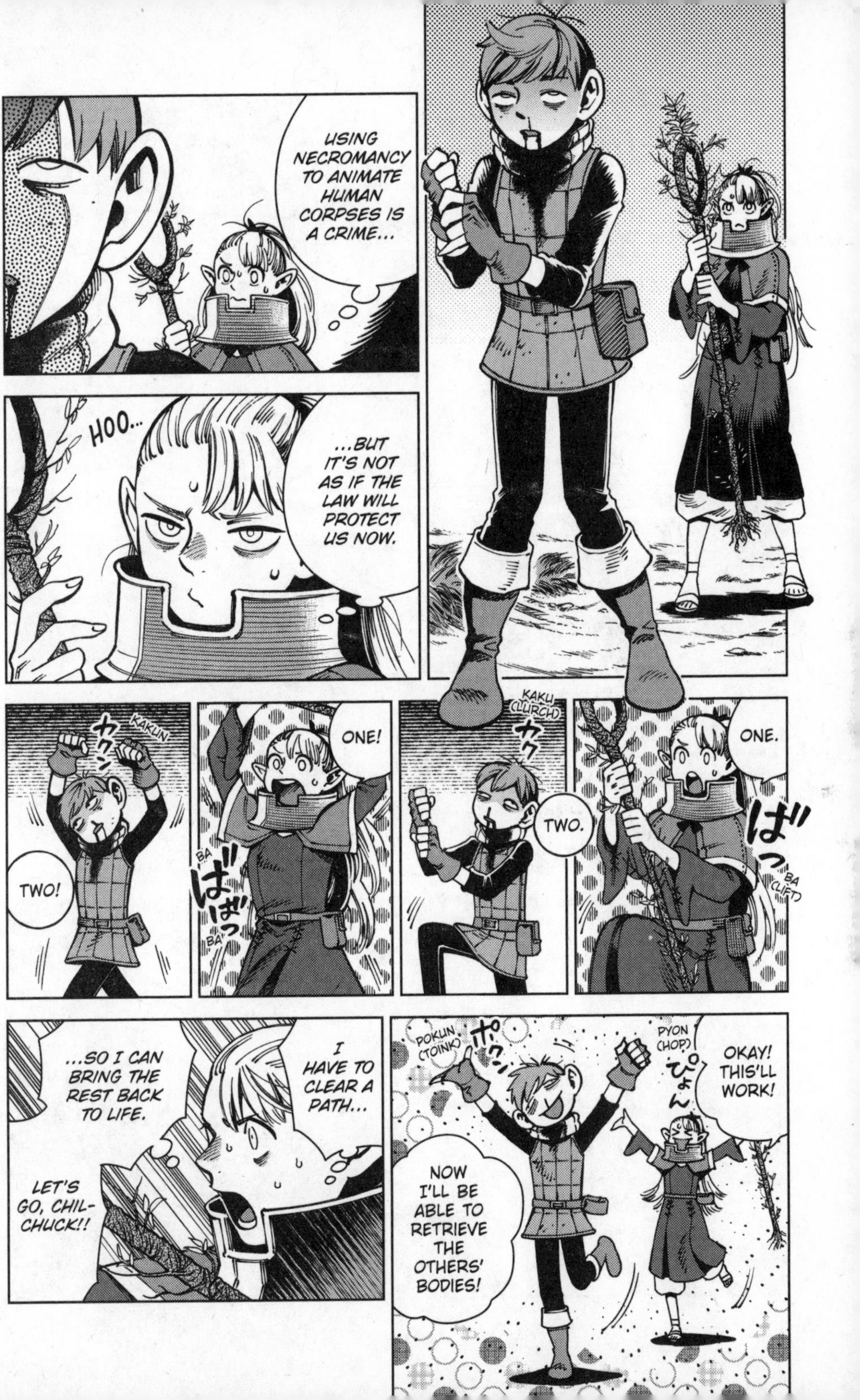
USING NECROMANCY TO ANIMATE HUMAN CORPSES IS A CRIME...
HOO...
...BUT IT'S NOT AS IF THE LAW WILL PROTECT US NOW.
ONE.
ばっ BA (LIFT)
KAKU (LURCH) カク
TWO.
ONE!
ばばっ BA BA
KAKUN カクン
TWO!
OKAY! THIS'LL WORK!
PYON (HOP) ぴょん
POKUN (TOINK) ポクッ
NOW I'LL BE ABLE TO RETRIEVE THE OTHERS' BODIES!
I HAVE TO CLEAR A PATH...
...SO I CAN BRING THE REST BACK TO LIFE.
LET'S GO, CHIL-CHUCK!!

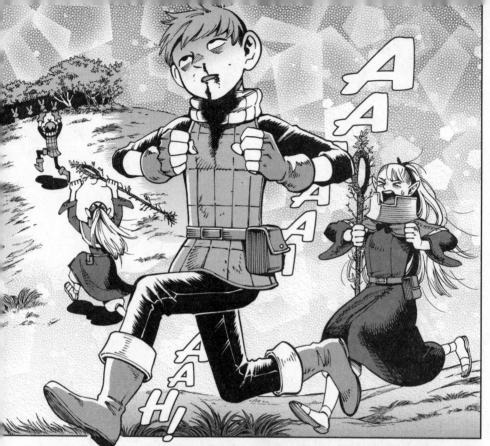

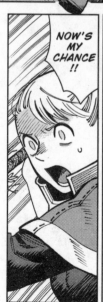

NOW'S MY CHANCE!!

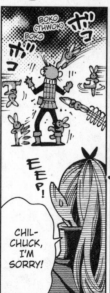

BOKO (THWOK)
BOKO (THWOK)

EEP!

CHIL-CHUCK, I'M SORRY!

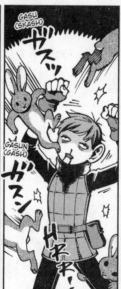

GASU (SKASH)

GASUN (GASH)

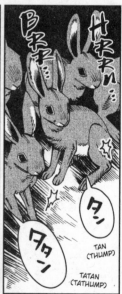

BRR...

HRRN...

TAN (THUMP)

TATAN (TATHUMP)

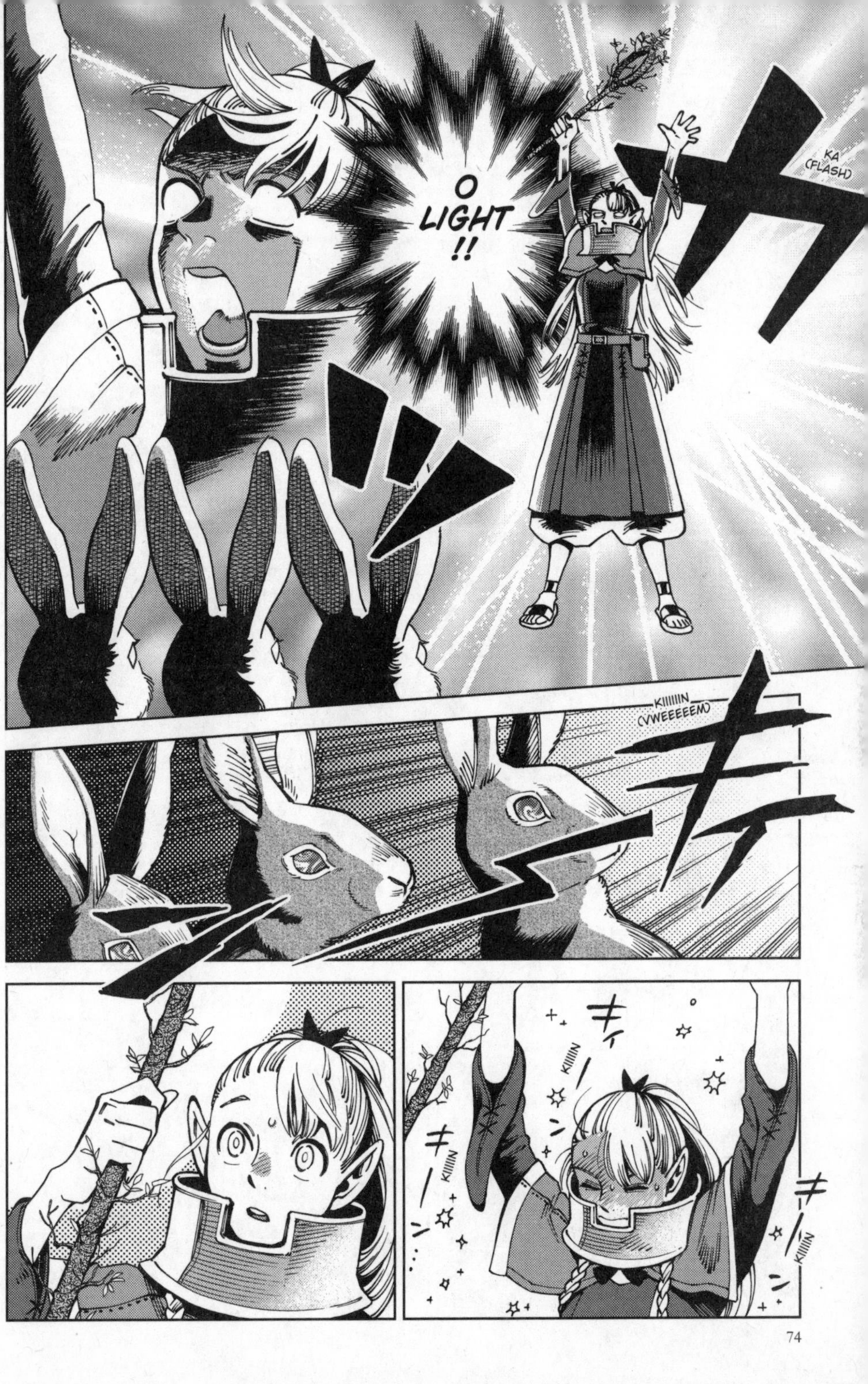
KA (FLASH)
O LIGHT!!
KIIIIIN (VWEEEEEM)
KIIIIN
KIIIIN
KIIIIN

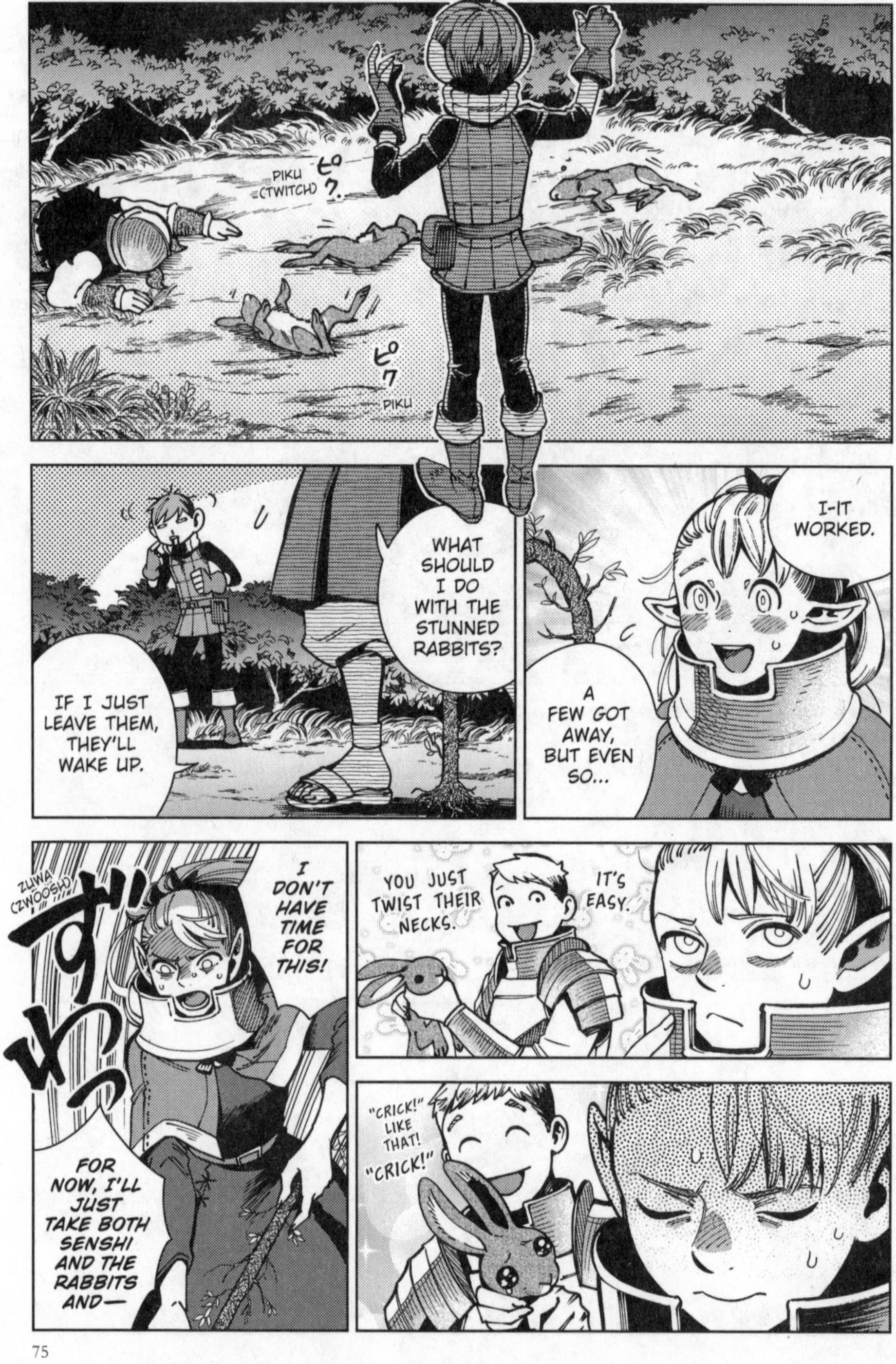
PIKU (TWITCH)
PIKU
I-IT WORKED.
A FEW GOT AWAY, BUT EVEN SO...
WHAT SHOULD I DO WITH THE STUNNED RABBITS?
IF I JUST LEAVE THEM, THEY'LL JUST WAKE UP.
IT'S EASY.
YOU JUST TWIST THEIR NECKS.
"CRICK!" LIKE THAT! "CRICK!"
ZUWA (ZWOOSH)
I DON'T HAVE TIME FOR THIS!
FOR NOW, I'LL JUST TAKE BOTH SENSHI AND THE RABBITS AND—

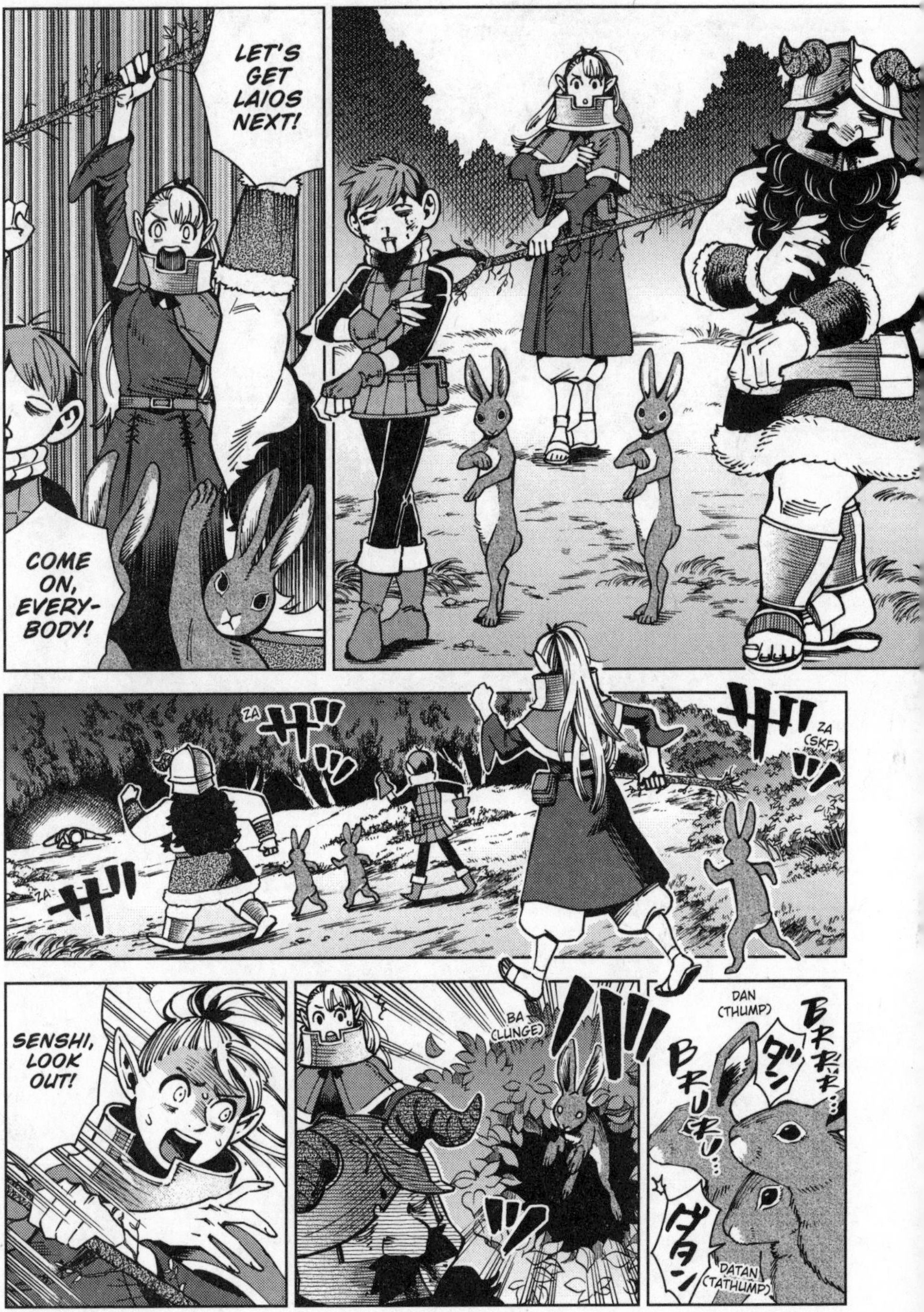
LET'S GET LAIOS NEXT!
COME ON, EVERY-BODY!
ZA (SKF)
ZA
ZA
DAN (THUMP)
BRRRR...
BRURU...
DATAN (TATHUMP)
BA (LUNGE)
SENSHI, LOOK OUT!

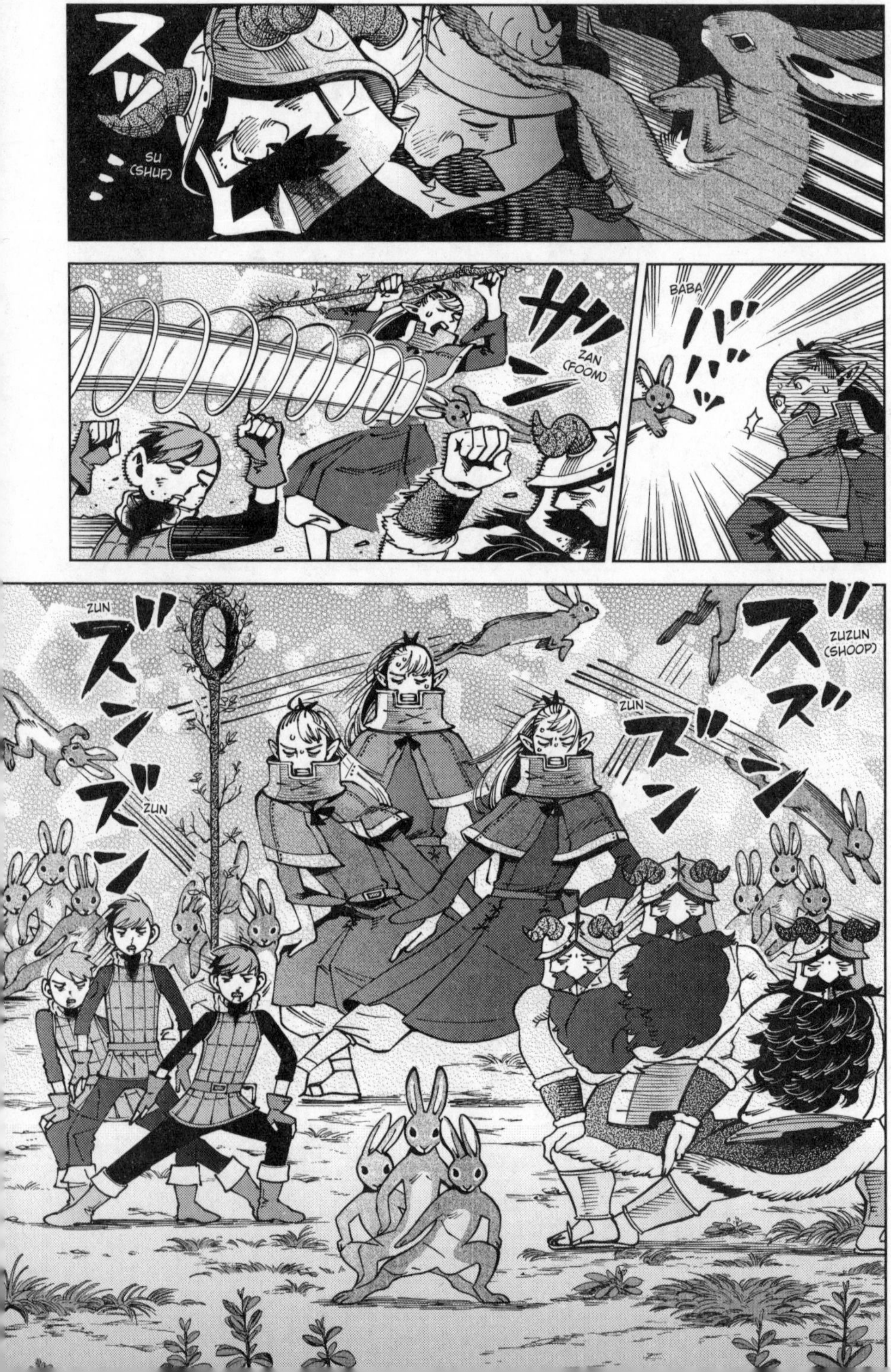

スッ
SU (SHUF)
バババッ
BABA
ザン
ZAN (FOOM)
ズズン
ZUZUN (SHOOP)
ZUN
ズン
ZUN
ズン
ZUN

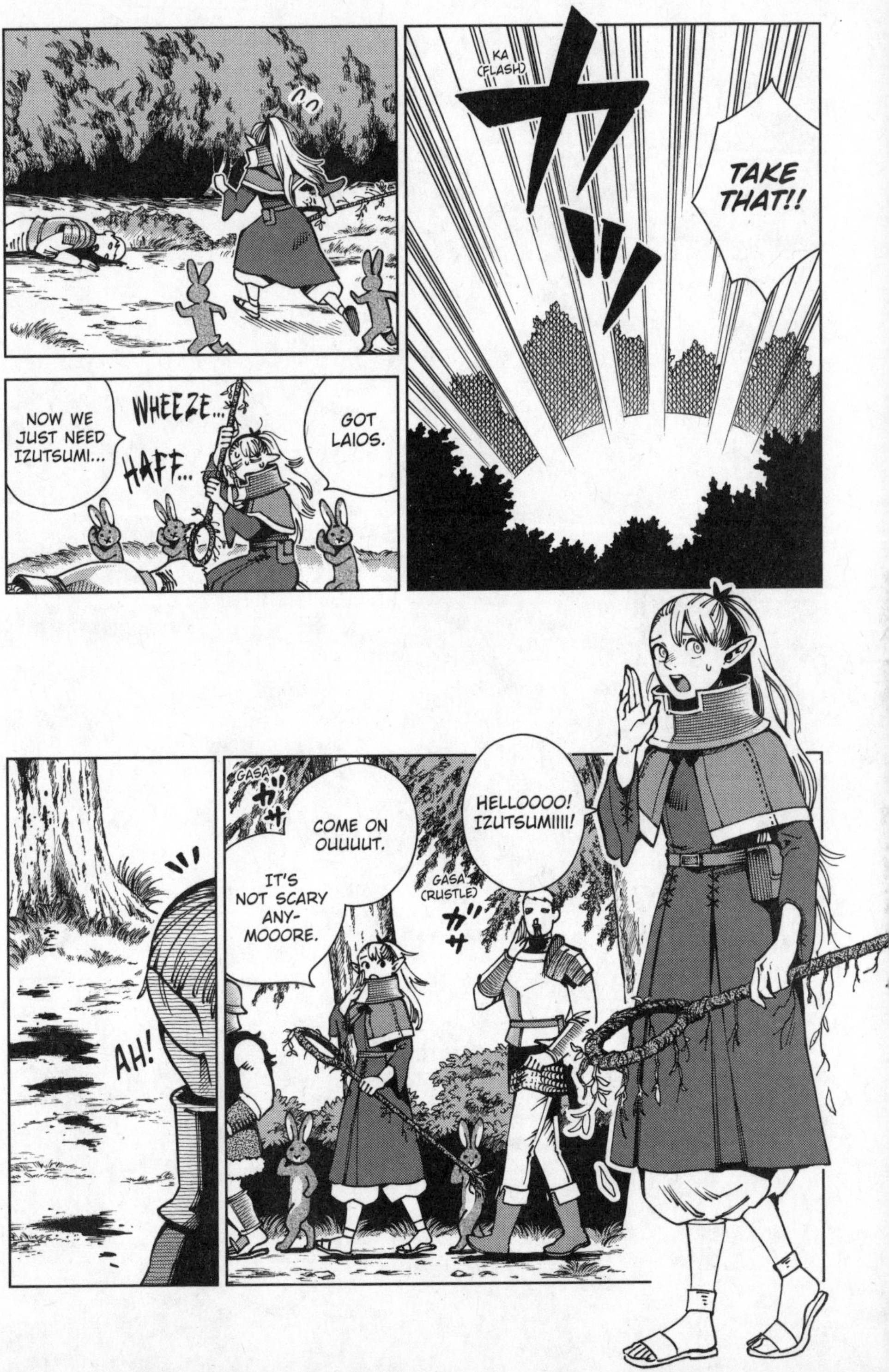
KA (FLASH)
TAKE THAT!!
GOT LAIOS.
WHEEZE...
HAFF...
NOW WE JUST NEED IZUTSUMI...
HELLOOOO! IZUTSUMIIIII!
GASA (RUSTLE)
COME ON OUUUUT.
IT'S NOT SCARY ANY-MOOORE.
GASA
AH!

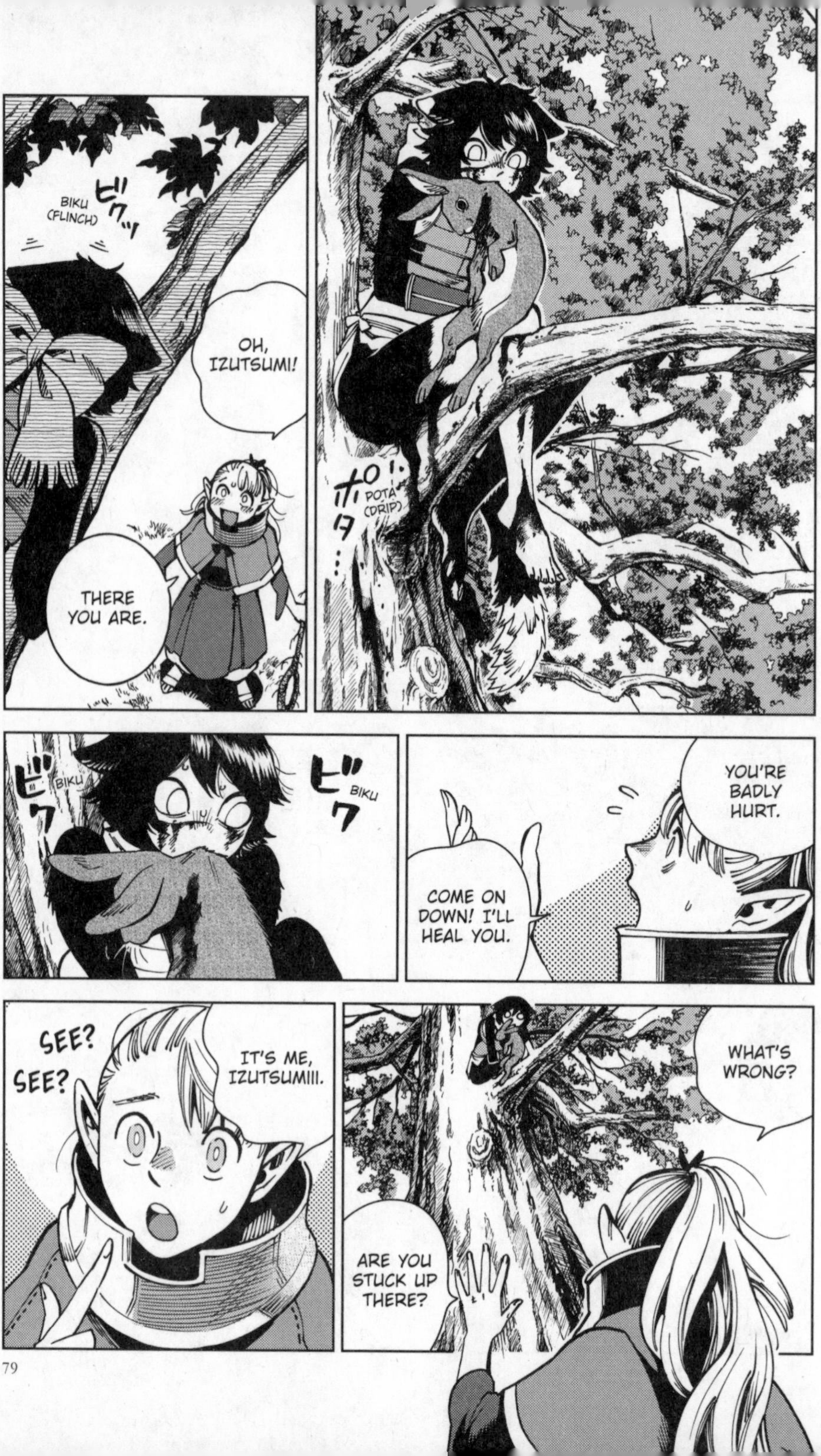
POTA (DRIP)
OH, IZUTSUMI!
BIKU (FLINCH)
THERE YOU ARE.
YOU'RE BADLY HURT.
COME ON DOWN! I'LL HEAL YOU.
BIKU
BIKU
WHAT'S WRONG?
ARE YOU STUCK UP THERE?
IT'S ME, IZUTSUMIII.
SEE? SEE?

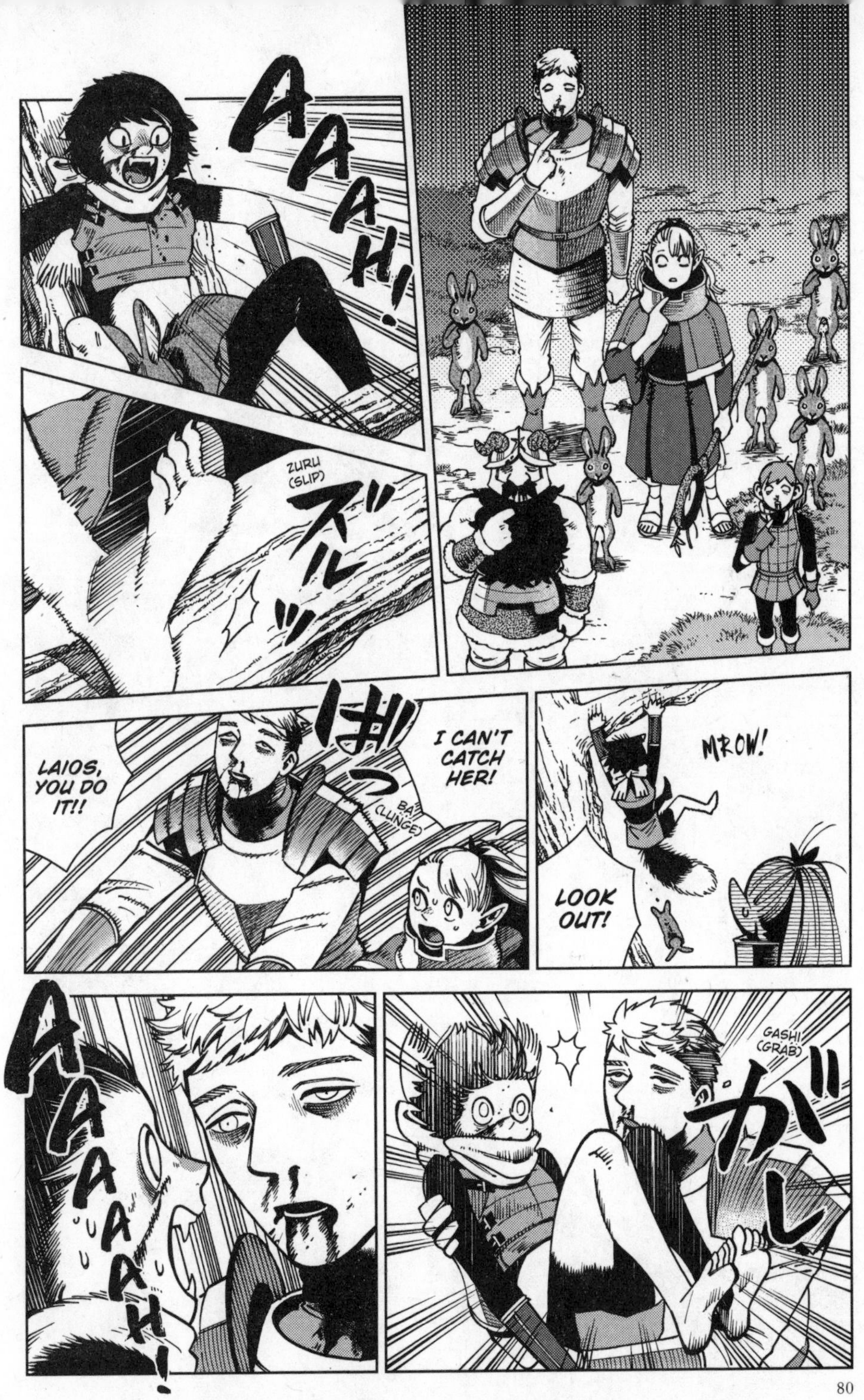
AAAH!
ZURU (SLIP)
ズルッ
MROW!
LOOK OUT!
I CAN'T CATCH HER!
ぱっ
BA (LUNGE)
LAIOS, YOU DO IT!!
GASHI (GRAB)
がしっ
AAAAAH!

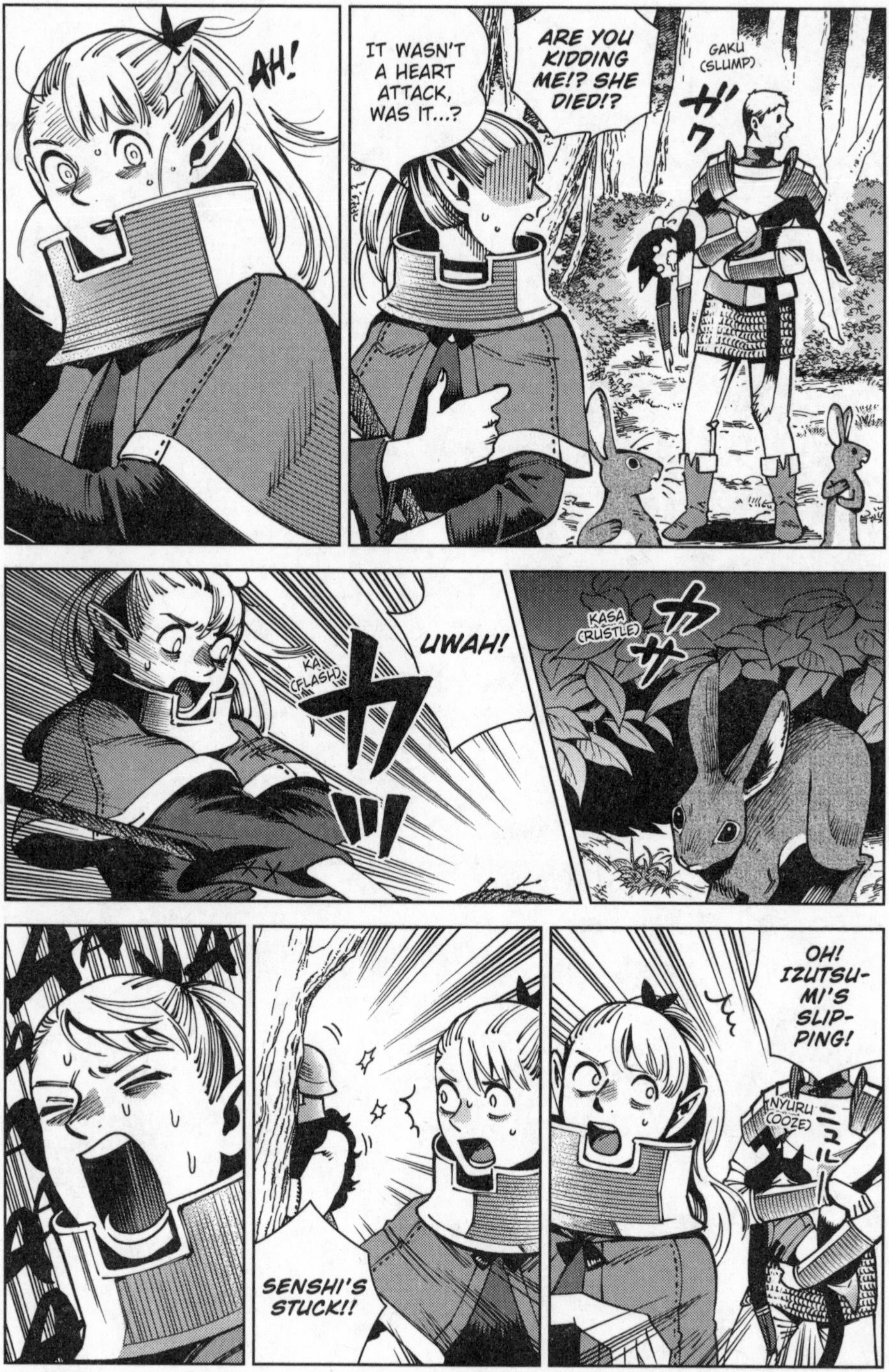
GAKU (SLUMP)
ガク
ARE YOU KIDDING ME!? SHE DIED!?
IT WASN'T A HEART ATTACK, WAS IT...?
AH!
KASA (RUSTLE)
カサ
UWAH!
KA (FLASH)
カッ
OH! IZUTSU-MI'S SLIP-PING!
NYURU (OOZE)
ニュル
SENSHI'S STUCK!!

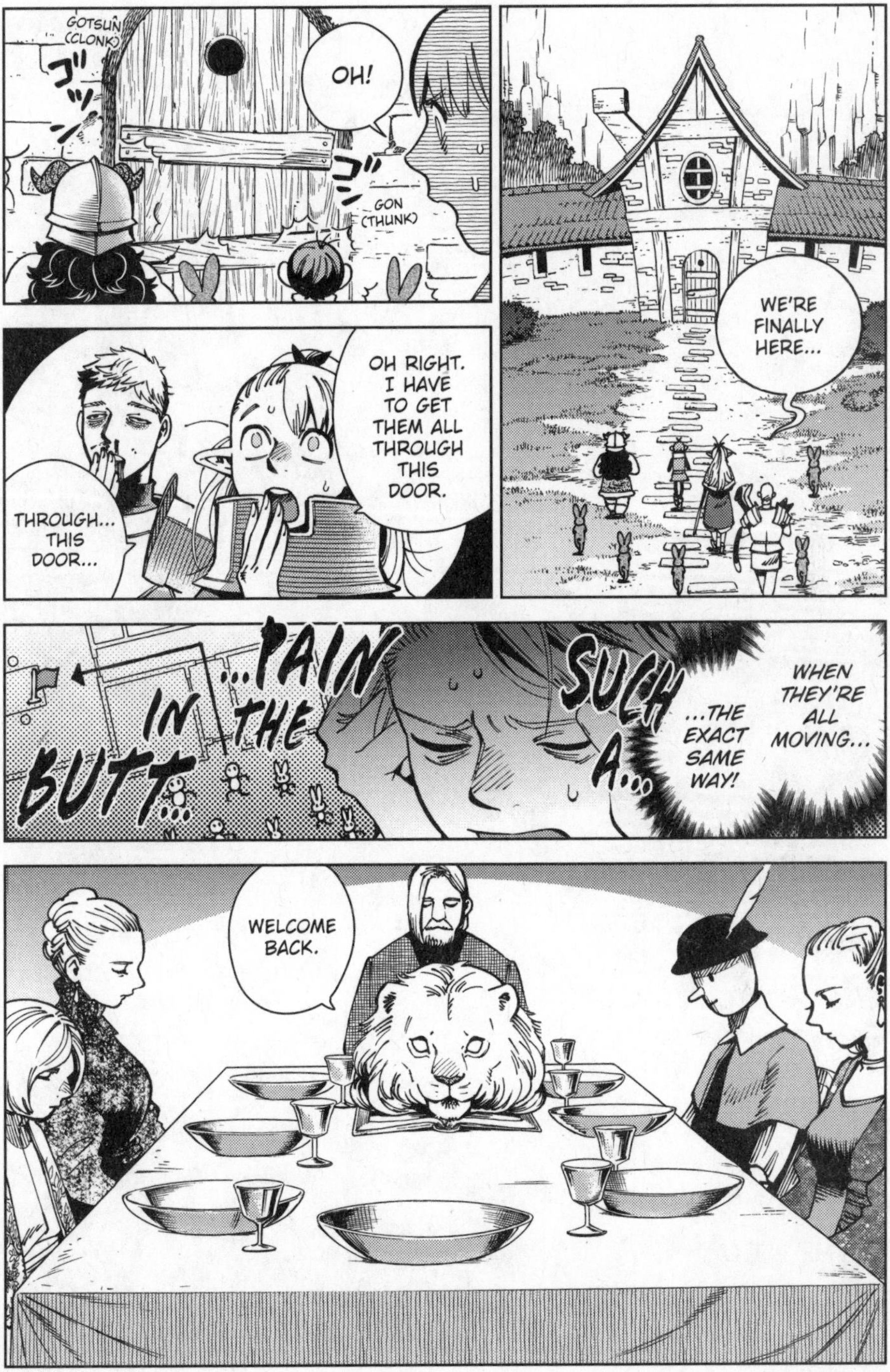
WE'RE FINALLY HERE...
GOTSUN (CLONK)
OH!
GON (THUNK)
OH RIGHT. I HAVE TO GET THEM ALL THROUGH THIS DOOR.
THROUGH... THIS DOOR...
WHEN THEY'RE ALL MOVING...
...THE EXACT SAME WAY!
SUCH A...
...PAIN IN THE BUTT...
WELCOME BACK.

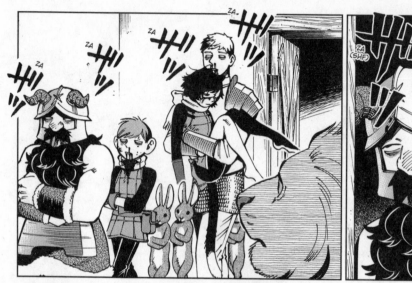

ZA ...ザッ

ZA ...ザッ

ZA ...ザッ

ZA ...ザッ

ZA (SHF) ザッ

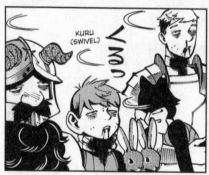

KURU (SWIVEL)

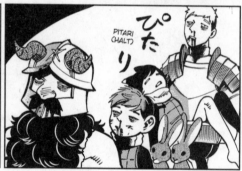

PITARI (CHALT)

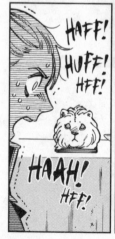

HAFF!

HUFF!

HFF!

HAAH!

HFF!

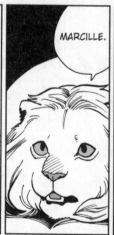

MARCILLE.

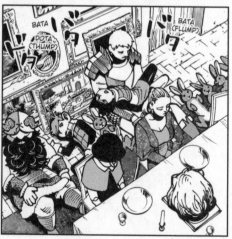

BATA

DOTA (THUMP)

BATA (FLUMP)

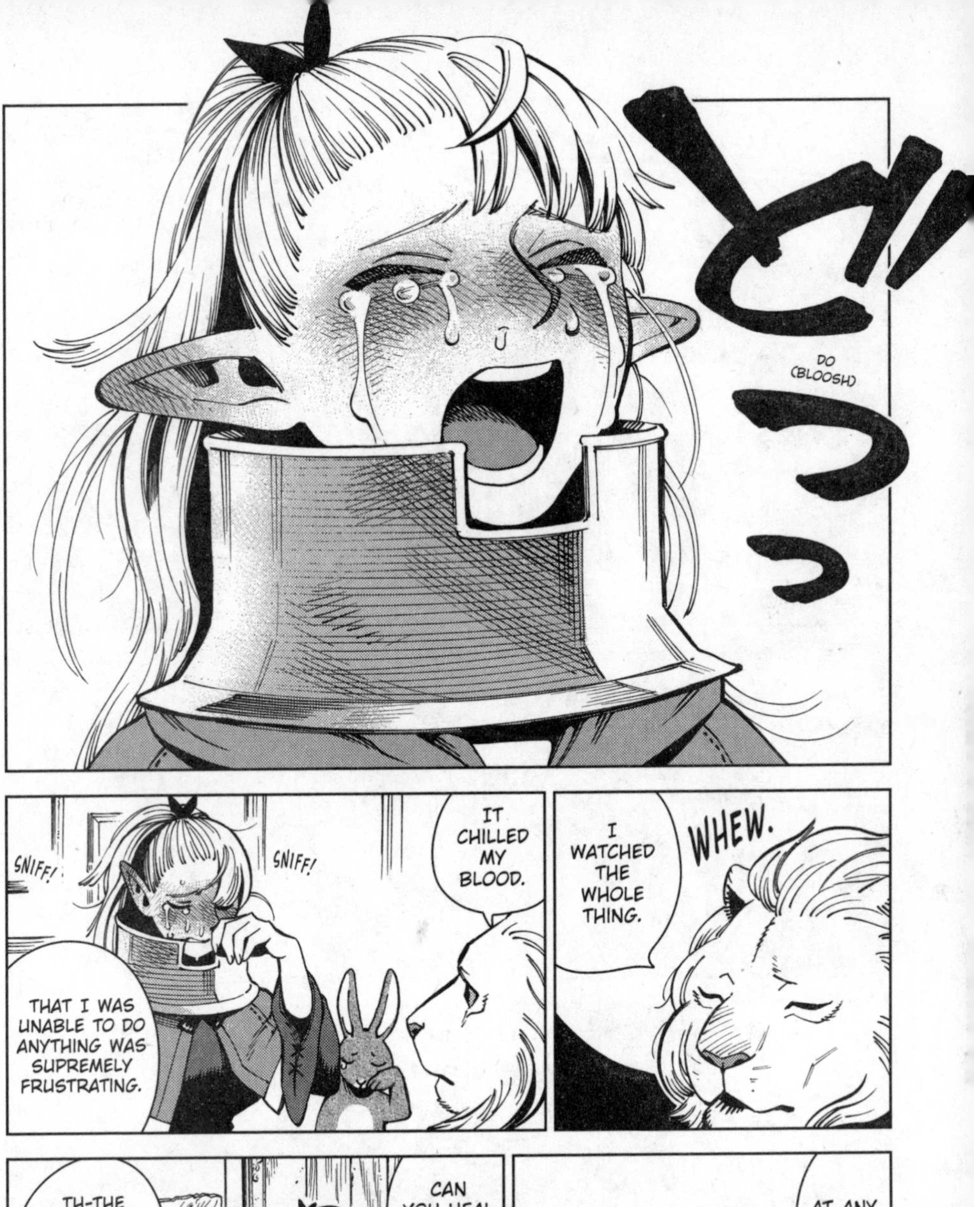
どっっ
DO (BLOOSH)
WHEW.
I WATCHED THE WHOLE THING.
IT CHILLED MY BLOOD.
SNIFF!
SNIFF!
THAT I WAS UNABLE TO DO ANYTHING WAS SUPREMELY FRUSTRATING.
AT ANY RATE...
...I'M GLAD YOU SURVIVED.
CAN YOU HEAL THEM?
TH-THE WOUNDS AREN'T COMPLICATED.
I JUST HAVE TO STICK THEM BACK TOGETHER, SO... PROBABLY.

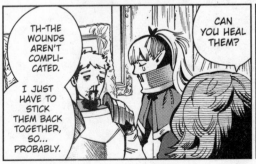

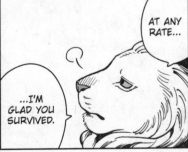

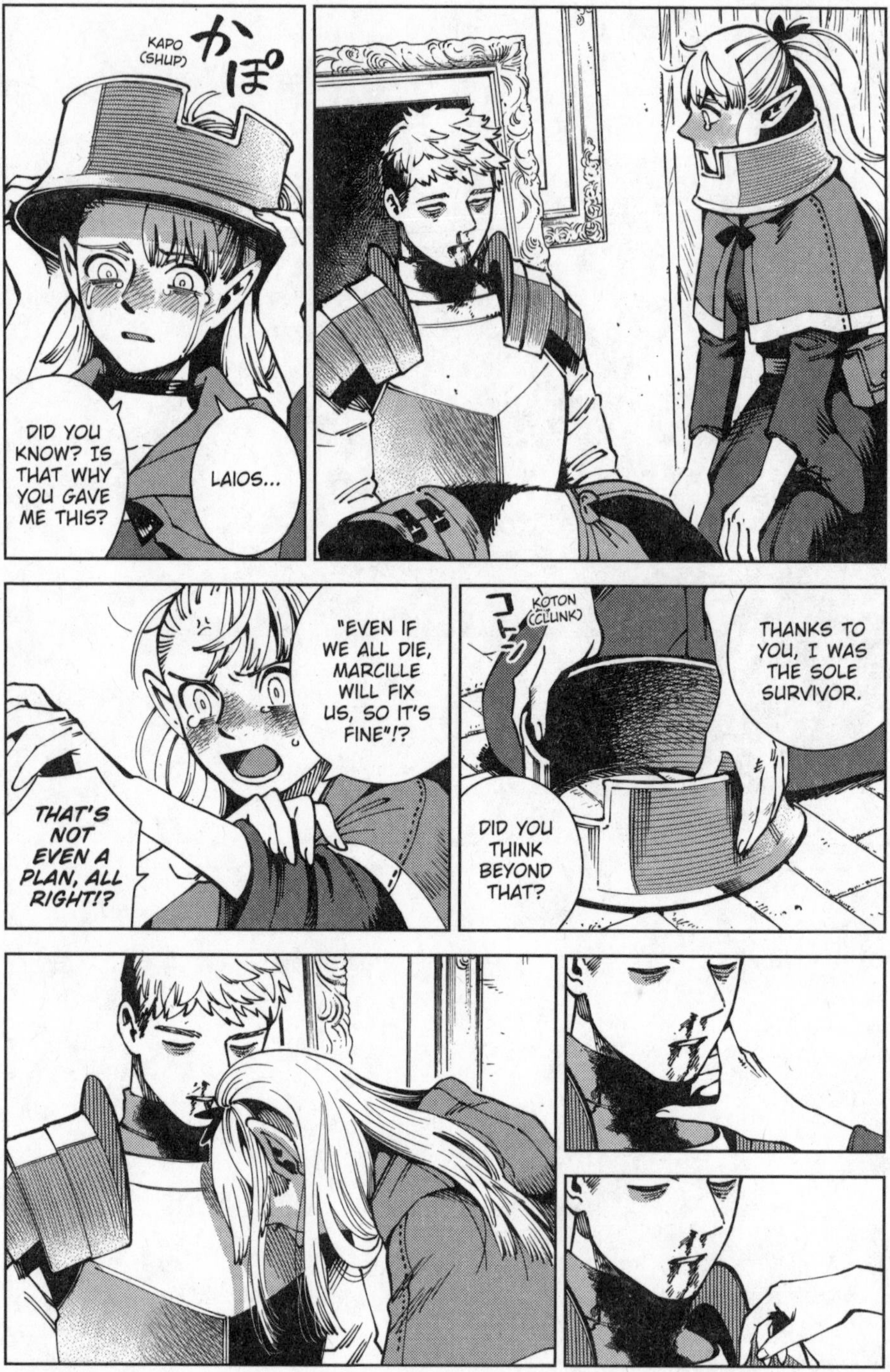

かぽ
KAPO (SHUP)
LAIOS...
DID YOU KNOW? IS THAT WHY YOU GAVE ME THIS?
KOTON (CLUNK)
THANKS TO YOU, I WAS THE SOLE SURVIVOR.
DID YOU THINK BEYOND THAT?
"EVEN IF WE ALL DIE, MARCILLE WILL FIX US, SO IT'S FINE"!?
THAT'S NOT EVEN A PLAN, ALL RIGHT!?

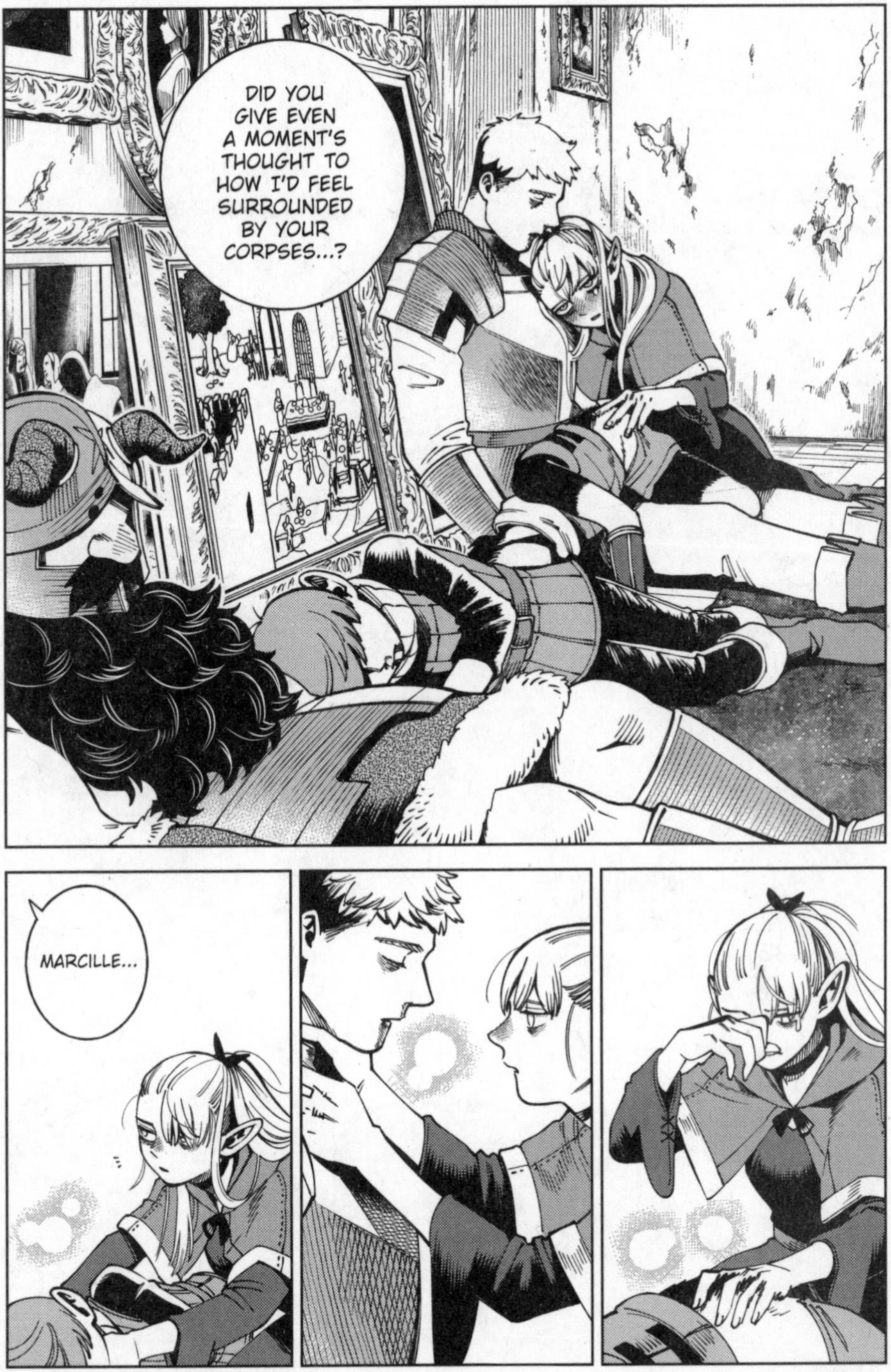
DID YOU GIVE EVEN A MOMENT'S THOUGHT TO HOW I'D FEEL SURROUNDED BY YOUR CORPSES...?
MARCILLE...

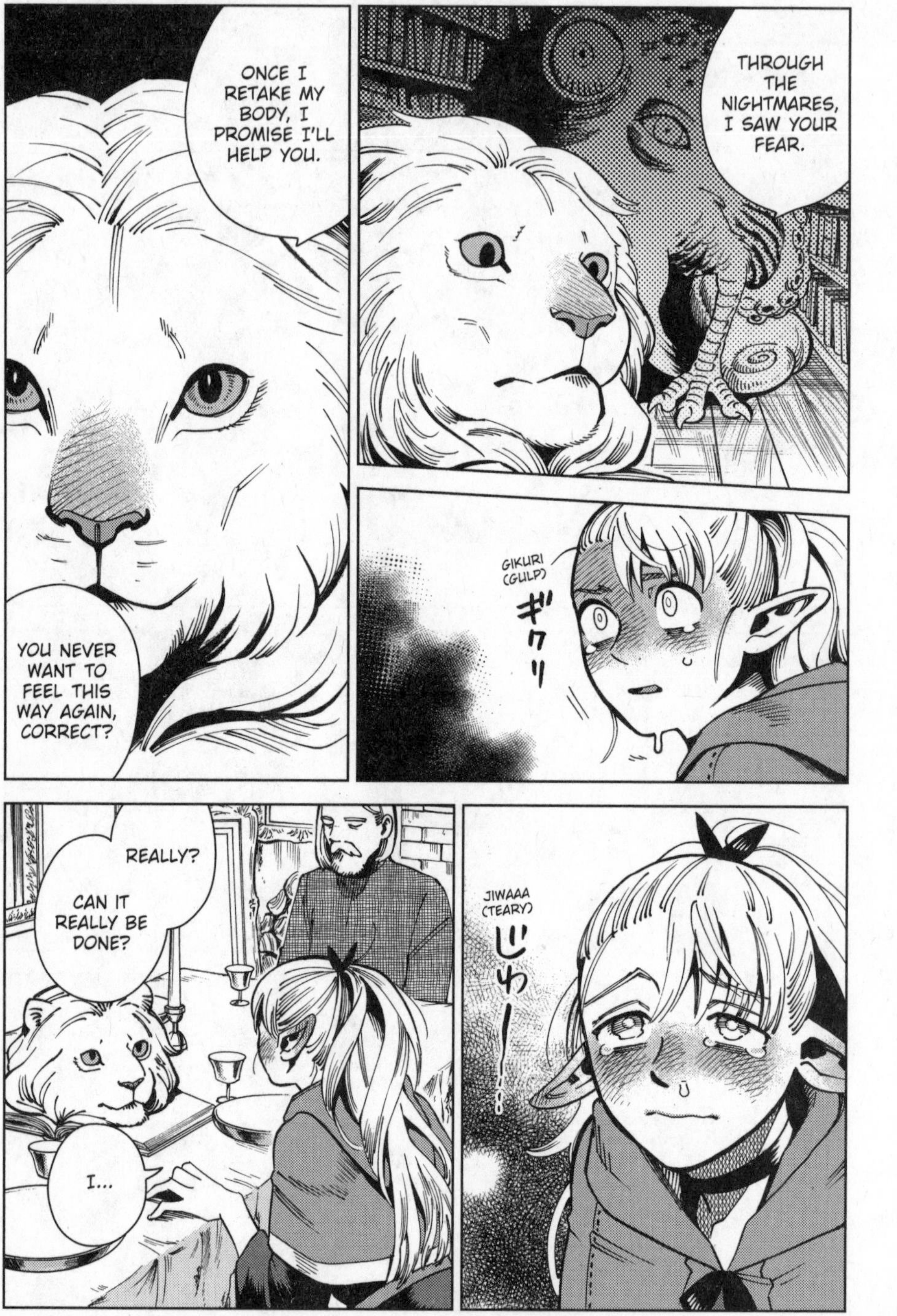
THROUGH THE NIGHTMARES, I SAW YOUR FEAR.
GIKURI (GULP)
ギクリ
ONCE I RETAKE MY BODY, I PROMISE I'LL HELP YOU.
YOU NEVER WANT TO FEEL THIS WAY AGAIN, CORRECT?
JIWAAA (TEARY)
じわーー…
REALLY?
CAN IT REALLY BE DONE?
I...

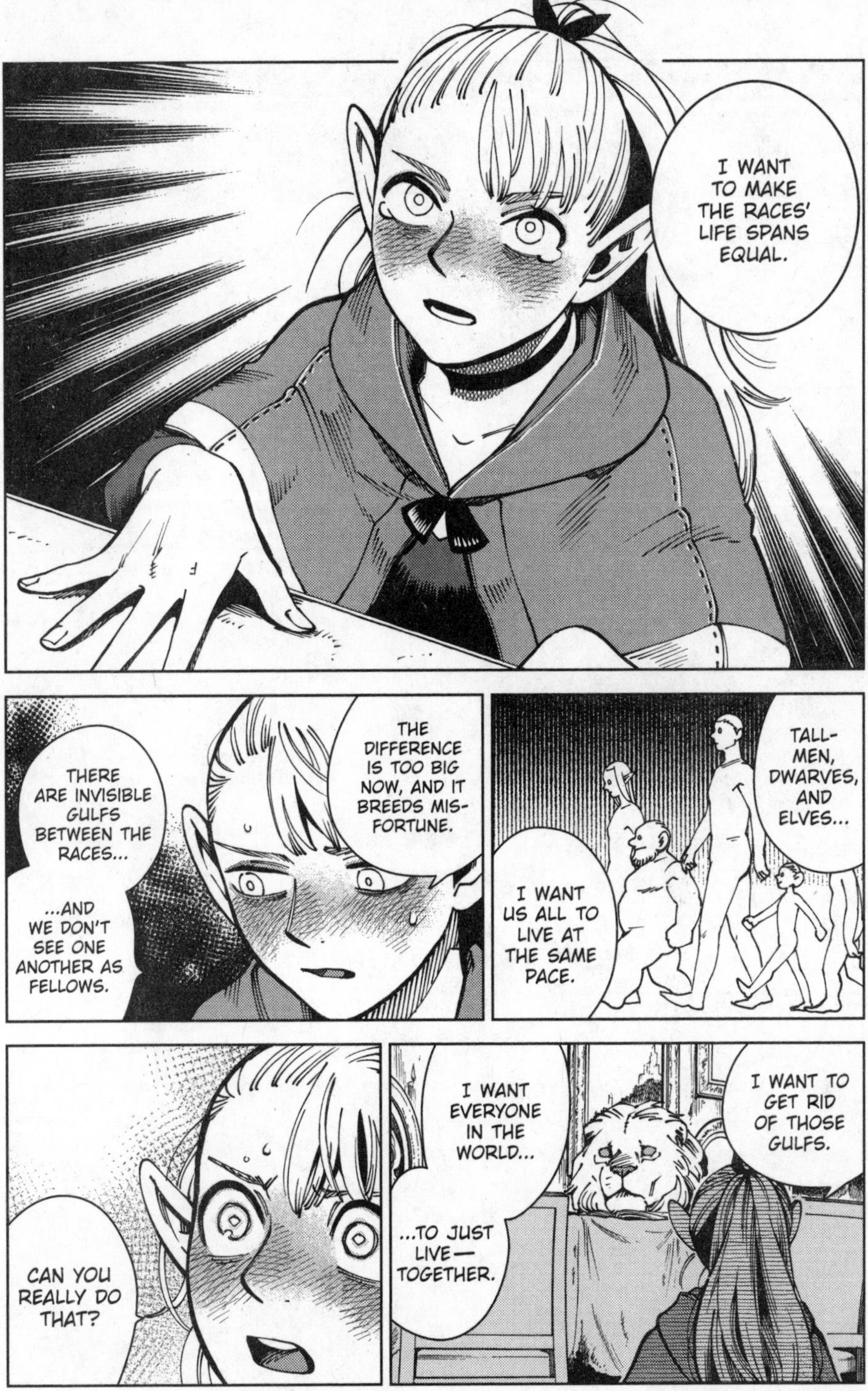
I WANT TO MAKE THE RACES' LIFE SPANS EQUAL.
TALL-MEN, DWARVES, AND ELVES...
I WANT US ALL TO LIVE AT THE SAME PACE.
THE DIFFERENCE IS TOO BIG NOW, AND IT BREEDS MIS-FORTUNE.
THERE ARE INVISIBLE GULFS BETWEEN THE RACES...
...AND WE DON'T SEE ONE ANOTHER AS FELLOWS.
I WANT TO GET RID OF THOSE GULFS.
I WANT EVERYONE IN THE WORLD...
...TO JUST LIVE—TOGETHER.
CAN YOU REALLY DO THAT?

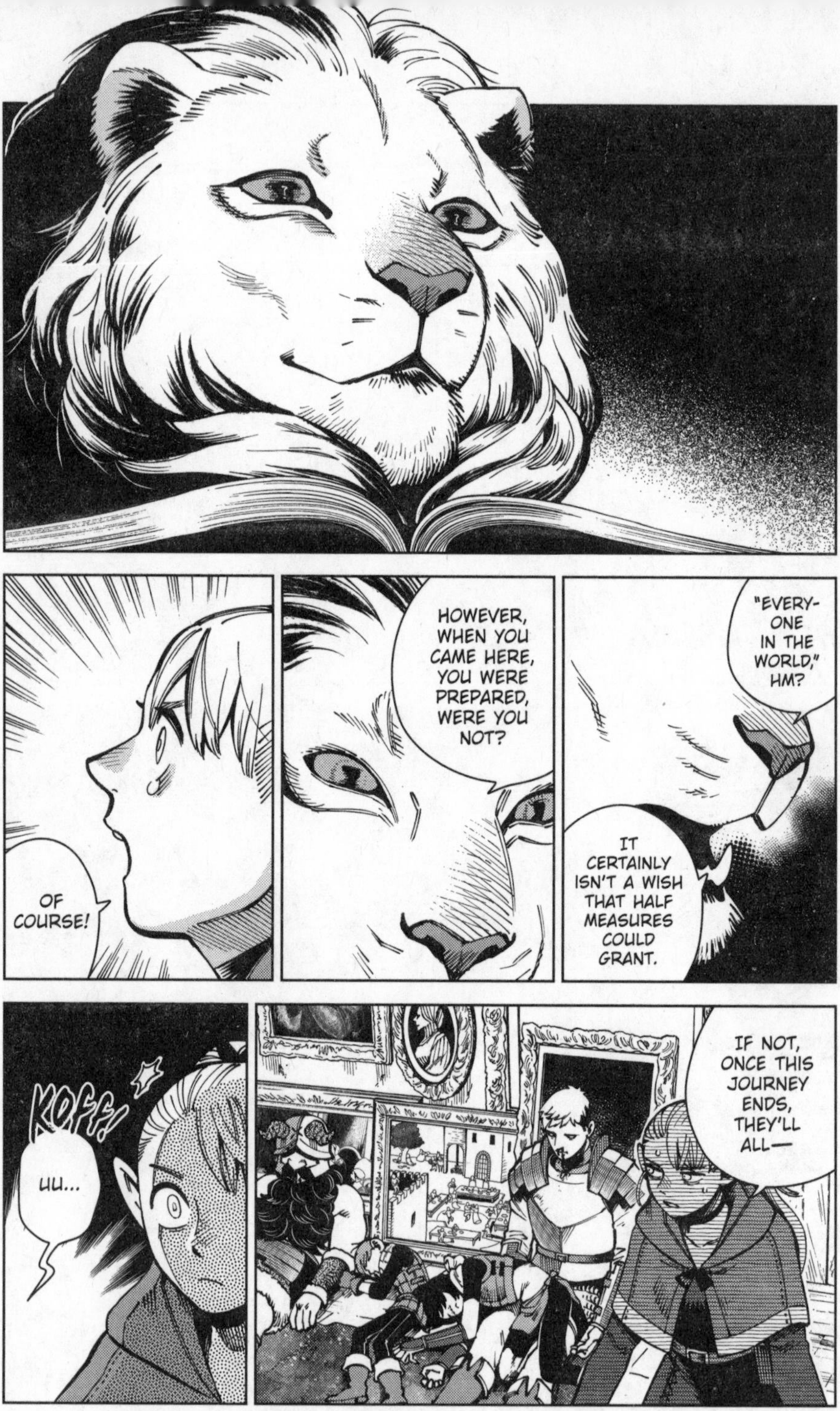
"EVERY-ONE IN THE WORLD," HM?
IT CERTAINLY ISN'T A WISH THAT HALF MEASURES COULD GRANT.
HOWEVER, WHEN YOU CAME HERE, YOU WERE PREPARED, WERE YOU NOT?
OF COURSE!
IF NOT, ONCE THIS JOURNEY ENDS, THEY'LL ALL—
KOFF!
UU...

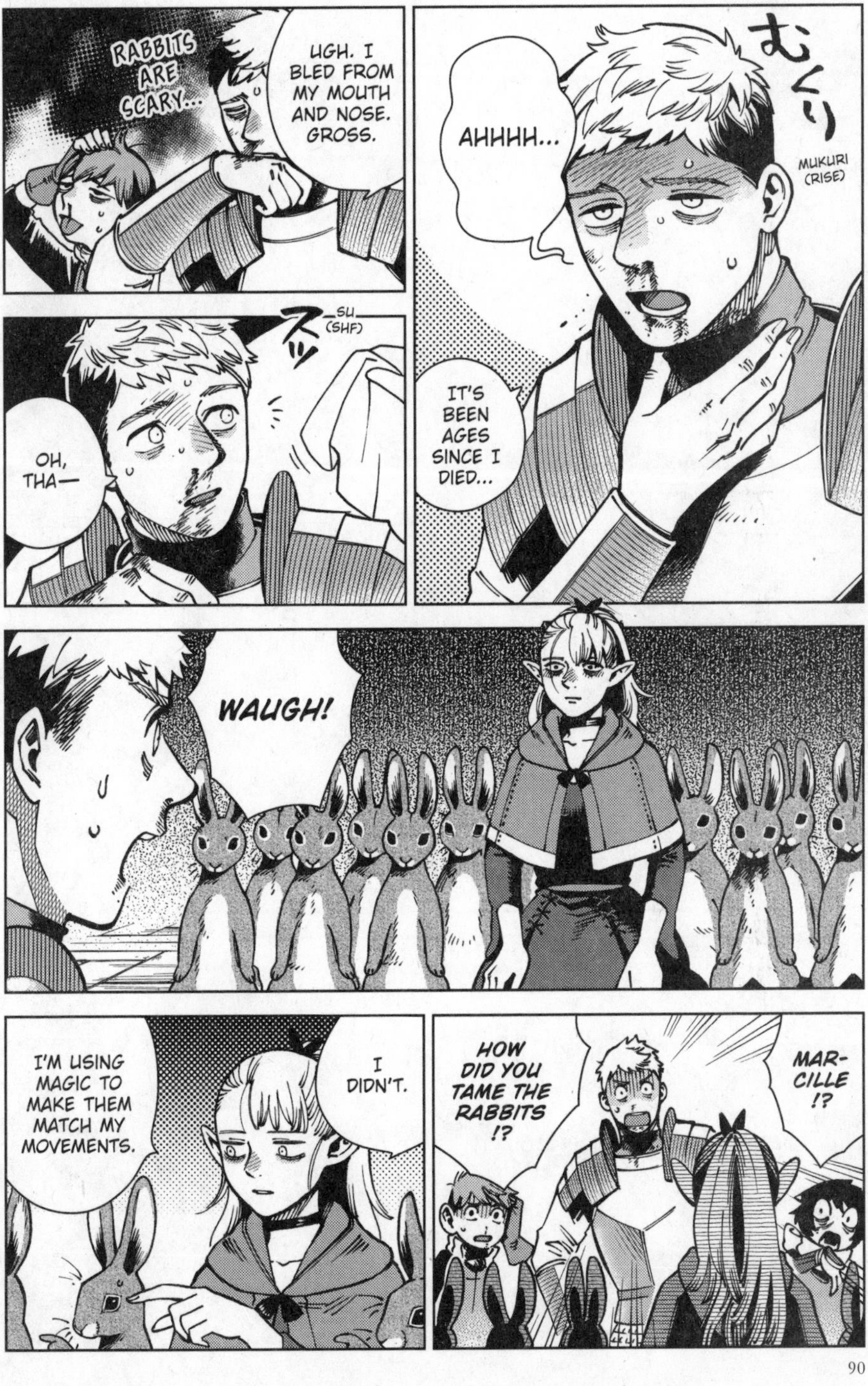

むくり
MUKURI (RISE)
AHHHH...
IT'S BEEN AGES SINCE I DIED...
UGH. I BLED FROM MY MOUTH AND NOSE. GROSS.
RABBITS ARE SCARY...
スッ
SU (SHF)
OH, THA—
WAUGH!
MAR-CILLE!?
HOW DID YOU TAME THE RABBITS!?
I DIDN'T.
I'M USING MAGIC TO MAKE THEM MATCH MY MOVEMENTS.

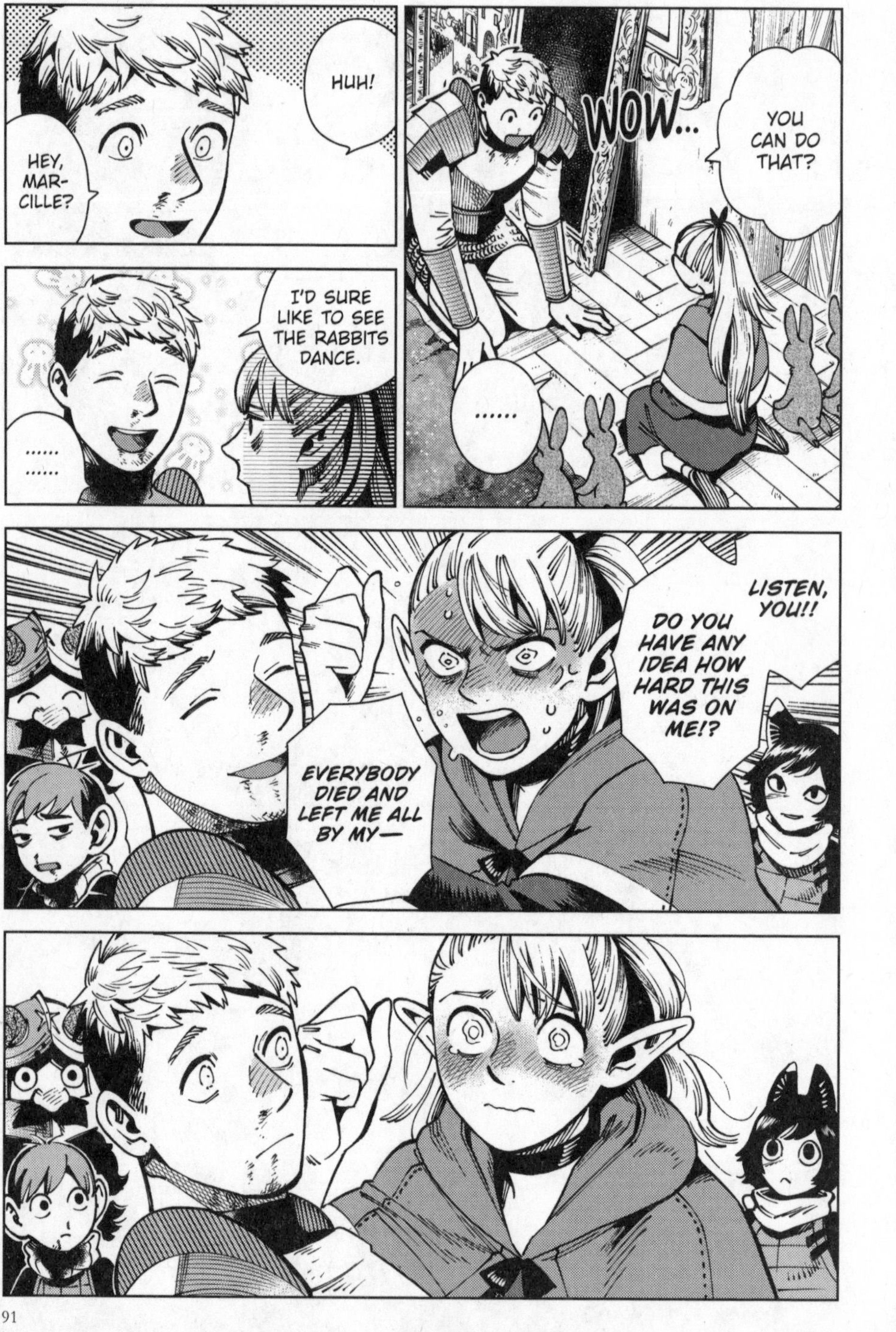

YOU CAN DO THAT?
WOW...
......
HUH!
HEY, MARCILLE?
I'D SURE LIKE TO SEE THE RABBITS DANCE.
....
LISTEN, YOU!!
DO YOU HAVE ANY IDEA HOW HARD THIS WAS ON ME!?
EVERYBODY DIED AND LEFT ME ALL BY MY—

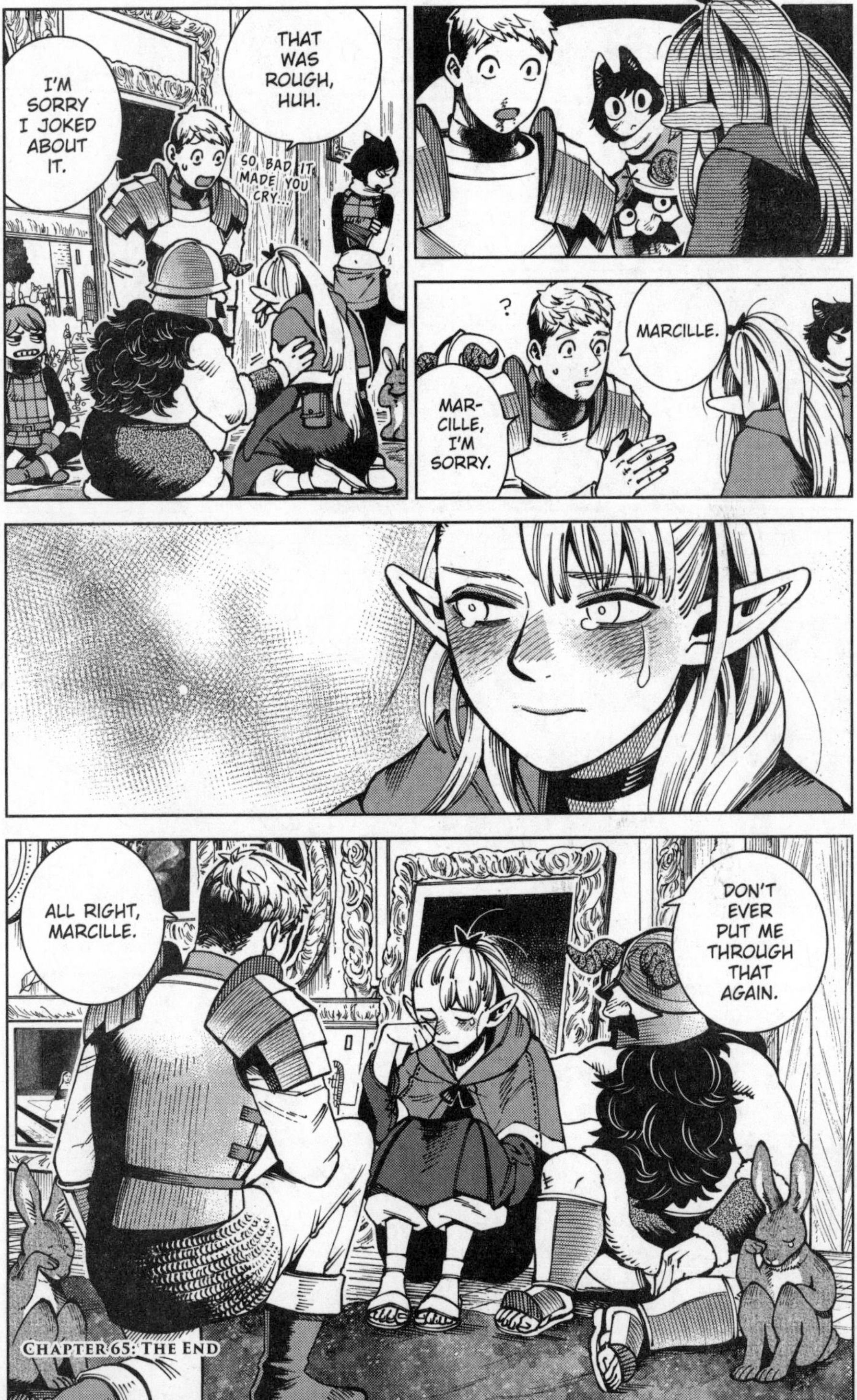
MARCILLE.
MAR-CILLE, I'M SORRY.
?
THAT WAS ROUGH, HUH.
SO, BAD IT MADE YOU CRY...
I'M SORRY I JOKED ABOUT IT.
DON'T EVER PUT ME THROUGH THAT AGAIN.
ALL RIGHT, MARCILLE.
CHAPTER 65: THE END

66. CURRY -1-

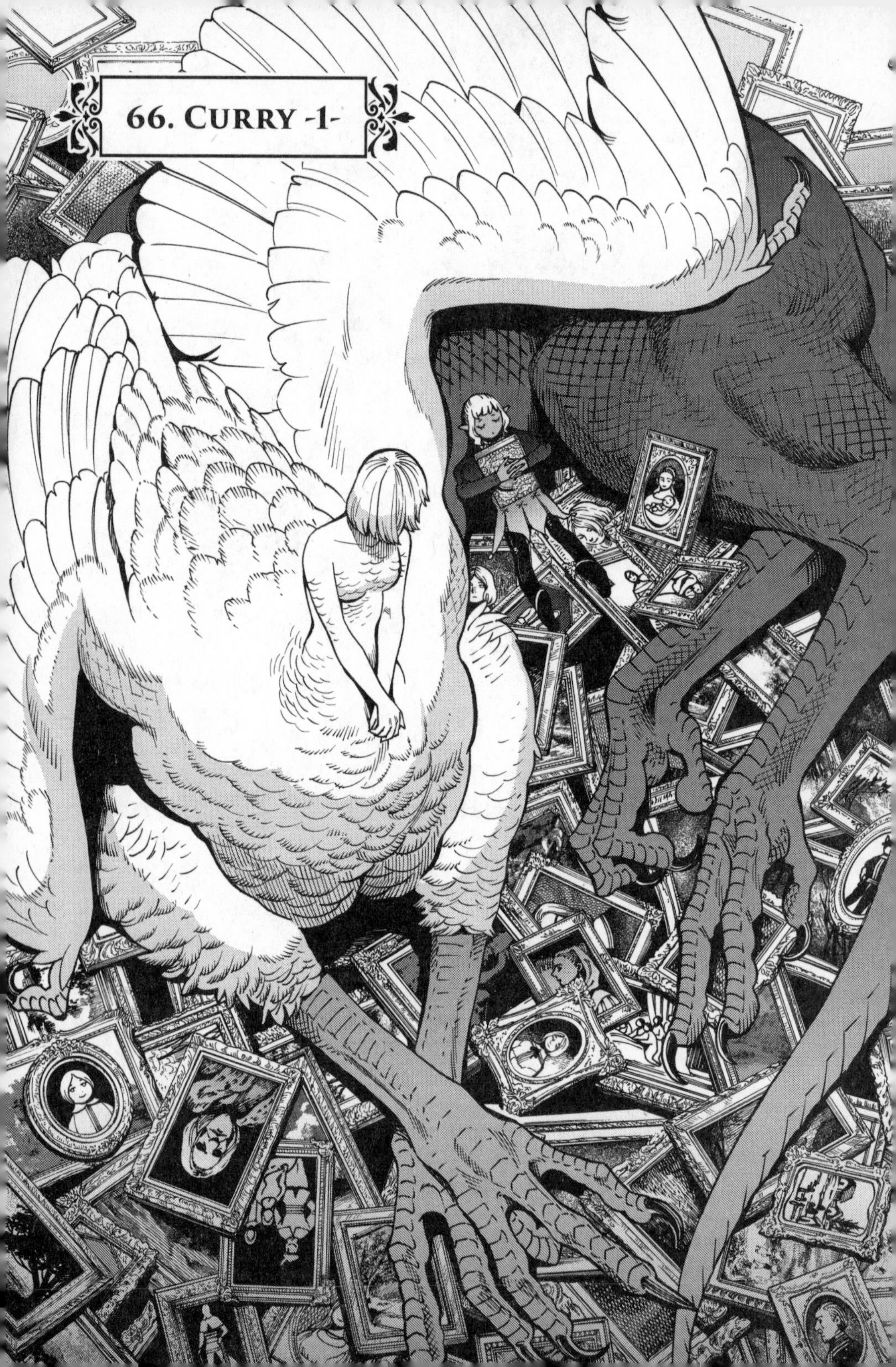

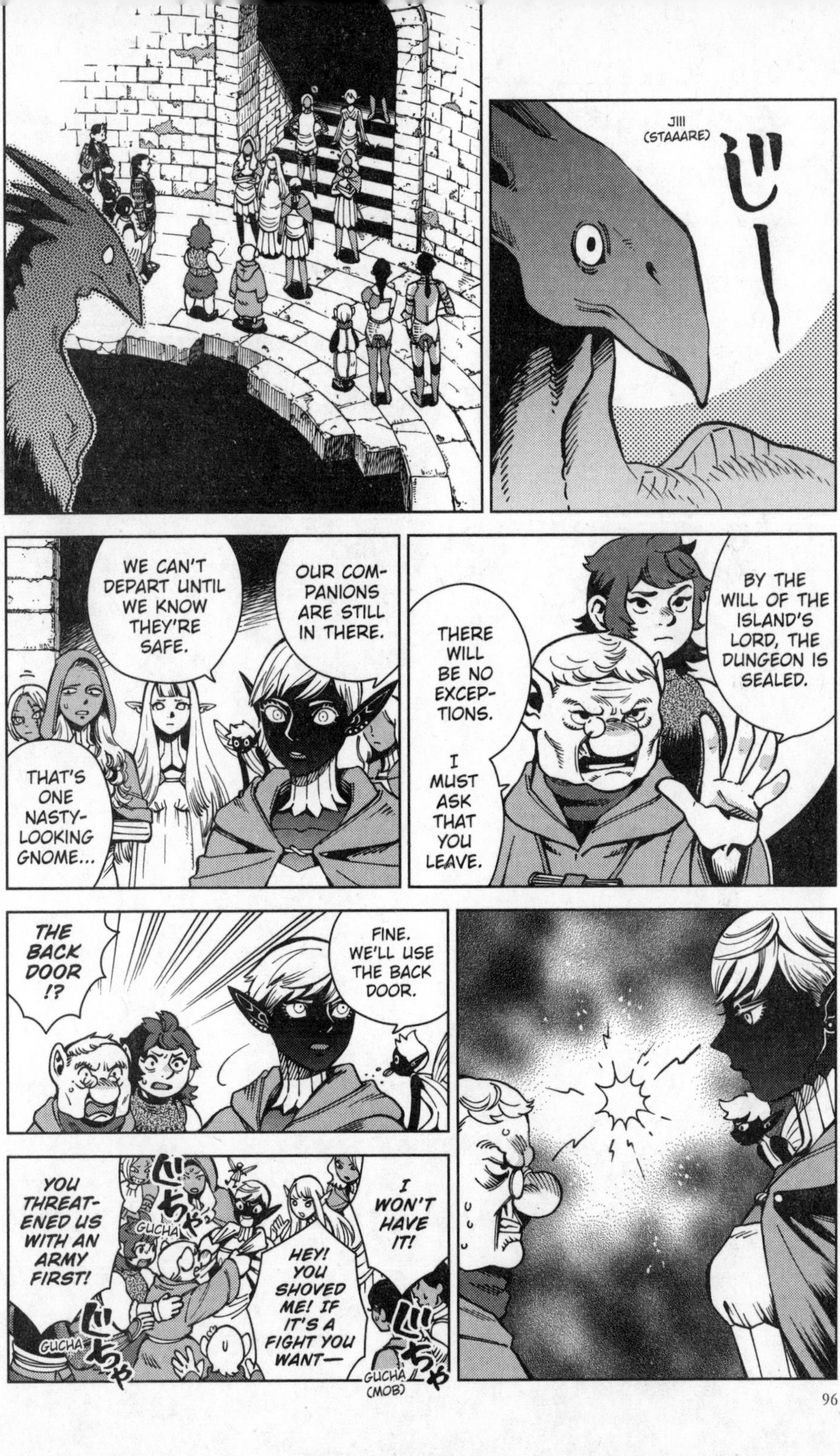
JIII (STAARE)
じー
BY THE WILL OF THE ISLAND'S LORD, THE DUNGEON IS SEALED.
THERE WILL BE NO EXCEPTIONS.
I MUST ASK THAT YOU LEAVE.
OUR COMPANIONS ARE STILL IN THERE.
WE CAN'T DEPART UNTIL WE KNOW THEY'RE SAFE.
THAT'S ONE NASTY-LOOKING GNOME...
FINE. WE'LL USE THE BACK DOOR.
THE BACK DOOR!?
I WON'T HAVE IT!
HEY! YOU SHOVED ME! IF IT'S A FIGHT YOU WANT—
YOU THREATENED US WITH AN ARMY FIRST!
GUCHA
GUCHA
GUCHA (MOB)

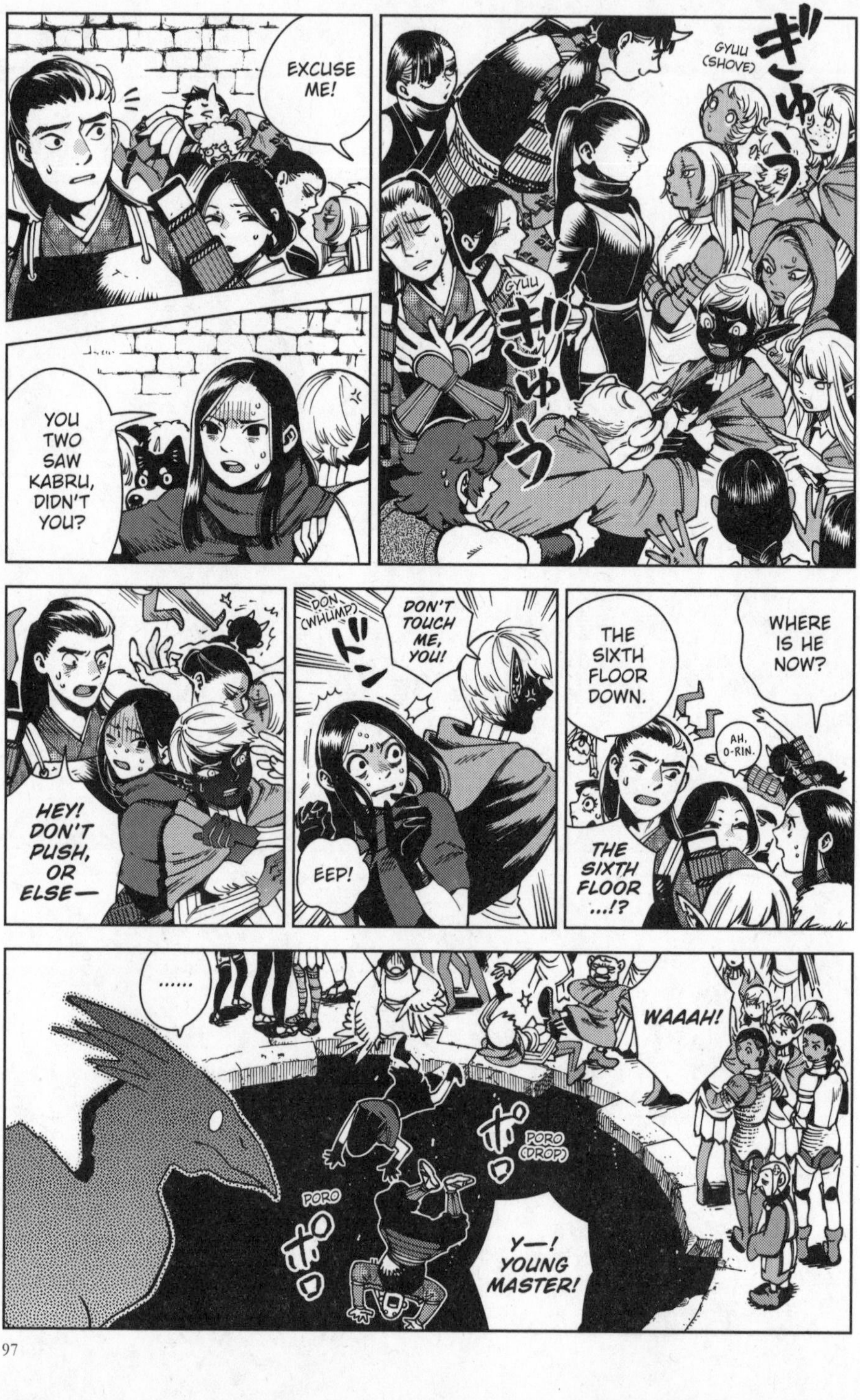

ぎゅう
GYUU (SHOVE)
ぎゅう
GYUU
EXCUSE ME!
YOU TWO SAW KABRU, DIDN'T YOU?
WHERE IS HE NOW?
THE SIXTH FLOOR DOWN.
AH, O-RIN.
THE SIXTH FLOOR ...!?
DON'T TOUCH ME, YOU!
ドン
DON (WHUMP)
EEP!
HEY! DON'T PUSH, OR ELSE—
WAAAH!
......
ポロ
PORO (DROP)
Y—! YOUNG MASTER!
ポロ
PORO

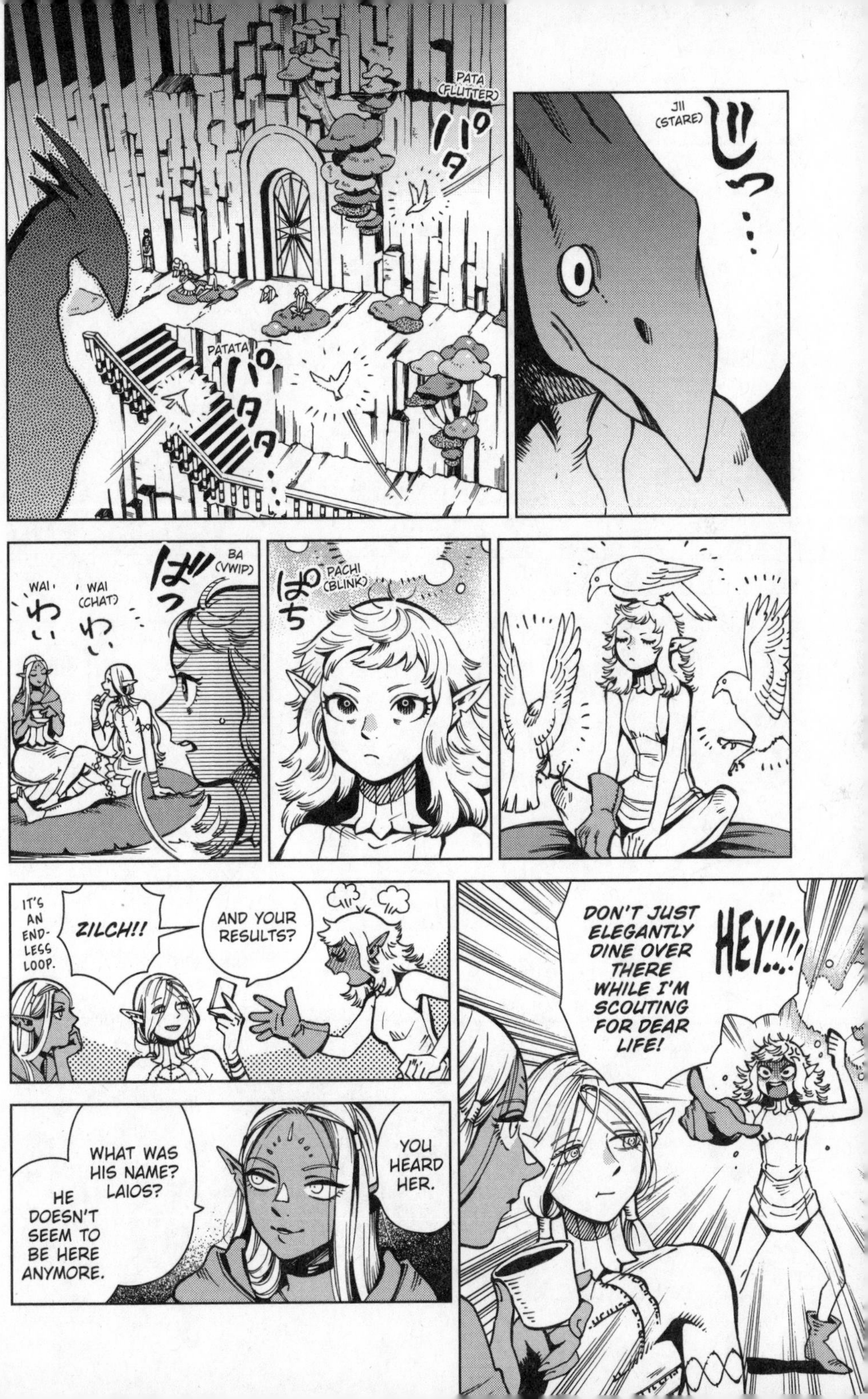

JII (STARE)
じっ…
PATA (FLUTTER)
パタ
PATATA
パタタタ…
PACHI (BLINK)
ぱち
BA (VWIP)
ぱっ
WAI
わい
WAI (CHAT)
わい
HEY!!!...
DON'T JUST ELEGANTLY DINE OVER THERE WHILE I'M SCOUTING FOR DEAR LIFE!
AND YOUR RESULTS?
ZILCH!!
IT'S AN ENDLESS LOOP.
YOU HEARD HER.
WHAT WAS HIS NAME? LAIOS?
HE DOESN'T SEEM TO BE HERE ANYMORE.

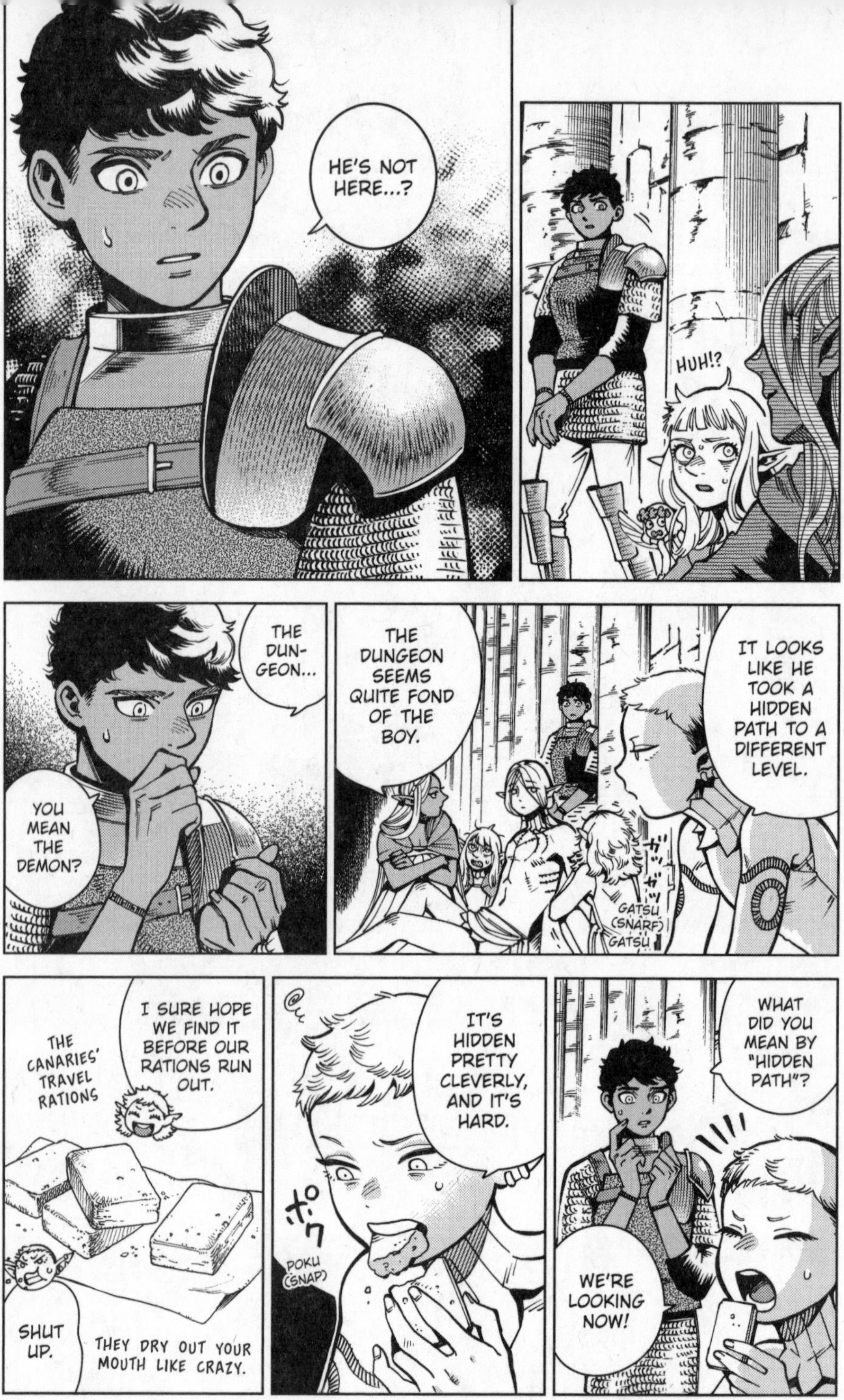
HUH!?
HE'S NOT HERE...?
IT LOOKS LIKE HE TOOK A HIDDEN PATH TO A DIFFERENT LEVEL.
THE DUNGEON SEEMS QUITE FOND OF THE BOY.
GATSU (SNARF) GATSU
THE DUN-GEON...
YOU MEAN THE DEMON?
WHAT DID YOU MEAN BY "HIDDEN PATH"?
WE'RE LOOKING NOW!
IT'S HIDDEN PRETTY CLEVERLY, AND IT'S HARD.
POKU (SNAP)
I SURE HOPE WE FIND IT BEFORE OUR RATIONS RUN OUT.
THE CANARIES' TRAVEL RATIONS
THEY DRY OUT YOUR MOUTH LIKE CRAZY.
SHUT UP.

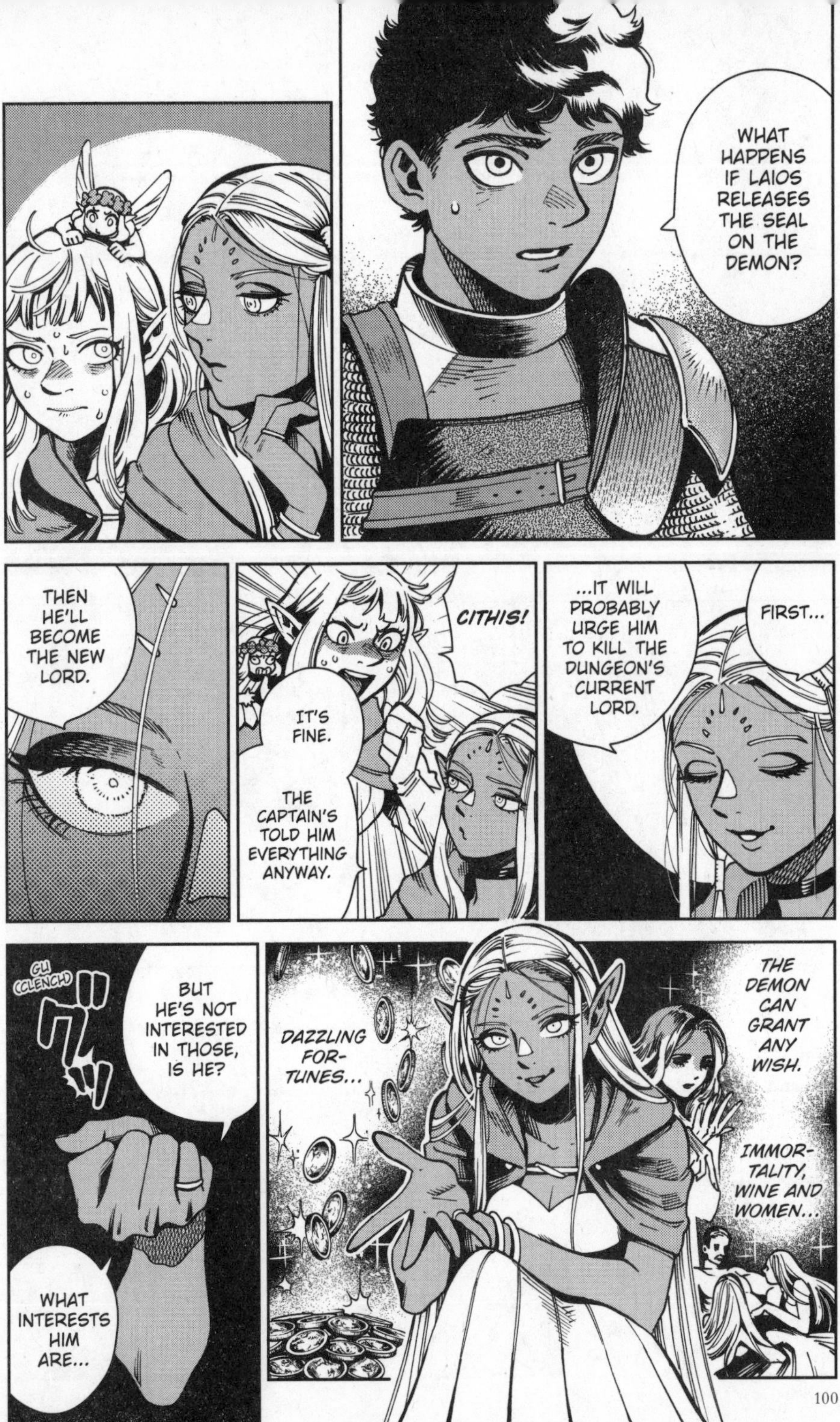
WHAT HAPPENS IF LAIOS RELEASES THE SEAL ON THE DEMON?
FIRST...
...IT WILL PROBABLY URGE HIM TO KILL THE DUNGEON'S CURRENT LORD.
CITHIS!
IT'S FINE.
THE CAPTAIN'S TOLD HIM EVERYTHING ANYWAY.
THEN HE'LL BECOME THE NEW LORD.
THE DEMON CAN GRANT ANY WISH.
IMMORTALITY, WINE AND WOMEN...
DAZZLING FORTUNES...
GU (CLENCH)
BUT HE'S NOT INTERESTED IN THOSE, IS HE?
WHAT INTERESTS HIM ARE...

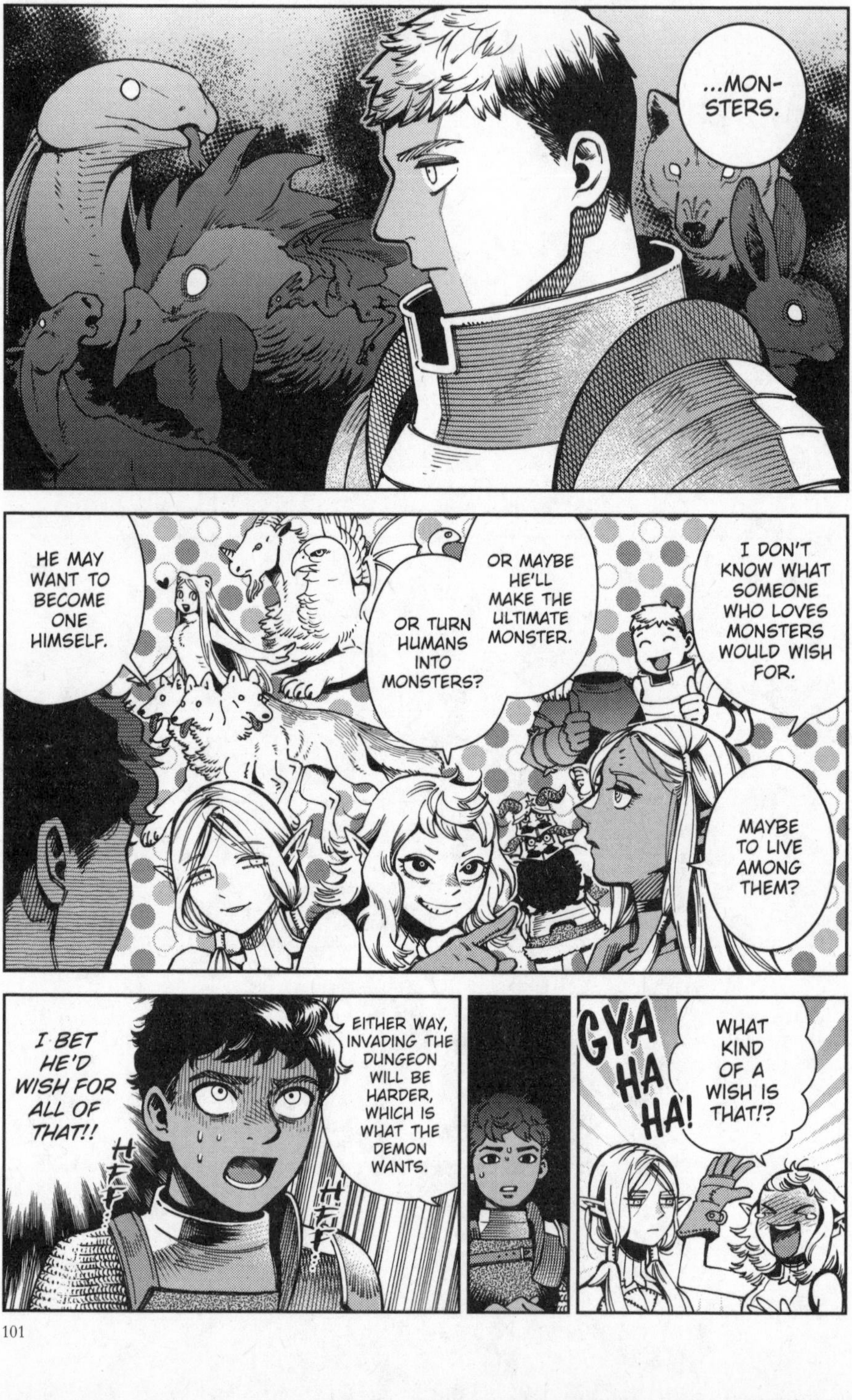

...MON-STERS.
I DON'T KNOW WHAT SOMEONE WHO LOVES MONSTERS WOULD WISH FOR.
MAYBE TO LIVE AMONG THEM?
OR MAYBE HE'LL MAKE THE ULTIMATE MONSTER.
OR TURN HUMANS INTO MONSTERS?
HE MAY WANT TO BECOME ONE HIMSELF.
WHAT KIND OF A WISH IS THAT!?
GYA HA HA!
EITHER WAY, INVADING THE DUNGEON WILL BE HARDER, WHICH IS WHAT THE DEMON WANTS.
I BET HE'D WISH FOR ALL OF THAT!!

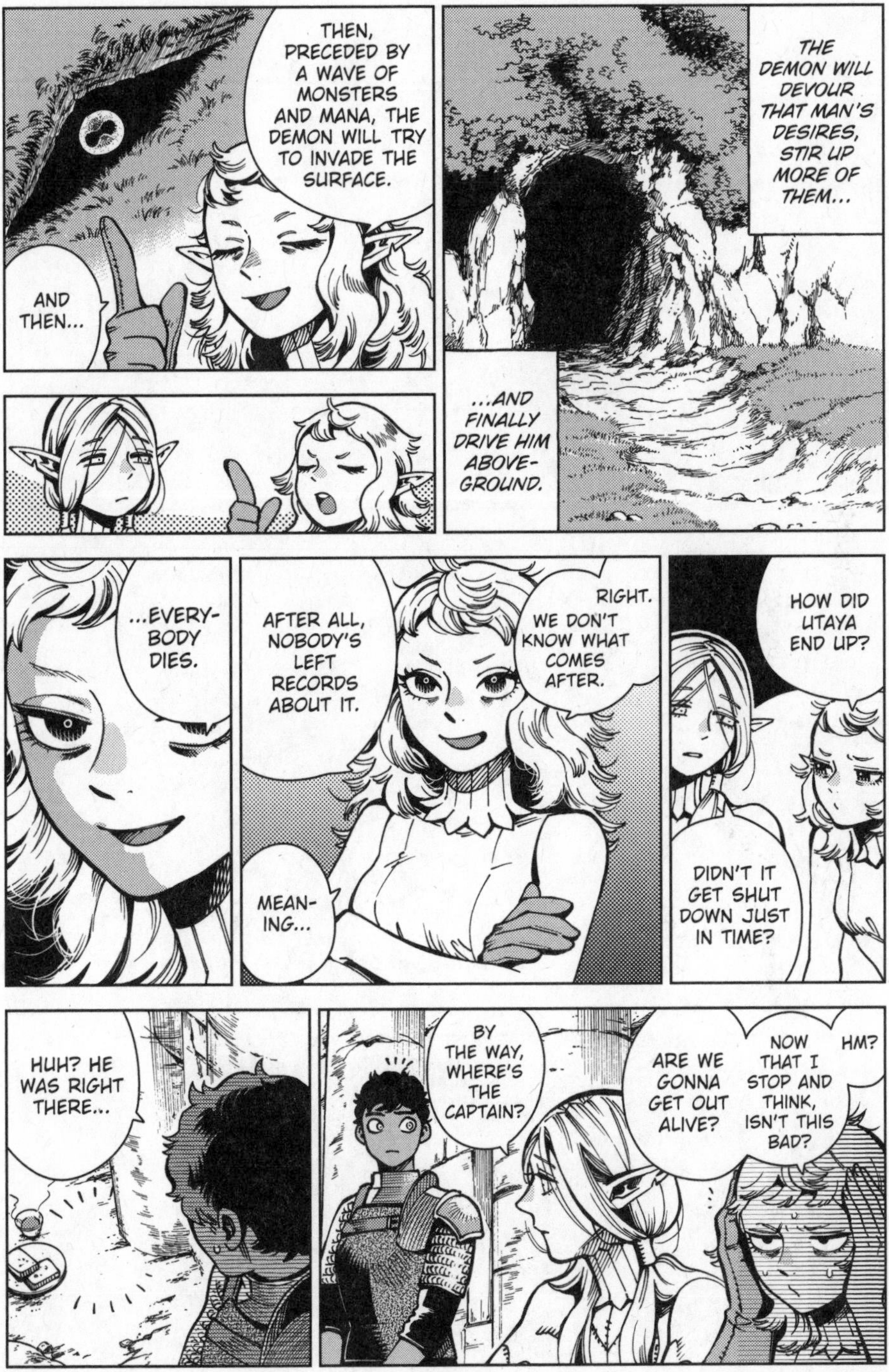
THE DEMON WILL DEVOUR THAT MAN'S DESIRES, STIR UP MORE OF THEM...
...AND FINALLY DRIVE HIM ABOVE-GROUND.
THEN, PRECEDED BY A WAVE OF MONSTERS AND MANA, THE DEMON WILL TRY TO INVADE THE SURFACE.
AND THEN...
HOW DID UTAYA END UP?
DIDN'T IT GET SHUT DOWN JUST IN TIME?
RIGHT.
WE DON'T KNOW WHAT COMES AFTER.
AFTER ALL, NOBODY'S LEFT RECORDS ABOUT IT.
MEAN-ING...
...EVERY-BODY DIES.
HM?
NOW THAT I STOP AND THINK, ISN'T THIS BAD?
ARE WE GONNA GET OUT ALIVE?
BY THE WAY, WHERE'S THE CAPTAIN?
HUH? HE WAS RIGHT THERE...

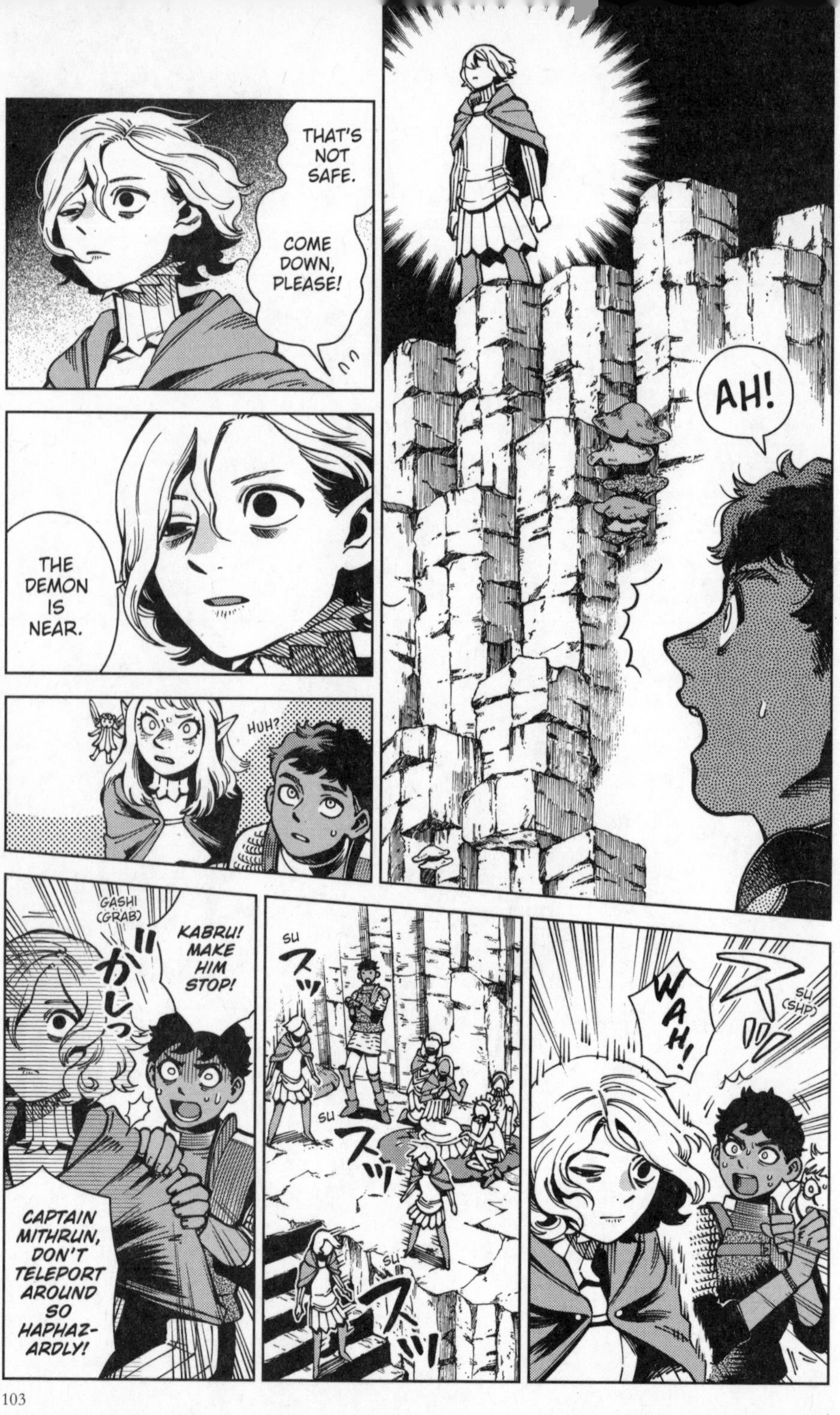
AH!
THAT'S NOT SAFE.
COME DOWN, PLEASE!
THE DEMON IS NEAR.
HUH?
WAH!
SU (SHP)
SU
SU
SU
GASHI (GRAB)
KABRU! MAKE HIM STOP!
CAPTAIN MITHRUN, DON'T TELEPORT AROUND SO HAPHAZARDLY!

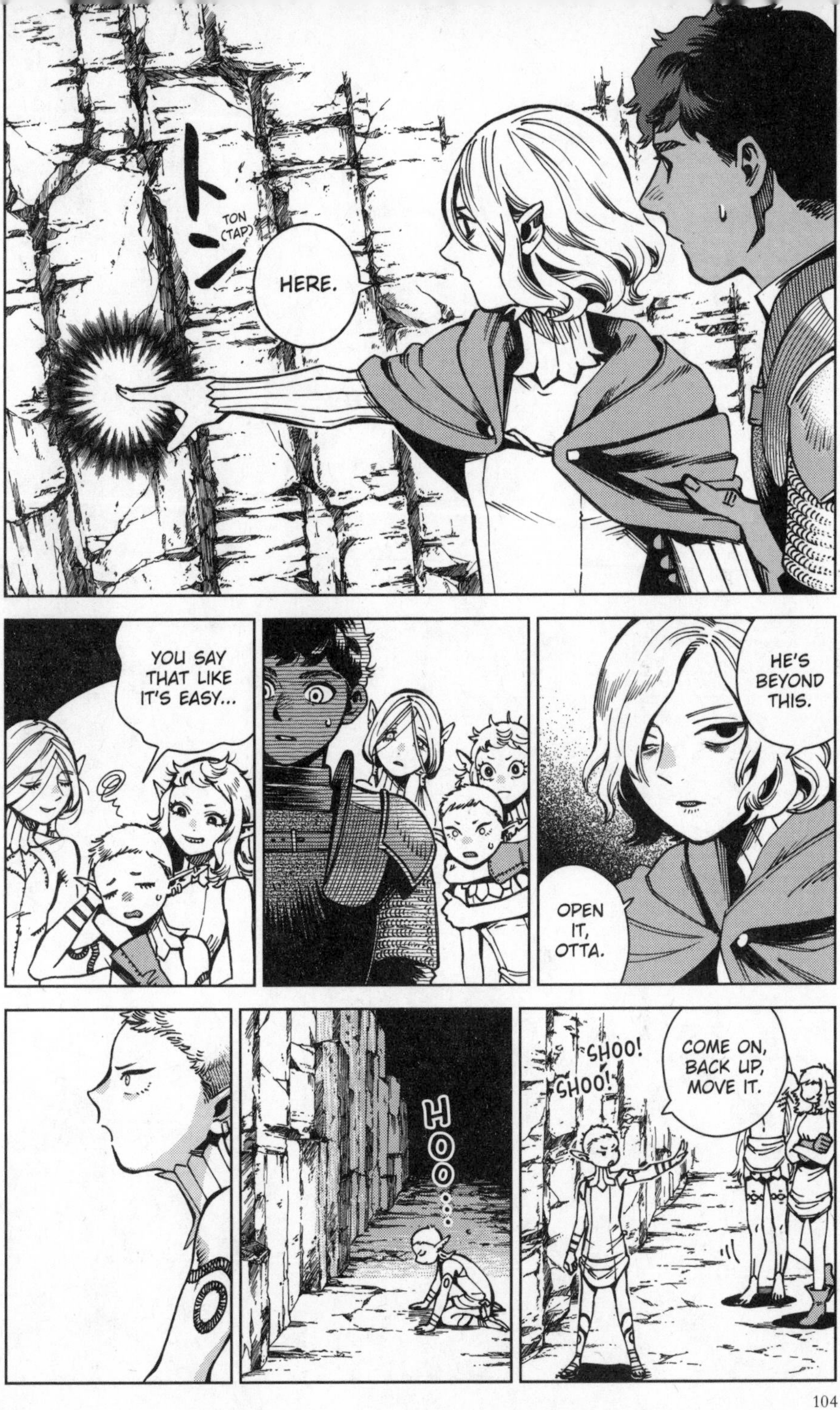
HERE.
TON (TAP)
HE'S BEYOND THIS.
OPEN IT, OTTA.
YOU SAY THAT LIKE IT'S EASY...
COME ON, BACK UP, MOVE IT.
SHOO! SHOO!
HOO...

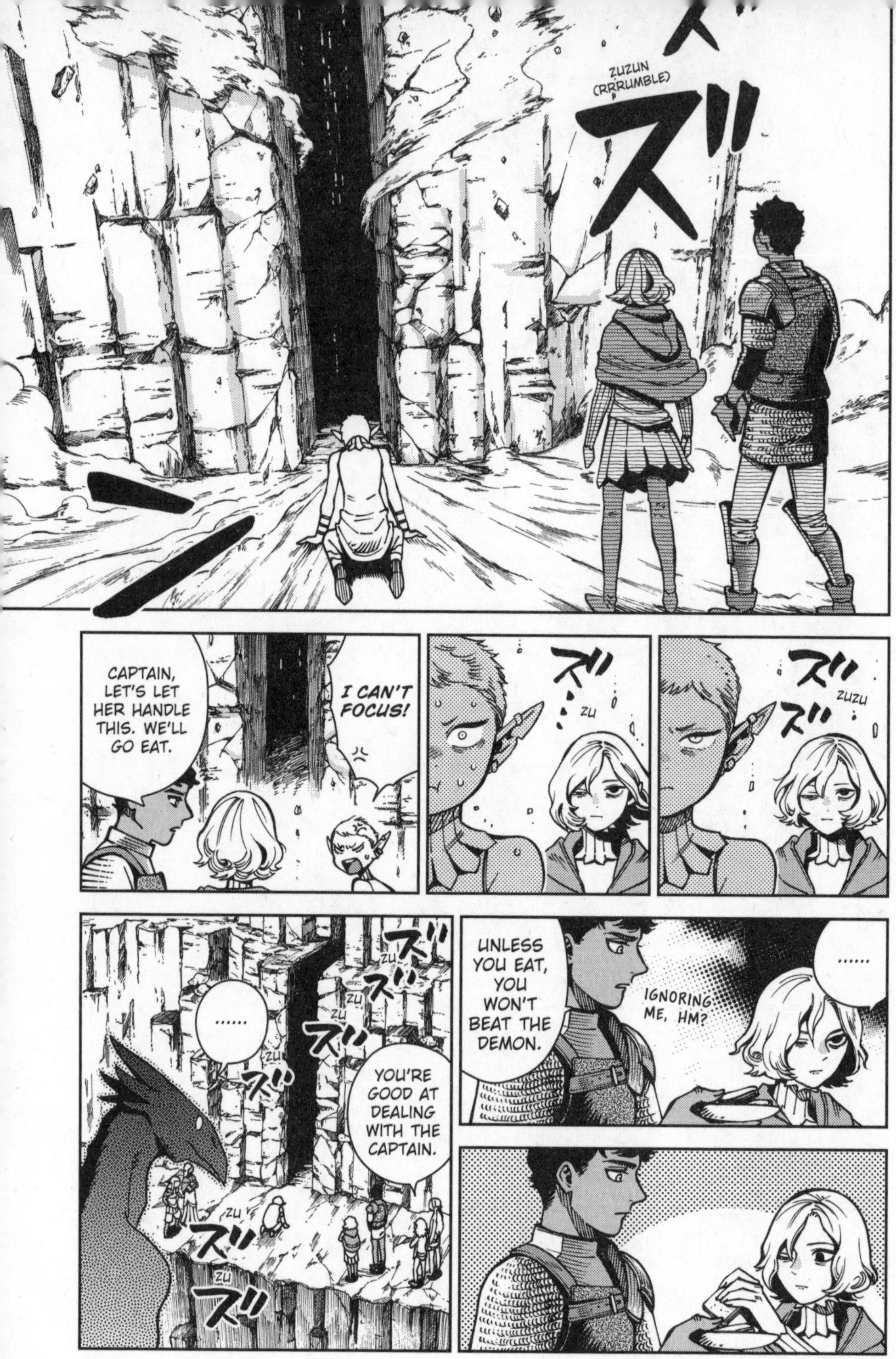
ZUZUN (RRRUMBLE)
ZUZU
ZU
CAPTAIN, LET'S LET HER HANDLE THIS. WE'LL GO EAT.
I CAN'T FOCUS!
......
UNLESS YOU EAT, YOU WON'T BEAT THE DEMON.
IGNORING ME, HM?
ZU
ZU
ZU
......
YOU'RE GOOD AT DEALING WITH THE CAPTAIN.
ZU
ZU

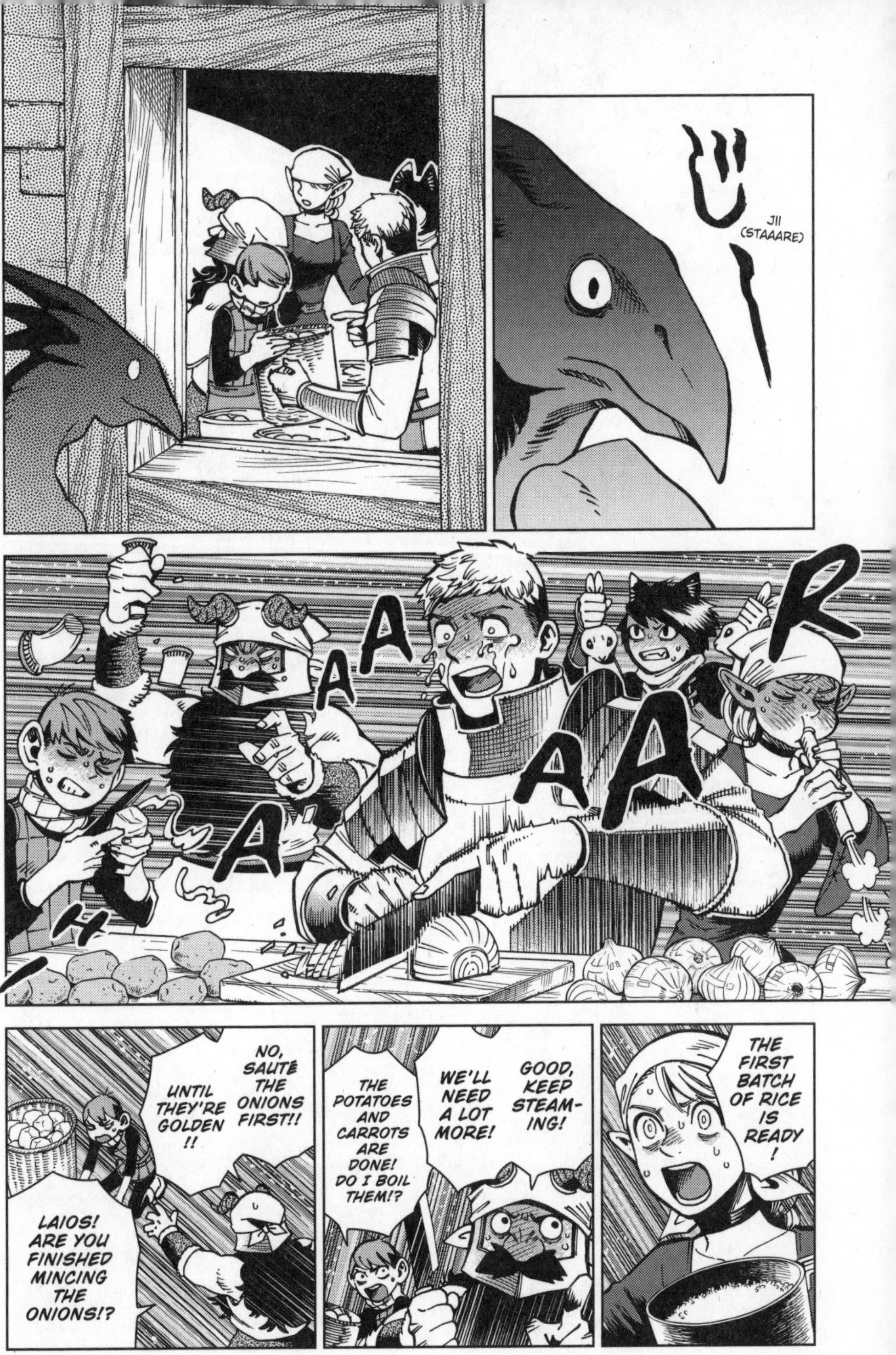
じー
JII (STAAARE)
HAAAAAR!
THE FIRST BATCH OF RICE IS READY!
GOOD, KEEP STEAMING!
WE'LL NEED A LOT MORE!
THE POTATOES AND CARROTS ARE DONE! DO I BOIL THEM!?
NO, SAUTE THE ONIONS FIRST!!
UNTIL THEY'RE GOLDEN!!
LAIOS! ARE YOU FINISHED MINCING THE ONIONS!?

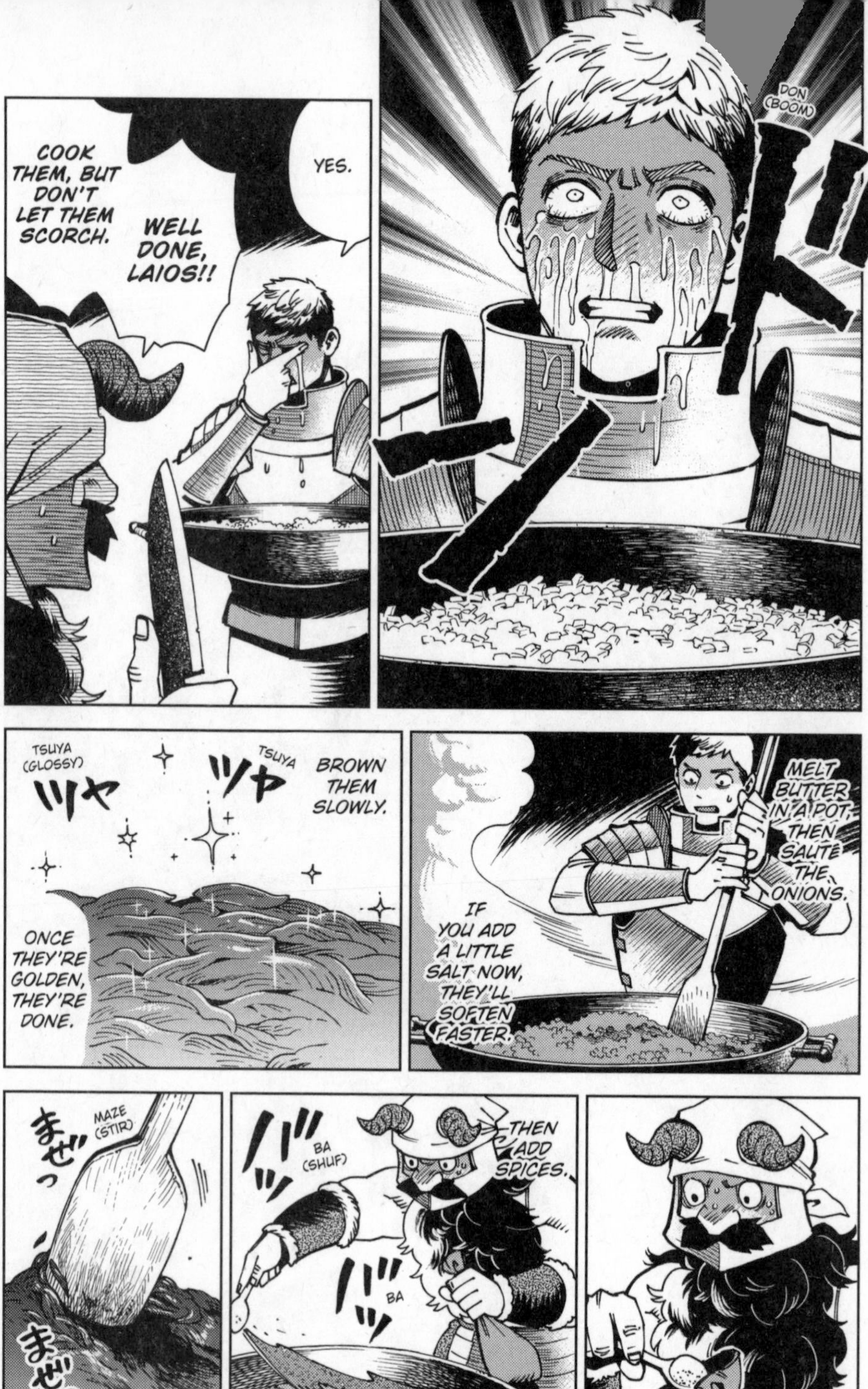
DON (BOOM)
ドン
COOK THEM, BUT DON'T LET THEM SCORCH.
YES.
WELL DONE, LAIOS!!
MELT BUTTER IN A POT, THEN SAUTE THE ONIONS.
IF YOU ADD A LITTLE SALT NOW, THEY'LL SOFTEN FASTER.
BROWN THEM SLOWLY.
TSUYA
ツヤ
TSUYA (GLOSSY)
ツヤ
ONCE THEY'RE GOLDEN, THEY'RE DONE.
THEN ADD SPICES.
BA (SHUF)
バッ
BA
バッ
MAZE (STIR)
まぜっ
まぜっ
MAZE

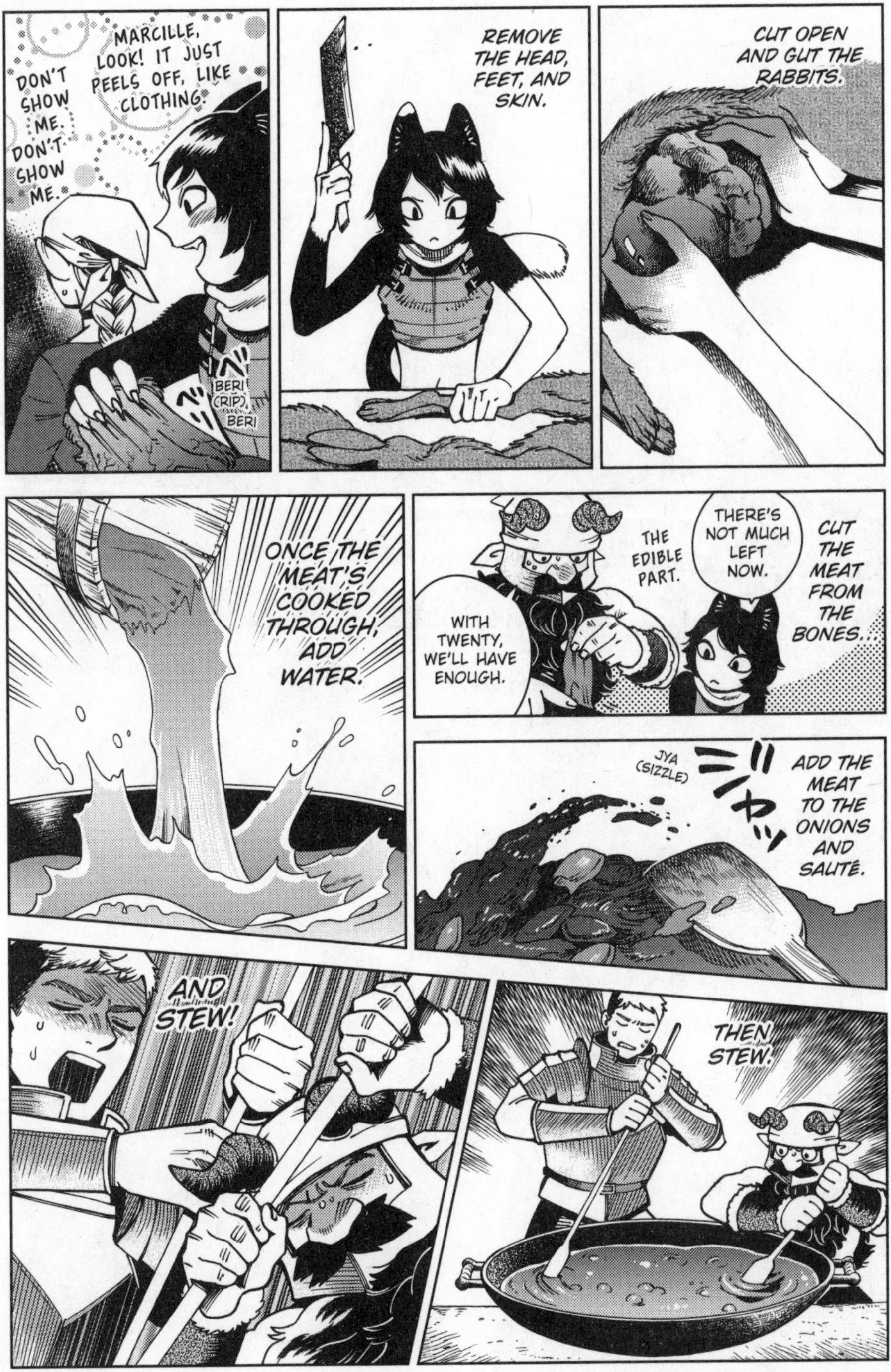
CUT OPEN AND GUT THE RABBITS.
REMOVE THE HEAD, FEET, AND SKIN.
MARCILLE, LOOK! IT JUST PEELS OFF, LIKE CLOTHING.
DON'T SHOW ME. DON'T SHOW ME.
BERI (RIP) BERI
CUT THE MEAT FROM THE BONES...
THERE'S NOT MUCH LEFT NOW.
THE EDIBLE PART.
WITH TWENTY, WE'LL HAVE ENOUGH.
ADD THE MEAT TO THE ONIONS AND SAUTÉ.
JYA (SIZZLE)
ONCE THE MEAT'S COOKED THROUGH, ADD WATER.
THEN STEW.
AND STEW!

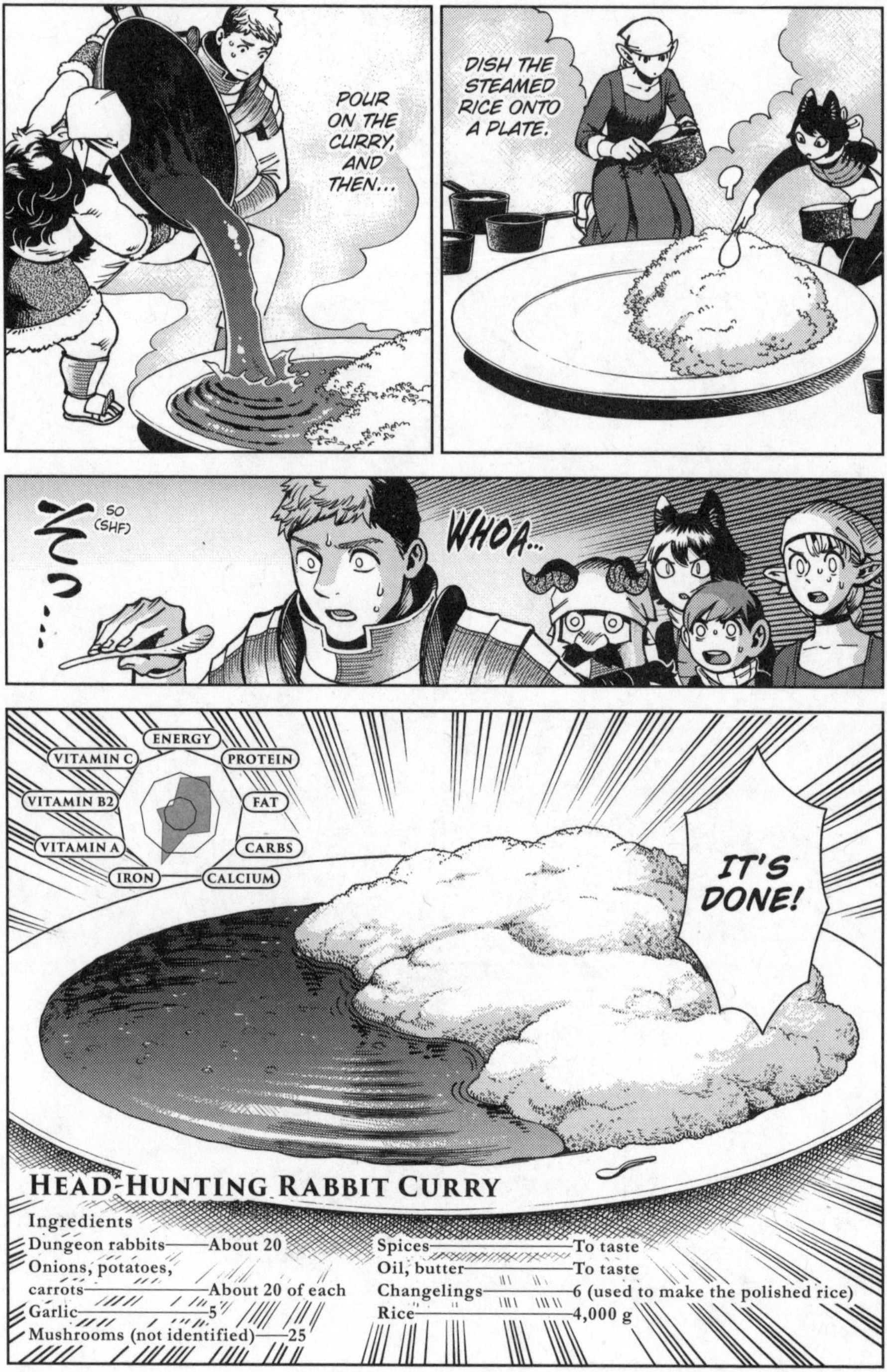
DISH THE STEAMED RICE ONTO A PLATE.
POUR ON THE CURRY, AND THEN...
WHOA...
そっ…
SO (SHF)
IT'S DONE!
ENERGY
PROTEIN
FAT
CARBS
CALCIUM
IRON
VITAMIN A
VITAMIN B2
VITAMIN C
HEAD-HUNTING RABBIT CURRY
Ingredients
Dungeon rabbits—About 20
Onions, potatoes, carrots—About 20 of each
Garlic—5
Mushrooms (not identified)—25
Spices—To taste
Oil, butter—To taste
Changelings—6 (used to make the polished rice)
Rice—4,000 g

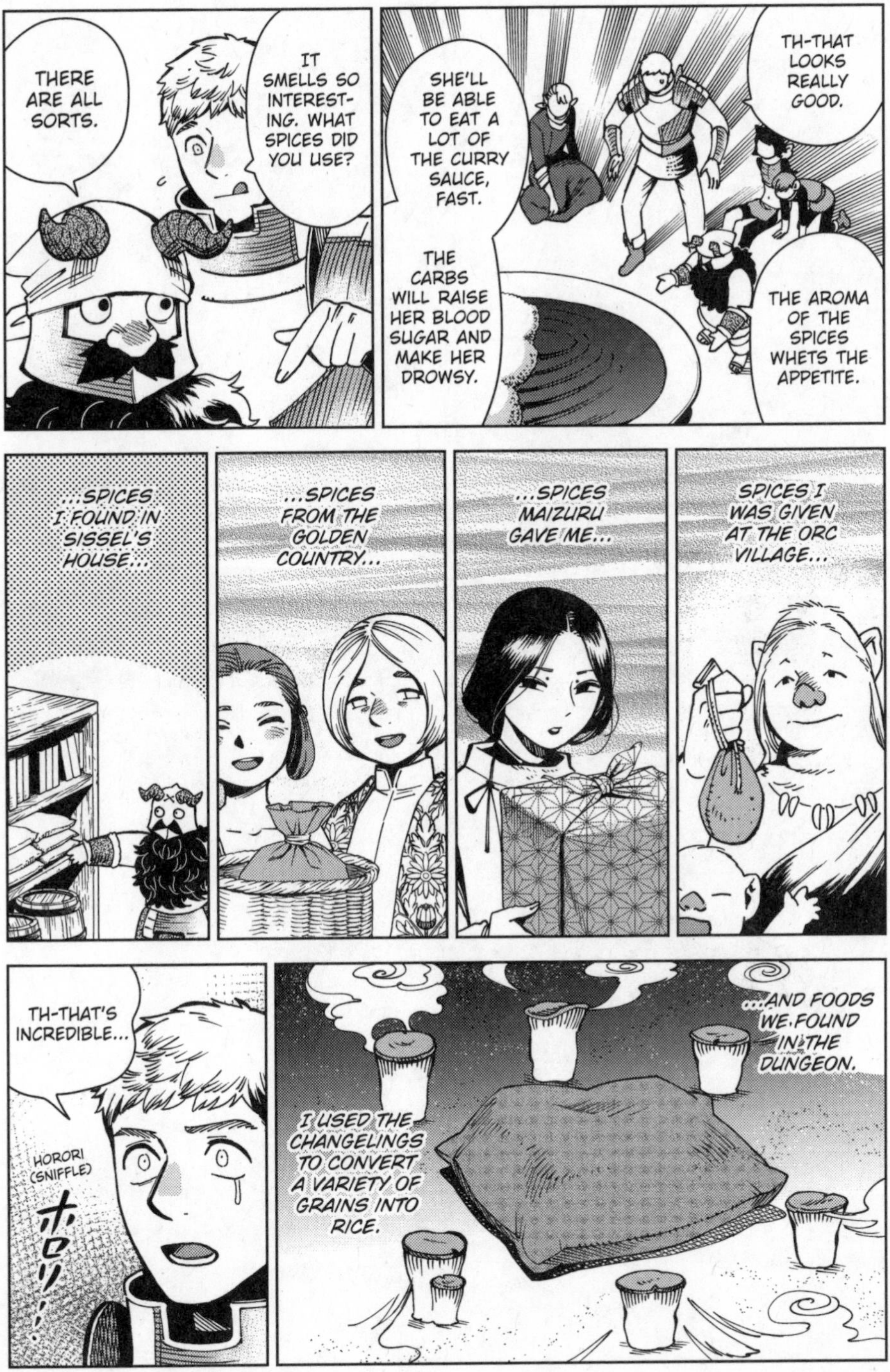
TH-THAT LOOKS REALLY GOOD.
THE AROMA OF THE SPICES WHETS THE APPETITE.
SHE'LL BE ABLE TO EAT A LOT OF THE CURRY SAUCE, FAST.
THE CARBS WILL RAISE HER BLOOD SUGAR AND MAKE HER DROWSY.
IT SMELLS SO INTEREST-ING. WHAT SPICES DID YOU USE?
THERE ARE ALL SORTS.
SPICES I WAS GIVEN AT THE ORC VILLAGE...
...SPICES MAIZURU GAVE ME...
...SPICES FROM THE GOLDEN COUNTRY...
...SPICES I FOUND IN SISSEL'S HOUSE...
...AND FOODS WE FOUND IN THE DUNGEON.
I USED THE CHANGELINGS TO CONVERT A VARIETY OF GRAINS INTO RICE.
TH-THAT'S INCREDIBLE...
HORORI (SNIFFLE)
ホロリ…

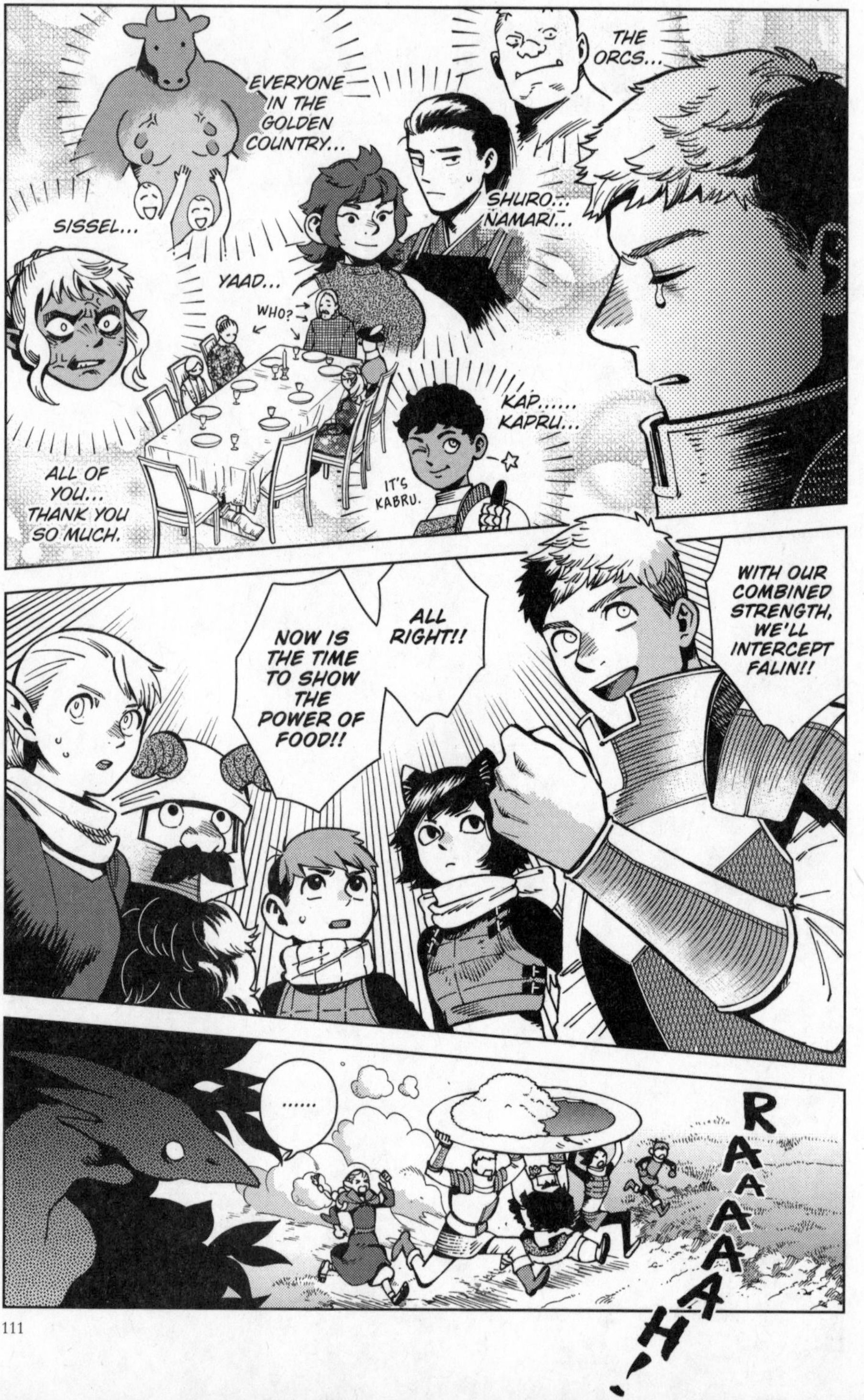
THE ORCS...
SHURO... NAMARI...
EVERYONE IN THE GOLDEN COUNTRY...
KAP...... KAPRU...
IT'S KABRU.
YAAD...
WHO?
SISSEL...
ALL OF YOU... THANK YOU SO MUCH.
WITH OUR COMBINED STRENGTH, WE'LL INTERCEPT FALIN!!
ALL RIGHT!!
NOW IS THE TIME TO SHOW THE POWER OF FOOD!!
RAAAAH!
......

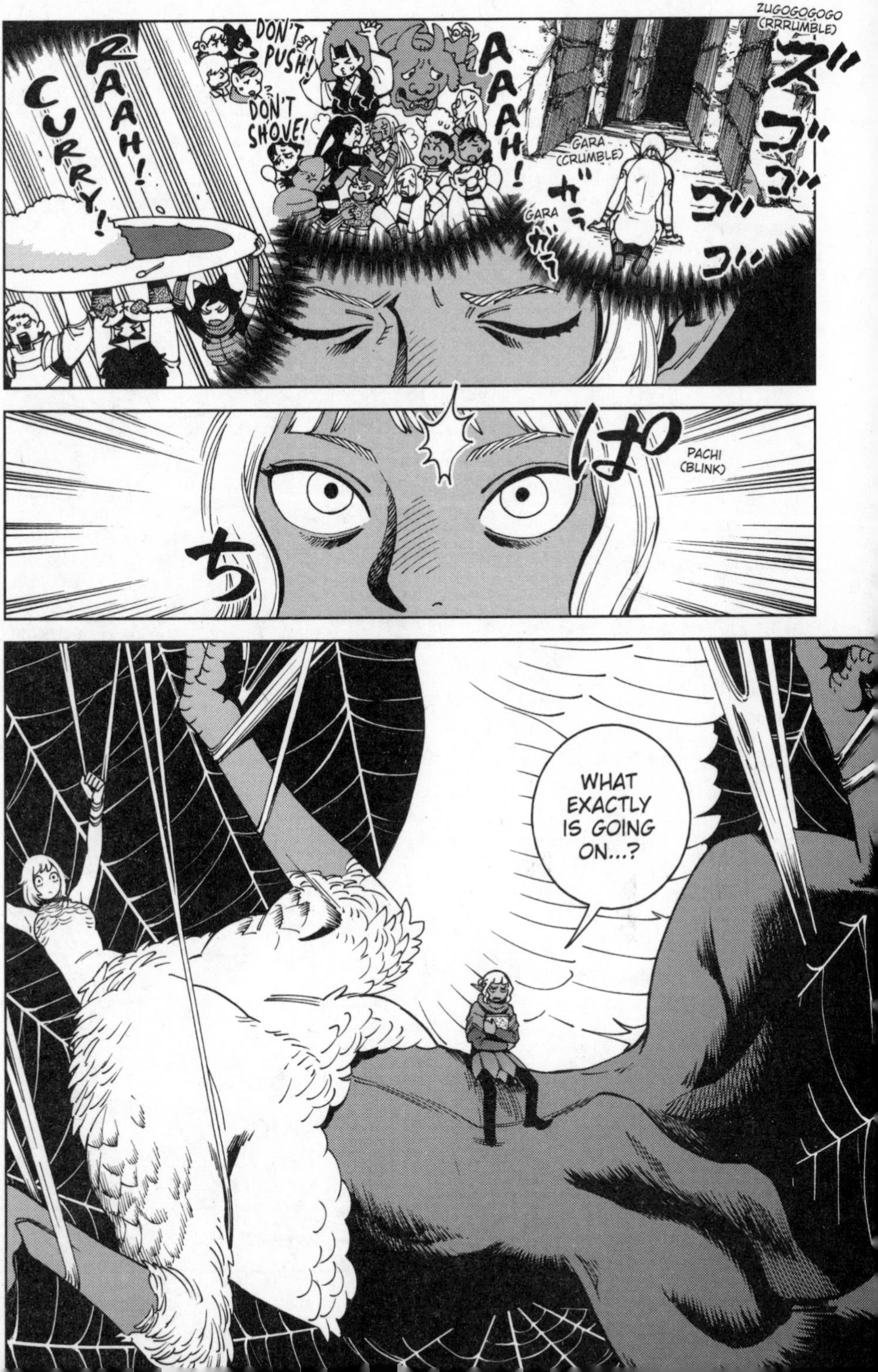
ZUGOGOGOGO (RRRUMBLE)
ズゴゴゴ
GARA (CRUMBLE)
ガラ
GARA
ガラ
AAAAH!
DON'T PUSH!
DON'T SHOVE!
RAAAH! CURRY!
PACHI (BLINK)
ぱち
WHAT EXACTLY IS GOING ON...?

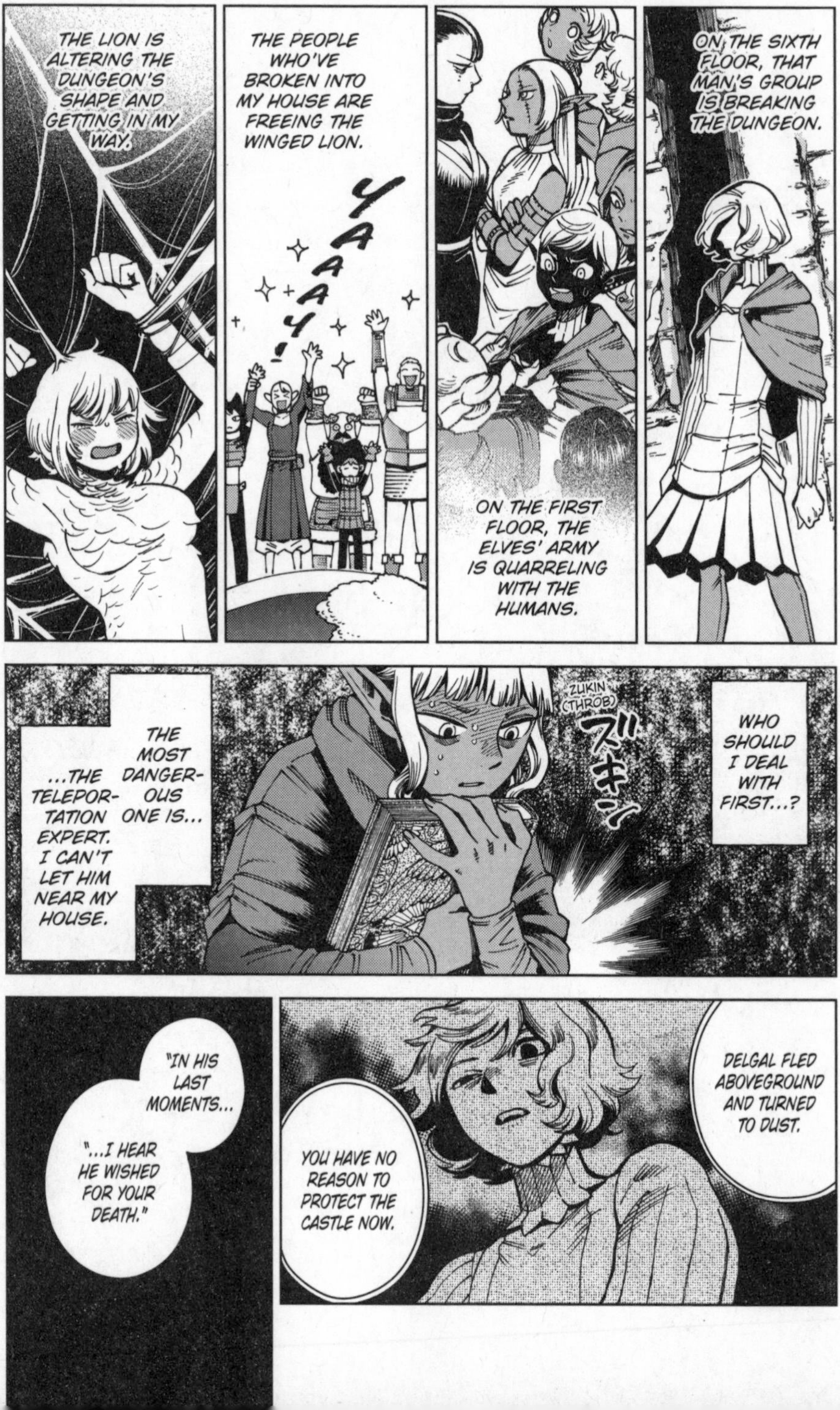
ON THE SIXTH FLOOR, THAT MAN'S GROUP IS BREAKING THE DUNGEON.
ON THE FIRST FLOOR, THE ELVES' ARMY IS QUARRELING WITH THE HUMANS.
THE PEOPLE WHO'VE BROKEN INTO MY HOUSE ARE FREEING THE WINGED LION.
YAAAAY!
THE LION IS ALTERING THE DUNGEON'S SHAPE AND GETTING IN MY WAY.
WHO SHOULD I DEAL WITH FIRST...?
ZUKIN (THROB)
THE MOST DANGER-OUS ONE IS...
...THE TELEPOR-TATION EXPERT. I CAN'T LET HIM NEAR MY HOUSE.
DELGAL FLED ABOVEGROUND AND TURNED TO DUST.
YOU HAVE NO REASON TO PROTECT THE CASTLE NOW.
"IN HIS LAST MOMENTS...
"...I HEAR HE WISHED FOR YOUR DEATH."

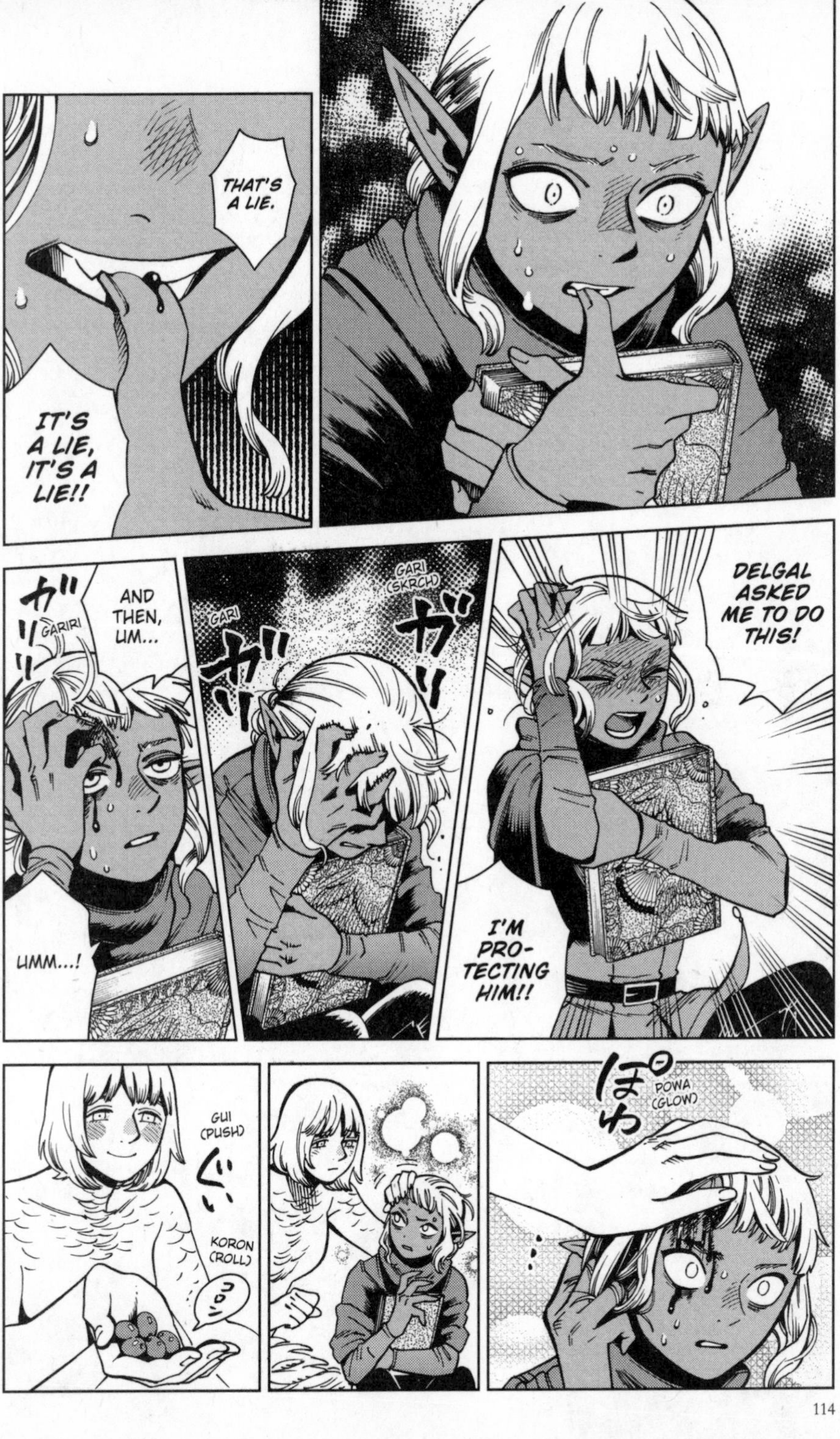
THAT'S A LIE.
IT'S A LIE, IT'S A LIE!!
DELGAL ASKED ME TO DO THIS!
I'M PRO-TECTING HIM!!
GARI (SKRCH)
GARI
GARIRI
AND THEN, UM...
UMM...!
POWA (GLOW)
GUI (PUSH)
KORON (ROLL)

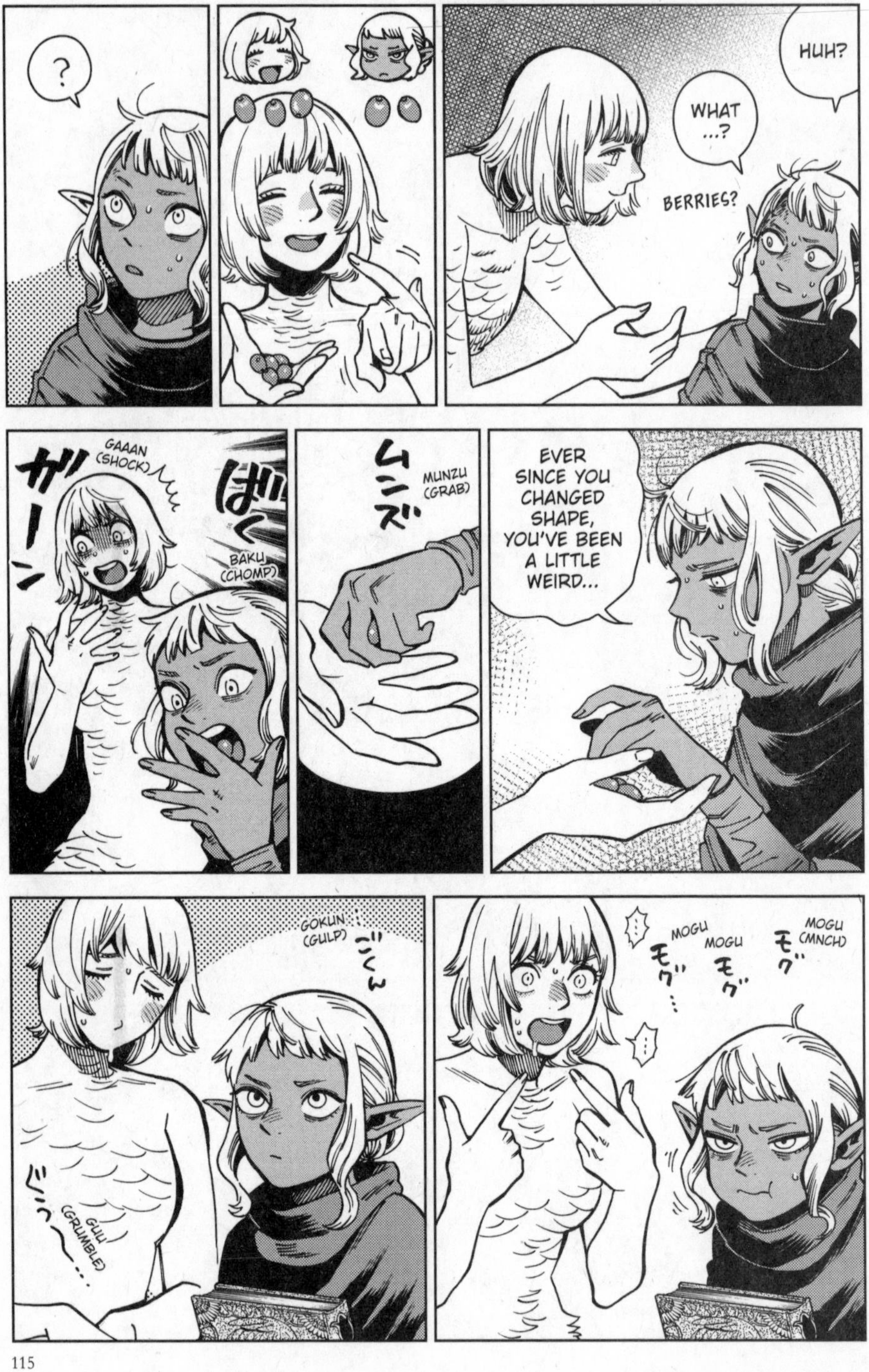
HUH?
WHAT ...?
BERRIES?
?
EVER SINCE YOU CHANGED SHAPE, YOU'VE BEEN A LITTLE WEIRD...
ムンズ
MUNZU (GRAB)
ばく
BAKU (CHOMP)
ガーン
GAAAN (SHOCK)
モグ
MOGU (MNCH)
MOGU
モグ
MOGU
モグ…
!
!
GOKUN (GULP)
ごくん
ぐぅ〜…
GUU (GRUMBLE)

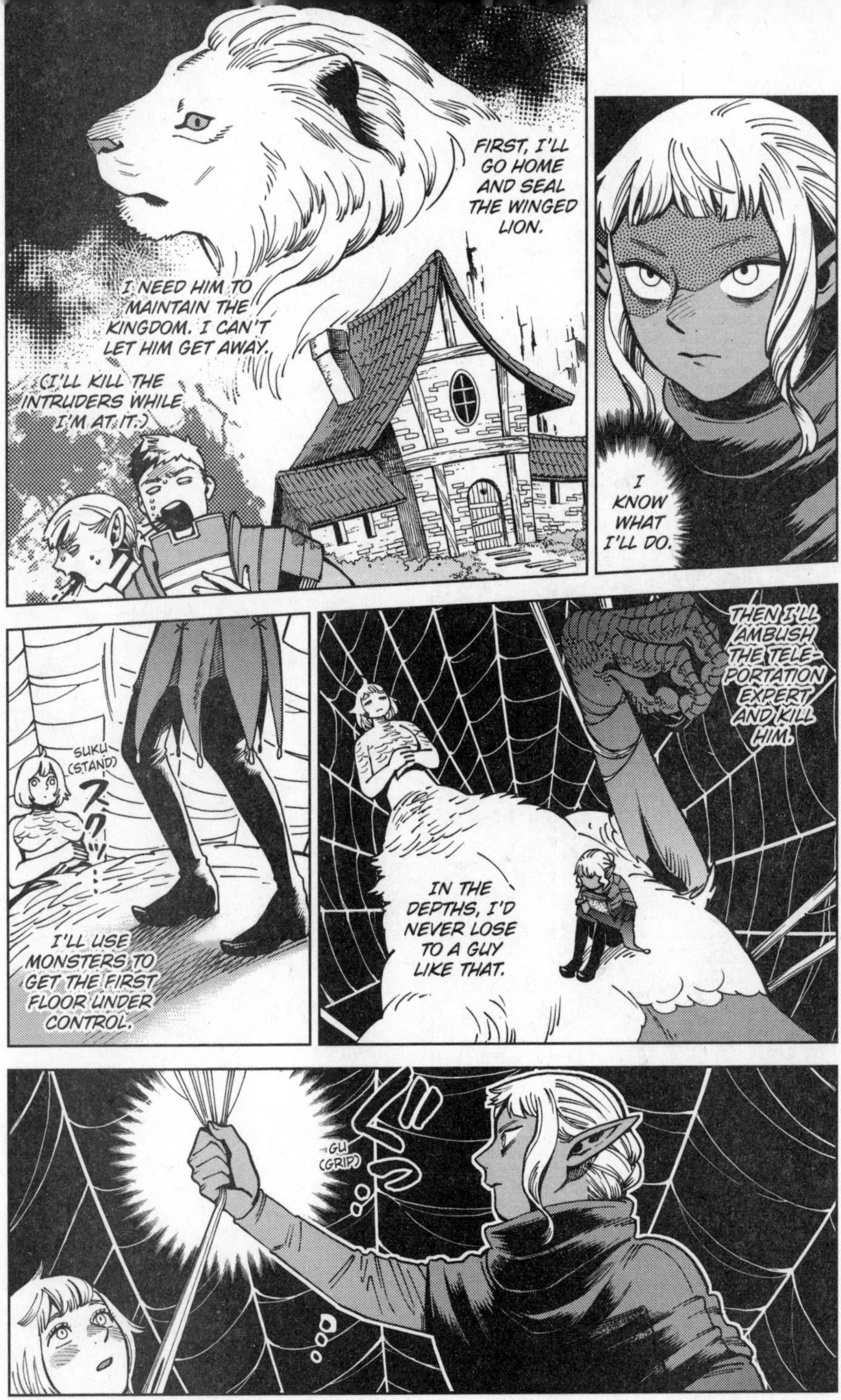
I KNOW WHAT I'LL DO.
FIRST, I'LL GO HOME AND SEAL THE WINGED LION.
I NEED HIM TO MAINTAIN THE KINGDOM. I CAN'T LET HIM GET AWAY.
(I'LL KILL THE INTRUDERS WHILE I'M AT IT.)
THEN I'LL AMBUSH THE TELE-PORTATION EXPERT AND KILL HIM.
IN THE DEPTHS, I'D NEVER LOSE TO A GUY LIKE THAT.
SUKU (STAND)
I'LL USE MONSTERS TO GET THE FIRST FLOOR UNDER CONTROL.
GU (GRIP)

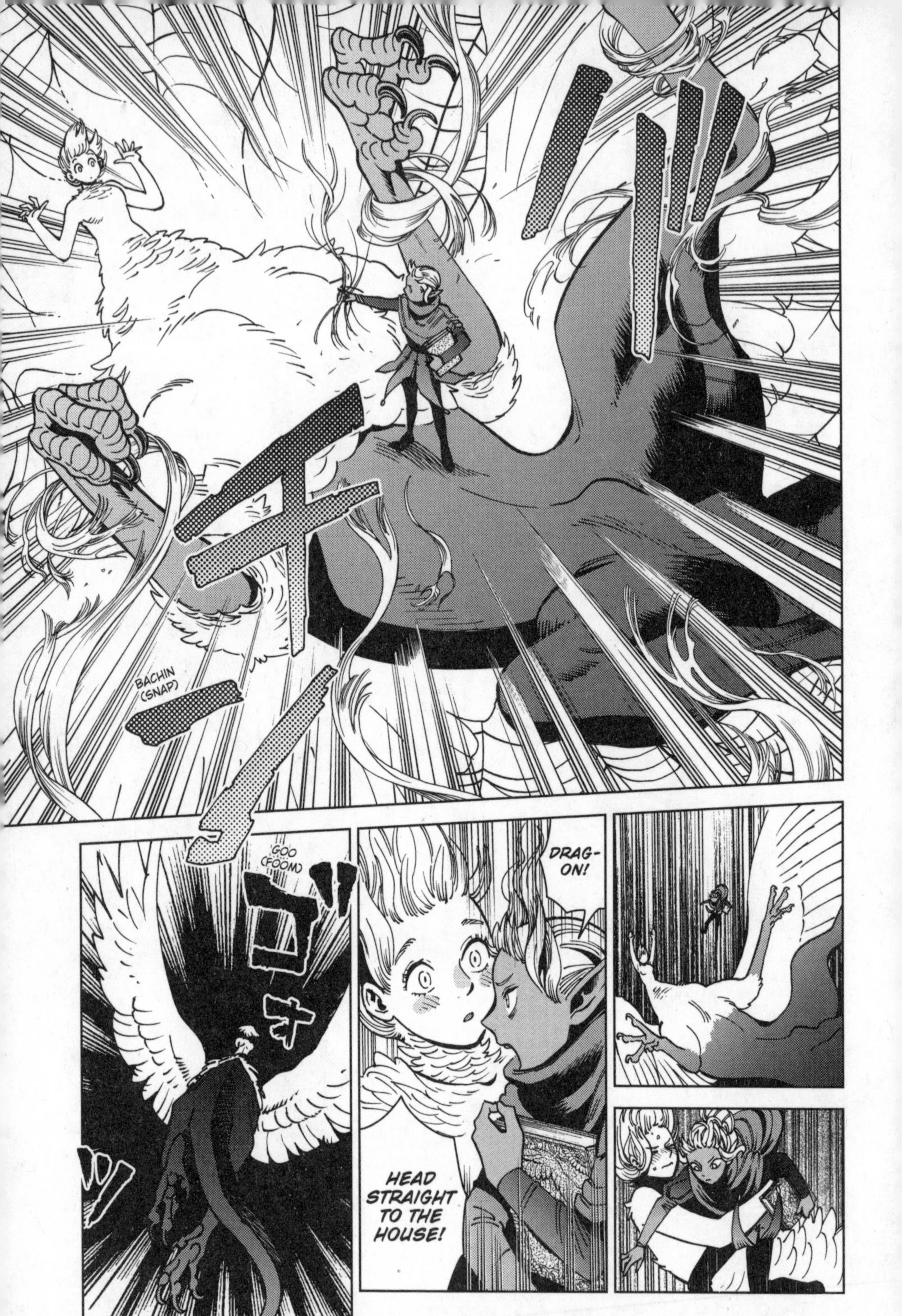
BACHIN
(SNAP)
DRAG-ON!
HEAD STRAIGHT TO THE HOUSE!
GOO
(FOOM)

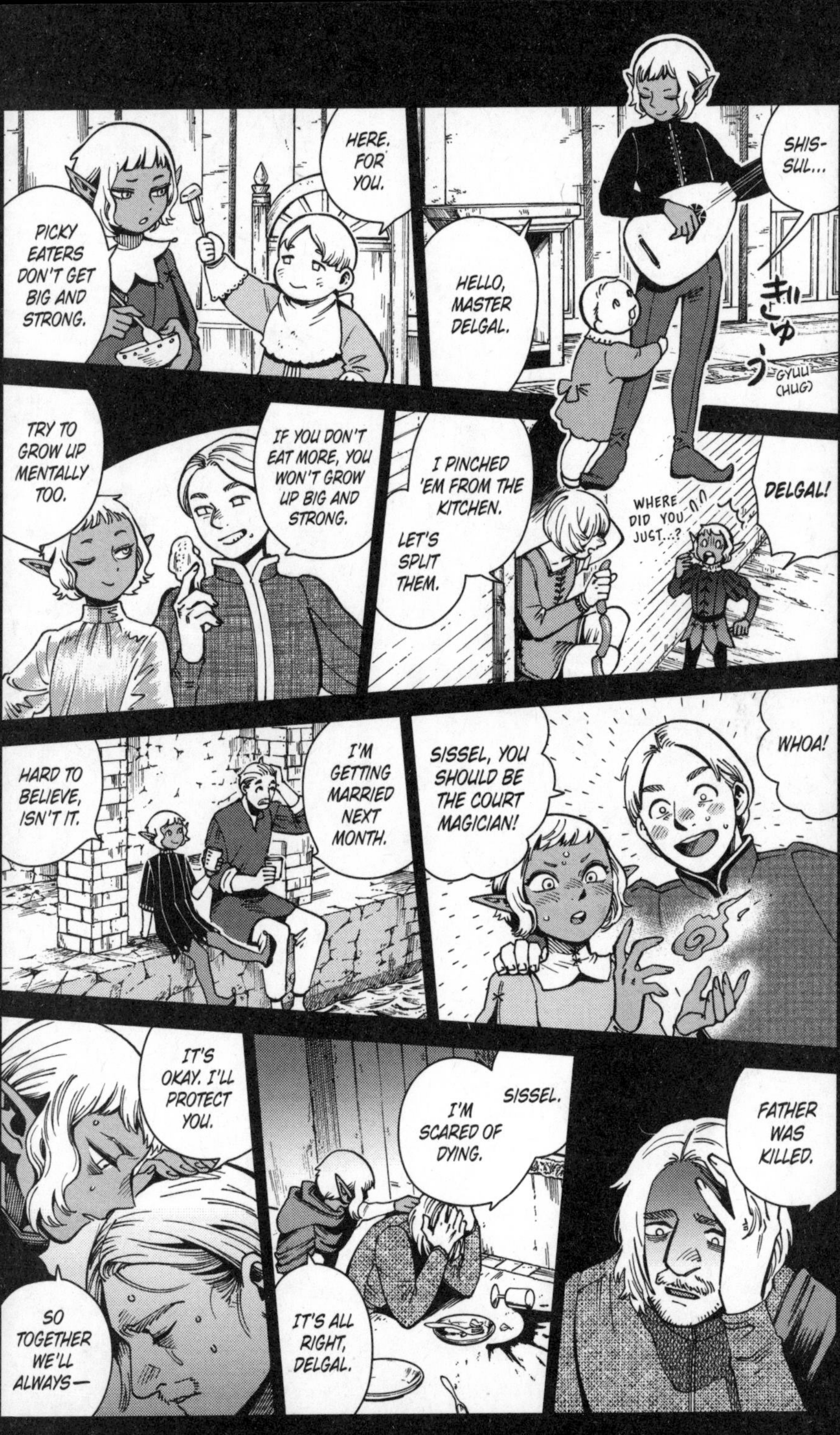
SHIS-SUL...
HELLO, MASTER DELGAL.
ぎゅう
GYUU (HUG)
HERE. FOR YOU.
PICKY EATERS DON'T GET BIG AND STRONG.
DELGAL!
WHERE DID YOU JUST...?
I PINCHED 'EM FROM THE KITCHEN.
LET'S SPLIT THEM.
IF YOU DON'T EAT MORE, YOU WON'T GROW UP BIG AND STRONG.
TRY TO GROW UP MENTALLY TOO.
WHOA!
SISSEL, YOU SHOULD BE THE COURT MAGICIAN!
I'M GETTING MARRIED NEXT MONTH.
HARD TO BELIEVE, ISN'T IT.
FATHER WAS KILLED.
SISSEL.
I'M SCARED OF DYING.
IT'S ALL RIGHT, DELGAL.
IT'S OKAY. I'LL PROTECT YOU.
SO TOGETHER WE'LL ALWAYS—

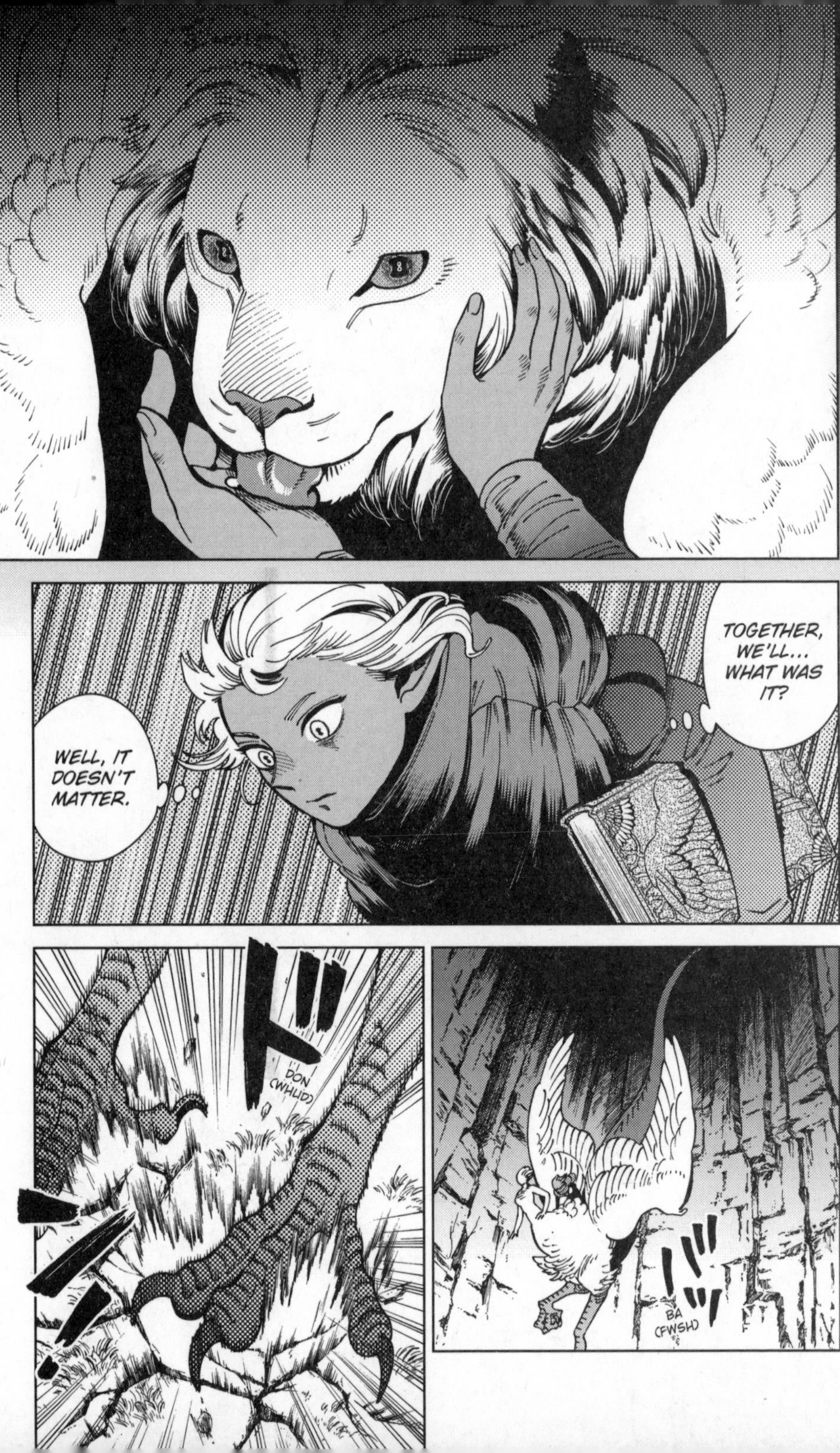
TOGETHER, WE'LL... WHAT WAS IT?
WELL, IT DOESN'T MATTER.
BA (FWSH)
DON (WHUD)

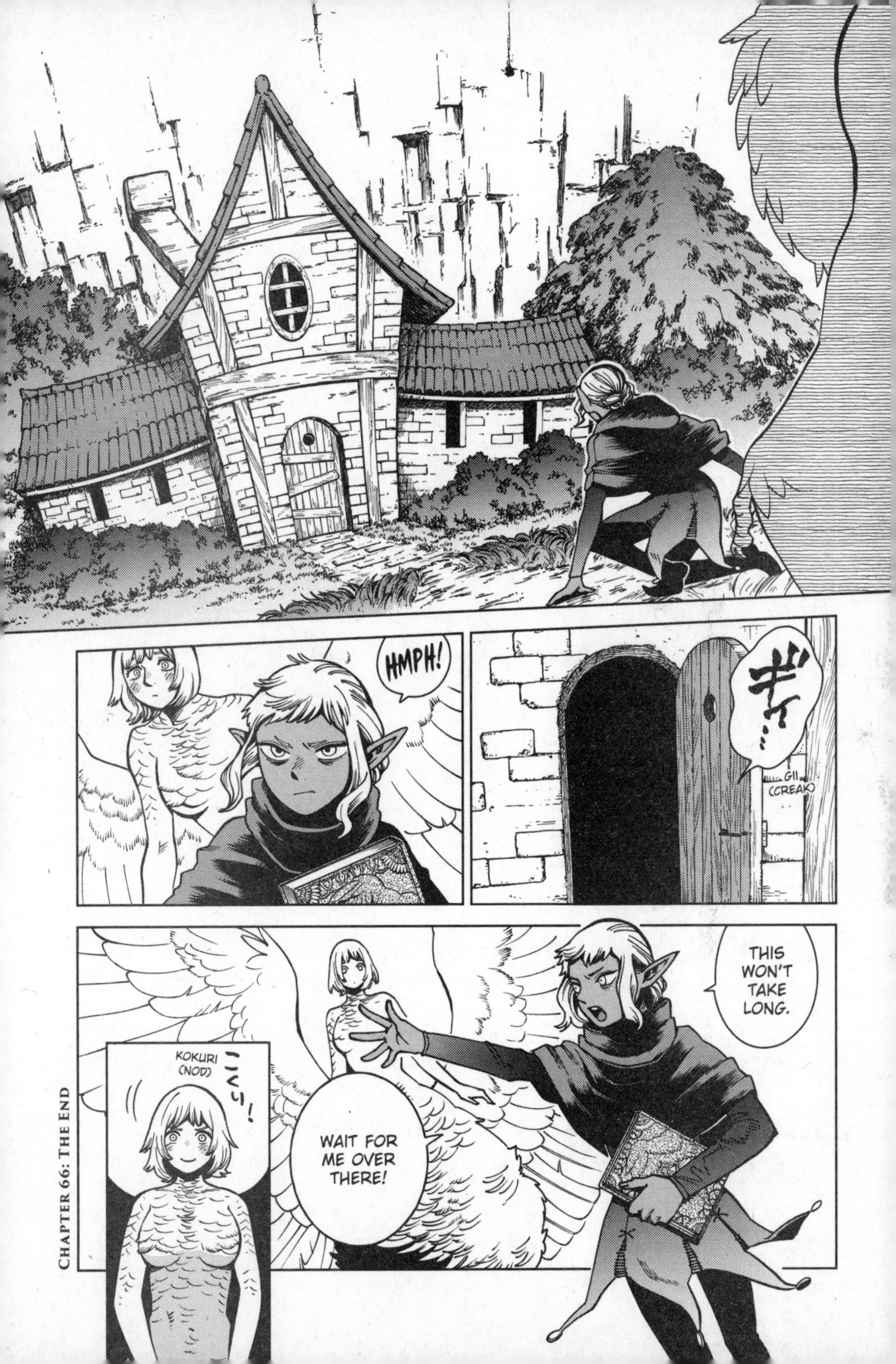
ギィ…
GII (CREAK)
HMPH!
THIS WON'T TAKE LONG.
WAIT FOR ME OVER THERE!
コクリ!
KOKURI (NOD)

Chapter 67

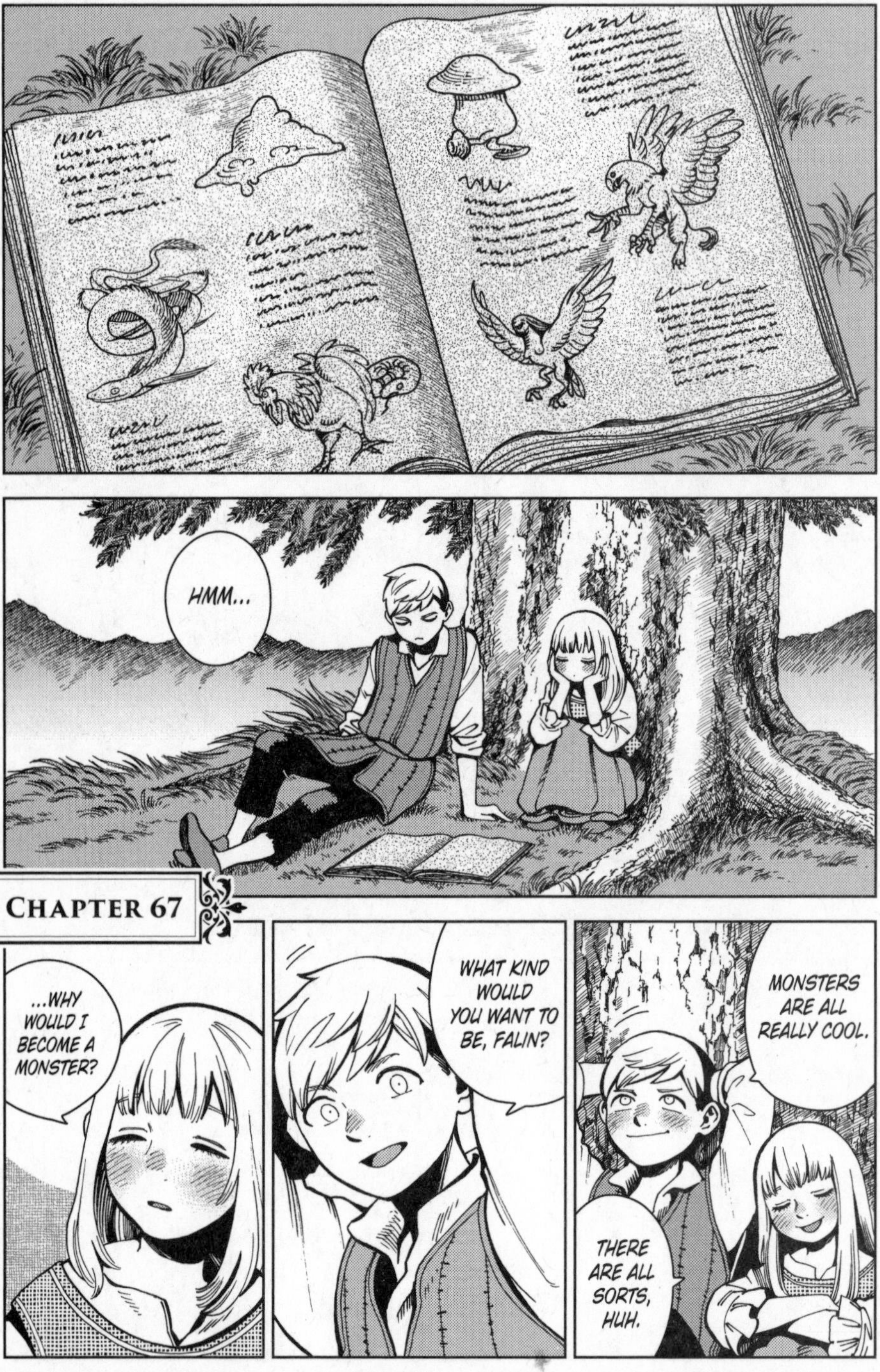
HMM...
MONSTERS ARE ALL REALLY COOL.
THERE ARE ALL SORTS, HUH.
WHAT KIND WOULD YOU WANT TO BE, FALIN?
...WHY WOULD I BECOME A MONSTER?

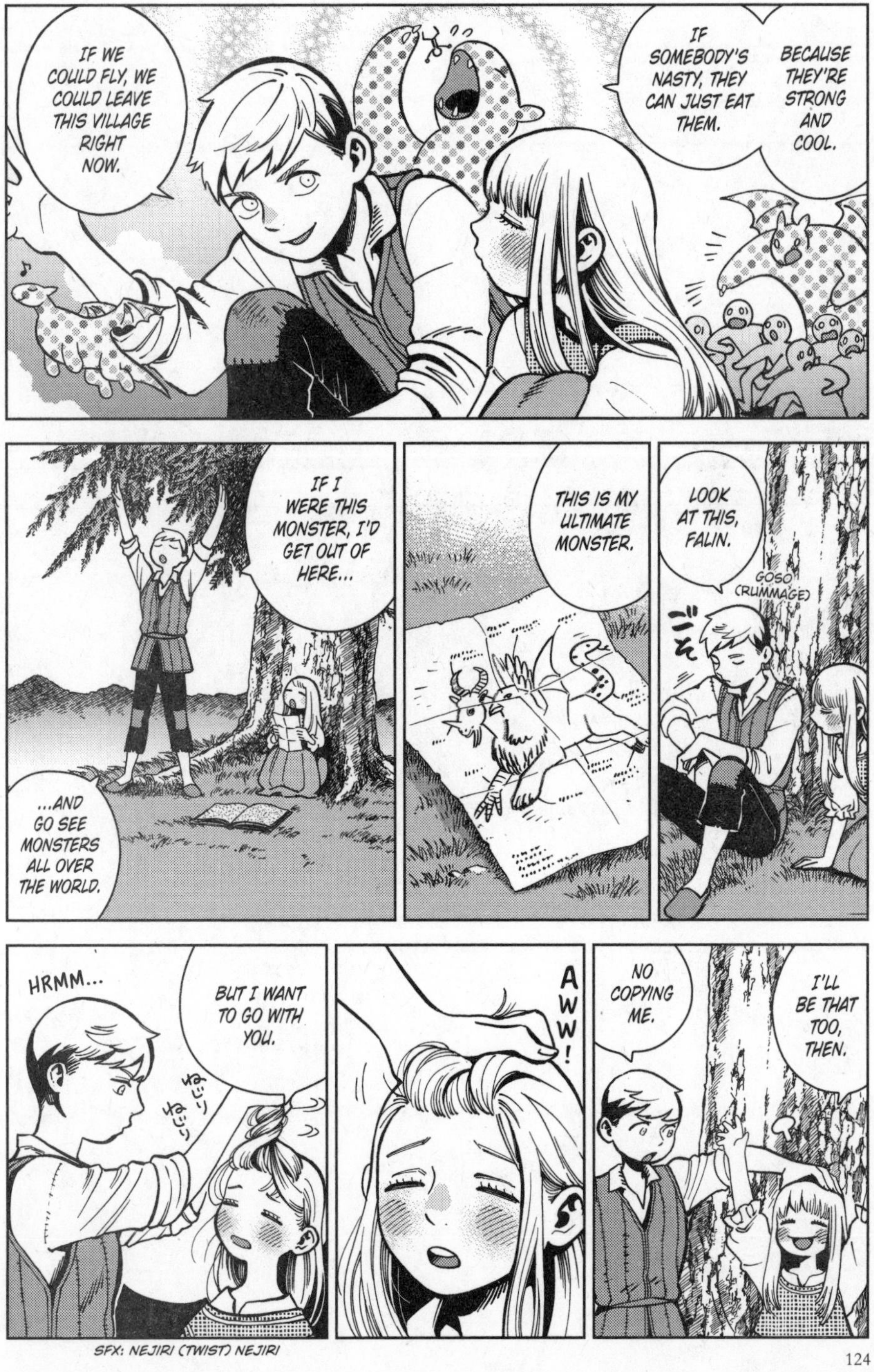
BECAUSE THEY'RE STRONG AND COOL.
IF SOMEBODY'S NASTY, THEY CAN JUST EAT THEM.
IF WE COULD FLY, WE COULD LEAVE THIS VILLAGE RIGHT NOW.
LOOK AT THIS, FALIN.
GOSO (RUMMAGE)
ごそ
THIS IS MY ULTIMATE MONSTER.
IF I WERE THIS MONSTER, I'D GET OUT OF HERE...
...AND GO SEE MONSTERS ALL OVER THE WORLD.
I'LL BE THAT TOO, THEN.
NO COPYING ME.
AWW!
BUT I WANT TO GO WITH YOU.
HRMM...
ねじり ねじり

SFX: NEJIRI (TWIST) NEJIRI

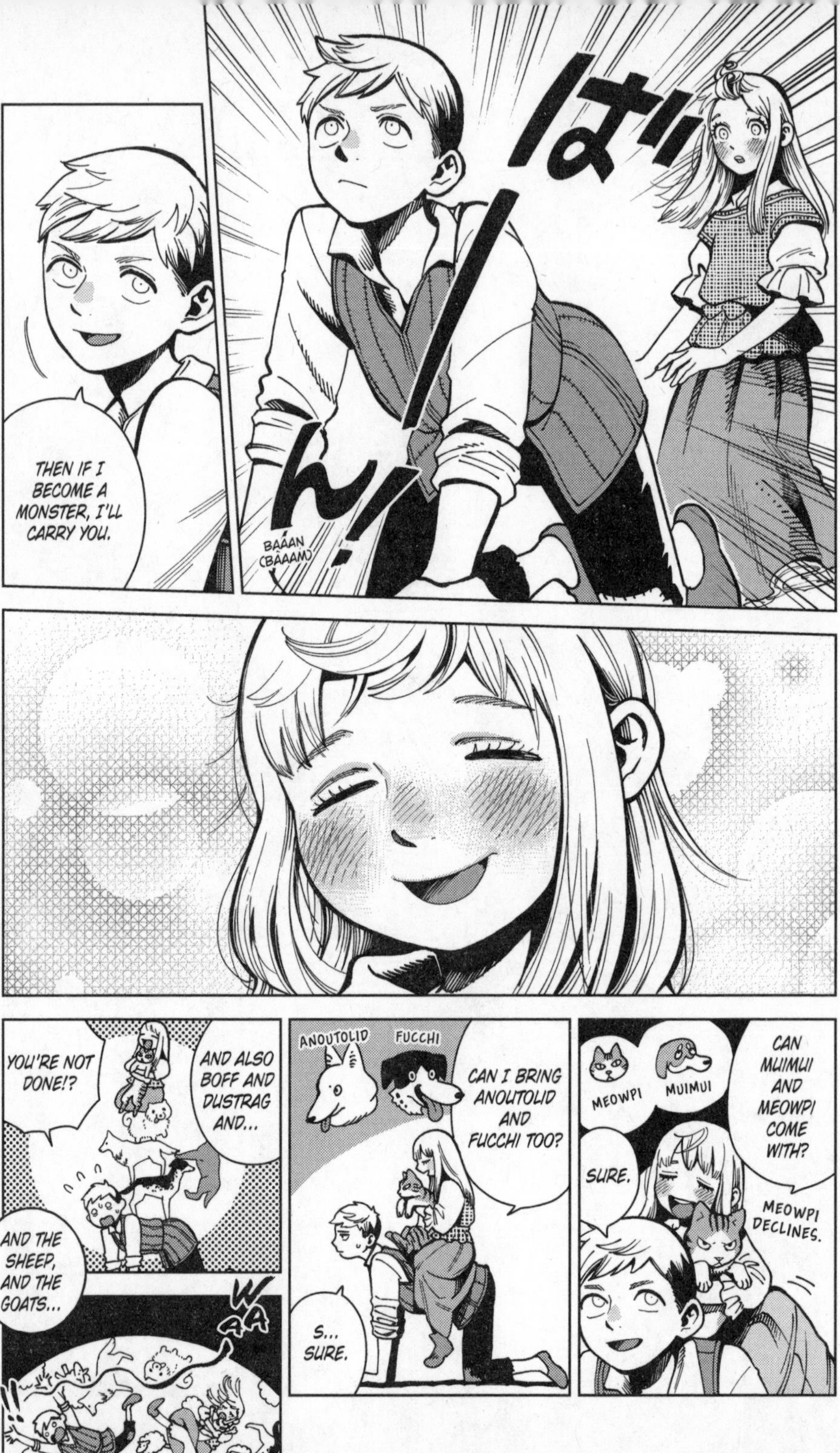
はい
ん!
BAÁAN (BÂAAM)
THEN IF I BECOME A MONSTER, I'LL CARRY YOU.
MEOWPI
MUIMUI
CAN MUIMUI AND MEOWPI COME WITH?
SURE.
MEOWPI DECLINES.
FUCCHI
ANOUTOLID
CAN I BRING ANOUTOLID AND FUCCHI TOO?
S... SURE.
AND ALSO BOFF AND DUSTRAG AND...
YOU'RE NOT DONE!?
AND THE SHEEP, AND THE GOATS...
WAA

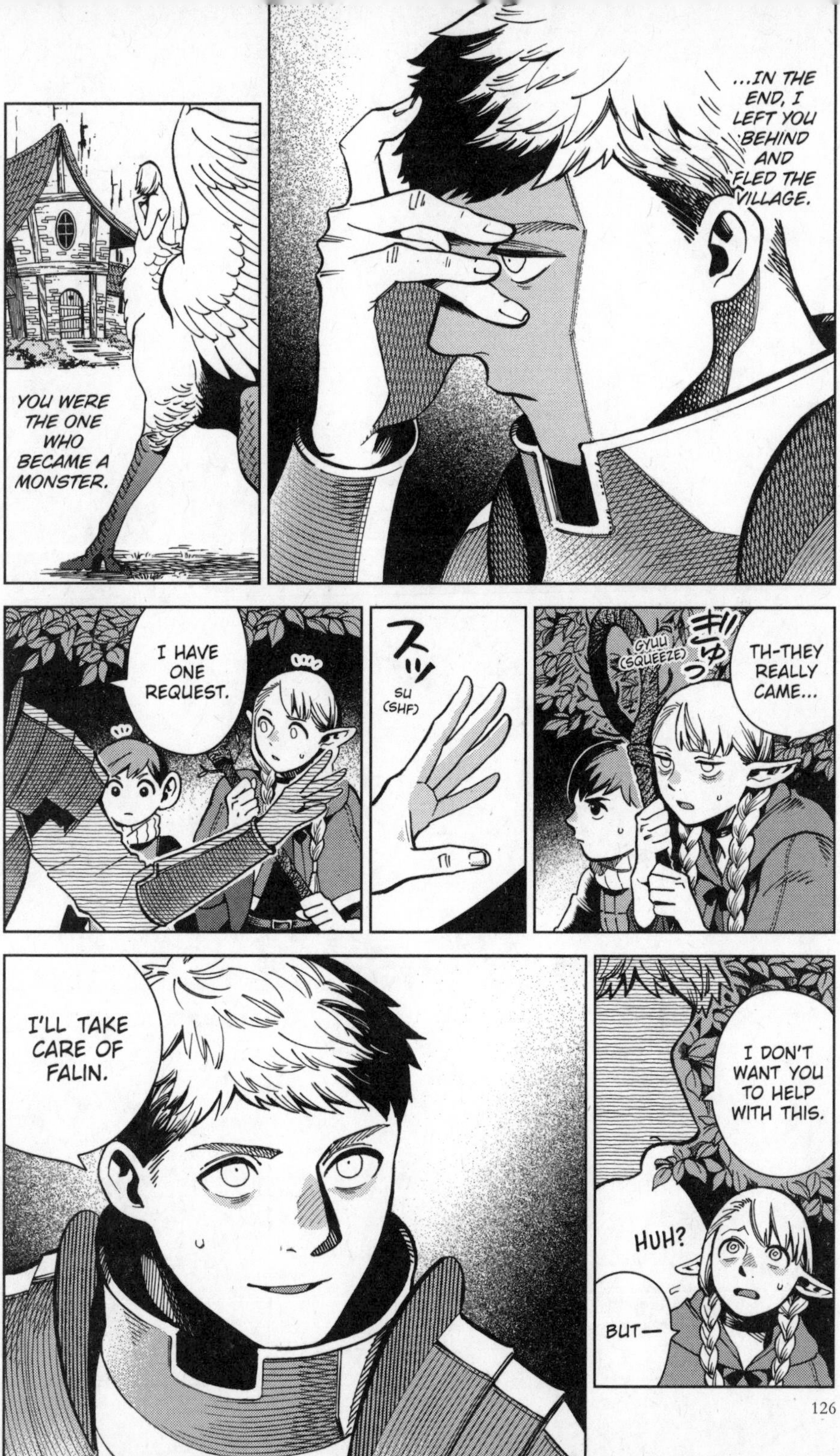
...IN THE END, I LEFT YOU BEHIND AND FLED THE VILLAGE.
YOU WERE THE ONE WHO BECAME A MONSTER.
ぎゅっ
GYUU (SQUEEZE)
TH-THEY REALLY CAME...
スッ
SU (SHF)
I HAVE ONE REQUEST.
I DON'T WANT YOU TO HELP WITH THIS.
HUH?
BUT—
I'LL TAKE CARE OF FALIN.

67. Curry -2-

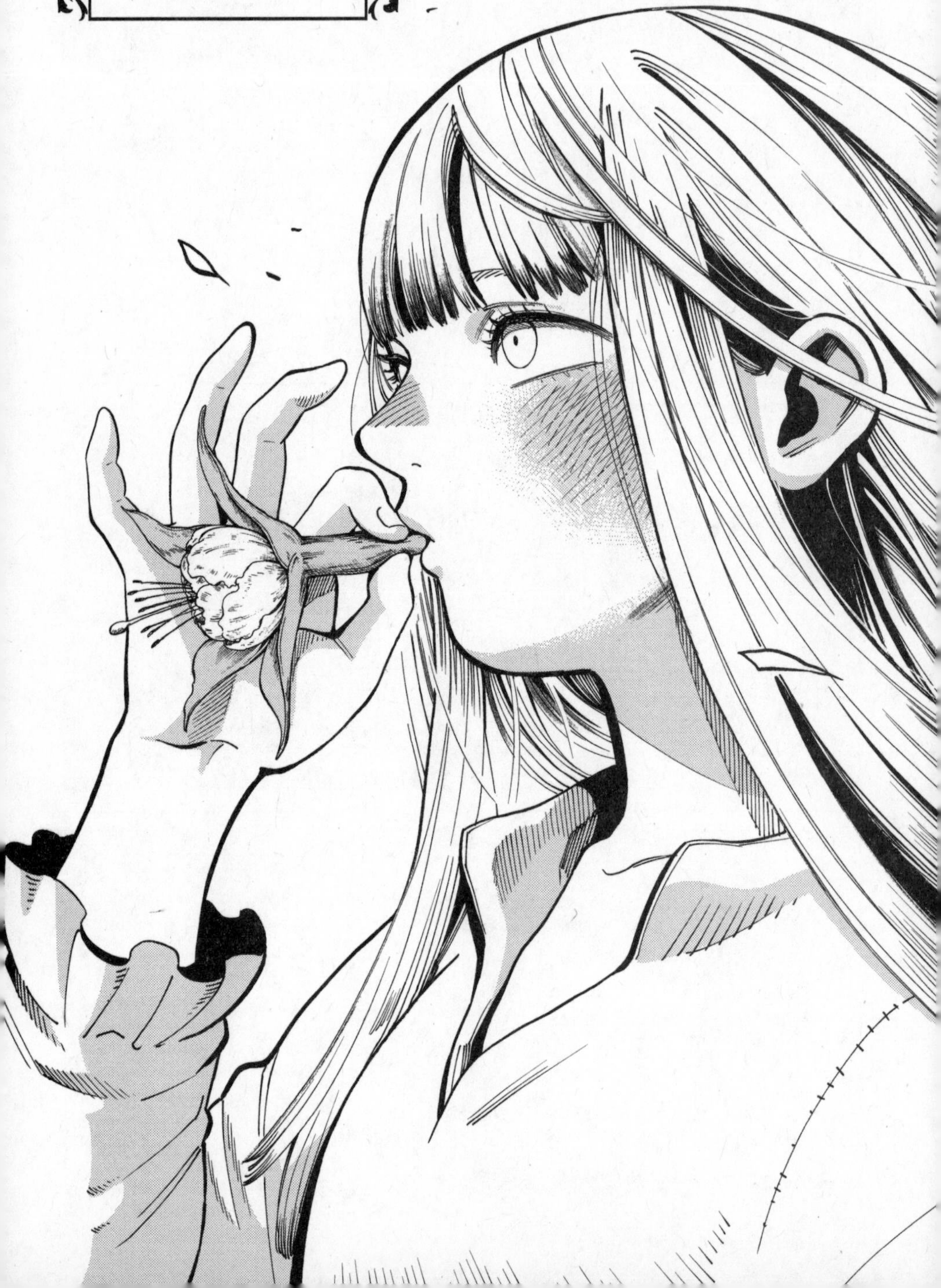

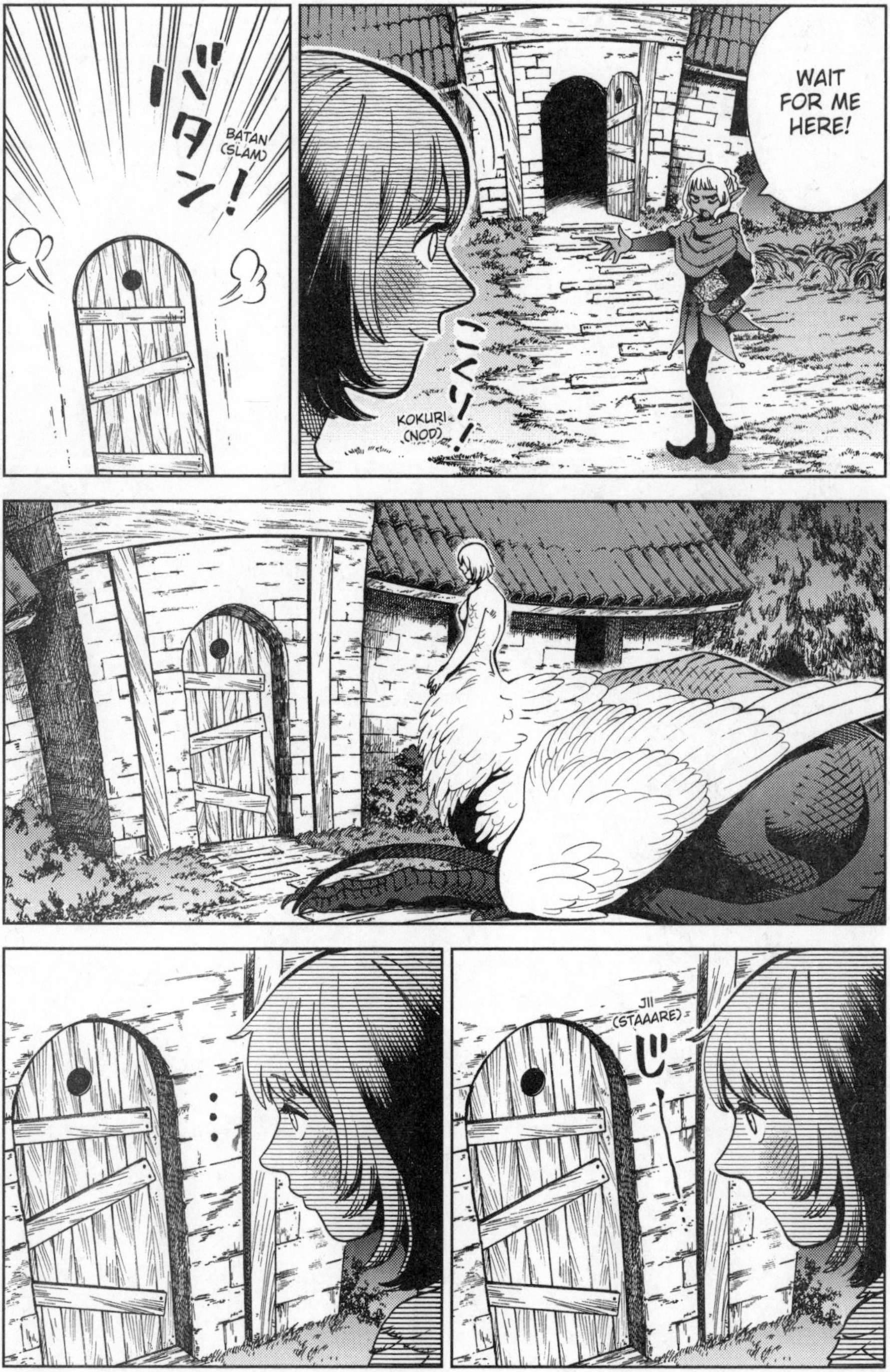

WAIT FOR ME HERE!
こくり！
KOKURI (NOD)
バタン！
BATAN (SLAM)
じー
JII (STAAARE)
…

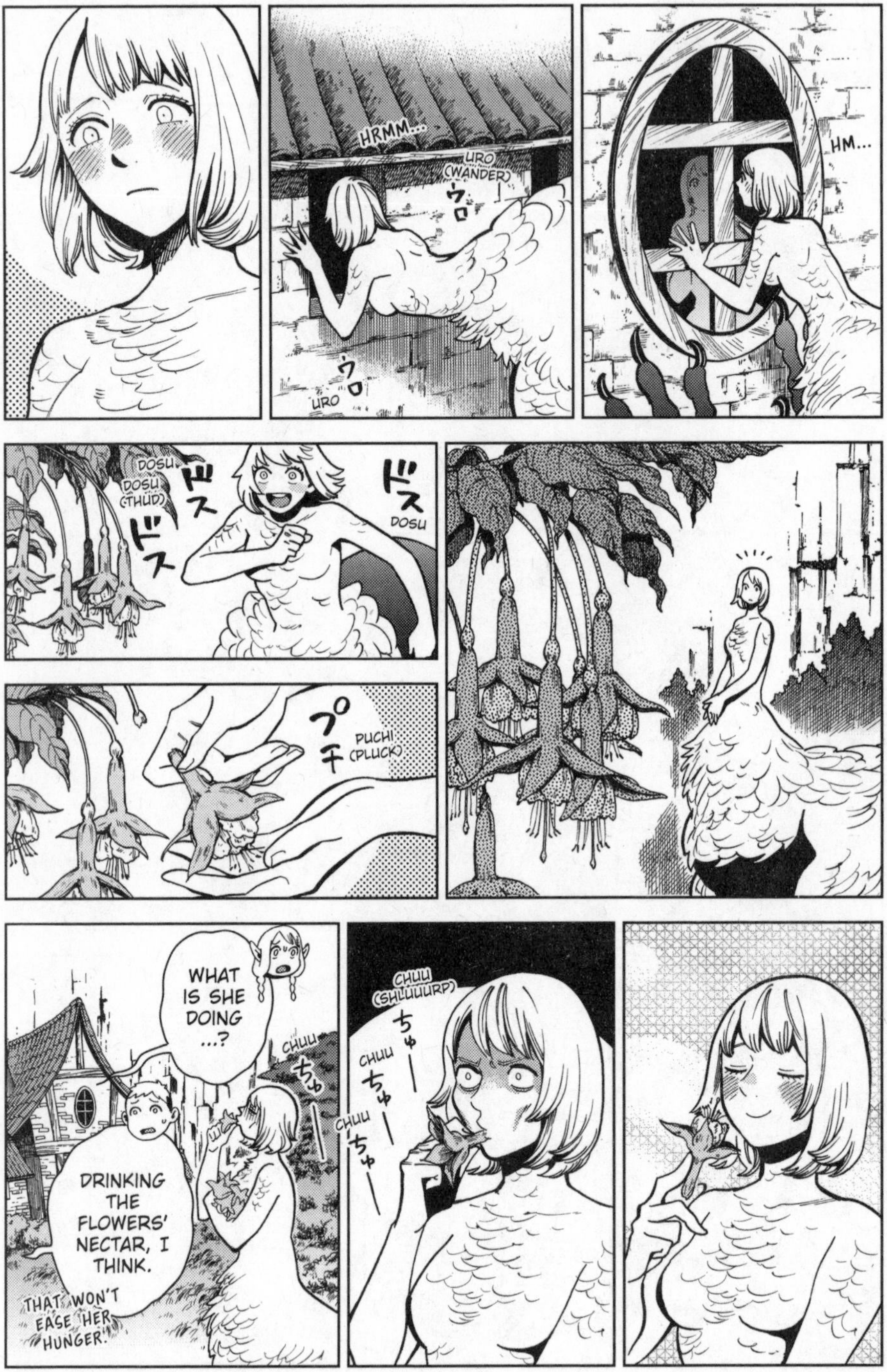

HM...
HRMM...
URO (WANDER)
ウロ
ウロ
URO
ドス
DOSU
DOSU DOSU (THUD)
ドス
ドス
プチ
PUCHI (PLUCK)
CHUU (SHLUUURP)
ちゅー
CHUU
ちゅー
CHUU
ちゅー
WHAT IS SHE DOING ...?
CHUU
ちゅー
DRINKING THE FLOWERS' NECTAR, I THINK.
THAT WON'T EASE HER HUNGER.

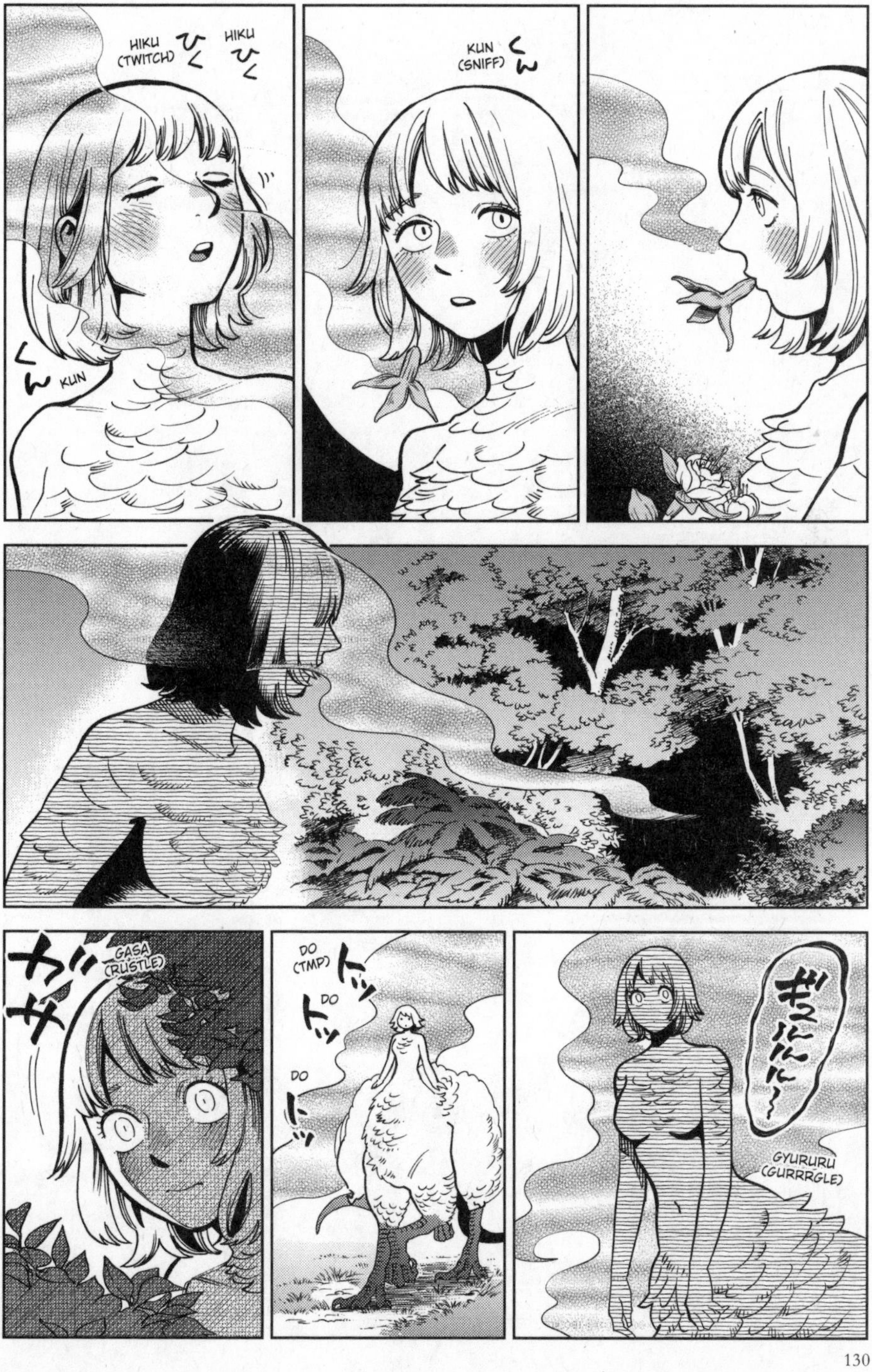
KUN (SNIFF) くん
HIKU (TWITCH) ひく
HIKU ひく
くん KUN
ギュルルル～
GYURURU (GURRRGLE)
DO (TMP) トッ
DO トッ
DO トッ
ガサ GASA (RUSTLE)

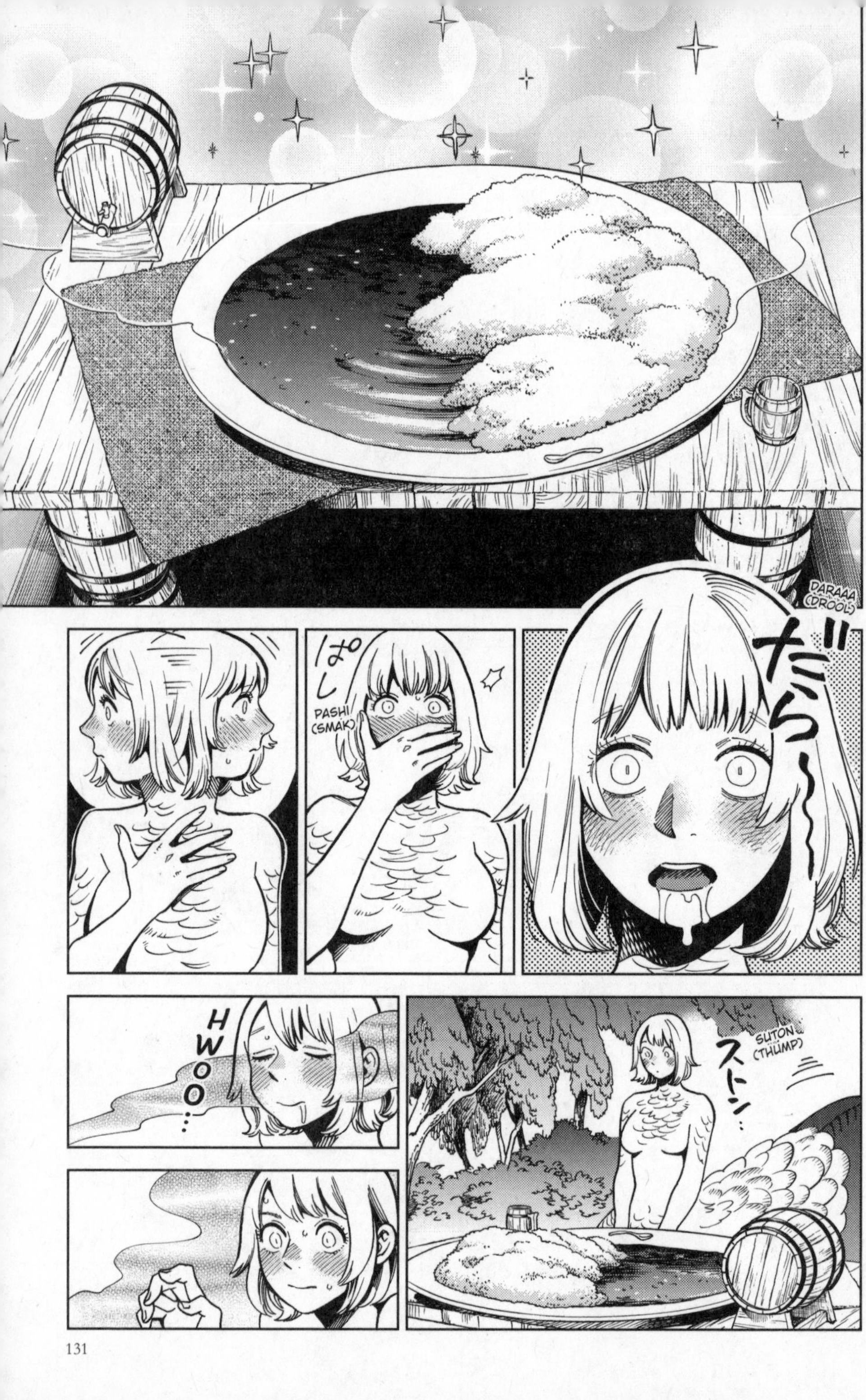
DARAAA (DROOL)
だら～
ぱし
PASHI (SMAK)
SUTON (THUMP)
ストン…
HWOO...

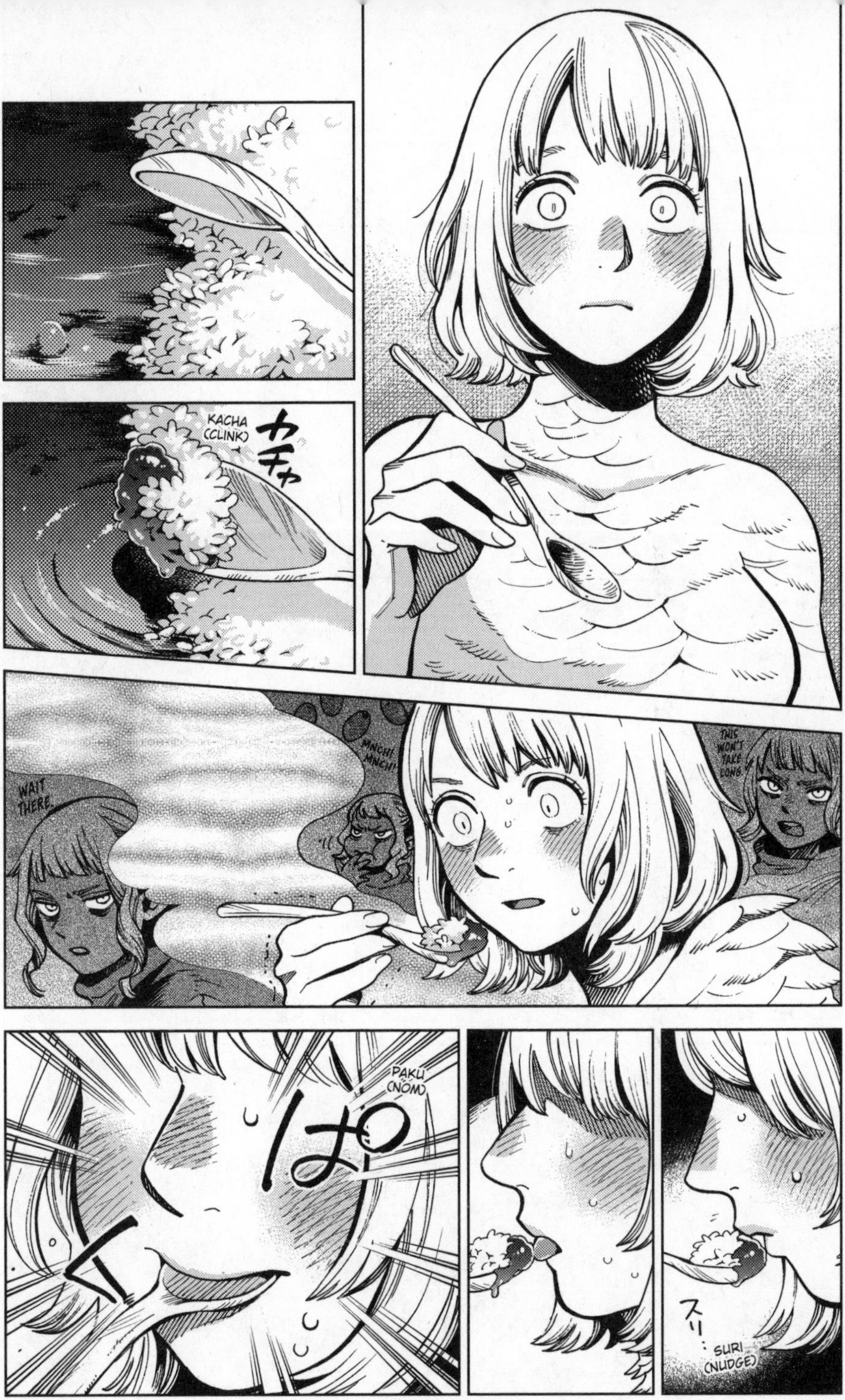
KACHA (CLINK)
カチャ
THIS WON'T TAKE LONG
MNCH! MNCH!
WAIT THERE.
スリ…
SURI (NUDGE)
PAKU (NOM)
ぱく

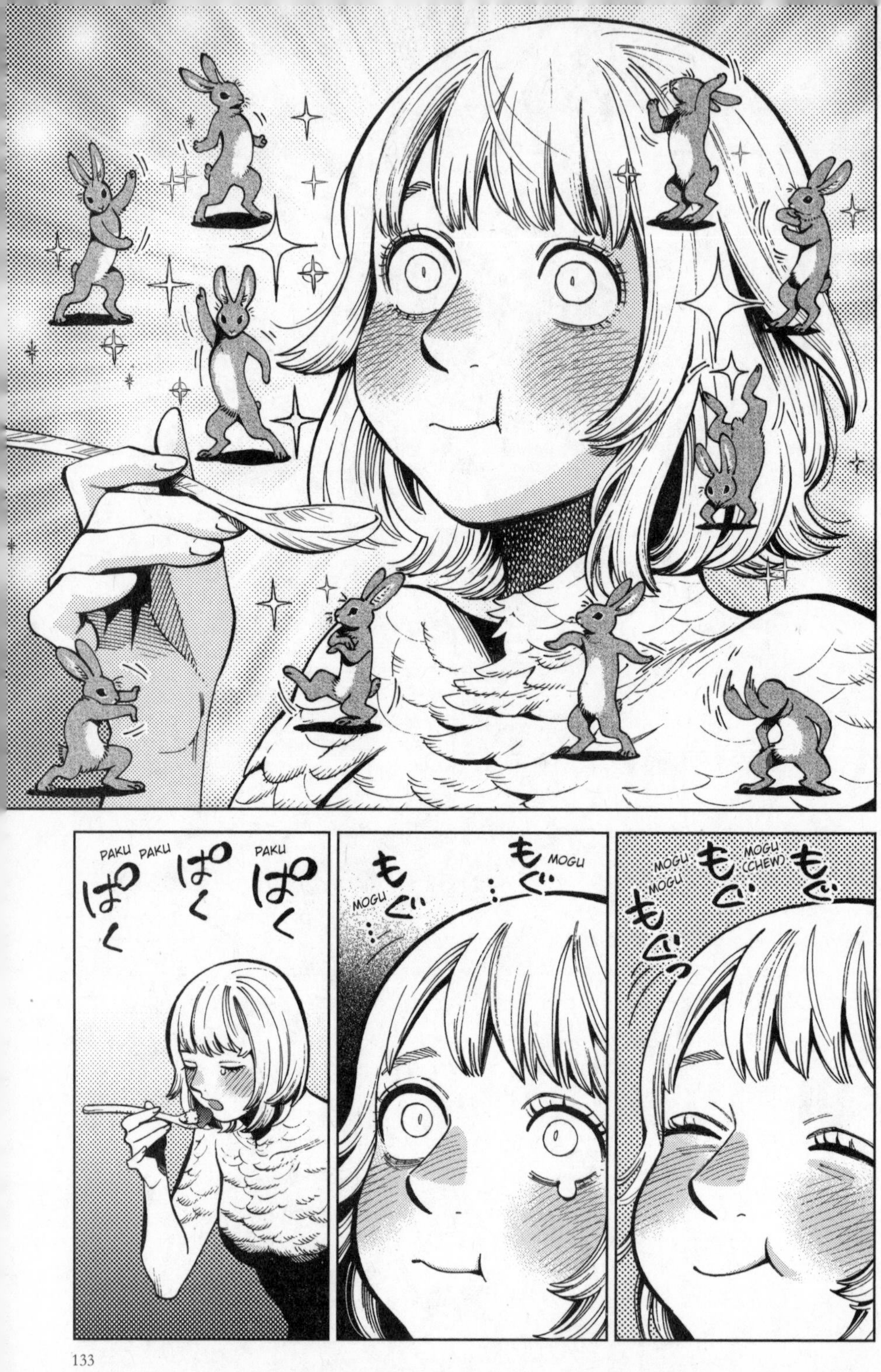
もぐ
MOGU (CHEW)
もぐ
MOGU
もぐっ
MOGU
…もぐ
MOGU
もぐ…
MOGU
ぱく
PAKU
ぱく
PAKU
ぱく
PAKU

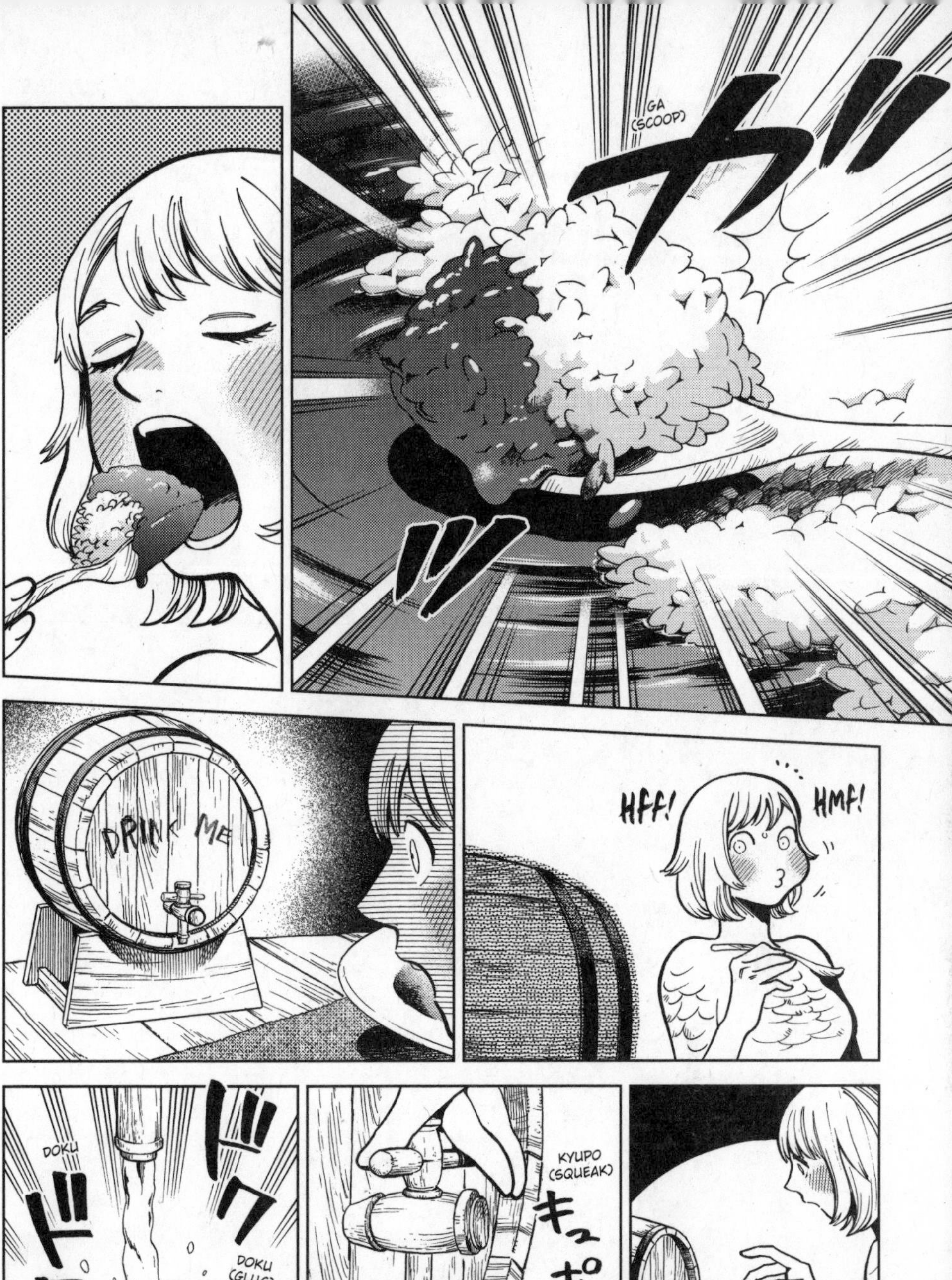
GA (SCOOP)
. . .
HFF!
HMF!
DRINK ME
DRINK ME
KYUPO (SQUEAK)
DOKU
DOKU (GLUG)

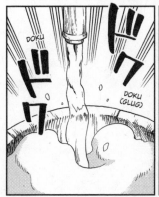

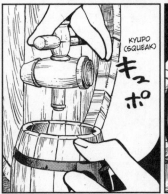

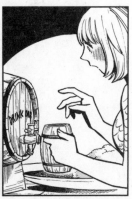

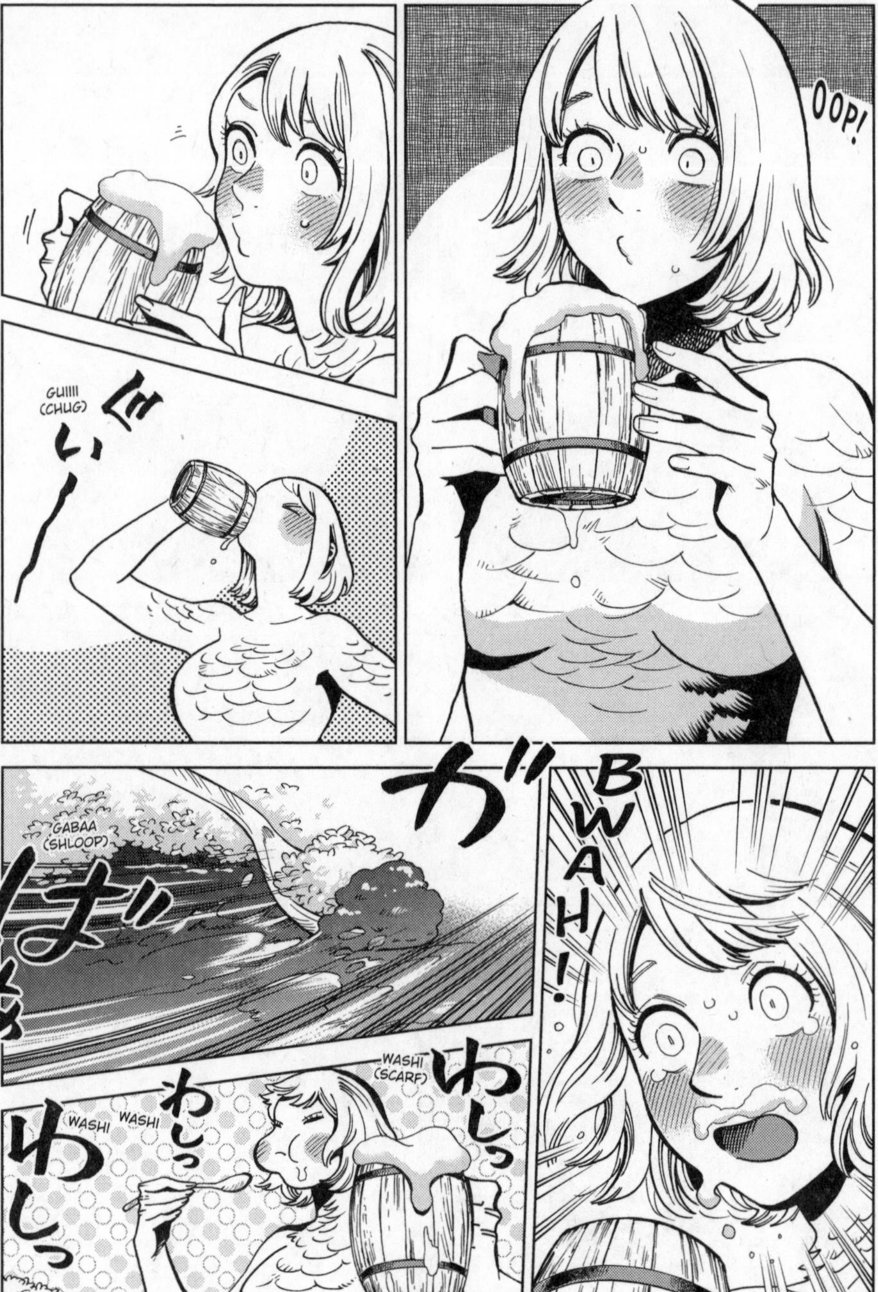
OOP!
GUIIII (CHUG)
ぐい〜
BWAH!
が
GABAA (SHLOOP)
ばあ
WASHI (SCARF)
わしっ
WASHI
わしっ
WASHI
わしっ

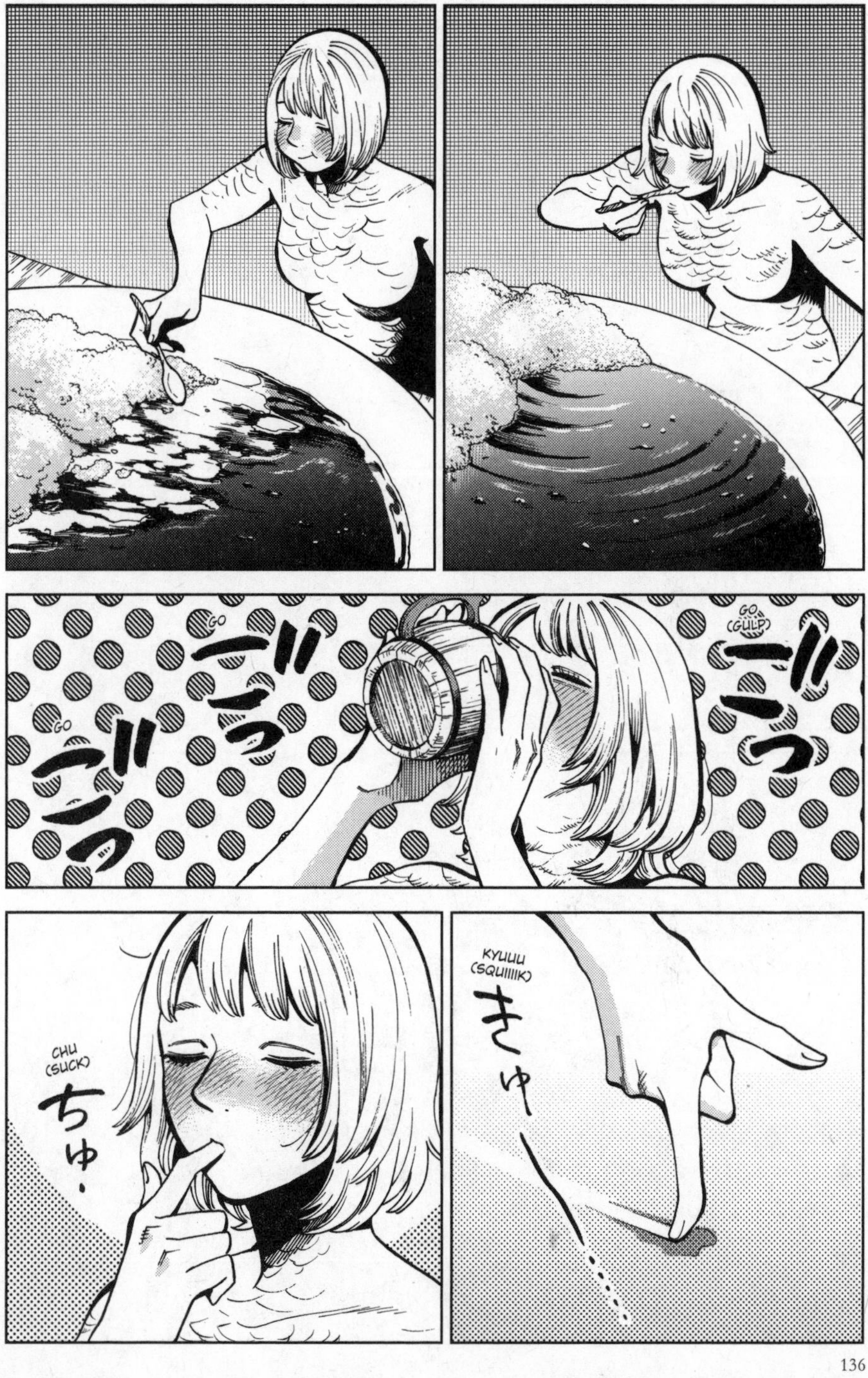
GO (GULP)
ごっ
GO
ごっ
GO
ごっ
KYUUU (SQUIIIIK)
きゅー
CHU (SUCK)
ちゅ

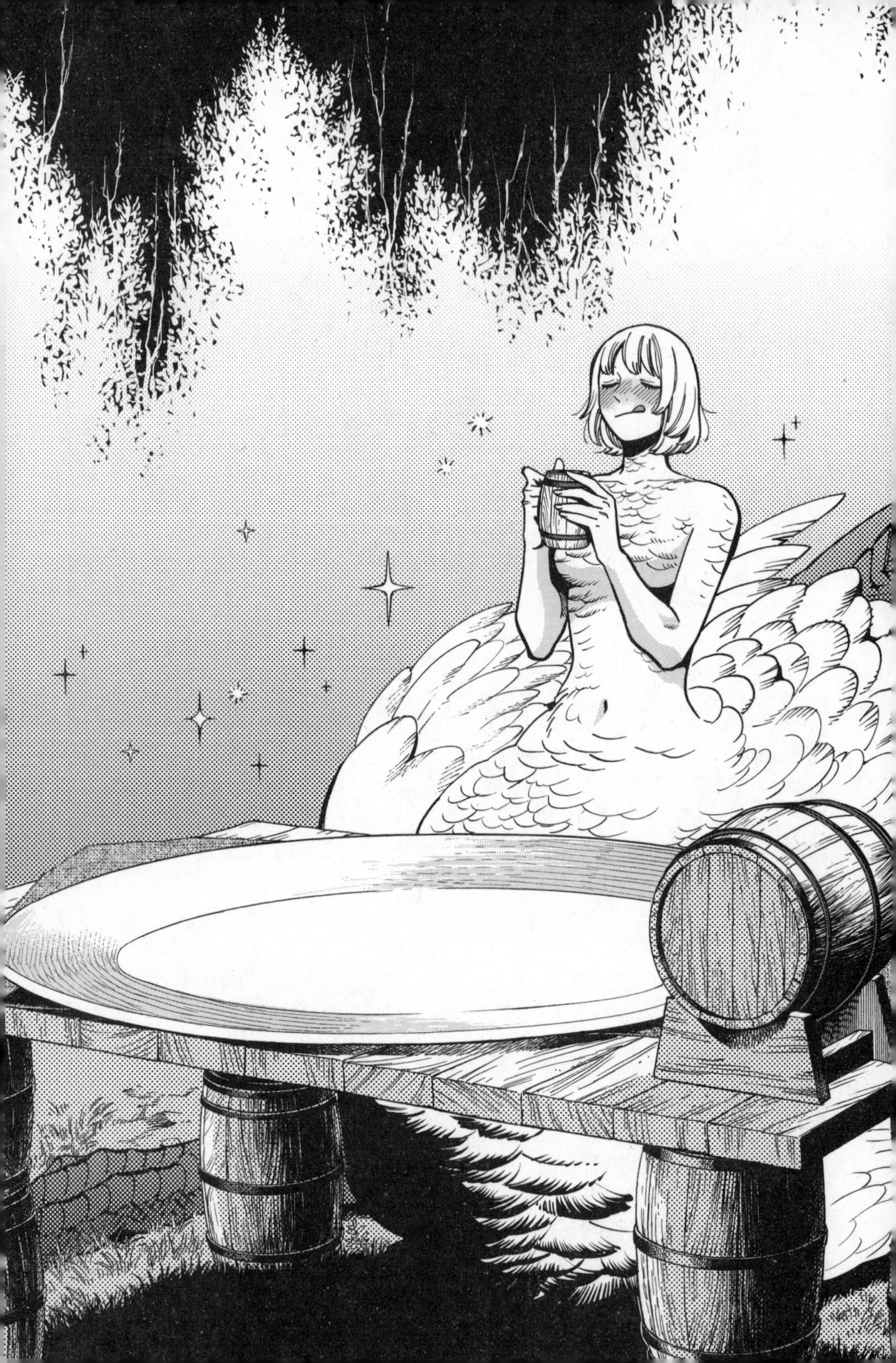

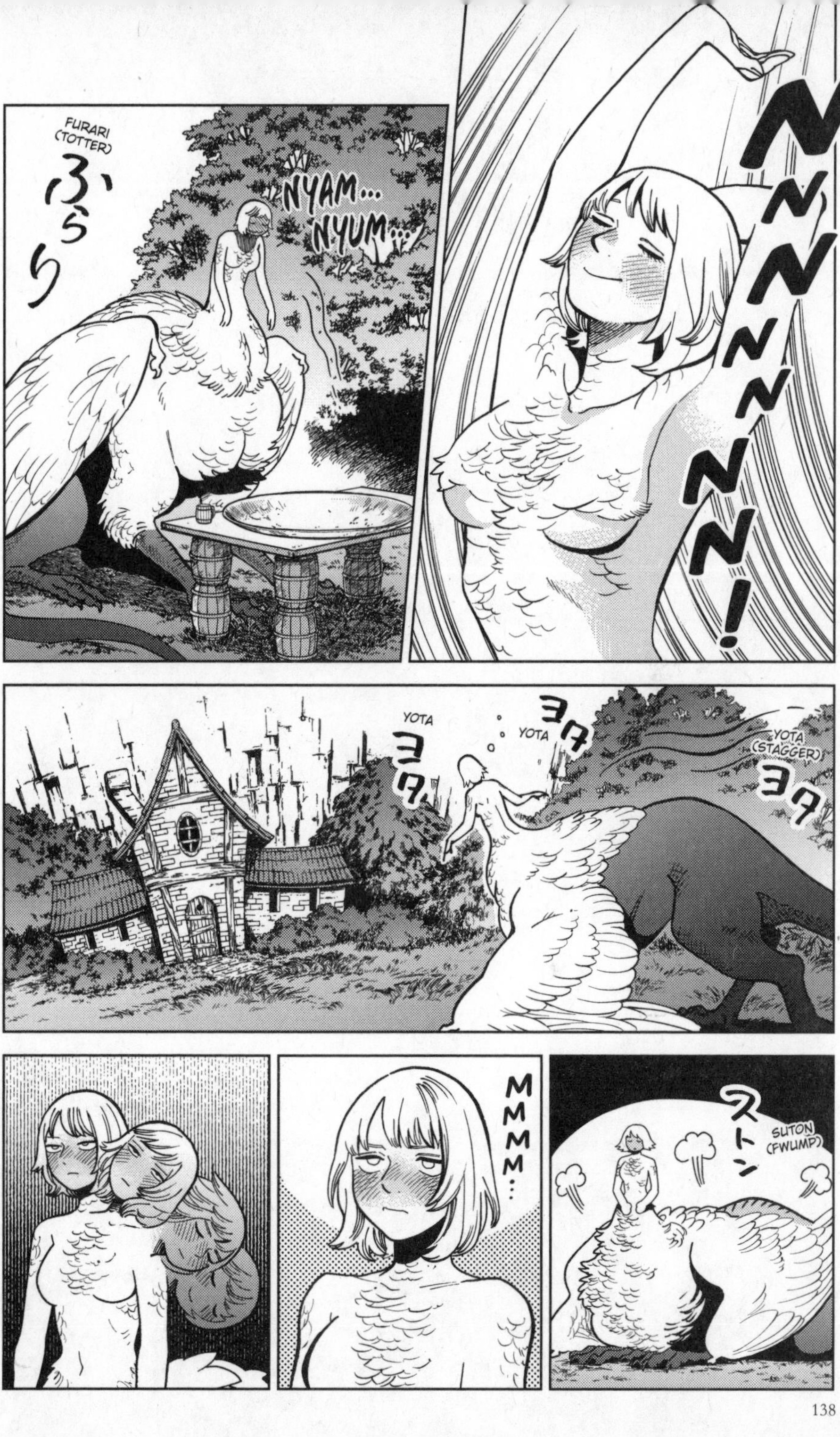
NNNNNNNNNN!
NYAM... NYUM...
FURARI (TOTTER)
ふらり
YOTA (STAGGER)
ヨタ
ヨタ
YOTA
YOTA
ヨタ
ストン
SUTON (FWUMP)
MMMM...

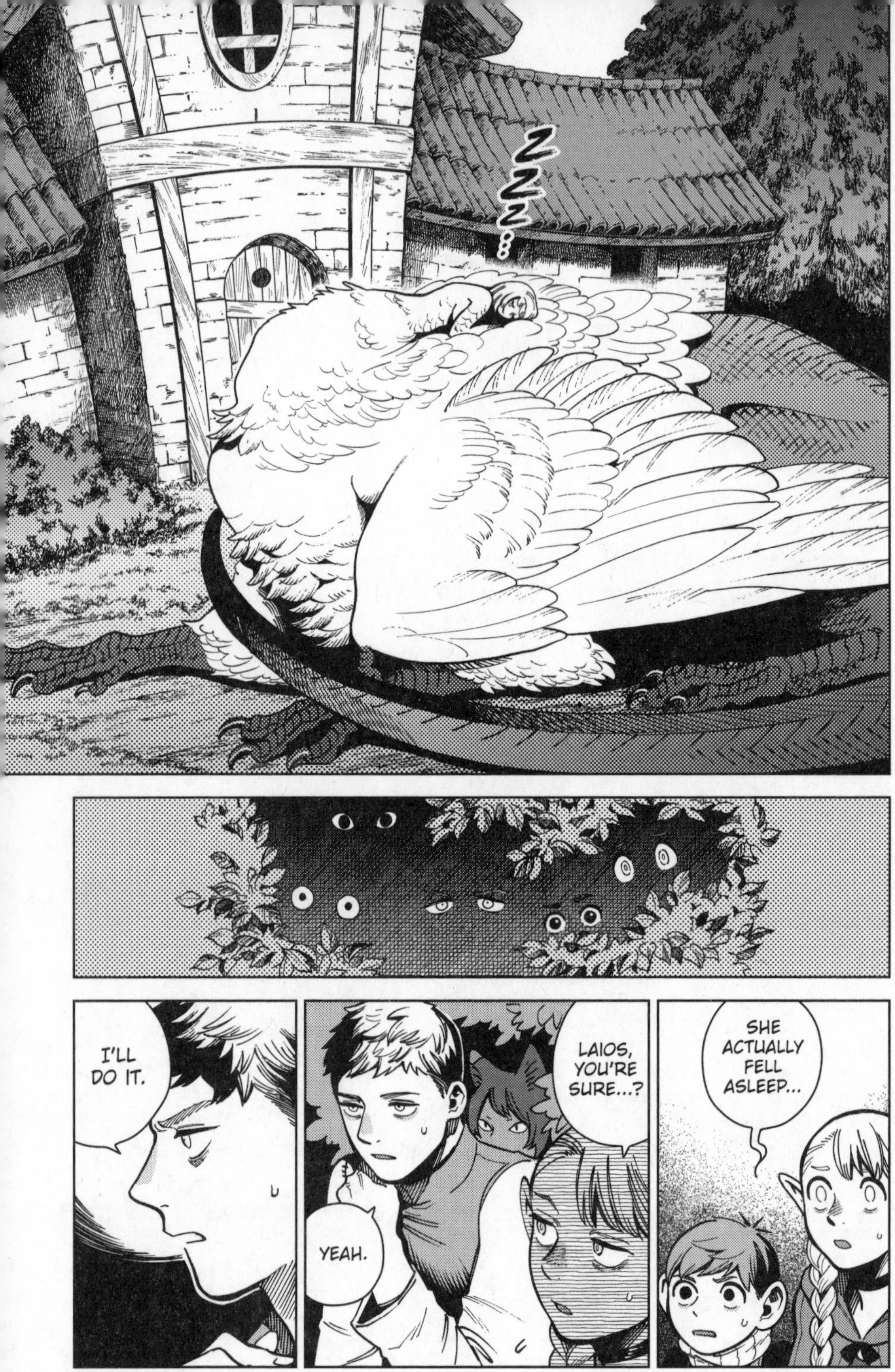
ZZZ...
SHE ACTUALLY FELL ASLEEP...
LAIOS, YOU'RE SURE...?
YEAH.
I'LL DO IT.

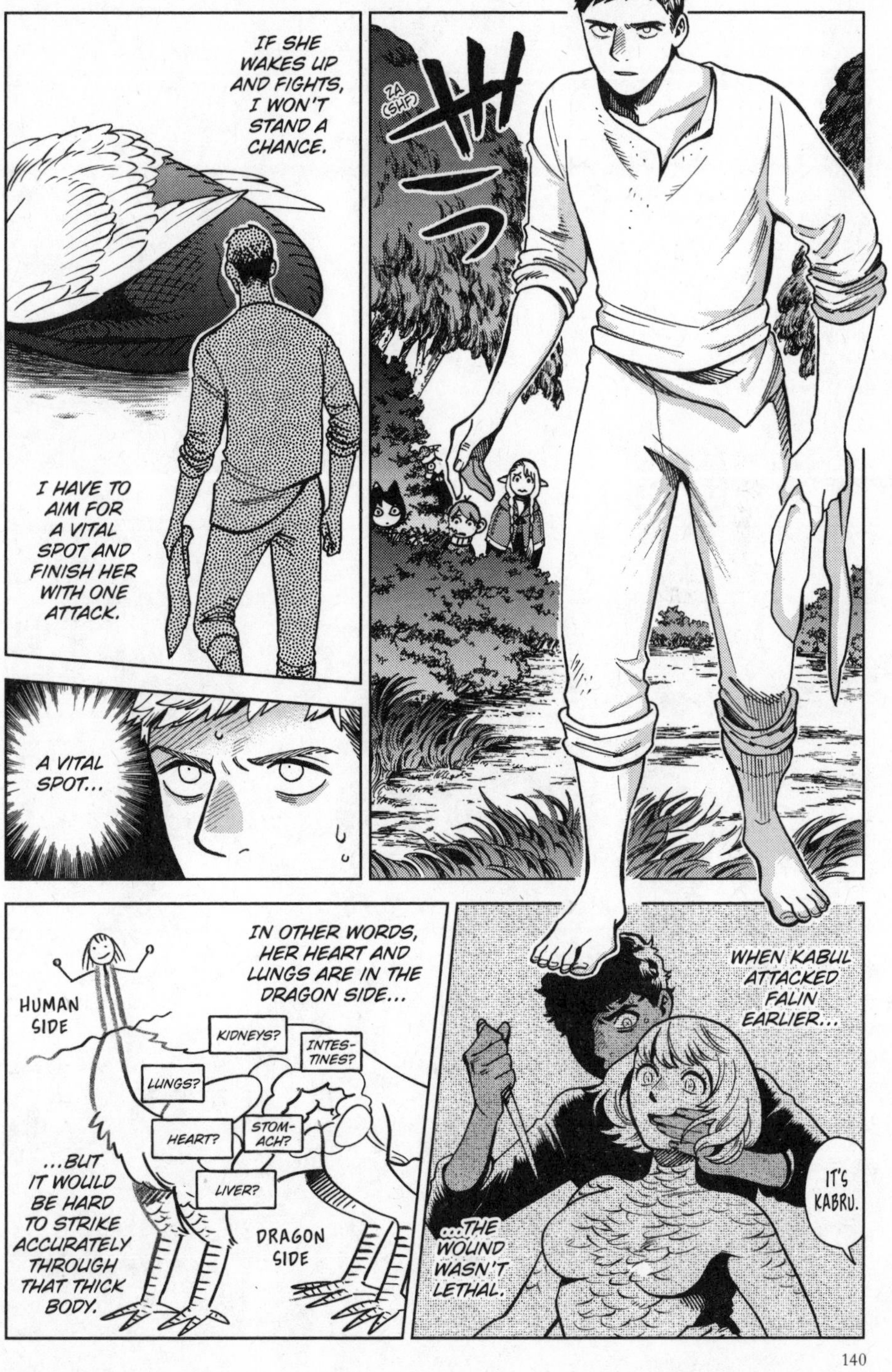
ZA (SHF)
IF SHE WAKES UP AND FIGHTS, I WON'T STAND A CHANCE.
I HAVE TO AIM FOR A VITAL SPOT AND FINISH HER WITH ONE ATTACK.
A VITAL SPOT...
WHEN KABUL ATTACKED FALIN EARLIER...
IT'S KABRU.
...THE WOUND WASN'T LETHAL.
IN OTHER WORDS, HER HEART AND LUNGS ARE IN THE DRAGON SIDE...
HUMAN SIDE
KIDNEYS?
INTES-TINES?
LUNGS?
HEART?
STOM-ACH?
LIVER?
DRAGON SIDE
...BUT IT WOULD BE HARD TO STRIKE ACCURATELY THROUGH THAT THICK BODY.

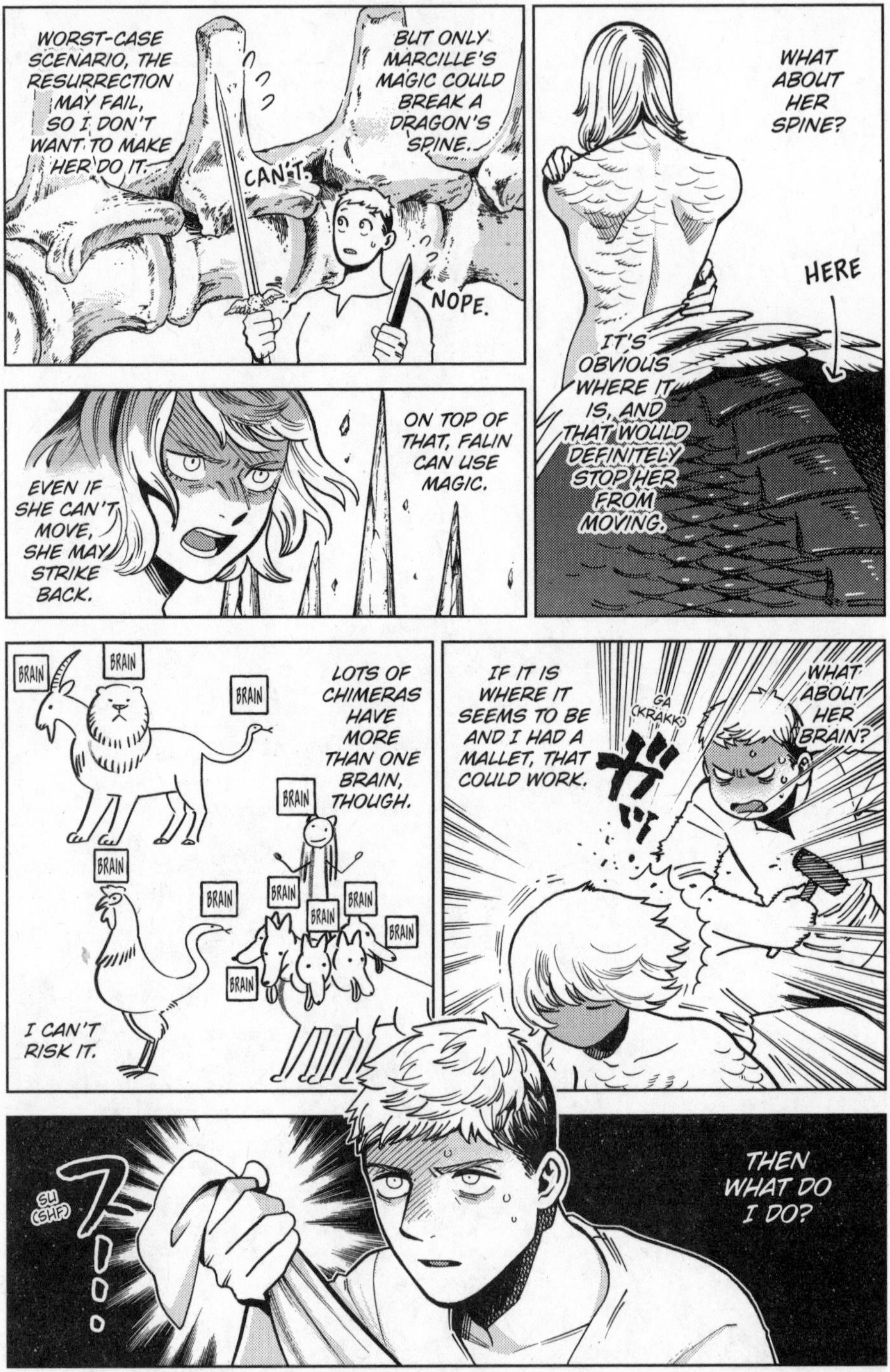
WHAT ABOUT HER SPINE?
HERE
IT'S OBVIOUS WHERE IT IS, AND THAT WOULD DEFINITELY STOP HER FROM MOVING.
BUT ONLY MARCILLE'S MAGIC COULD BREAK A DRAGON'S SPINE.
WORST-CASE SCENARIO, THE RESURRECTION MAY FAIL, SO I DON'T WANT TO MAKE HER DO IT.
CAN'T.
NOPE.
ON TOP OF THAT, FALIN CAN USE MAGIC.
EVEN IF SHE CAN'T MOVE, SHE MAY STRIKE BACK.
WHAT ABOUT HER BRAIN?
GA (KRAKK)
IF IT IS WHERE IT SEEMS TO BE AND I HAD A MALLET, THAT COULD WORK.
LOTS OF CHIMERAS HAVE MORE THAN ONE BRAIN, THOUGH.
BRAIN
BRAIN
BRAIN
BRAIN
BRAIN
BRAIN
BRAIN
BRAIN
BRAIN
BRAIN
BRAIN
I CAN'T RISK IT.
THEN WHAT DO I DO?
SU (SHF)

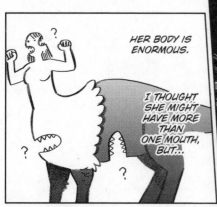

HER BODY IS ENORMOUS.

I THOUGHT SHE MIGHT HAVE MORE THAN ONE MOUTH, BUT...

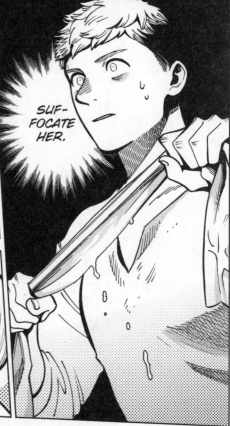

SUF-FOCATE HER.

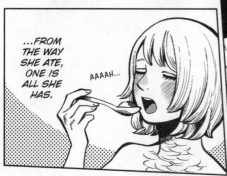

...FROM THE WAY SHE ATE, ONE IS ALL SHE HAS.

AAAAH...

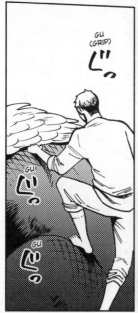

GU (GRIP)

じっ

GU じっ

GU じっ

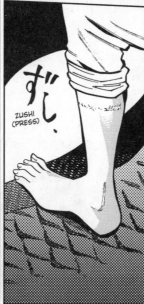

ずし

ZUSHI (PRESS)

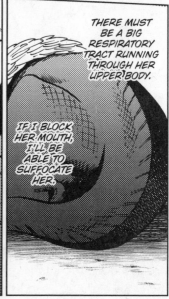

THERE MUST BE A BIG RESPIRATORY TRACT RUNNING THROUGH HER UPPER BODY.

IF I BLOCK HER MOUTH, I'LL BE ABLE TO SUFFOCATE HER.

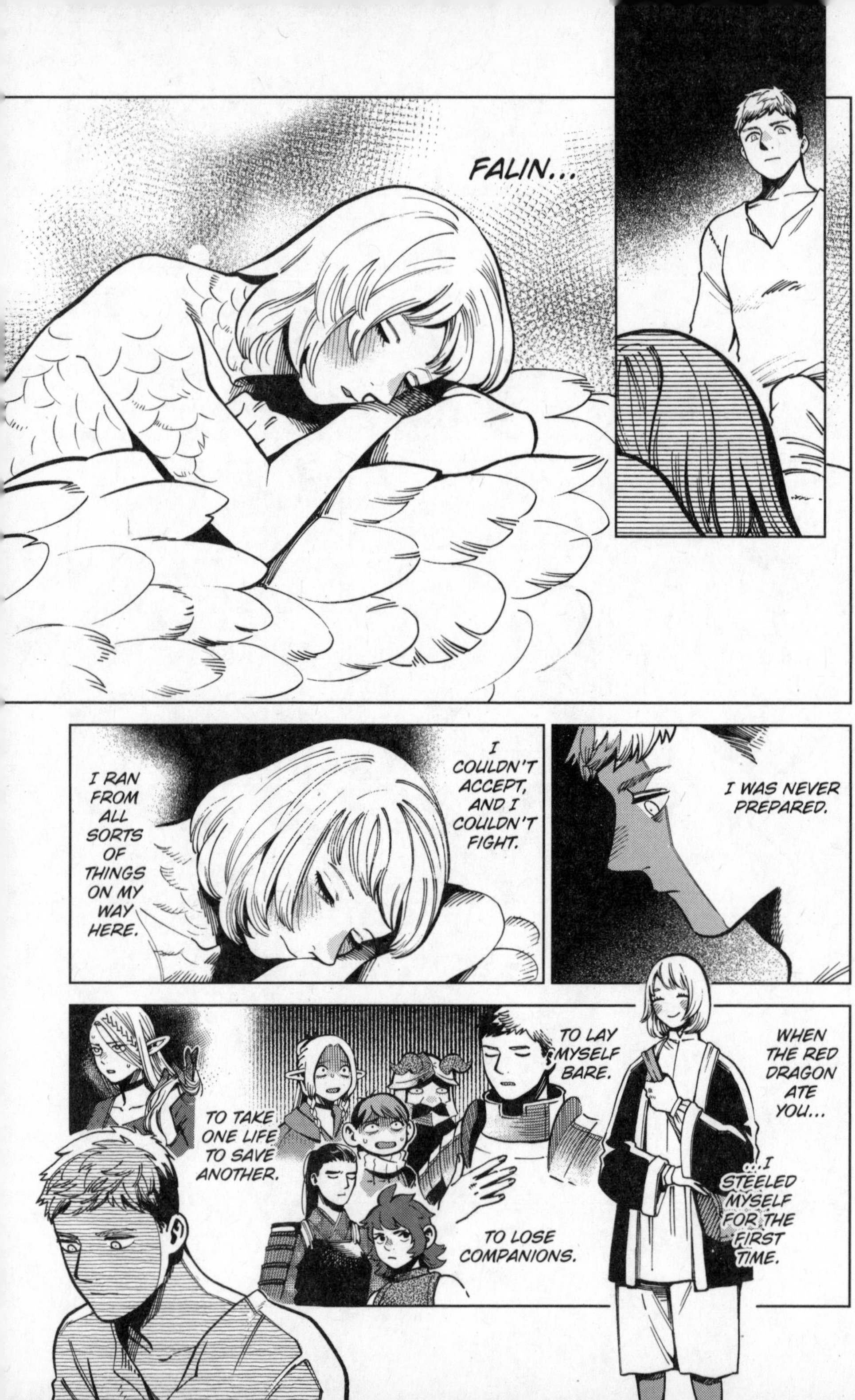
FALIN...
I WAS NEVER PREPARED.
I COULDN'T ACCEPT, AND I COULDN'T FIGHT.
I RAN FROM ALL SORTS OF THINGS ON MY WAY HERE.
WHEN THE RED DRAGON ATE YOU...
...I STEELED MYSELF FOR THE FIRST TIME.
TO LAY MYSELF BARE.
TO TAKE ONE LIFE TO SAVE ANOTHER.
TO LOSE COMPANIONS.

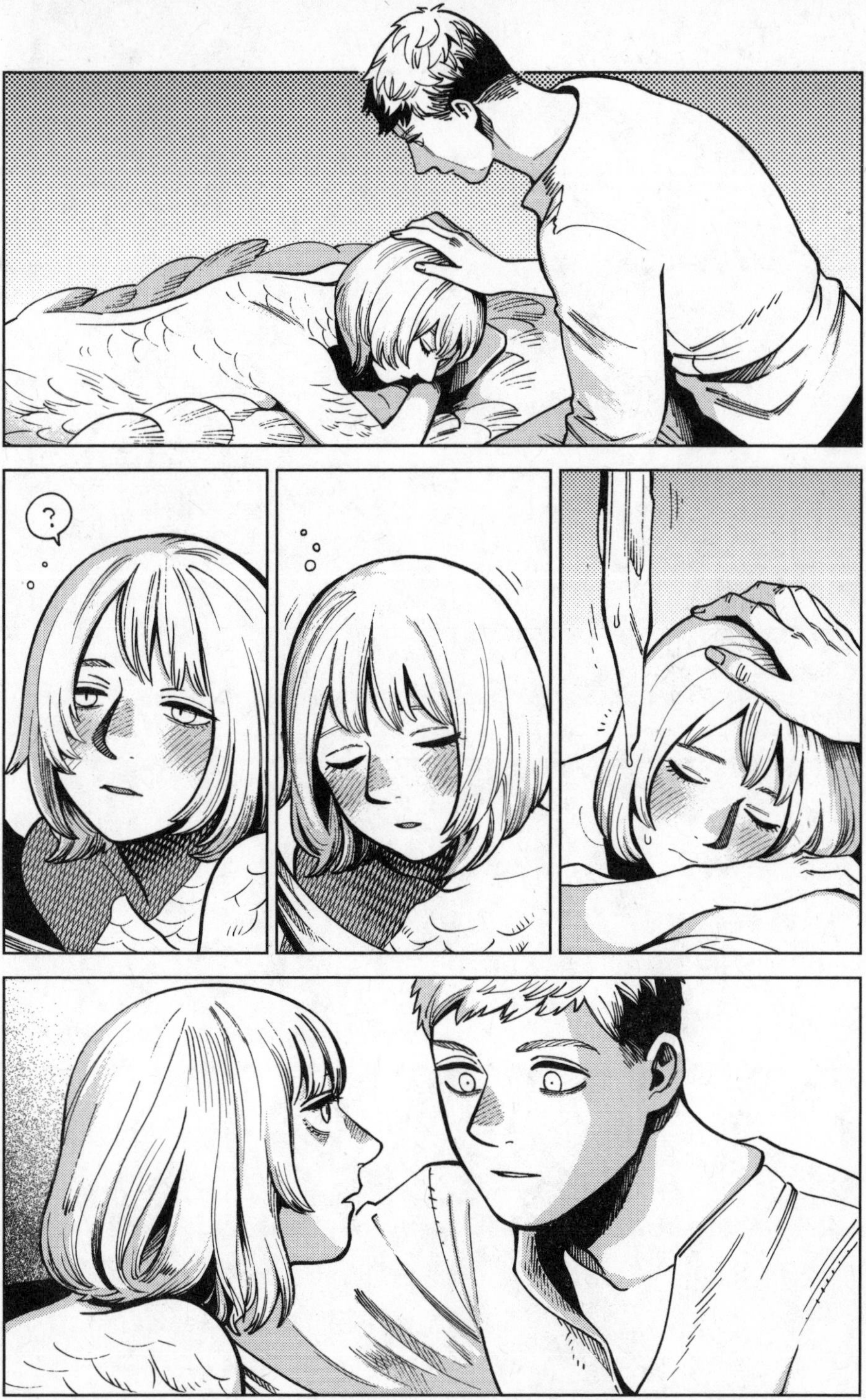
?

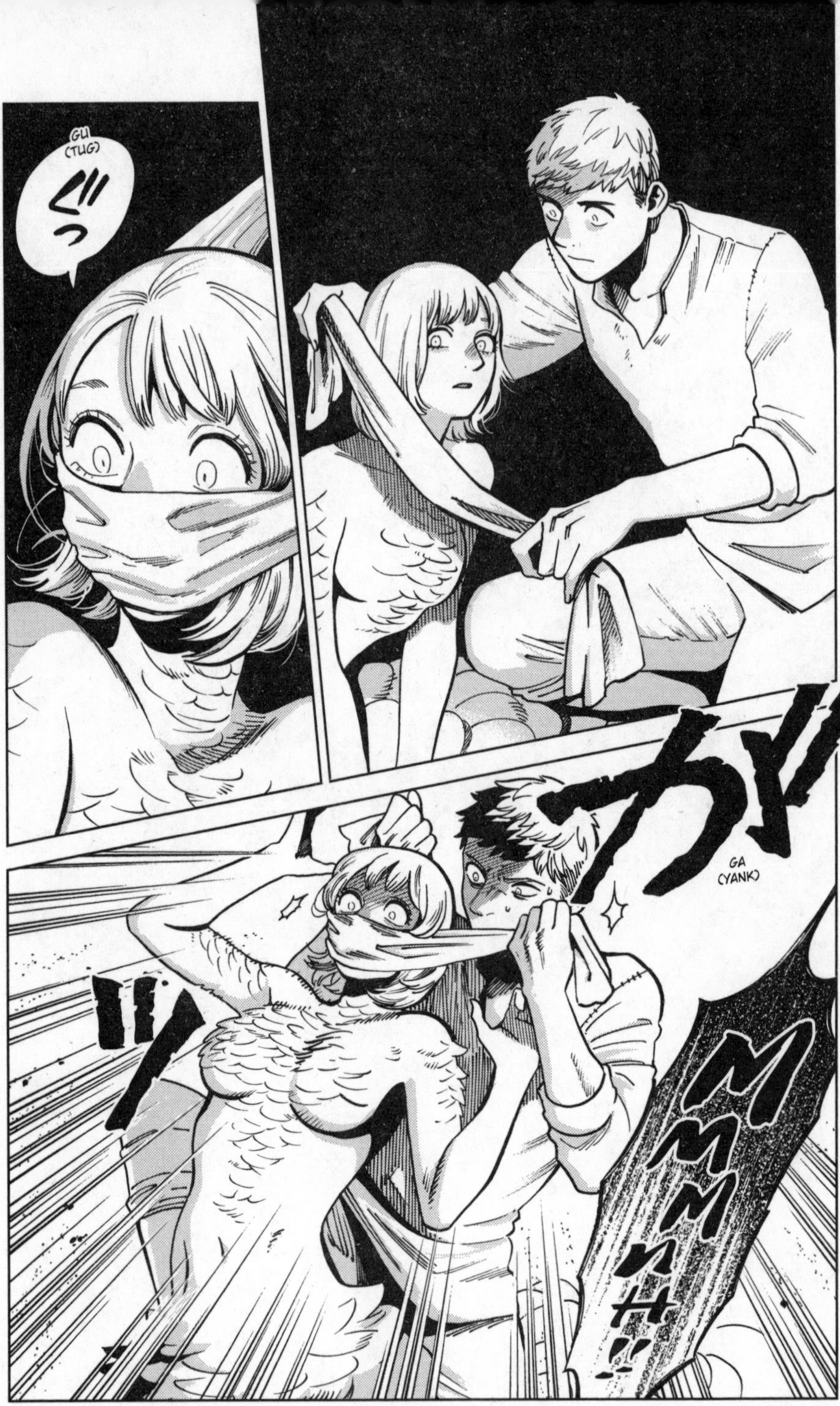
ぐっ
GU (TUG)
ガッ
GA (YANK)
MMMMH!!

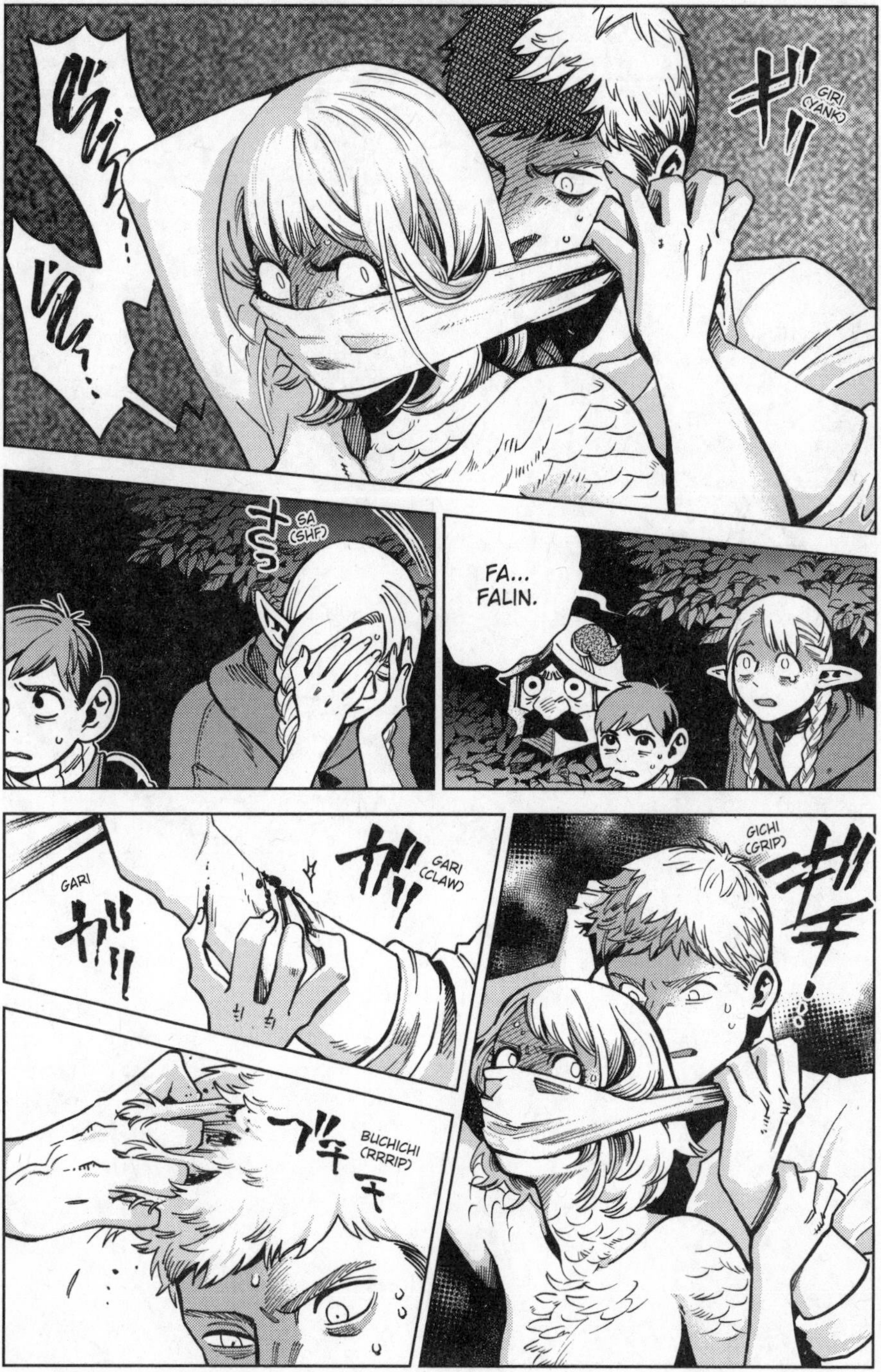
GIRI (YANK)
FA... FALIN.
SA (SHF)
GICHI (GRIP)
GARI (CLAW)
GARI
BUCHICHI (RRRIP)

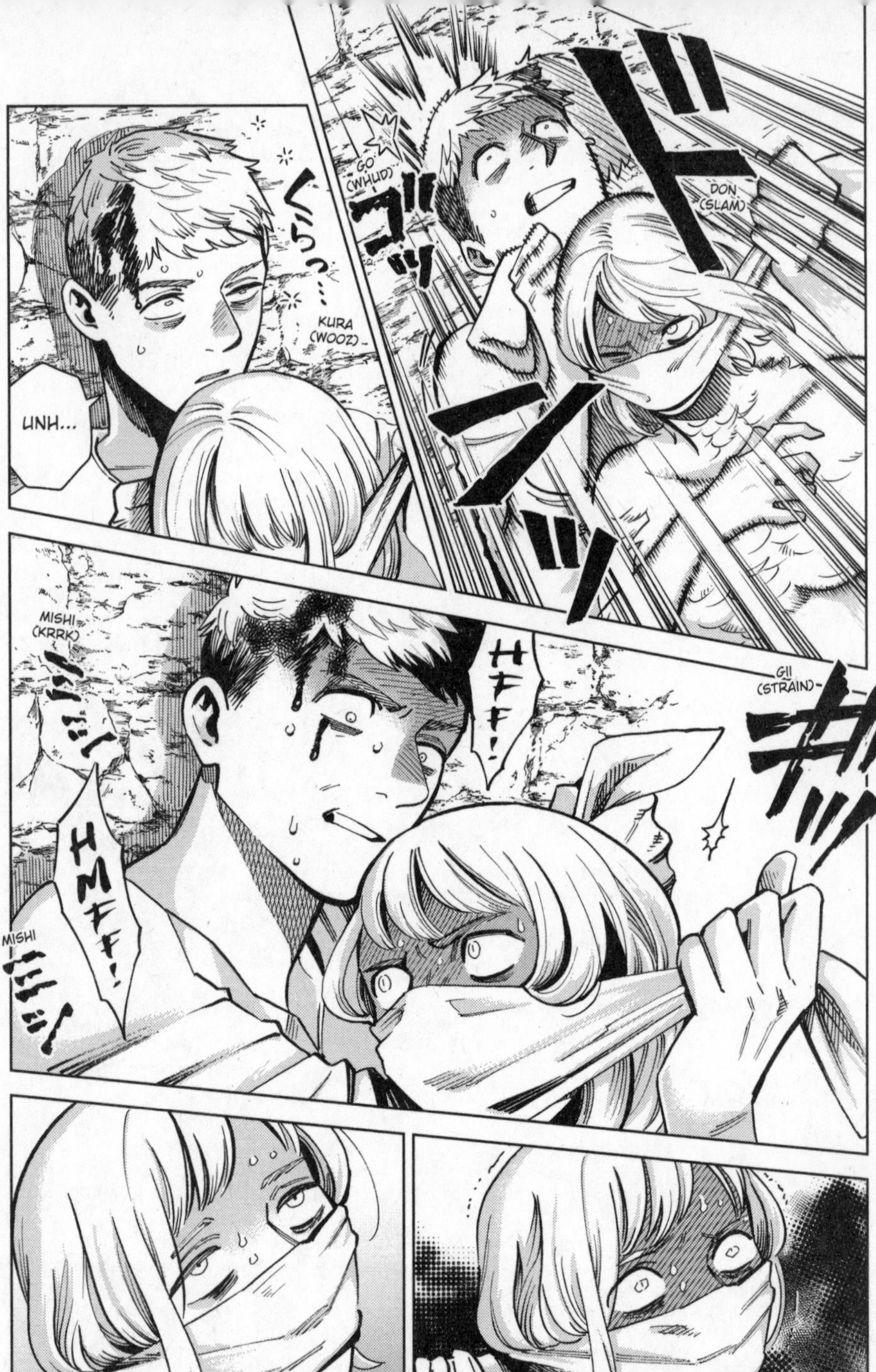

DON (SLAM)
ドンッ
GO (WHUD)
ゴッ
KURA (WOOZ)
くらっ…
UNH...
GII (STRAIN)
ギッ
HFFF!
MISHI (KRRK)
ミシッ
HMFFF!
MISHI
ミシッ

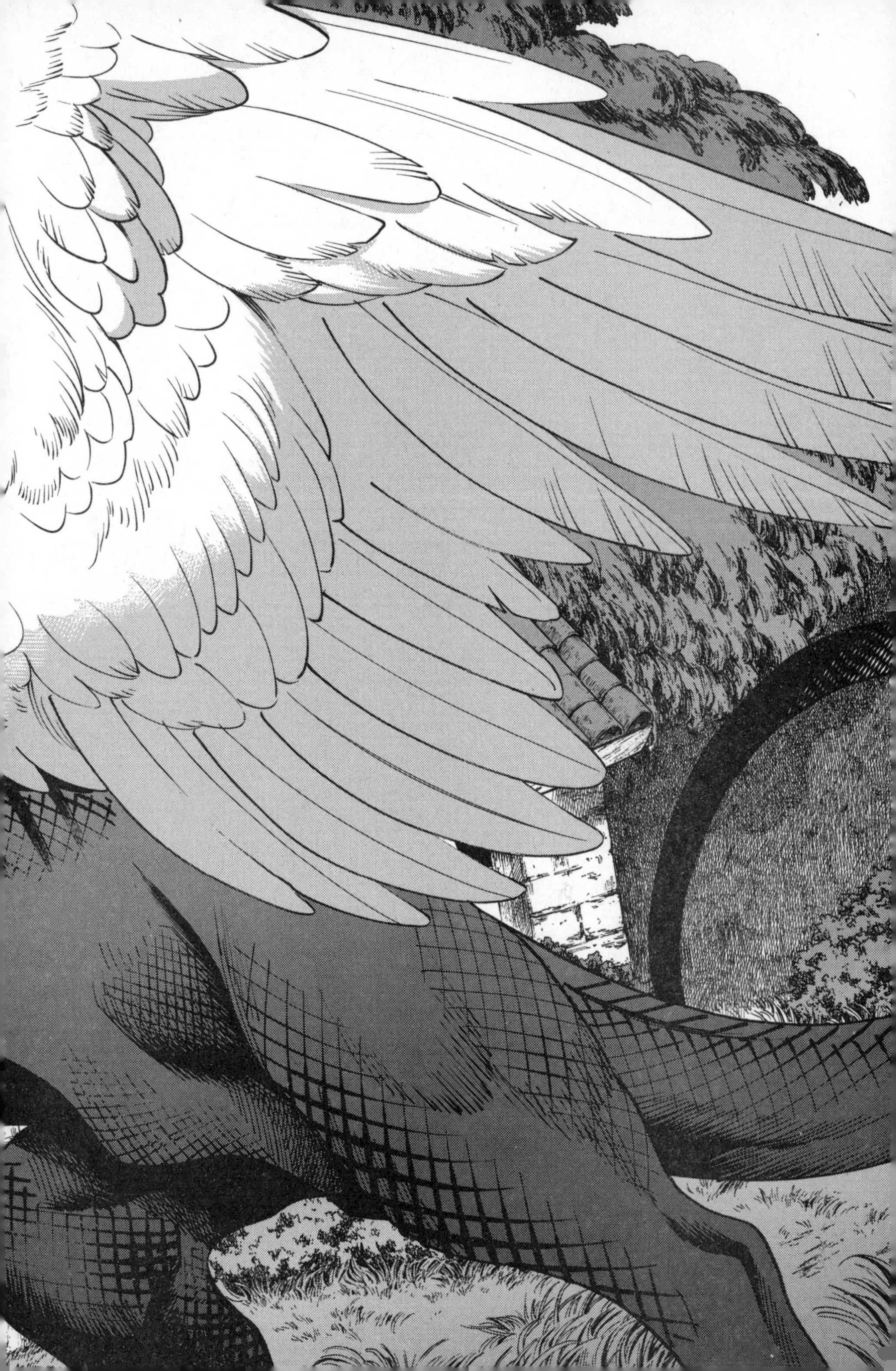

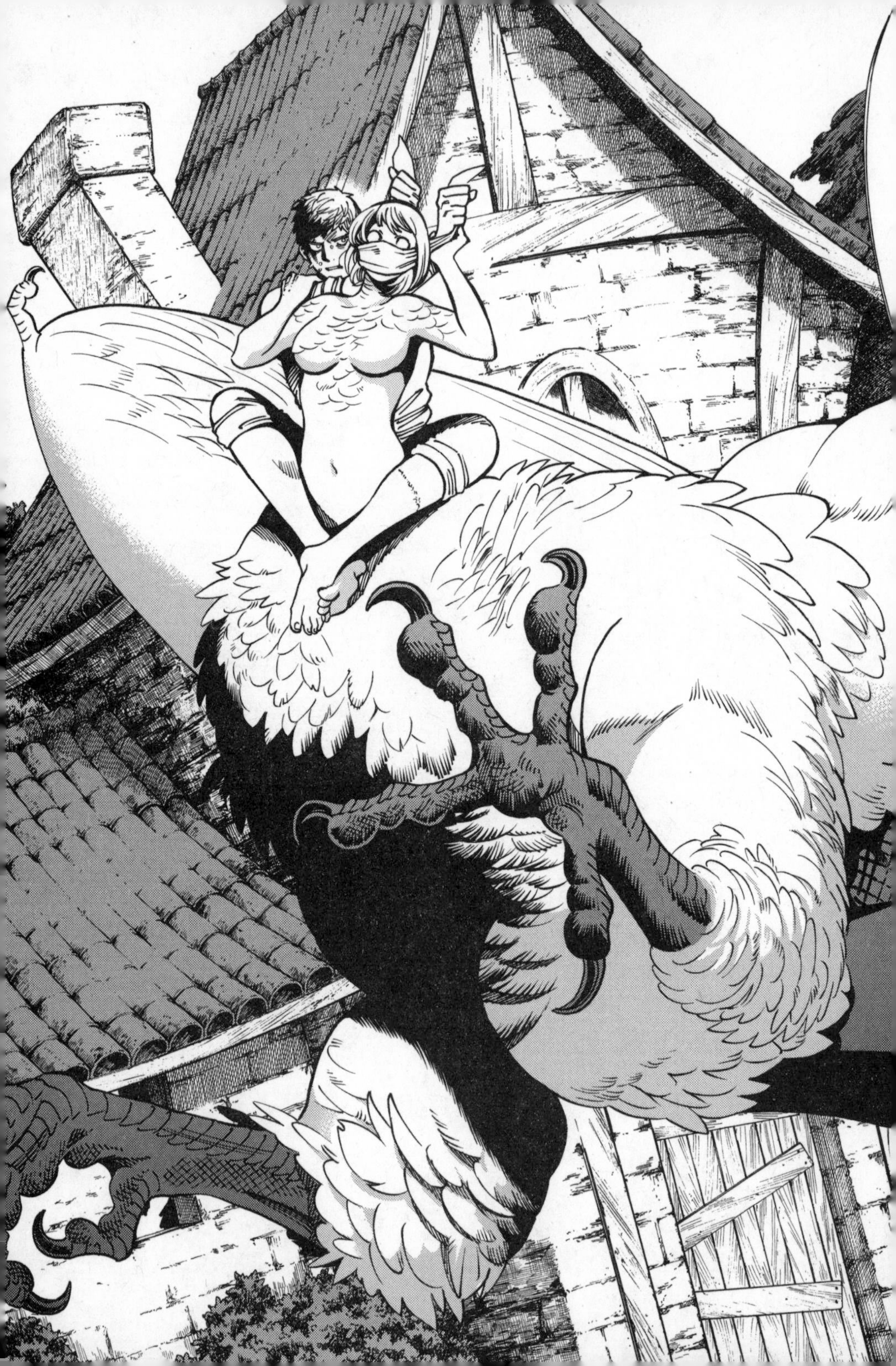

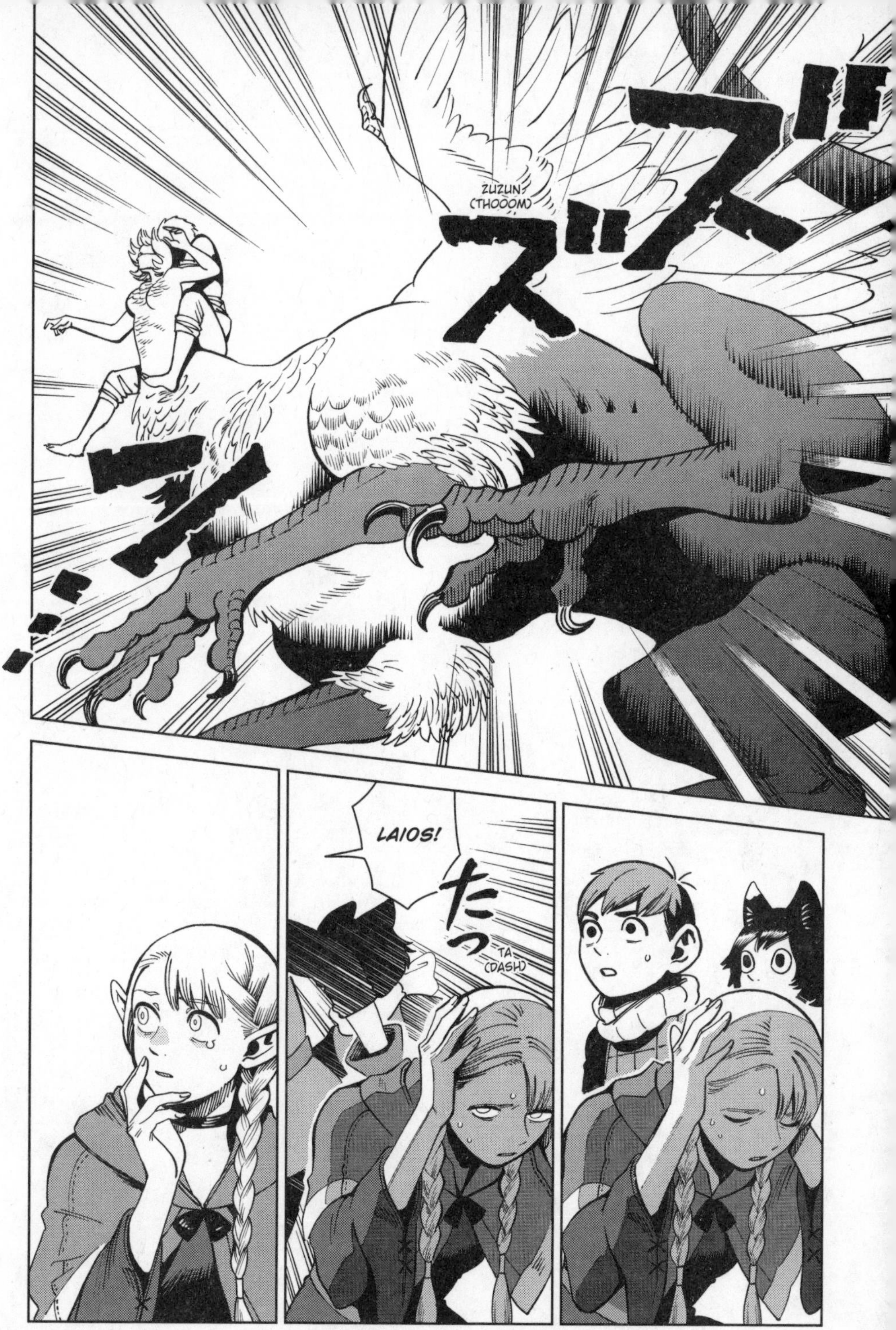
ZUZUN
(THOOOM)
LAIOS!
たっ
TA
(DASH)

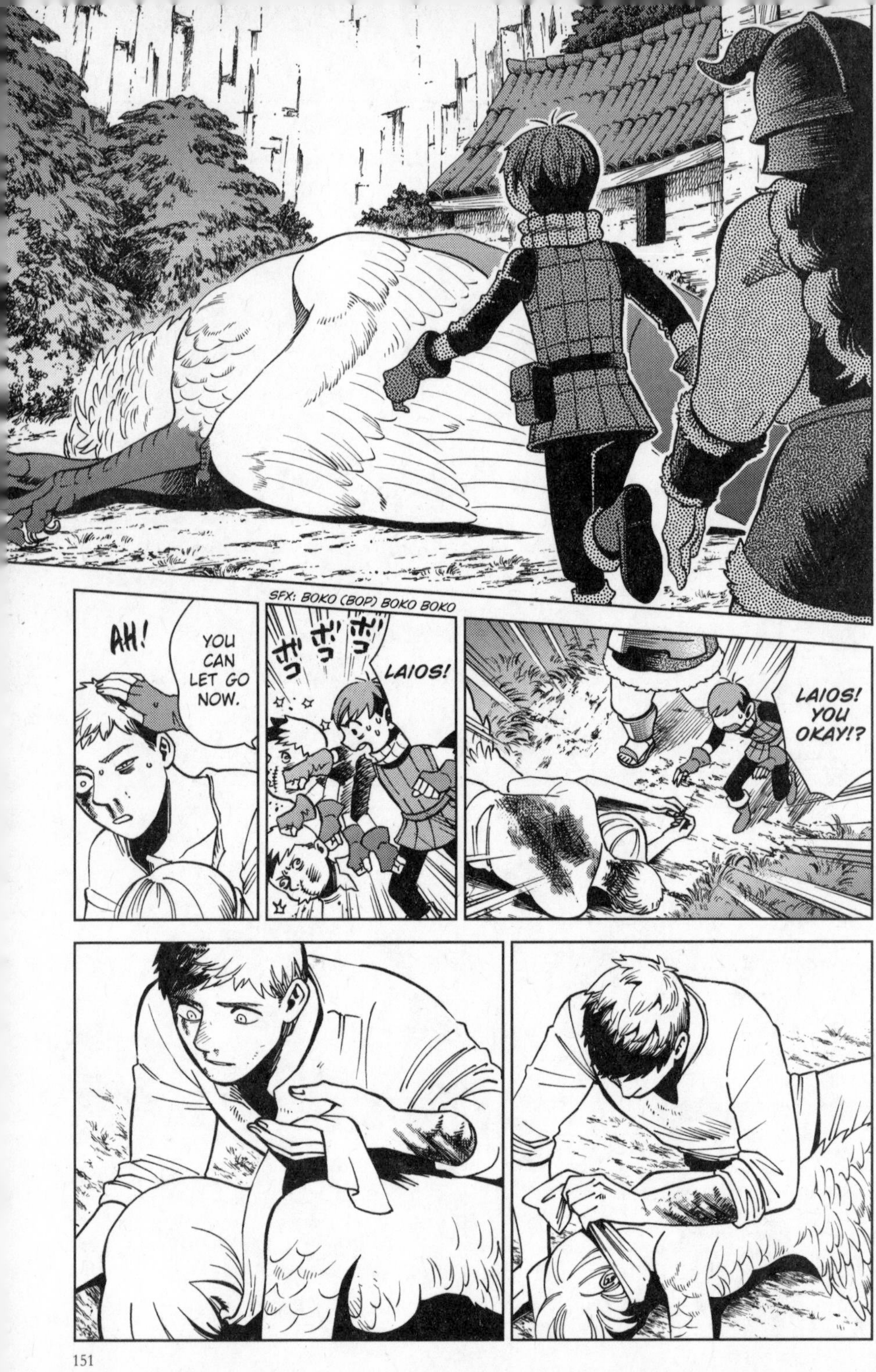
LAIOS! YOU OKAY!?
SFX: BOKO (BOP) BOKO BOKO
LAIOS!
AH!
YOU CAN LET GO NOW.

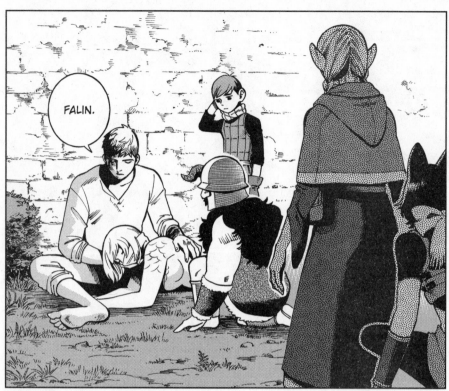

FALIN.

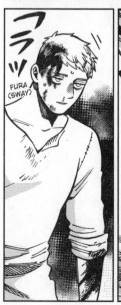

FURA
(SWAY)

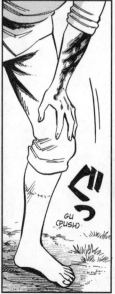

GU
(PUSH)

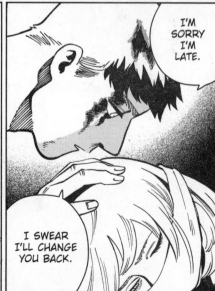

I'M SORRY I'M LATE.

I SWEAR I'LL CHANGE YOU BACK.

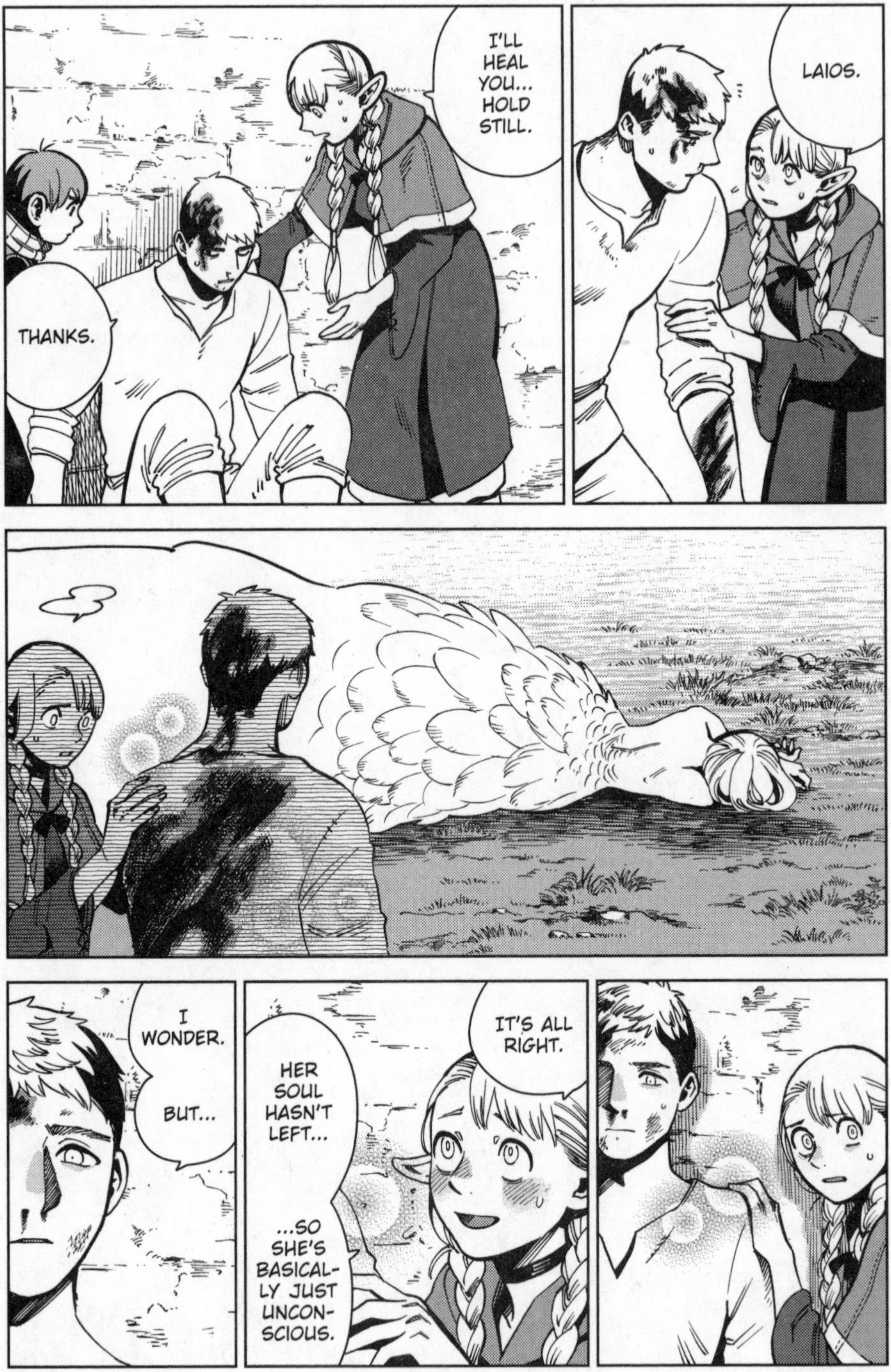
LAIOS.
I'LL HEAL YOU... HOLD STILL.
THANKS.
IT'S ALL RIGHT.
HER SOUL HASN'T LEFT...
...SO SHE'S BASICALLY JUST UNCONSCIOUS.
I WONDER.
BUT...

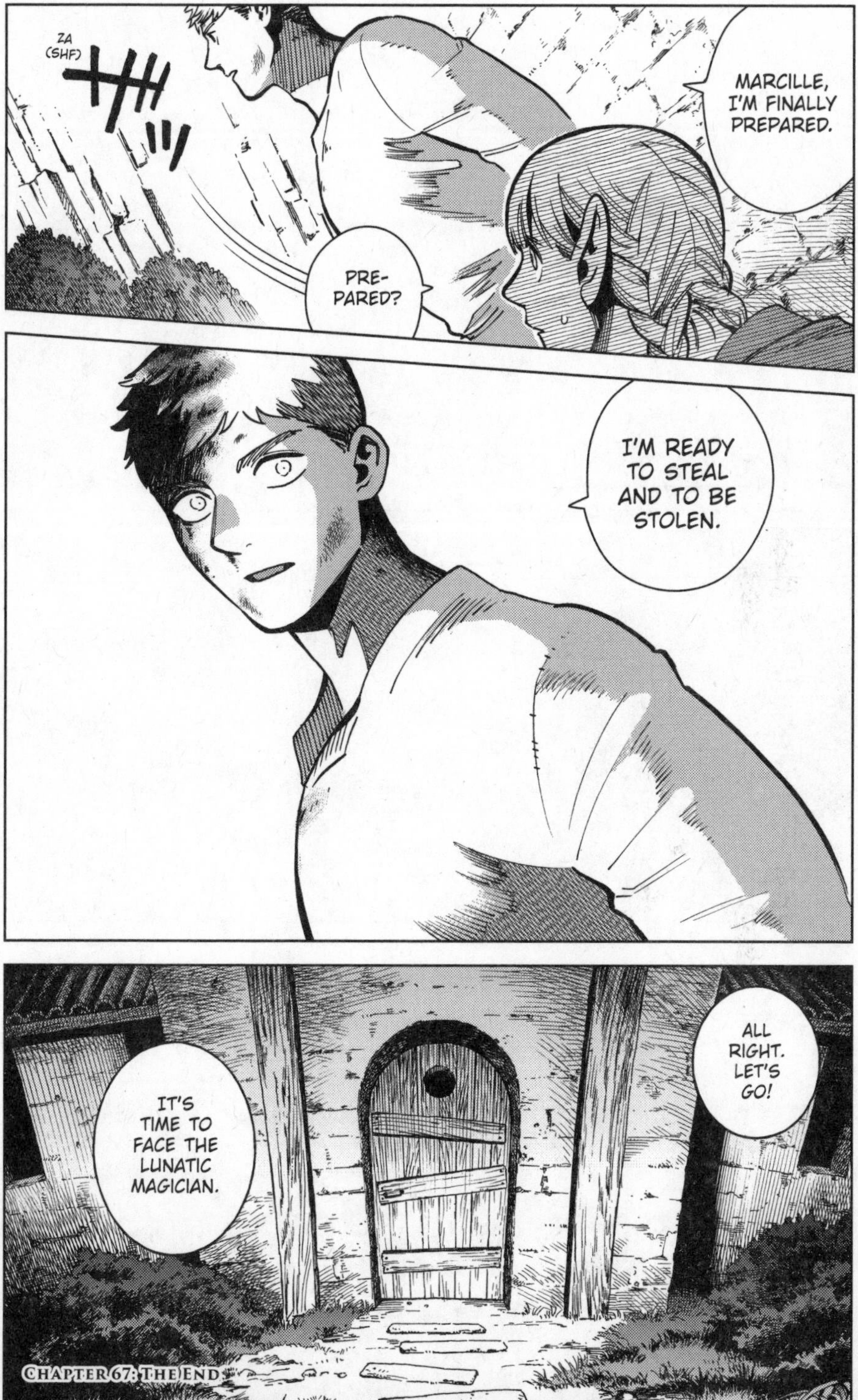
MARCILLE, I'M FINALLY PREPARED.
PRE-PARED?
ZA (SHF)
I'M READY TO STEAL AND TO BE STOLEN.
ALL RIGHT. LET'S GO!
IT'S TIME TO FACE THE LUNATIC MAGICIAN.
Chapter 67: The End

68. Sissel -1-

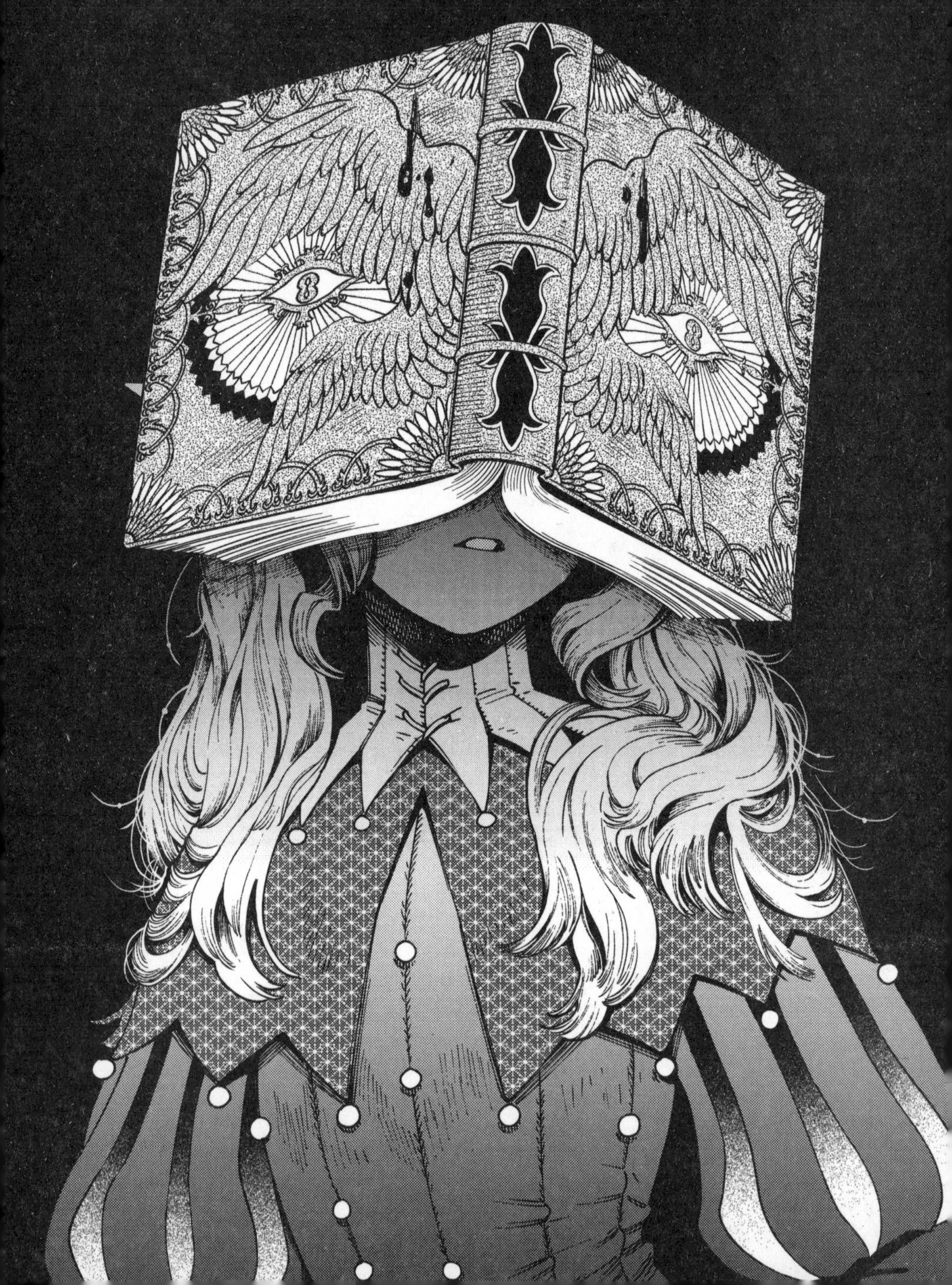

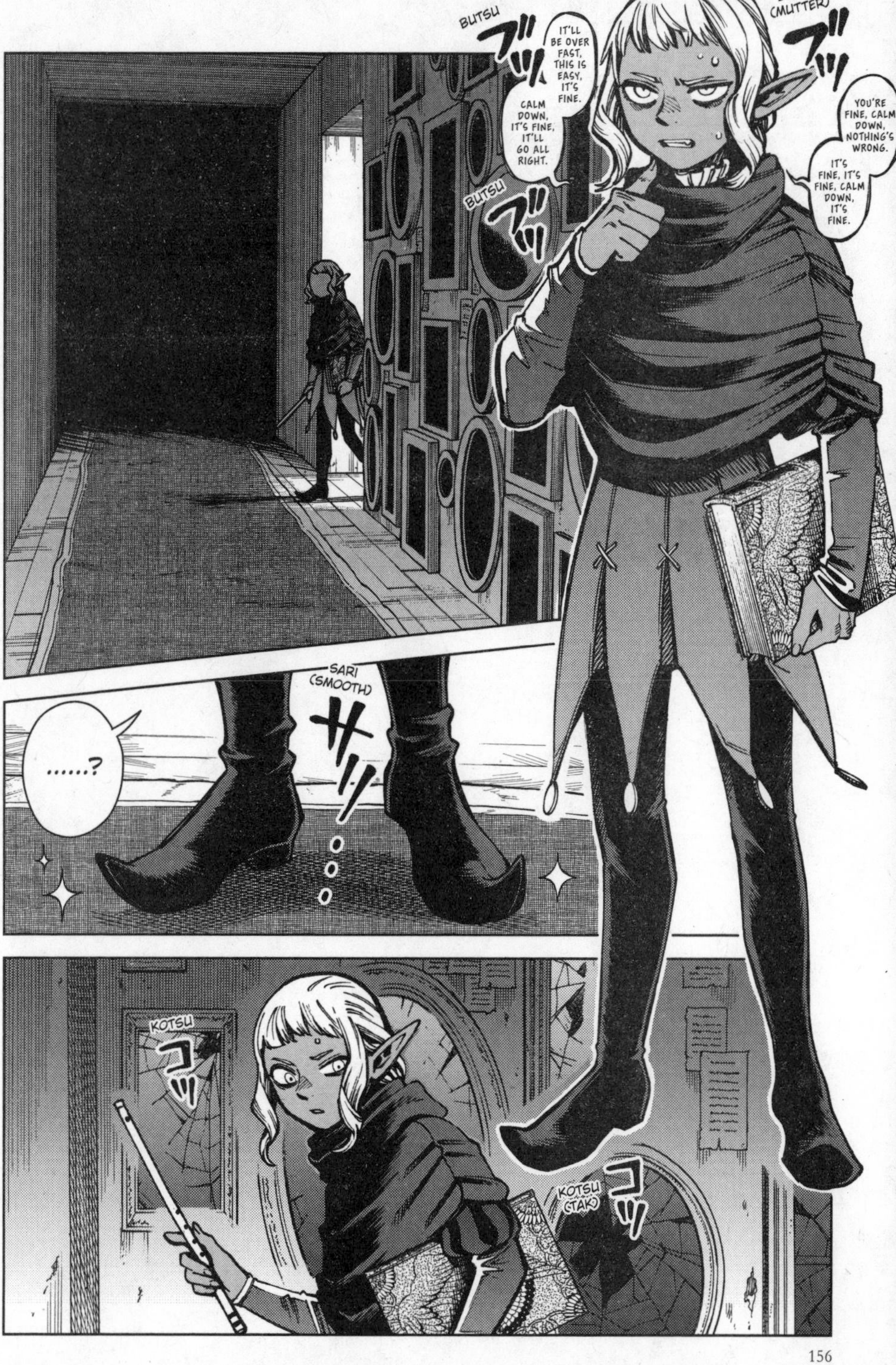
BUTSU (MUTTER)
YOU'RE FINE, CALM DOWN, NOTHING'S WRONG.
IT'S FINE, IT'S FINE, CALM DOWN, IT'S FINE.
IT'LL BE OVER FAST, THIS IS EASY, IT'S FINE.
BUTSU
CALM DOWN, IT'S FINE, IT'LL GO ALL RIGHT.
BUTSU
SARI (SMOOTH)
......?
KOTSU (TAK)
KOTSU

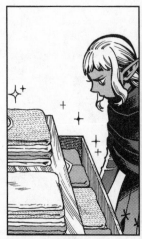

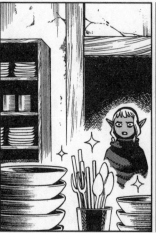

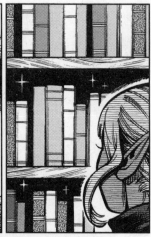

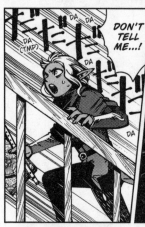

DON'T TELL ME...!

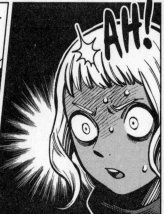

AH!

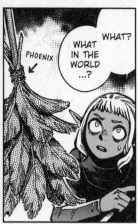

PHOENIX ↙

WHAT IN THE WORLD ...?

WHAT?

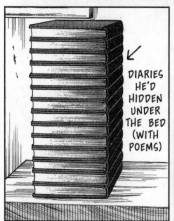

DIARIES HE'D HIDDEN UNDER THE BED (WITH POEMS) ↖

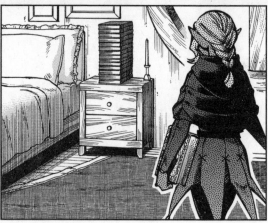

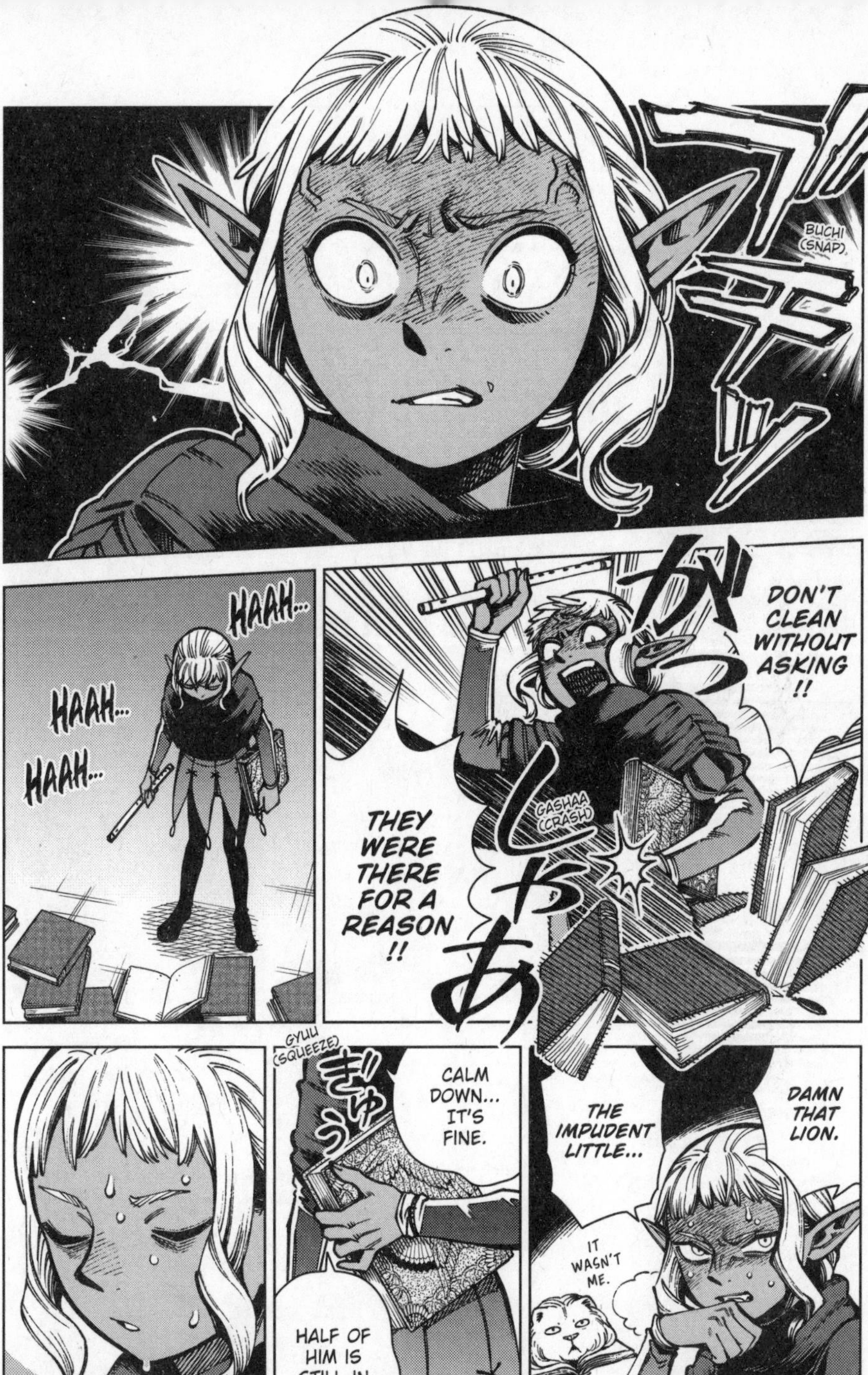
BUCHI (SNAP)
DON'T CLEAN WITHOUT ASKING!!
THEY WERE THERE FOR A REASON!!
GASHAA (CRASH)
HAAH...
HAAH...
HAAH...
DAMN THAT LION.
THE IMPUDENT LITTLE...
IT WASN'T ME.
GYUU (SQUEEZE)
CALM DOWN... IT'S FINE.
HALF OF HIM IS STILL IN HERE.

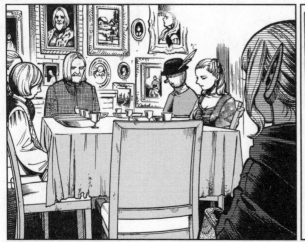
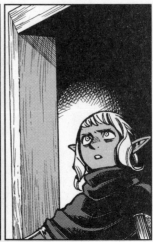

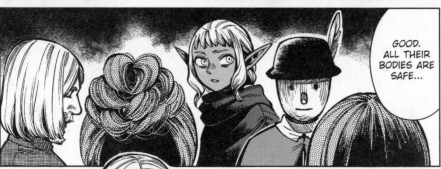

GOOD. ALL THEIR BODIES ARE SAFE...

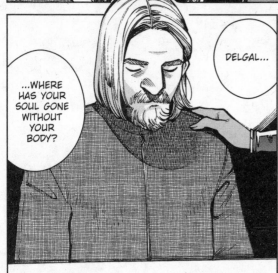

...WHERE HAS YOUR SOUL GONE WITHOUT YOUR BODY?

DELGAL...

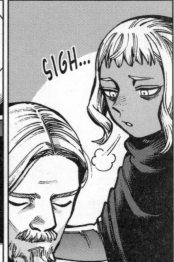

SIGH...

159

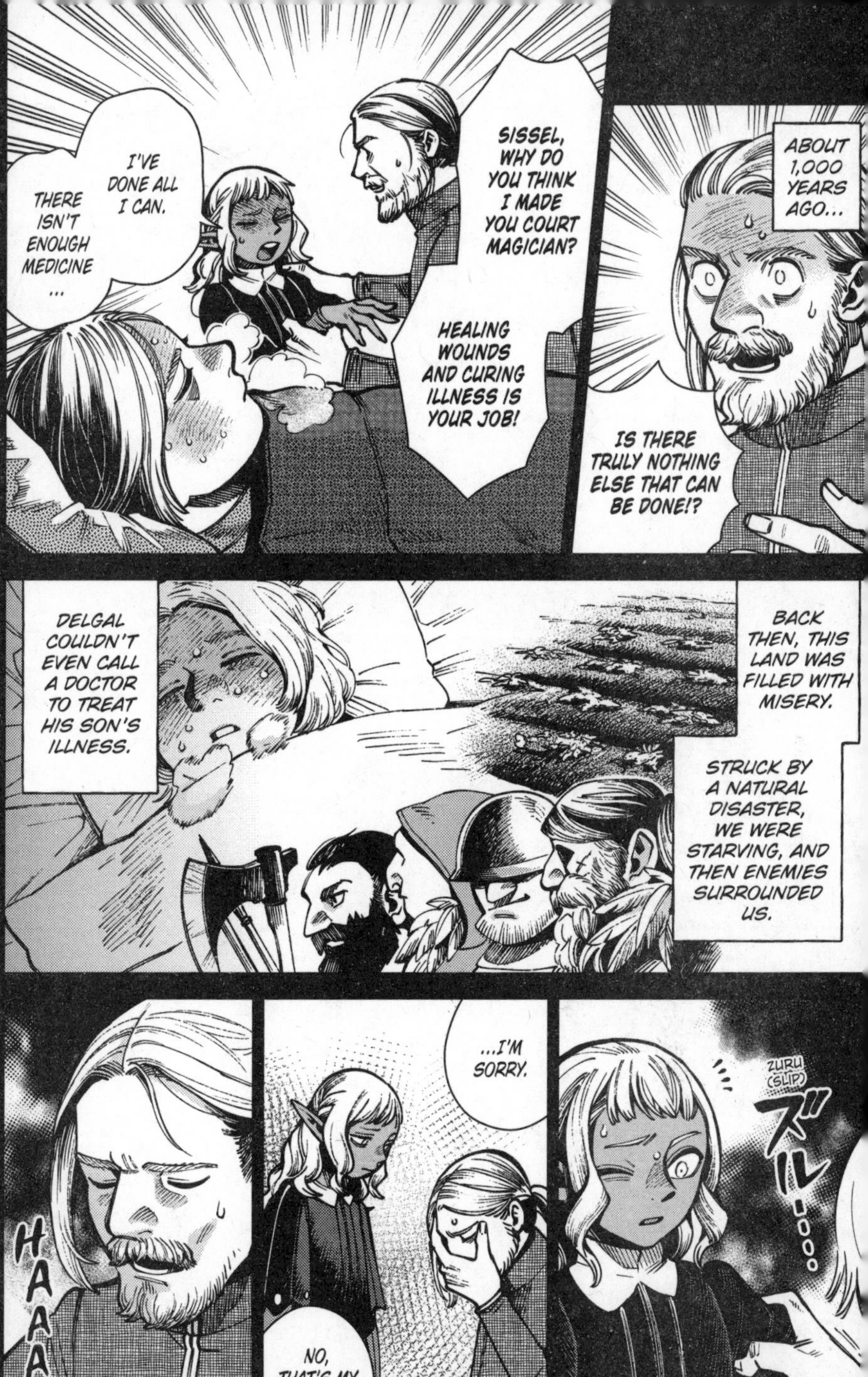
ABOUT 1,000 YEARS AGO...
IS THERE TRULY NOTHING ELSE THAT CAN BE DONE!?
SISSEL, WHY DO YOU THINK I MADE YOU COURT MAGICIAN?
HEALING WOUNDS AND CURING ILLNESS IS YOUR JOB!
I'VE DONE ALL I CAN.
THERE ISN'T ENOUGH MEDICINE...
BACK THEN, THIS LAND WAS FILLED WITH MISERY.
STRUCK BY A NATURAL DISASTER, WE WERE STARVING, AND THEN ENEMIES SURROUNDED US.
DELGAL COULDN'T EVEN CALL A DOCTOR TO TREAT HIS SON'S ILLNESS.
ZURU (SLIP)
ズル…
...I'M SORRY.
NO, THAT'S MY LINE.
HAAAH...

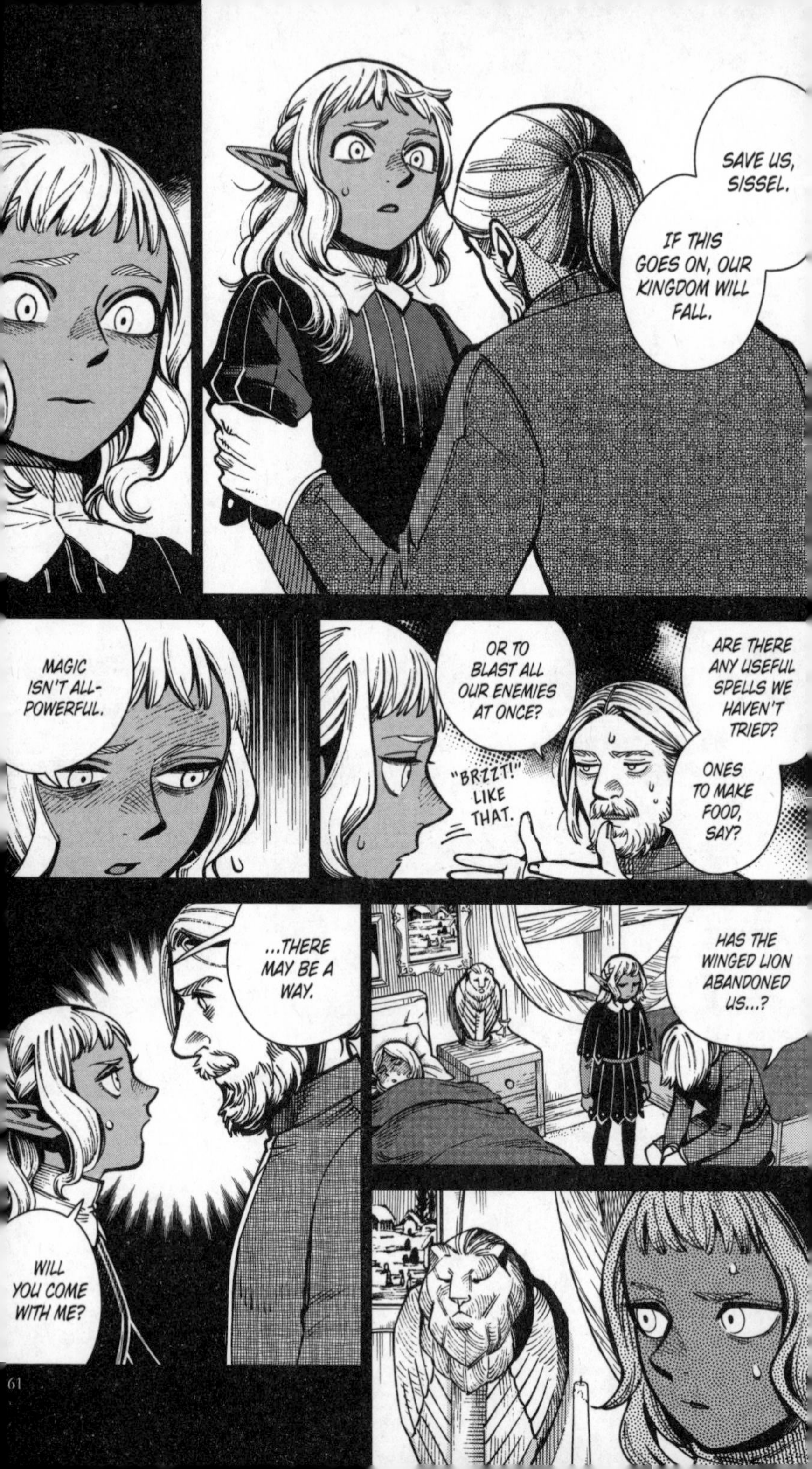
SAVE US, SISSEL.
IF THIS GOES ON, OUR KINGDOM WILL FALL.
ARE THERE ANY USEFUL SPELLS WE HAVEN'T TRIED?
ONES TO MAKE FOOD, SAY?
OR TO BLAST ALL OUR ENEMIES AT ONCE?
"BRZZT!" LIKE THAT.
MAGIC ISN'T ALL-POWERFUL.
HAS THE WINGED LION ABANDONED US...?
...THERE MAY BE A WAY.
WILL YOU COME WITH ME?

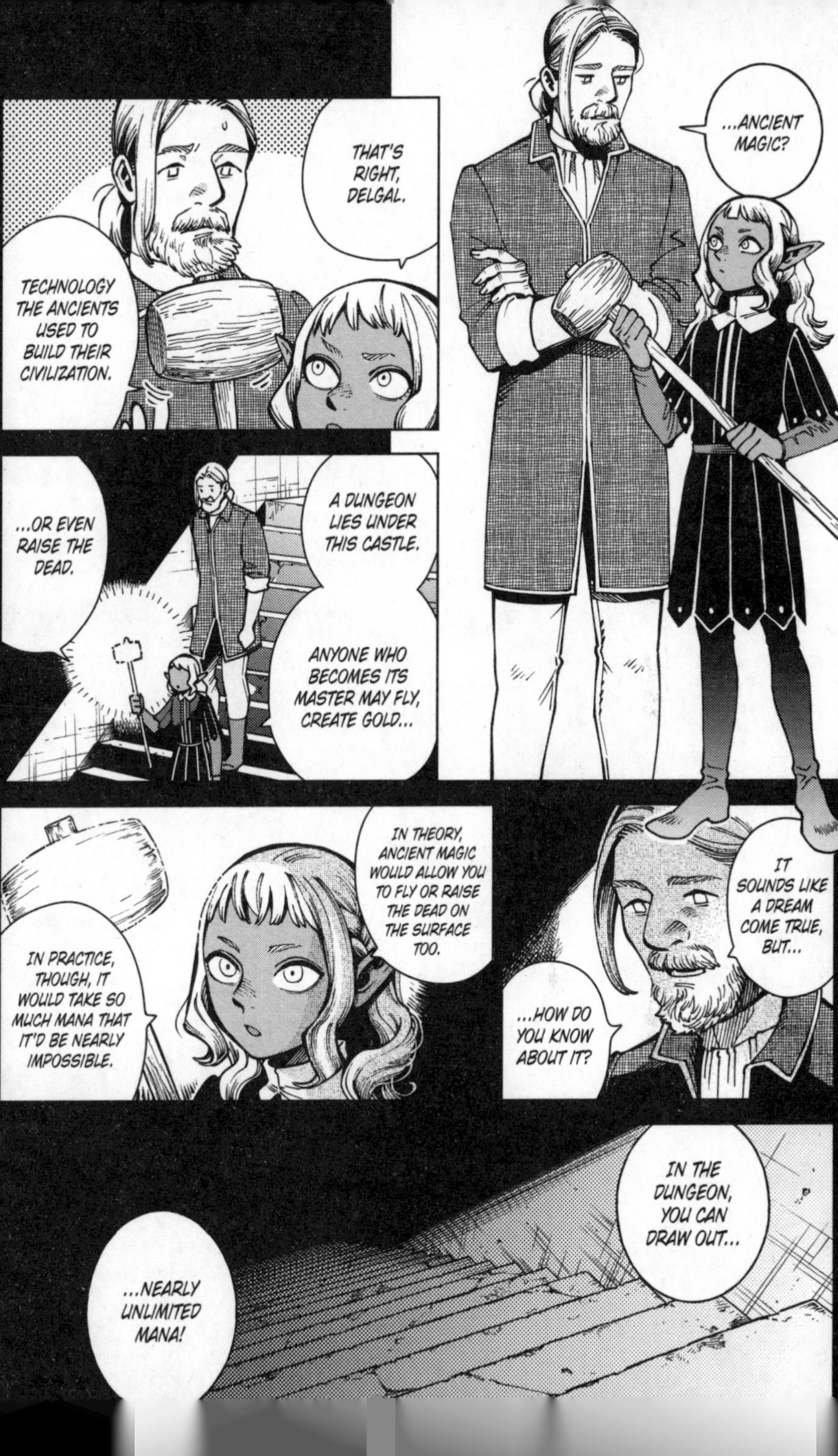
...ANCIENT MAGIC?
THAT'S RIGHT, DELGAL.
TECHNOLOGY THE ANCIENTS USED TO BUILD THEIR CIVILIZATION.
A DUNGEON LIES UNDER THIS CASTLE.
ANYONE WHO BECOMES ITS MASTER MAY FLY, CREATE GOLD...
...OR EVEN RAISE THE DEAD.
IT SOUNDS LIKE A DREAM COME TRUE, BUT...
...HOW DO YOU KNOW ABOUT IT?
IN THEORY, ANCIENT MAGIC WOULD ALLOW YOU TO FLY OR RAISE THE DEAD ON THE SURFACE TOO.
IN PRACTICE, THOUGH, IT WOULD TAKE SO MUCH MANA THAT IT'D BE NEARLY IMPOSSIBLE.
IN THE DUNGEON, YOU CAN DRAW OUT...
...NEARLY UNLIMITED MANA!

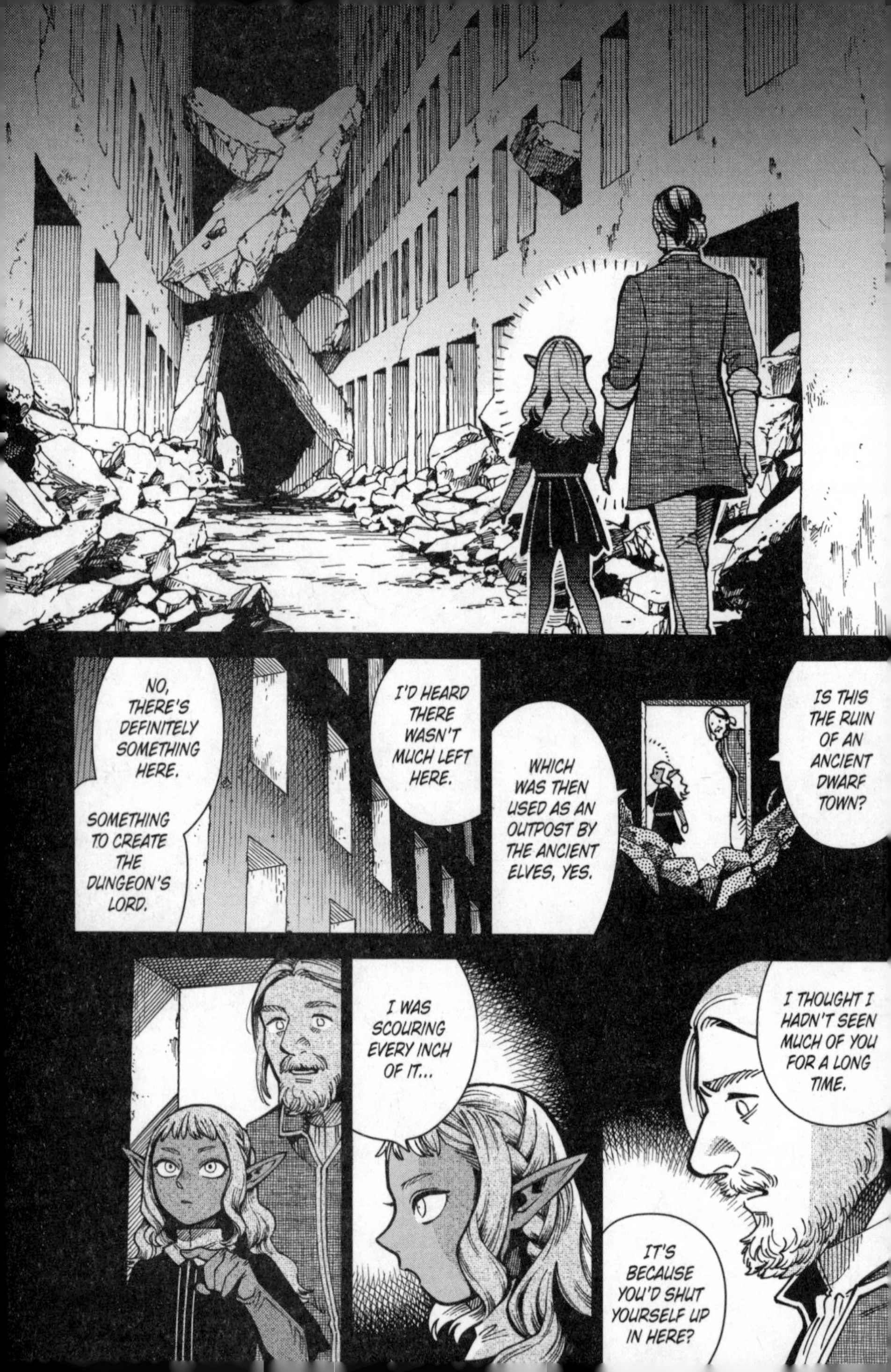
IS THIS THE RUIN OF AN ANCIENT DWARF TOWN?
WHICH WAS THEN USED AS AN OUTPOST BY THE ANCIENT ELVES, YES.
I'D HEARD THERE WASN'T MUCH LEFT HERE.
NO, THERE'S DEFINITELY SOMETHING HERE.
SOMETHING TO CREATE THE DUNGEON'S LORD.
I THOUGHT I HADN'T SEEN MUCH OF YOU FOR A LONG TIME.
IT'S BECAUSE YOU'D SHUT YOURSELF UP IN HERE?
I WAS SCOURING EVERY INCH OF IT...

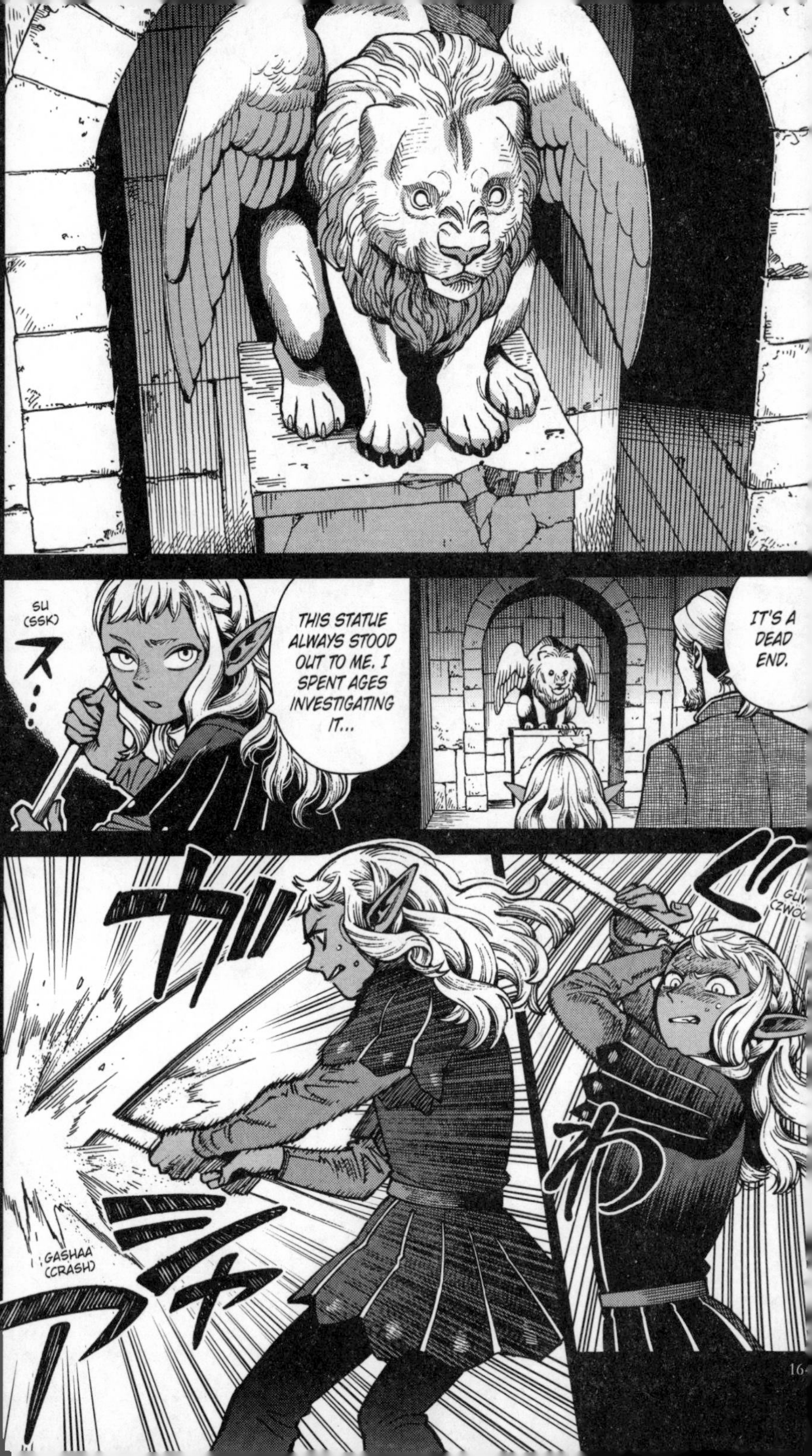
IT'S A DEAD END.
SU (SSK)
THIS STATUE ALWAYS STOOD OUT TO ME. I SPENT AGES INVESTIGATING IT...
GASHAA (CRASH)

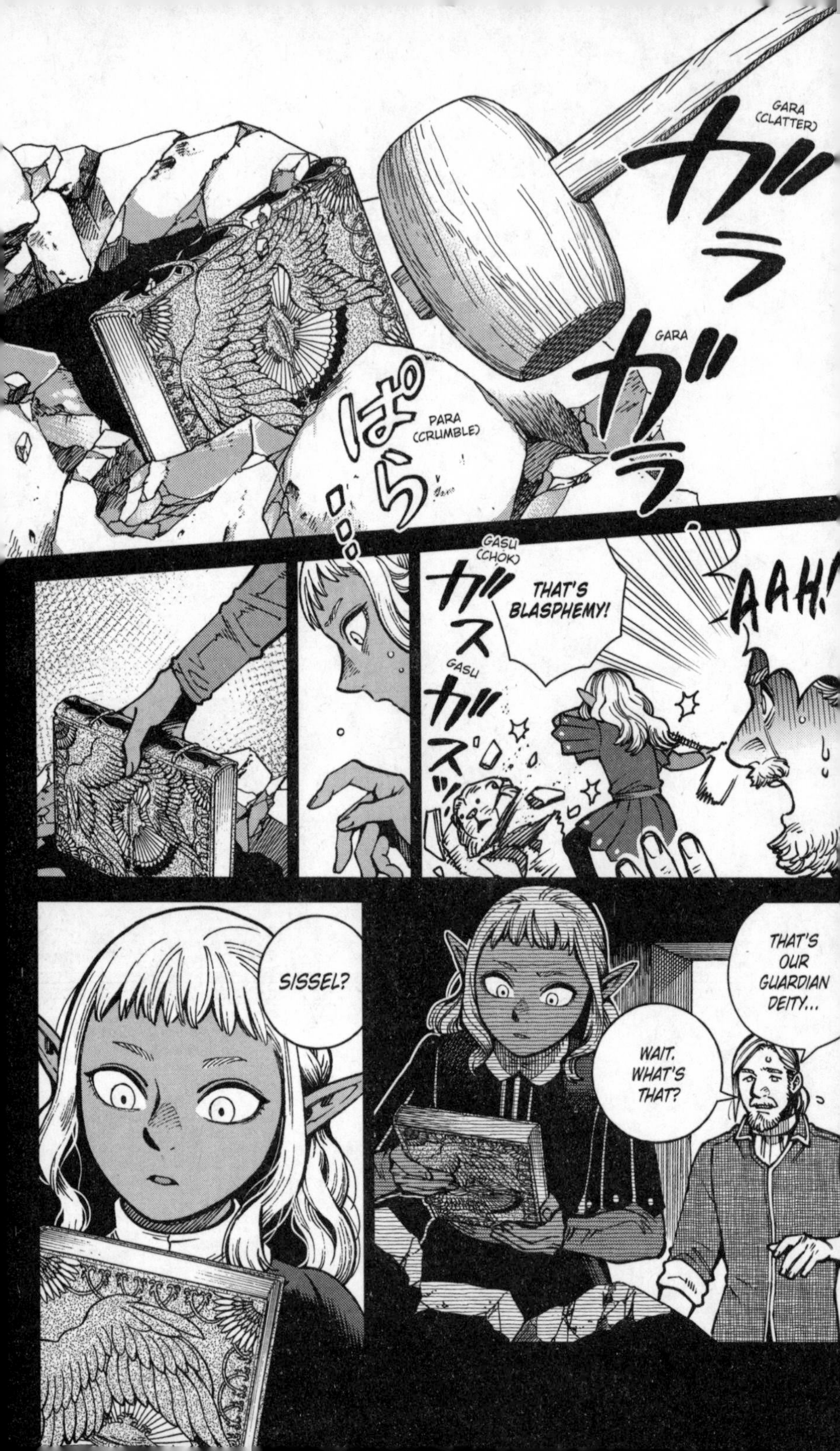
GARA (CLATTER)
ガラ
GARA
ガラ
PARA (CRUMBLE)
ぱら
AAH!
GASU (CHOK)
ガス
THAT'S BLASPHEMY!
GASU
ガスッ
THAT'S OUR GUARDIAN DEITY...
WAIT. WHAT'S THAT?
SISSEL?

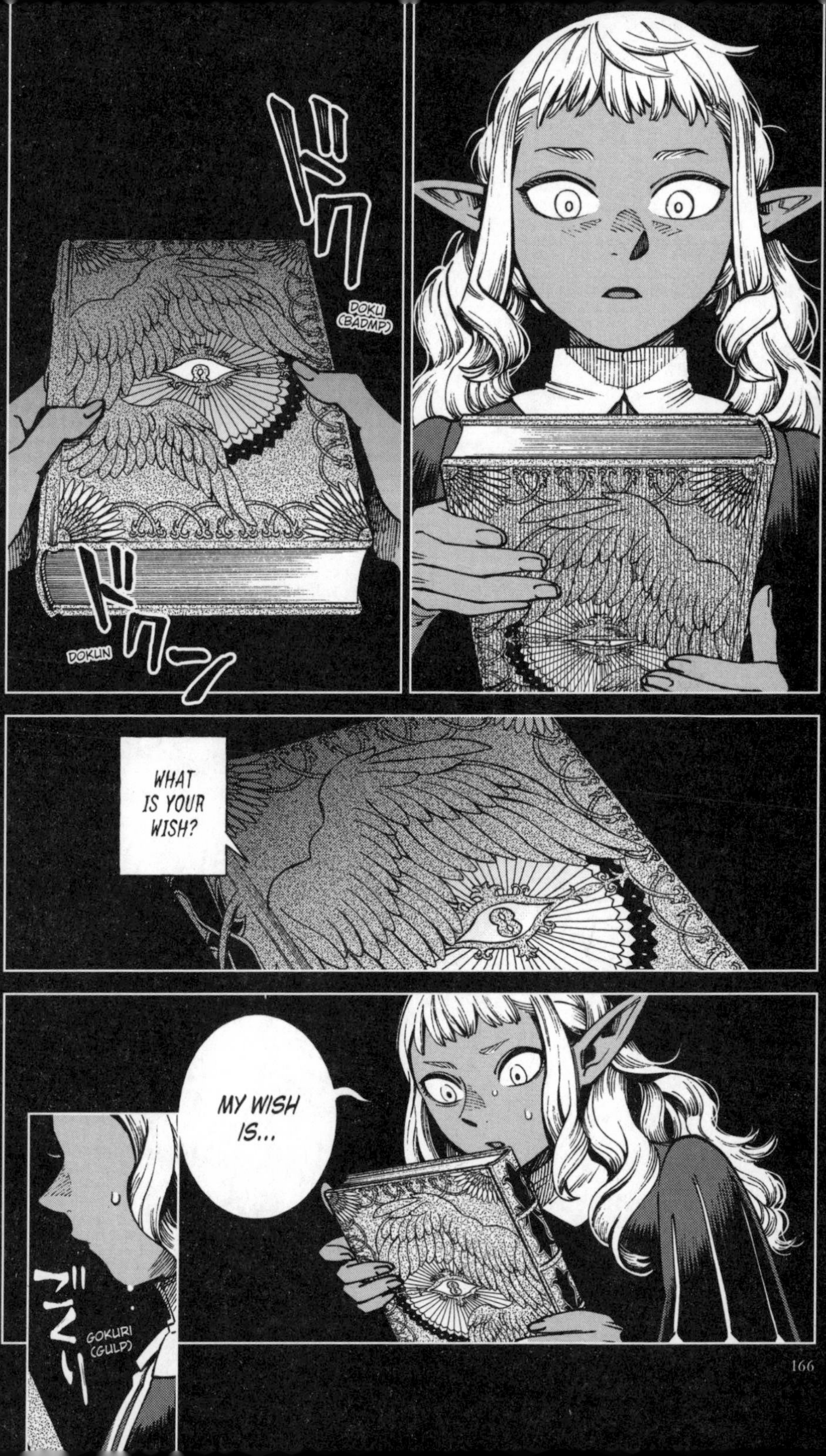
DOKU (BADMP)
DOKUN
WHAT IS YOUR WISH?
MY WISH IS...
GOKURI (GULP)

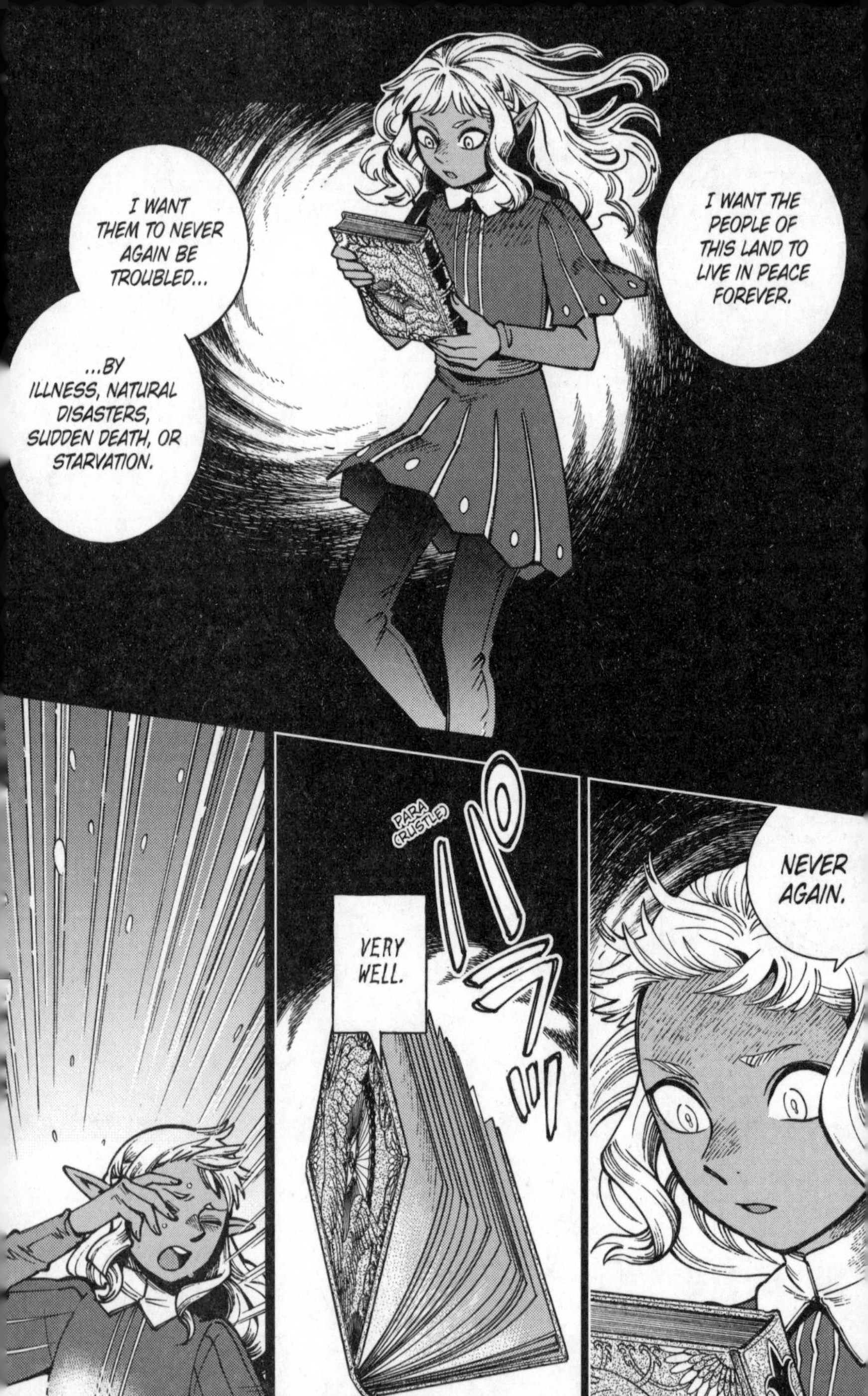
I WANT THE PEOPLE OF THIS LAND TO LIVE IN PEACE FOREVER.
I WANT THEM TO NEVER AGAIN BE TROUBLED...
...BY ILLNESS, NATURAL DISASTERS, SUDDEN DEATH, OR STARVATION.
NEVER AGAIN.
PARA (RUSTLE)
VERY WELL.

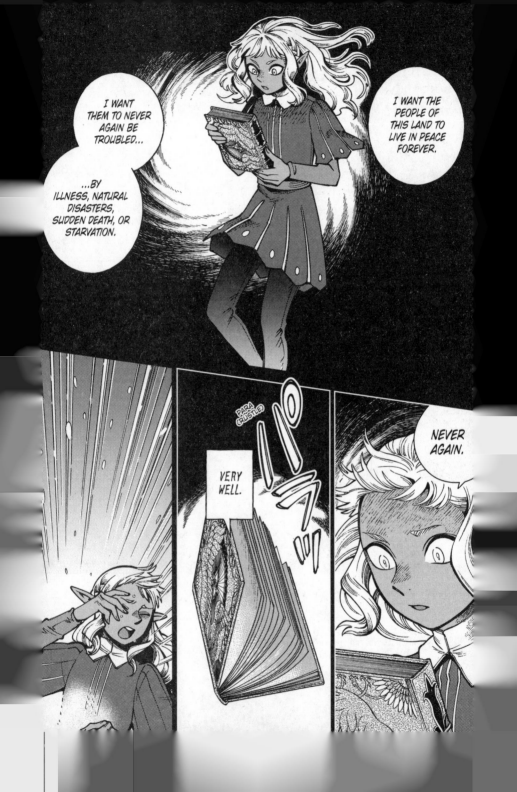

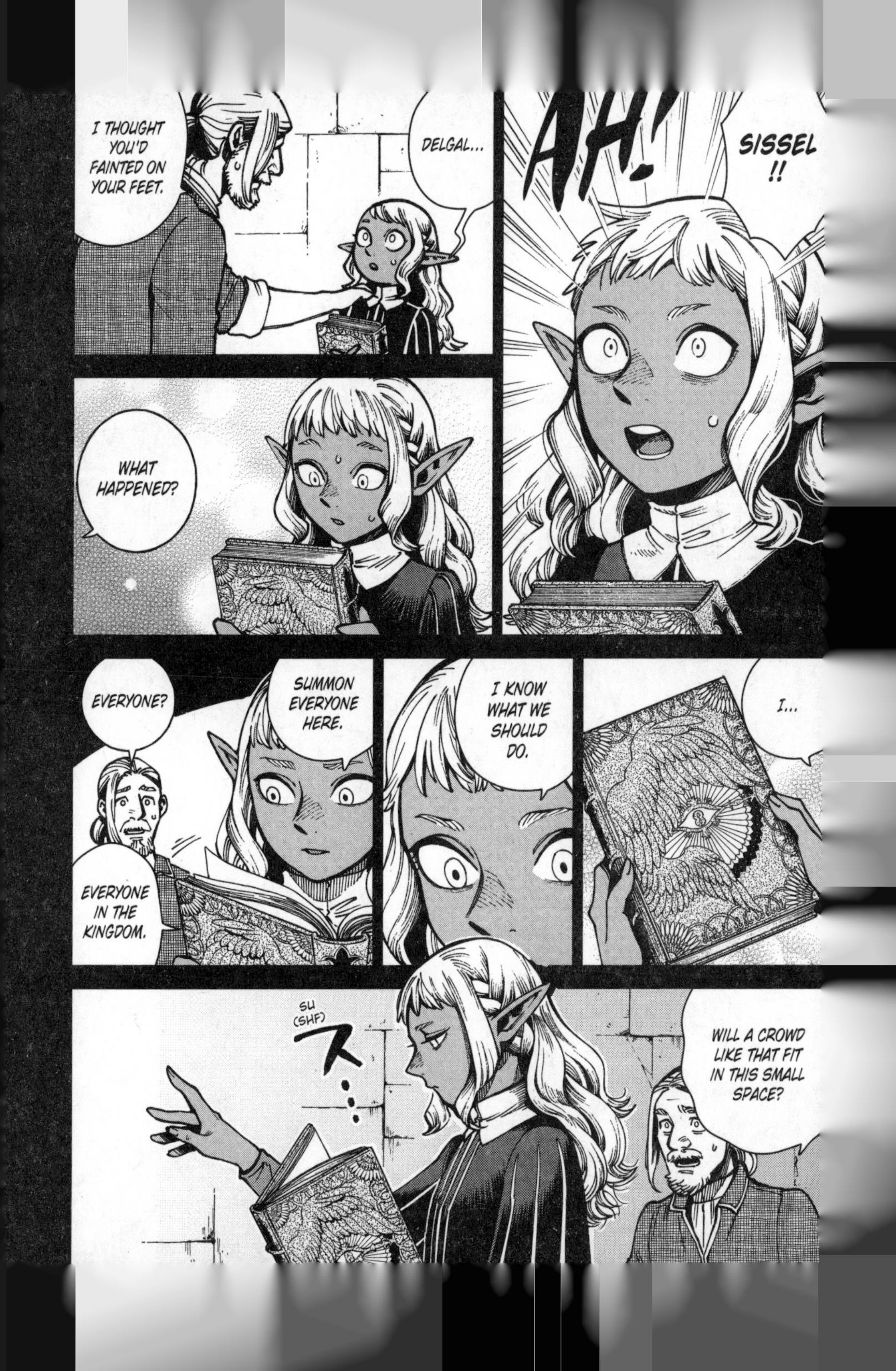
AH!
SISSEL!!
DELGAL...
I THOUGHT YOU'D FAINTED ON YOUR FEET.
WHAT HAPPENED?
I...
I KNOW WHAT WE SHOULD DO.
SUMMON EVERYONE HERE.
EVERYONE?
EVERYONE IN THE KINGDOM.
WILL A CROWD LIKE THAT FIT IN THIS SMALL SPACE?
SU (SHF)
ス...

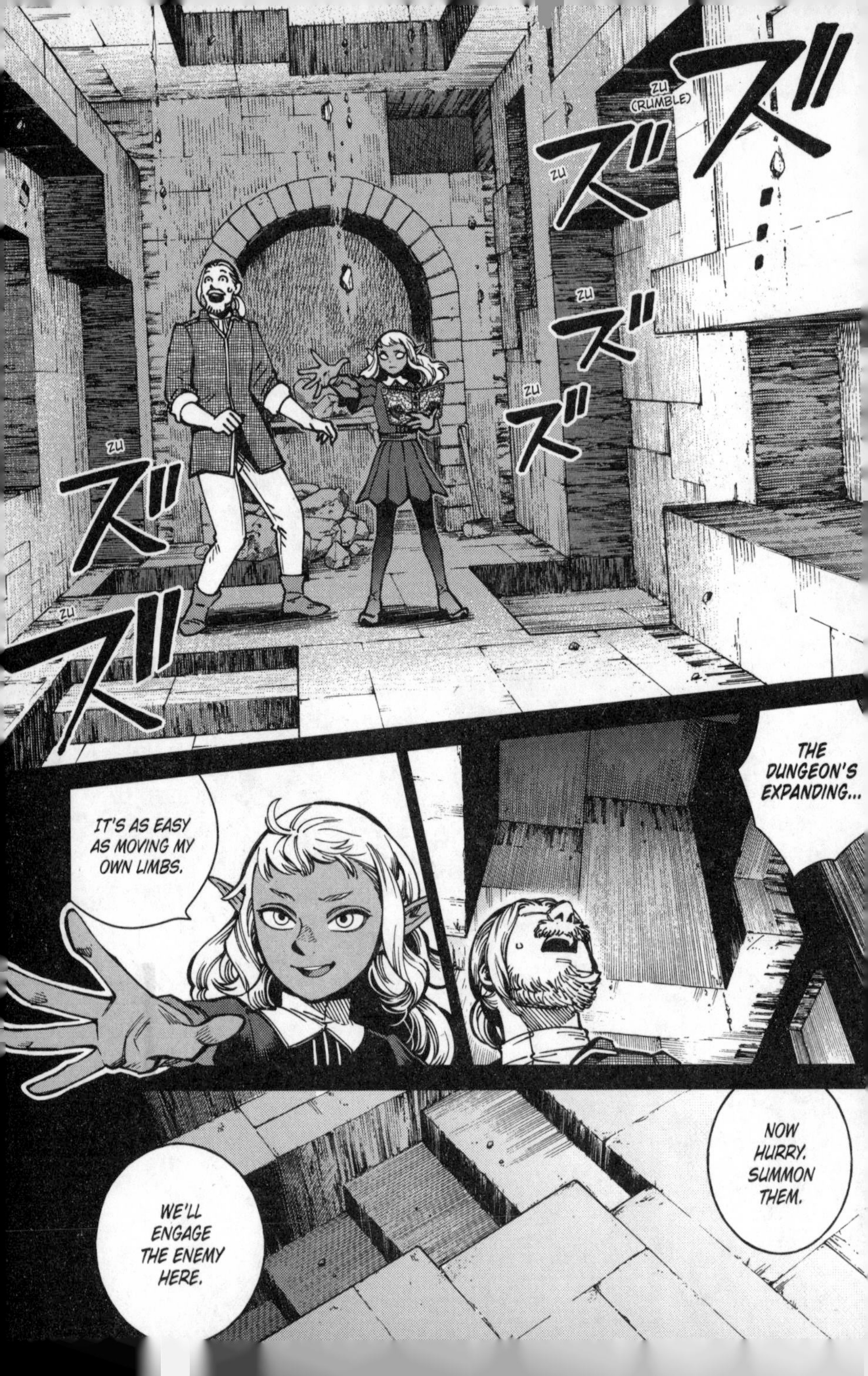
ZU (RUMBLE)
ZU
ZU
ZU
ZU
ZU
THE DUNGEON'S EXPANDING...
IT'S AS EASY AS MOVING MY OWN LIMBS.
NOW HURRY. SUMMON THEM.
WE'LL ENGAGE THE ENEMY HERE.

AAAH!
EEEP!
THIS LOOKS BAD.
わあ
WAA (CLAMOR)
わあ
WAA
WAA
わあ
RETREAT! RETREAT!

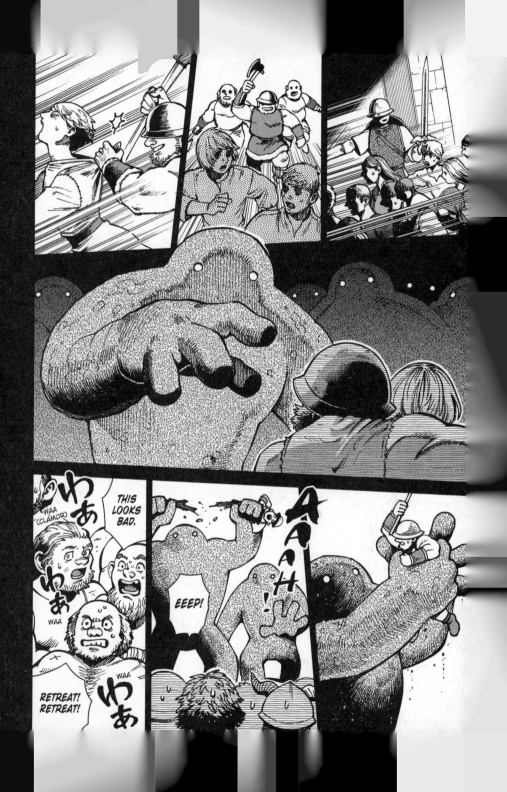

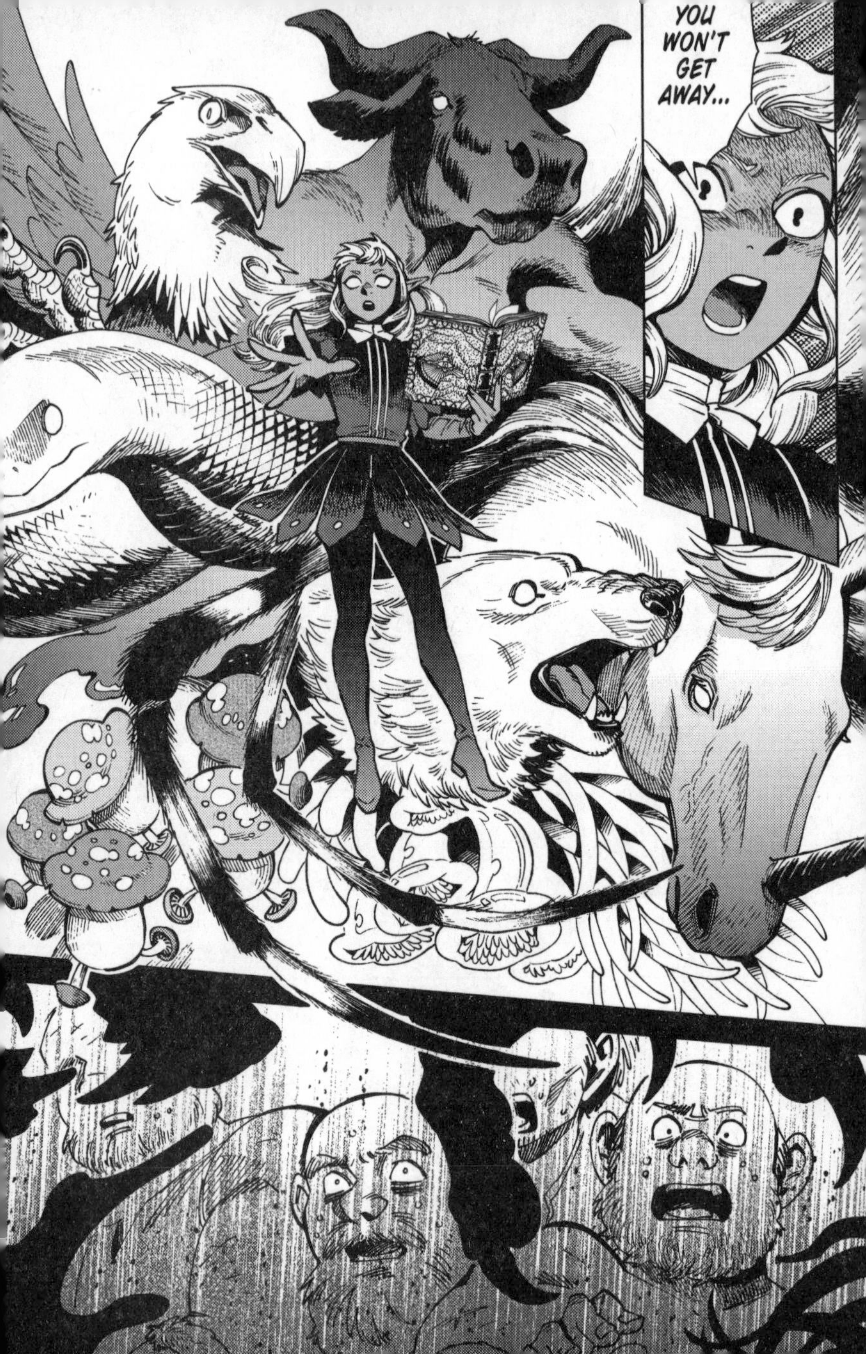
YOU WON'T GET AWAY...

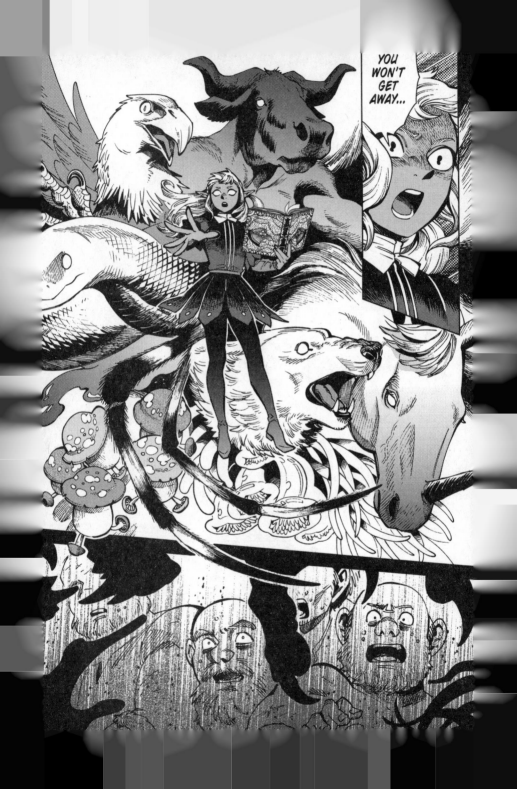

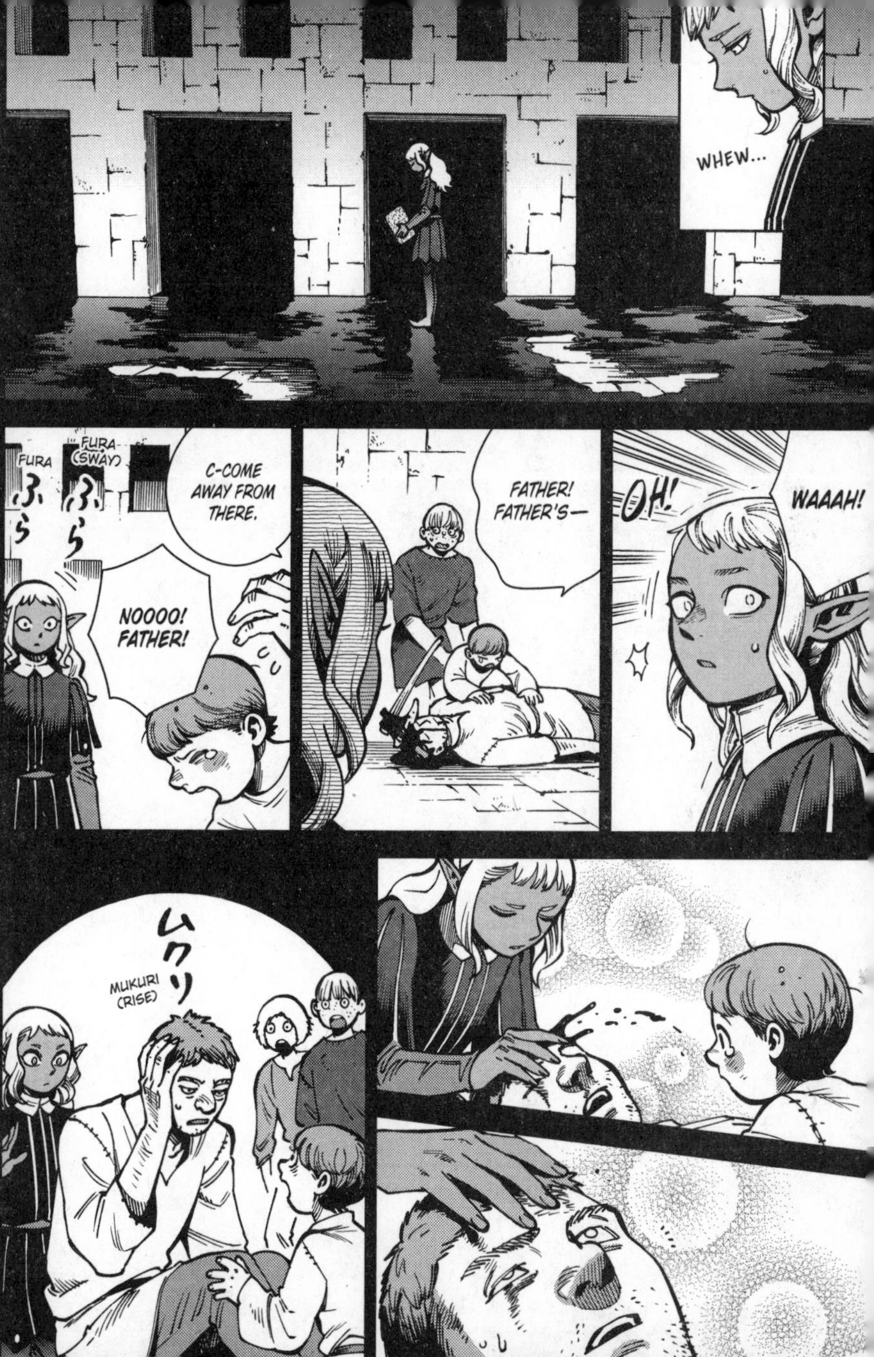

WHEW...
WAAAH!
OH!
FATHER! FATHER'S—
C-COME AWAY FROM THERE.
ふら
FURA (SWAY)
ふら
FURA
NOOOO! FATHER!
ムクリ
MUKURI (RISE)

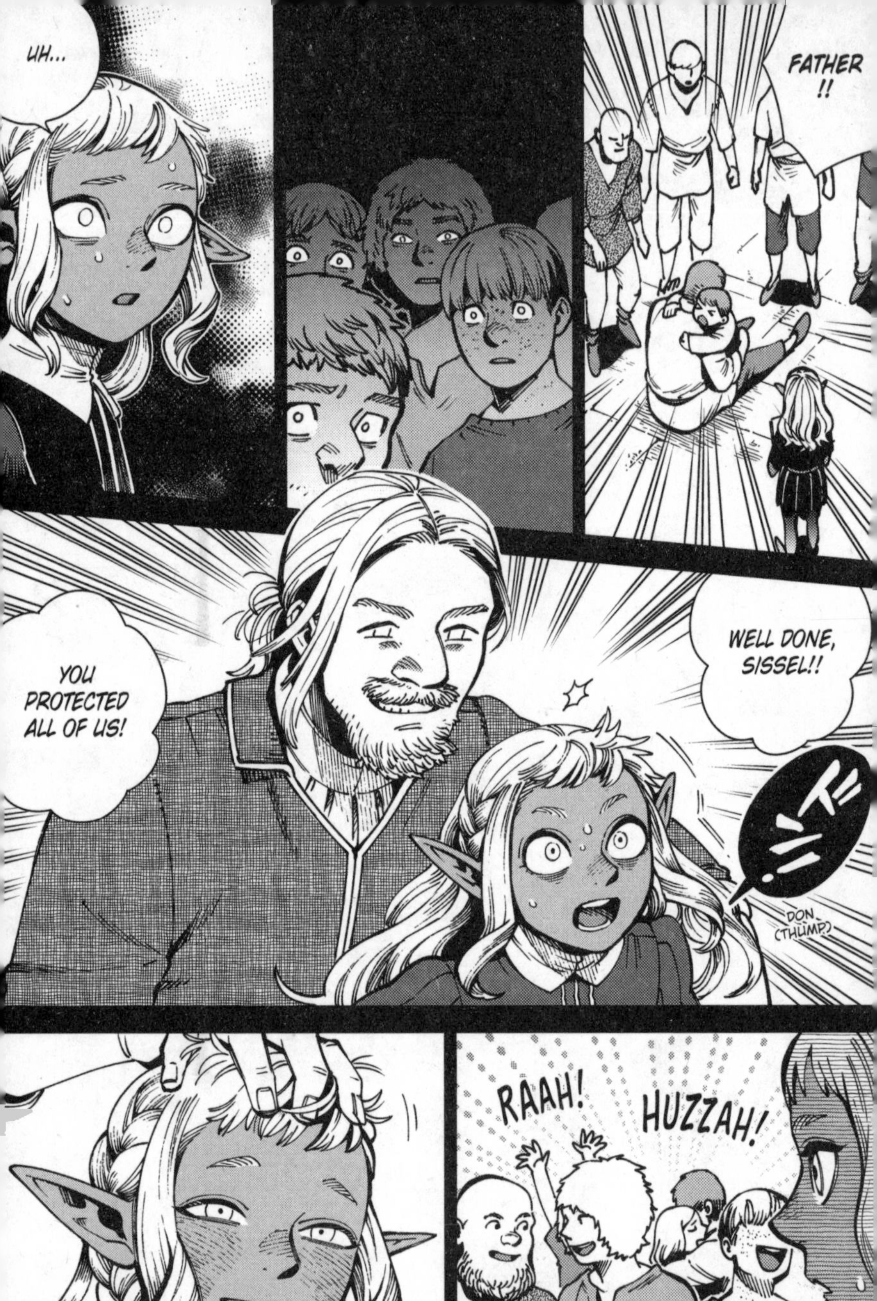
FATHER !!
UH...
WELL DONE, SISSEL!!
DON (THUMP)
YOU PROTECTED ALL OF US!
HUZZAH!
RAAH!

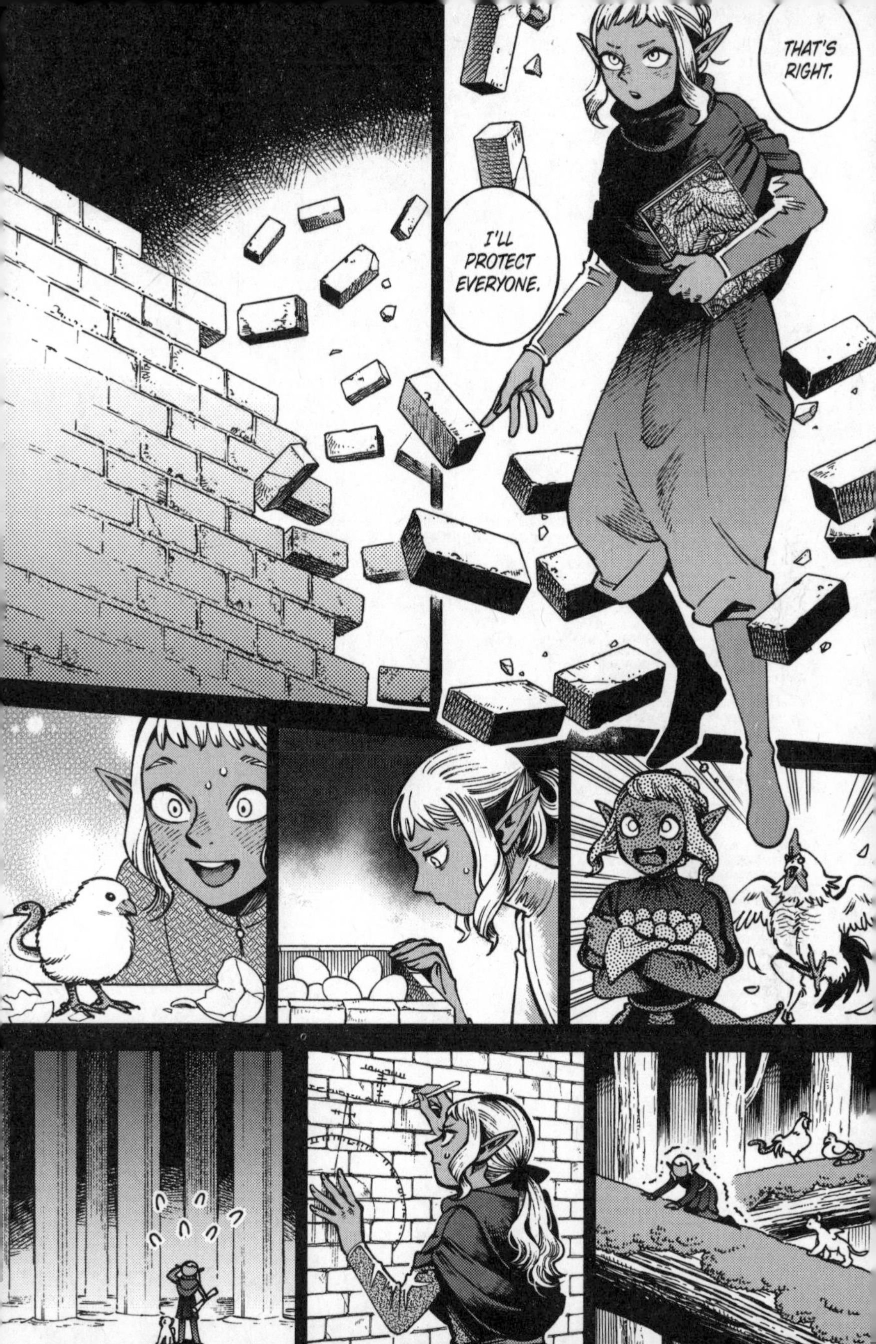
THAT'S RIGHT.
I'LL PROTECT EVERYONE.

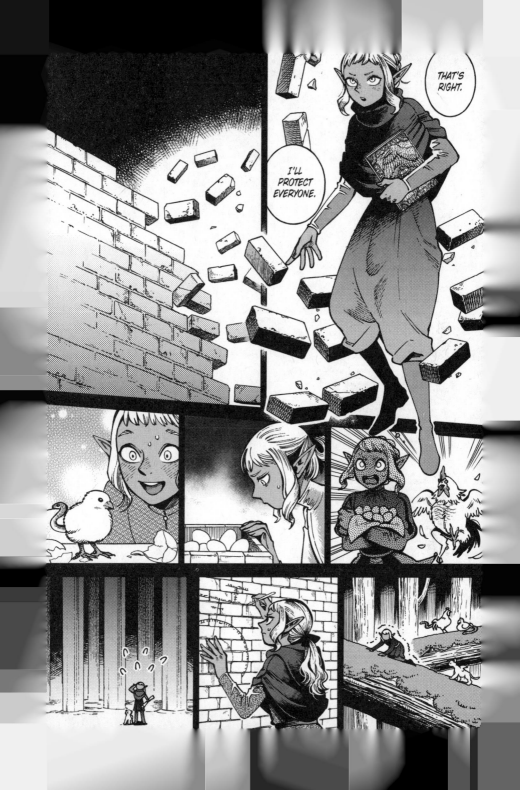

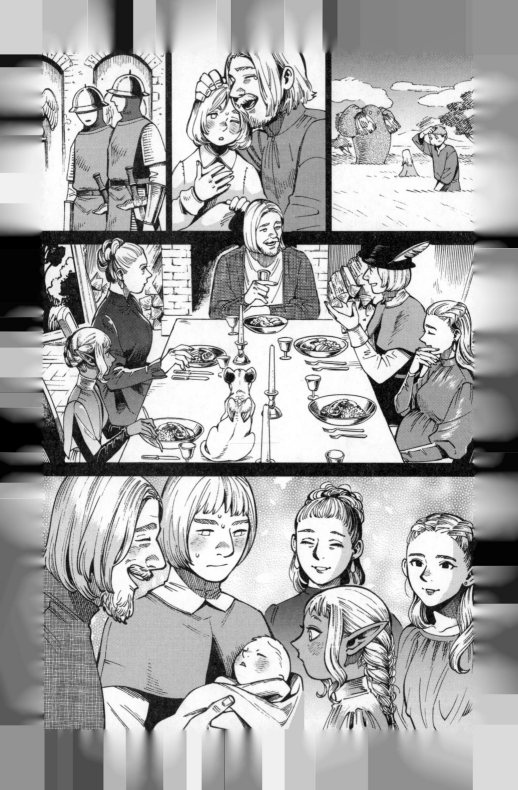

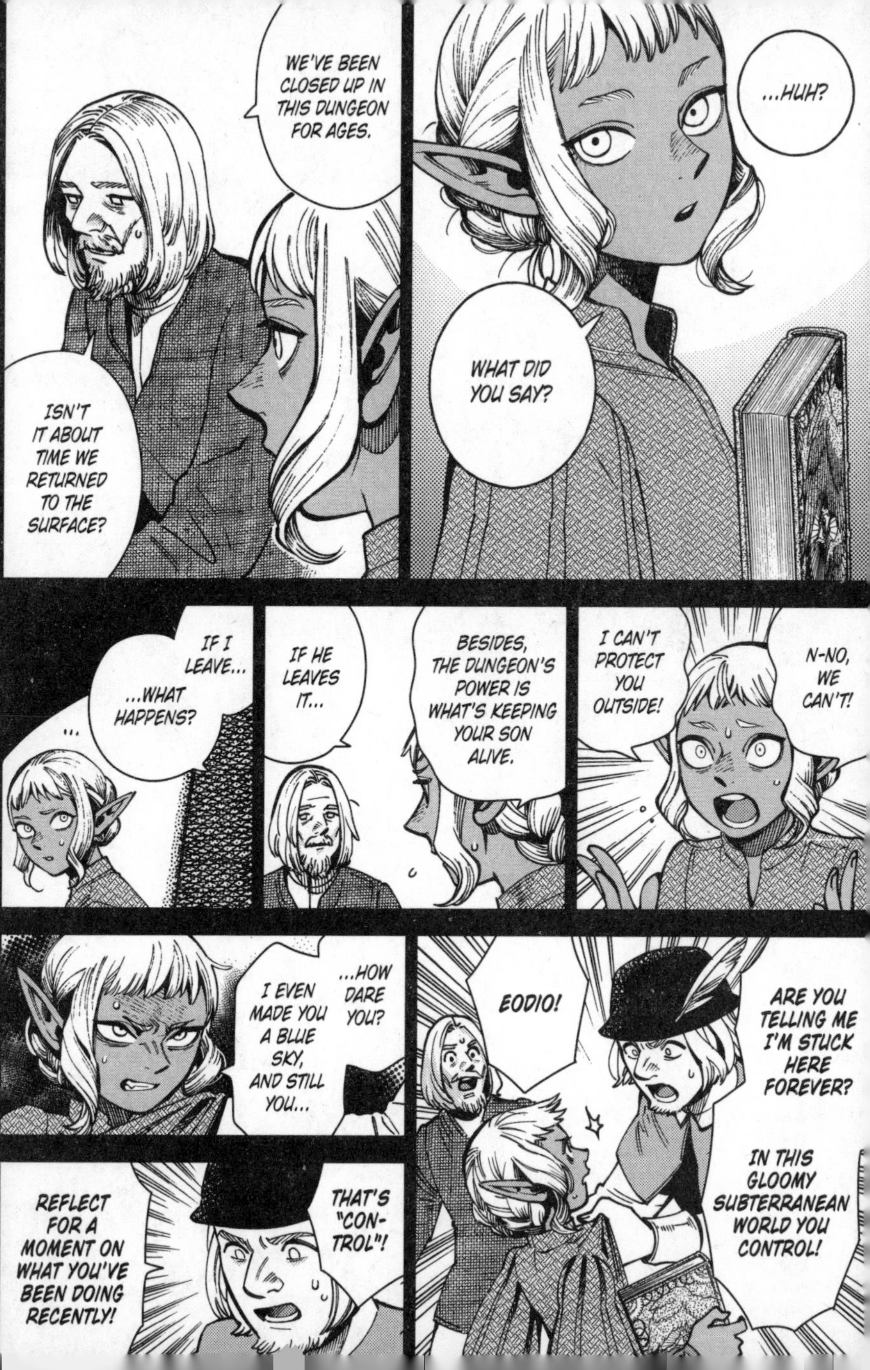

...HUH?
WHAT DID YOU SAY?
WE'VE BEEN CLOSED UP IN THIS DUNGEON FOR AGES.
ISN'T IT ABOUT TIME WE RETURNED TO THE SURFACE?
N-NO, WE CAN'T!
I CAN'T PROTECT YOU OUTSIDE!
BESIDES, THE DUNGEON'S POWER IS WHAT'S KEEPING YOUR SON ALIVE.
IF HE LEAVES IT...
IF I LEAVE...
...WHAT HAPPENS?
...
EODIO!
ARE YOU TELLING ME I'M STUCK HERE FOREVER?
IN THIS GLOOMY SUBTERRANEAN WORLD YOU CONTROL!
...HOW DARE YOU?
I EVEN MADE YOU A BLUE SKY, AND STILL YOU...
THAT'S "CON-TROL"!
REFLECT FOR A MOMENT ON WHAT YOU'VE BEEN DOING RECENTLY!

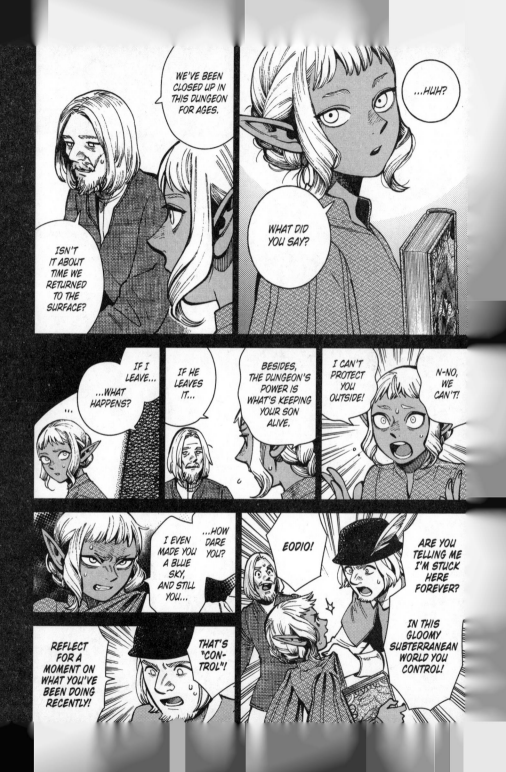

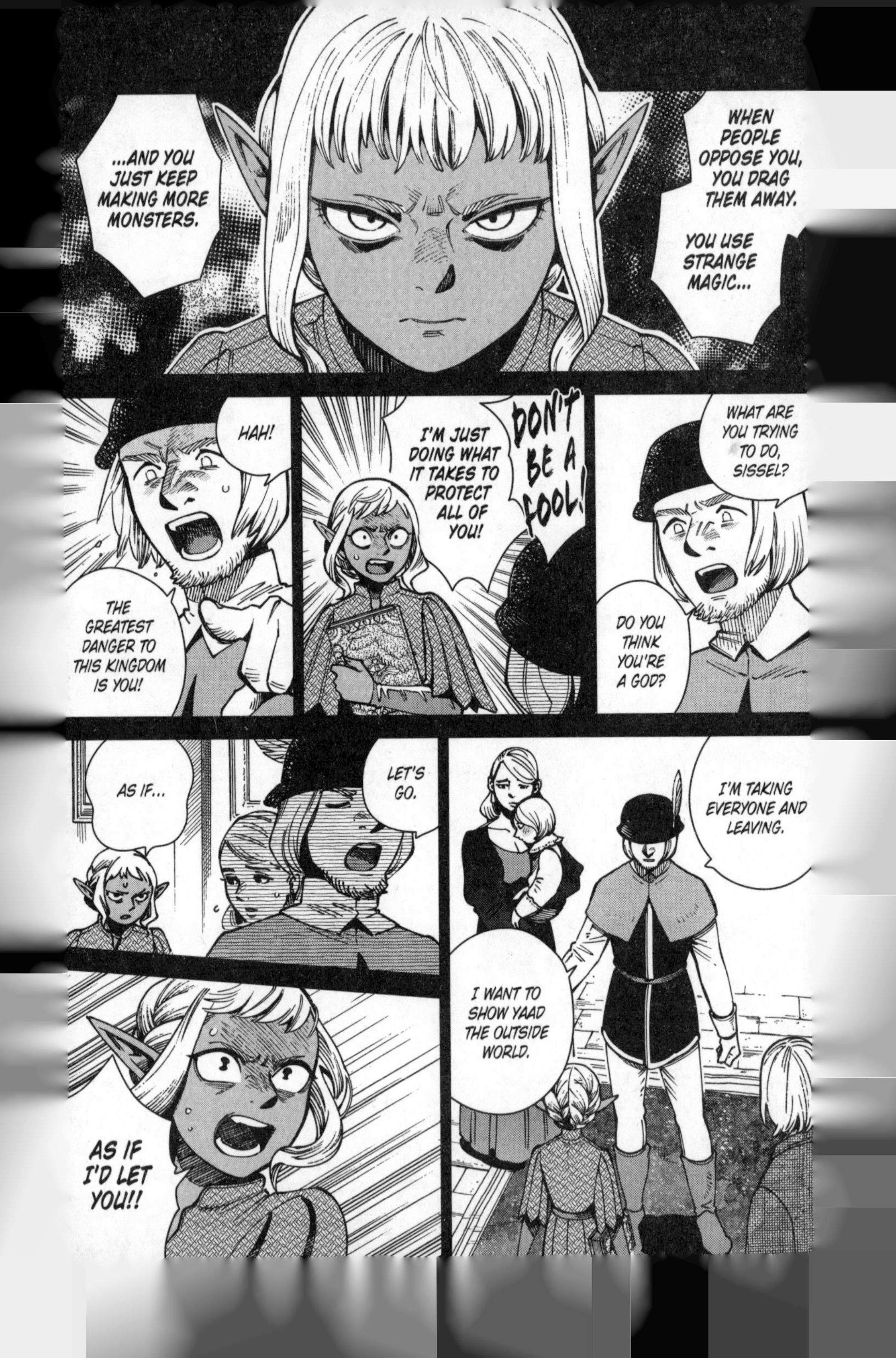
WHEN PEOPLE OPPOSE YOU, YOU DRAG THEM AWAY.
YOU USE STRANGE MAGIC...
...AND YOU JUST KEEP MAKING MORE MONSTERS.
WHAT ARE YOU TRYING TO DO, SISSEL?
DO YOU THINK YOU'RE A GOD?
DON'T BE A FOOL!
I'M JUST DOING WHAT IT TAKES TO PROTECT ALL OF YOU!
HAH!
THE GREATEST DANGER TO THIS KINGDOM IS YOU!
I'M TAKING EVERYONE AND LEAVING.
I WANT TO SHOW YAAD THE OUTSIDE WORLD.
LET'S GO.
AS IF...
AS IF I'D LET YOU!!

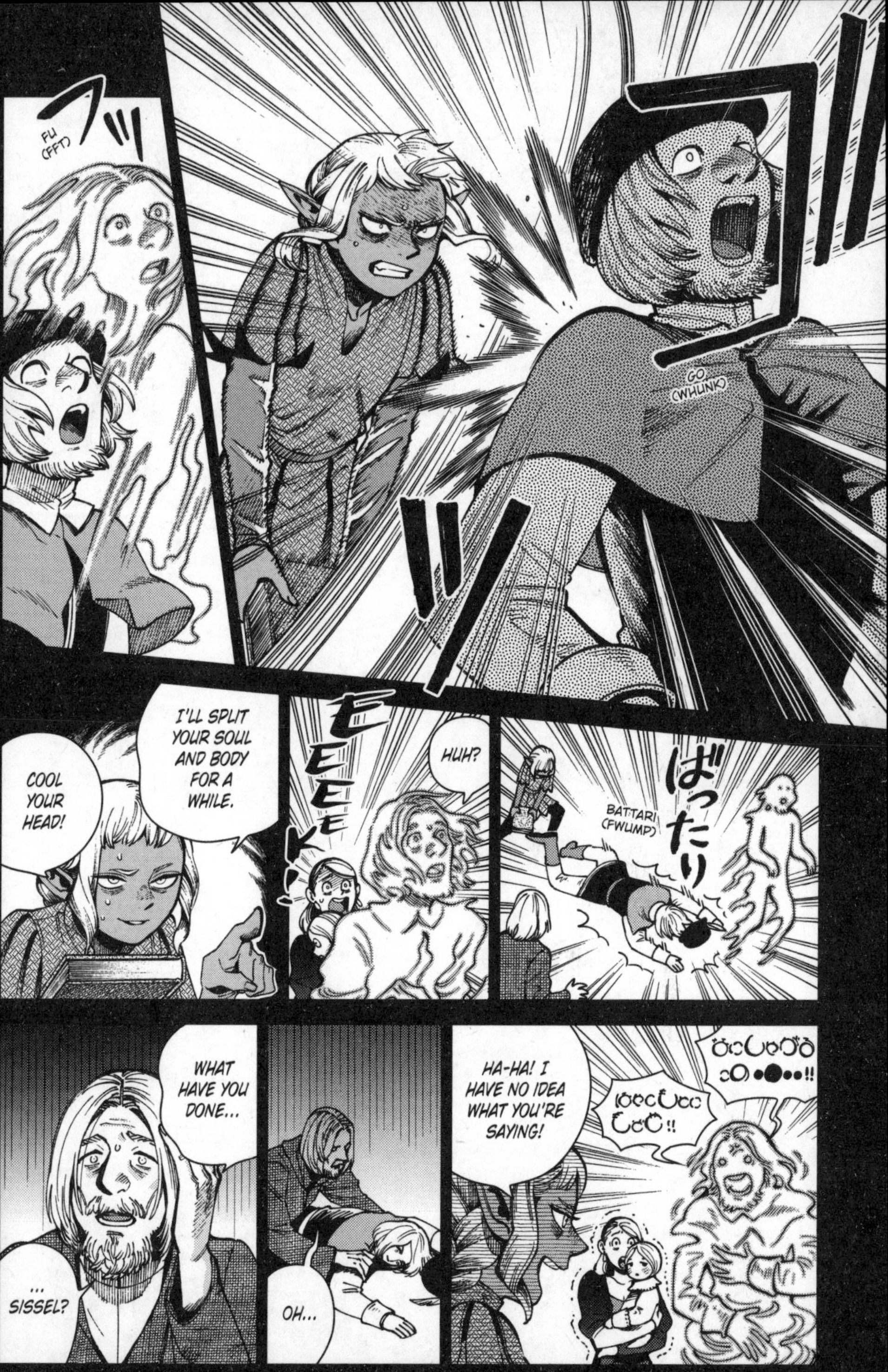
GO (WHUNK)
FU (FFT)
ばったり
BATTARI (FWUMP)
HUH?
EEEEEK
I'LL SPLIT YOUR SOUL AND BODY FOR A WHILE.
COOL YOUR HEAD!
HA-HA! I HAVE NO IDEA WHAT YOU'RE SAYING!
OH...
WHAT HAVE YOU DONE...
...SISSEL?

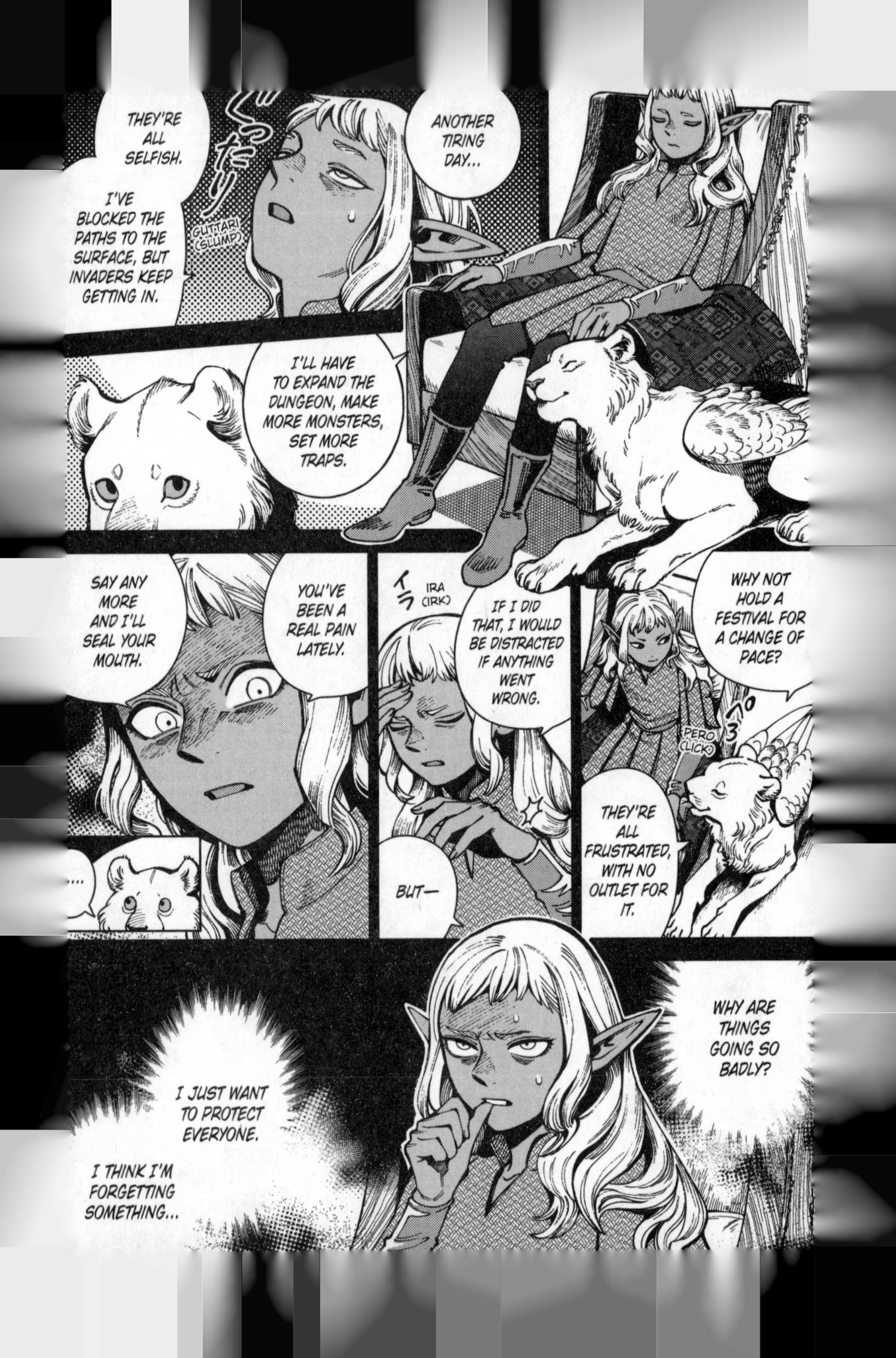
ANOTHER TIRING DAY...
GUTTARI (SLUMP)
THEY'RE ALL SELFISH.
I'VE BLOCKED THE PATHS TO THE SURFACE, BUT INVADERS KEEP GETTING IN.
I'LL HAVE TO EXPAND THE DUNGEON, MAKE MORE MONSTERS, SET MORE TRAPS.
WHY NOT HOLD A FESTIVAL FOR A CHANGE OF PACE?
PERO (LICK)
THEY'RE ALL FRUSTRATED, WITH NO OUTLET FOR IT.
IRA (IRK)
IF I DID THAT, I WOULD BE DISTRACTED IF ANYTHING WENT WRONG.
BUT—
YOU'VE BEEN A REAL PAIN LATELY.
SAY ANY MORE AND I'LL SEAL YOUR MOUTH.
....
WHY ARE THINGS GOING SO BADLY?
I JUST WANT TO PROTECT EVERYONE.
I THINK I'M FORGETTING SOMETHING...

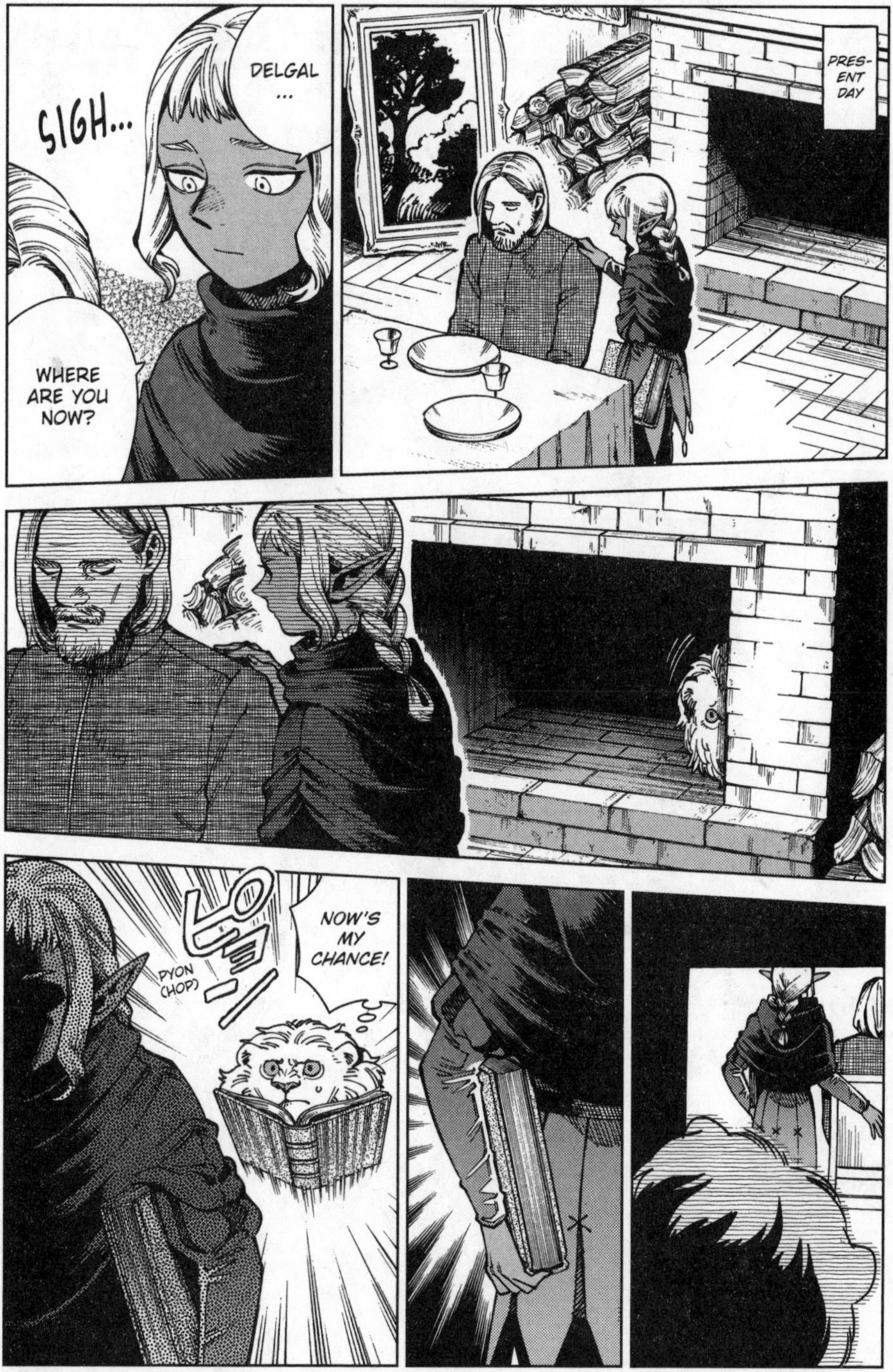
PRESENT DAY
DELGAL ...
SIGH...
WHERE ARE YOU NOW?
NOW'S MY CHANCE!
PYON (HOP)

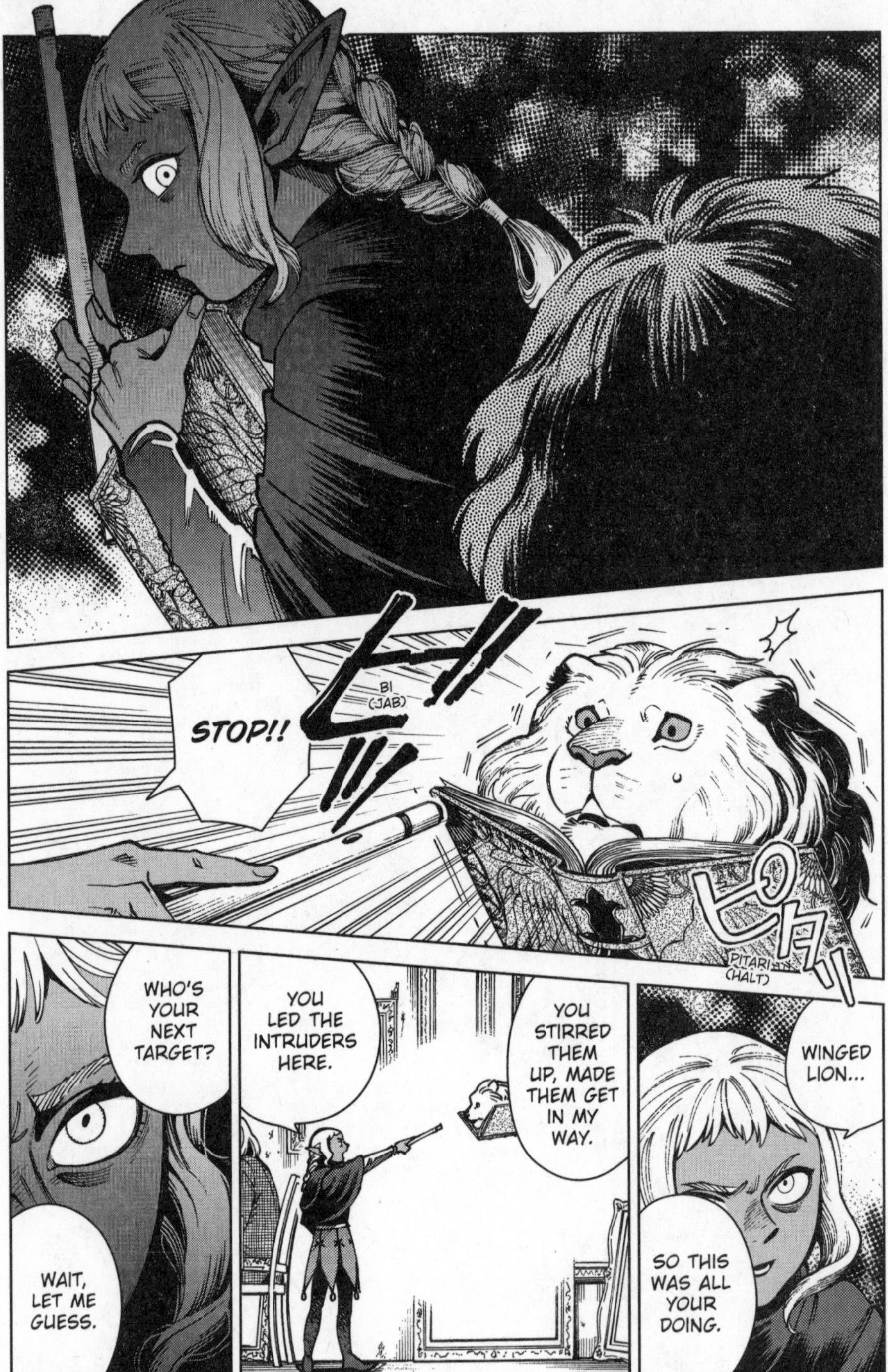
BI (JAB)
STOP!!
PITARI (HALT)
WINGED LION...
SO THIS WAS ALL YOUR DOING.
YOU STIRRED THEM UP, MADE THEM GET IN MY WAY.
YOU LED THE INTRUDERS HERE.
WHO'S YOUR NEXT TARGET?
WAIT, LET ME GUESS.

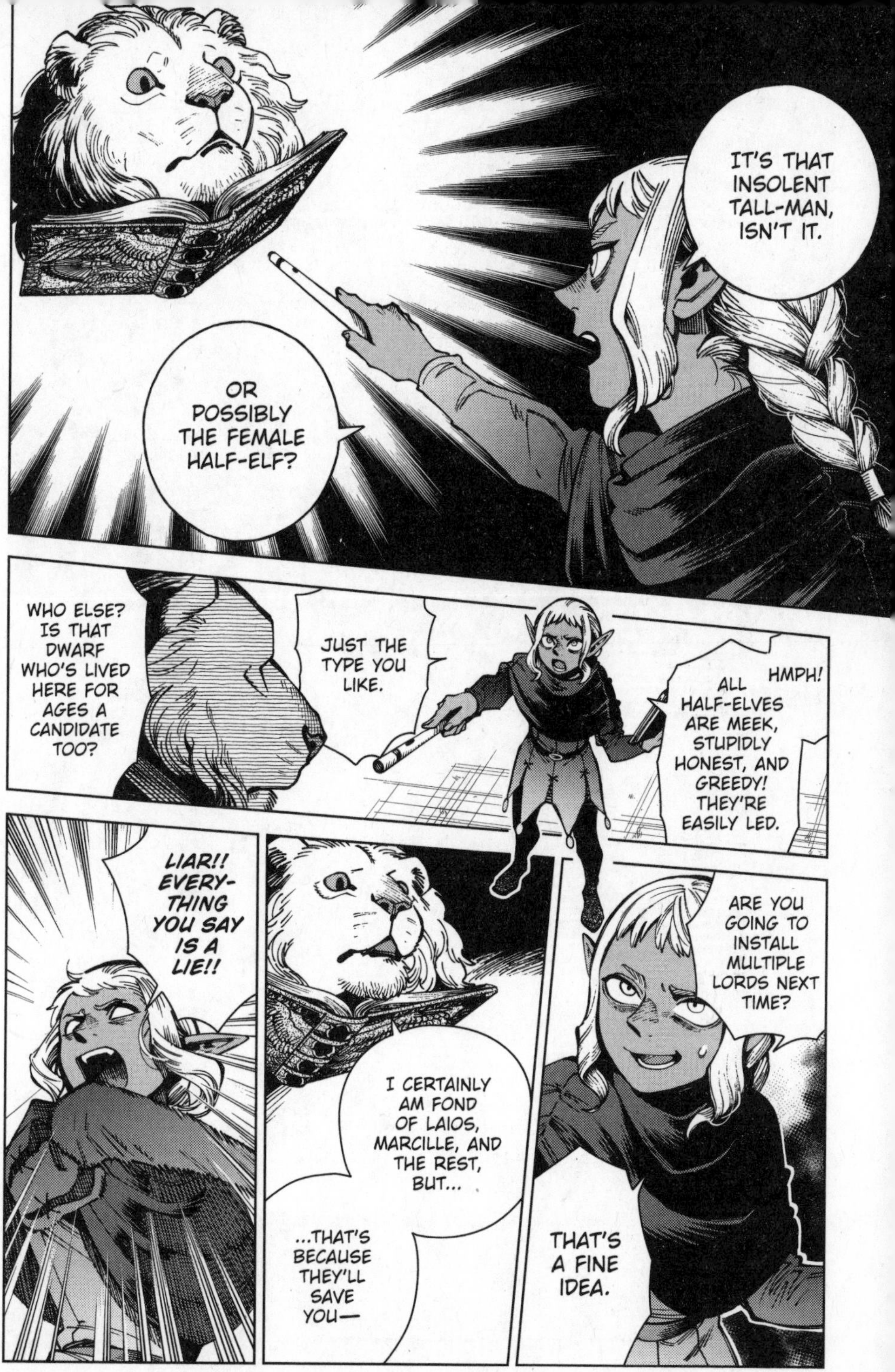
IT'S THAT INSOLENT TALL-MAN, ISN'T IT.
OR POSSIBLY THE FEMALE HALF-ELF?
HMPH!
ALL HALF-ELVES ARE MEEK, STUPIDLY HONEST, AND GREEDY! THEY'RE EASILY LED.
JUST THE TYPE YOU LIKE.
WHO ELSE? IS THAT DWARF WHO'S LIVED HERE FOR AGES A CANDIDATE TOO?
ARE YOU GOING TO INSTALL MULTIPLE LORDS NEXT TIME?
THAT'S A FINE IDEA.
I CERTAINLY AM FOND OF LAIOS, MARCILLE, AND THE REST, BUT...
...THAT'S BECAUSE THEY'LL SAVE YOU—
LIAR!! EVERY-THING YOU SAY IS A LIE!!

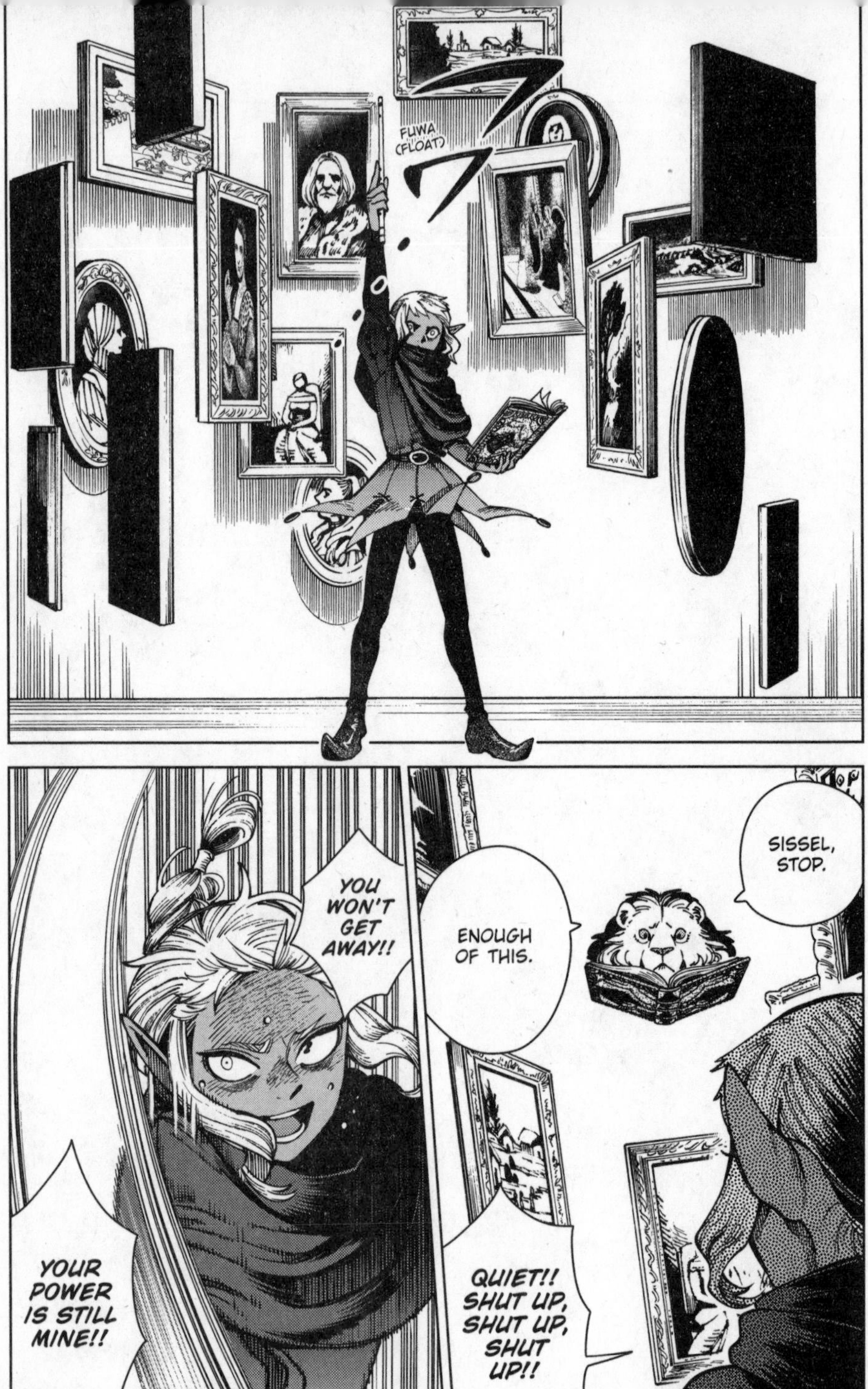
FUWA (FLOAT)
SISSEL, STOP.
ENOUGH OF THIS.
QUIET!! SHUT UP, SHUT UP, SHUT UP!!
YOU WON'T GET AWAY!!
YOUR POWER IS STILL MINE!!

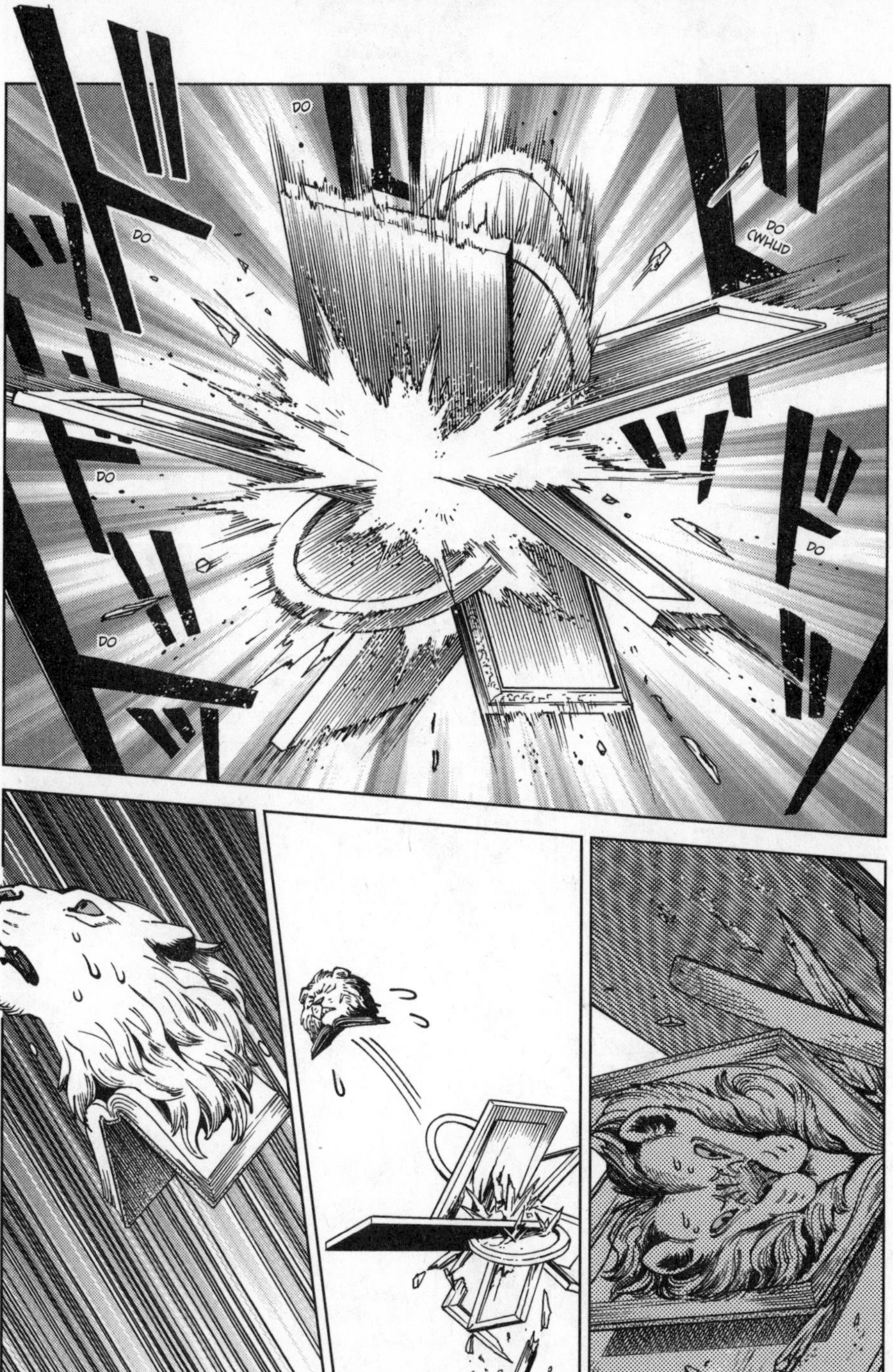
DO
CWHUD
DO
DO
DO
DO
DO

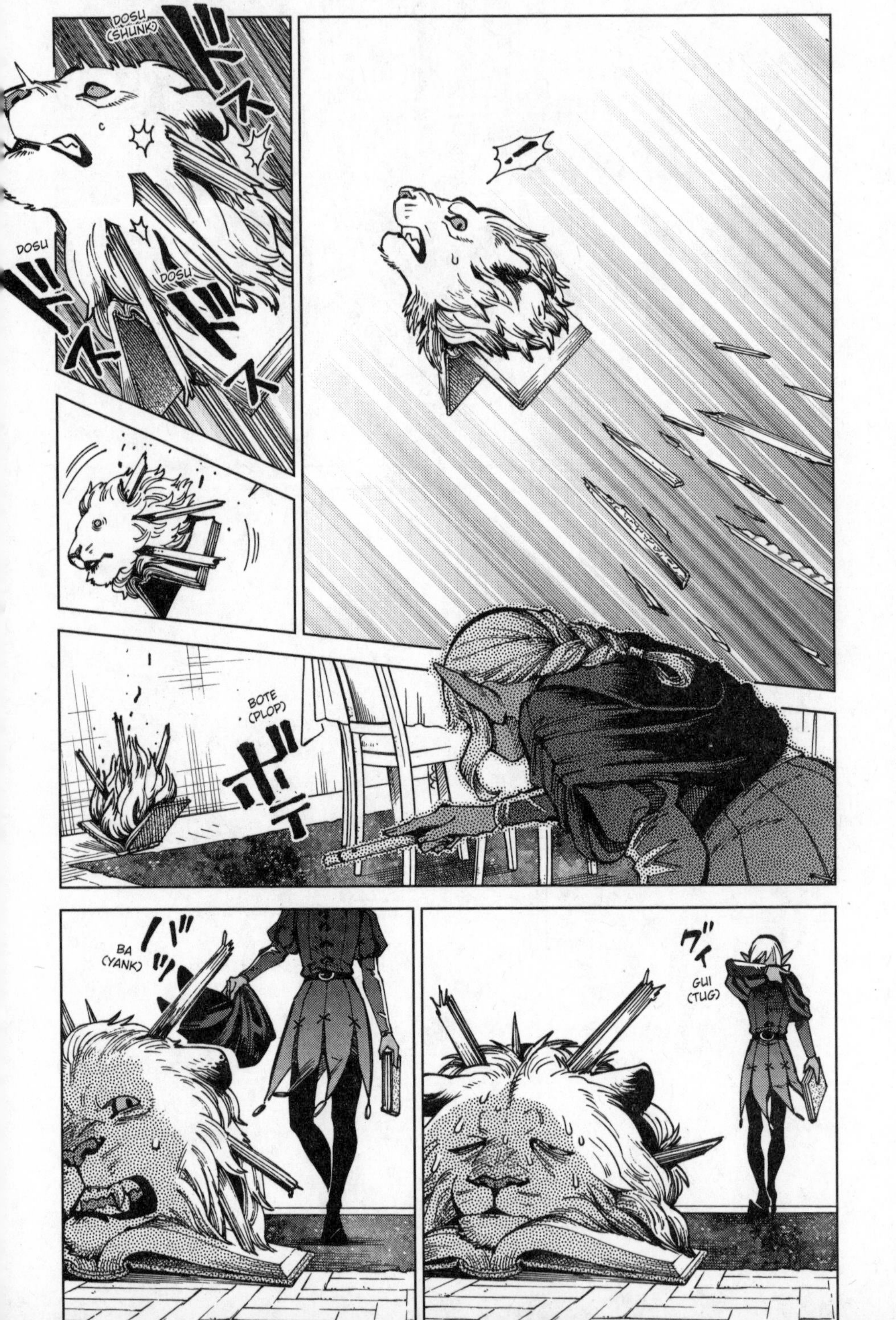
!
ドス
DOSU (SHUNK)
ドス
DOSU
ドス
DOSU
ボテ
BOTE (PLOP)
グイ
GUI (TUG)
バッ
BA (YANK)

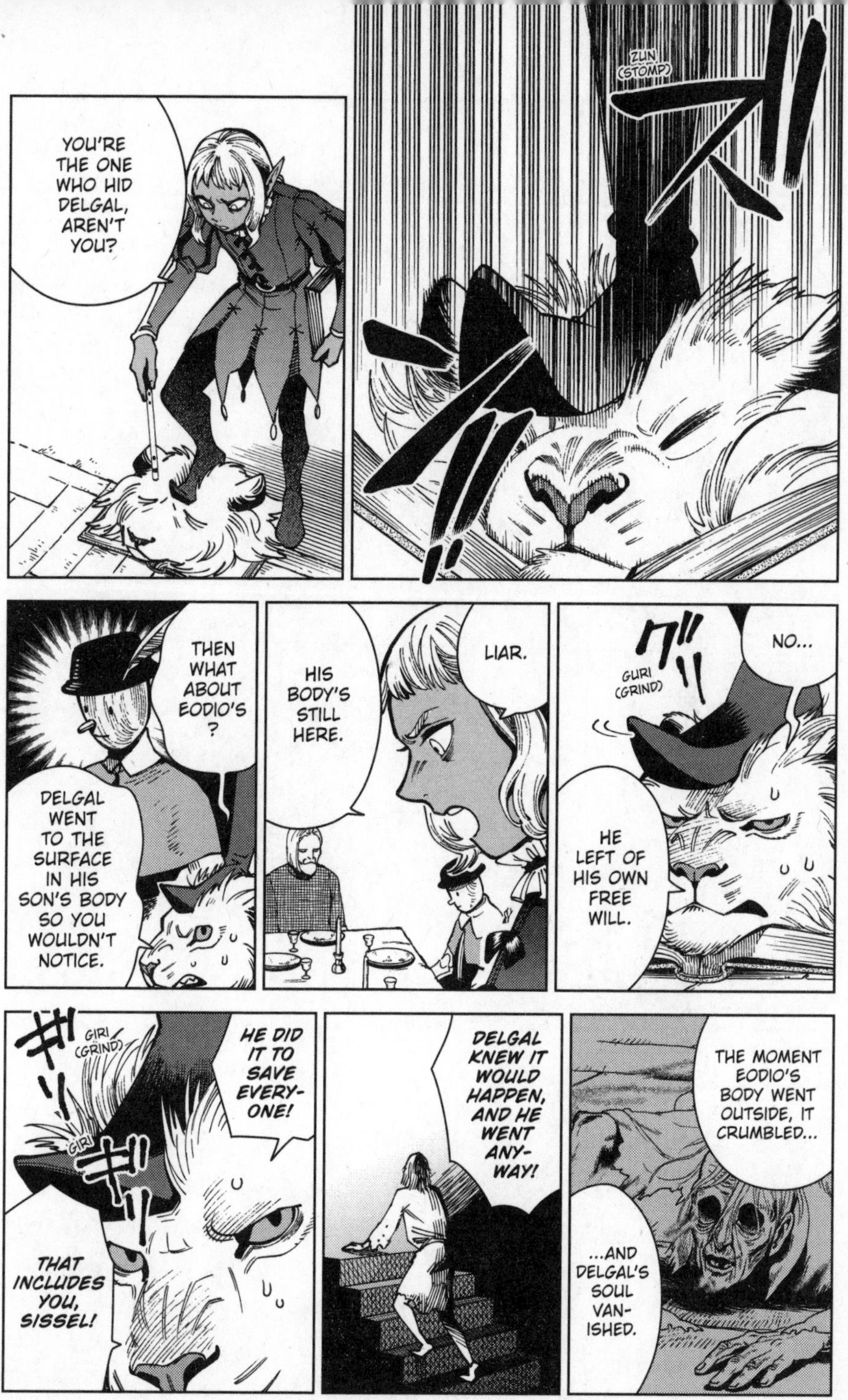
ZUN (STOMP)
YOU'RE THE ONE WHO HID DELGAL, AREN'T YOU?
NO...
GURI (GRIND)
HE LEFT OF HIS OWN FREE WILL.
LIAR.
HIS BODY'S STILL HERE.
THEN WHAT ABOUT EODIO'S?
DELGAL WENT TO THE SURFACE IN HIS SON'S BODY SO YOU WOULDN'T NOTICE.
THE MOMENT EODIO'S BODY WENT OUTSIDE, IT CRUMBLED...
...AND DELGAL'S SOUL VANISHED.
DELGAL KNEW IT WOULD HAPPEN, AND HE WENT ANYWAY!
HE DID IT TO SAVE EVERYONE!
GIRI (GRIND)
GIRI
THAT INCLUDES YOU, SISSEL!

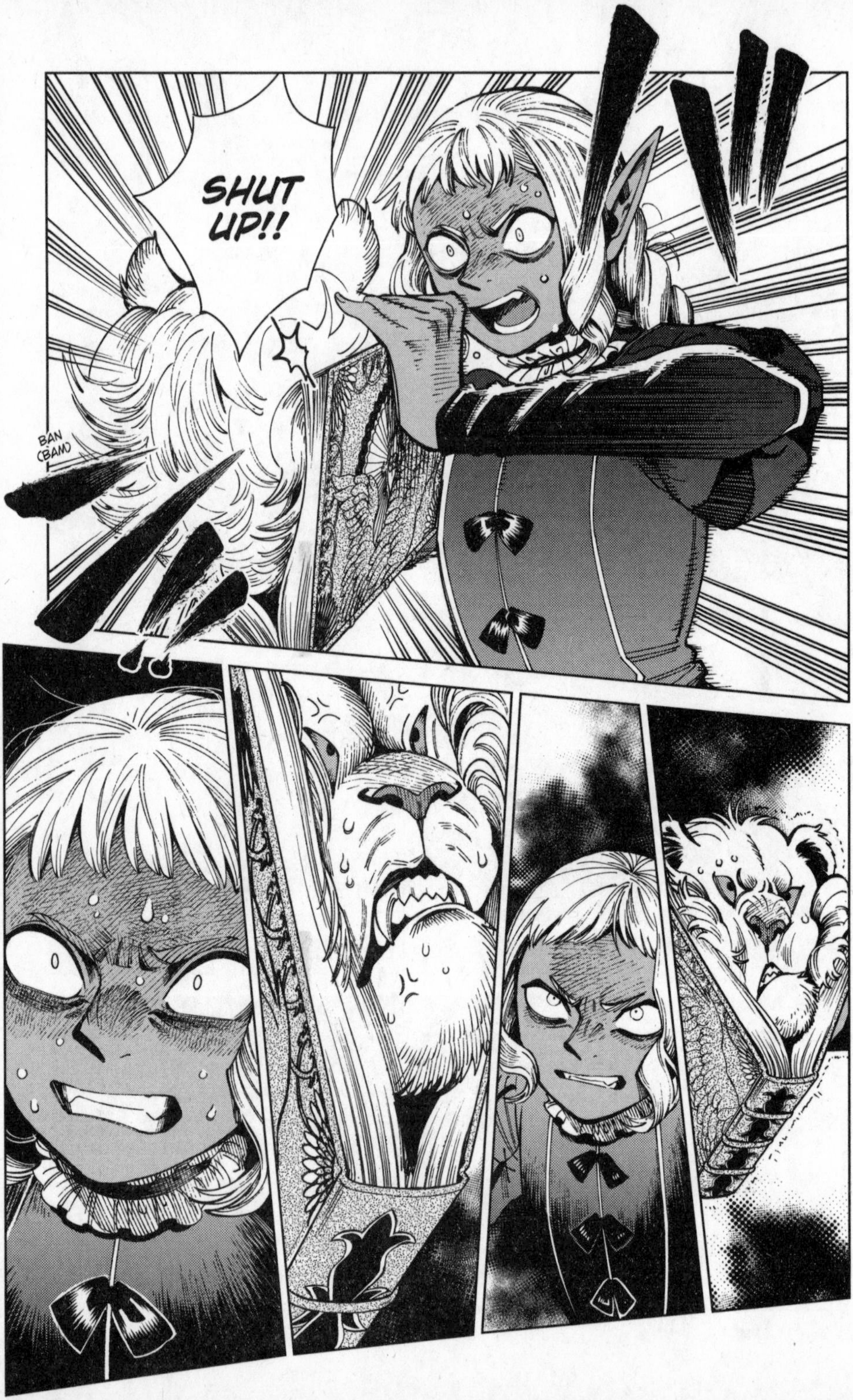
SHUT UP!!
BAN (BAM)

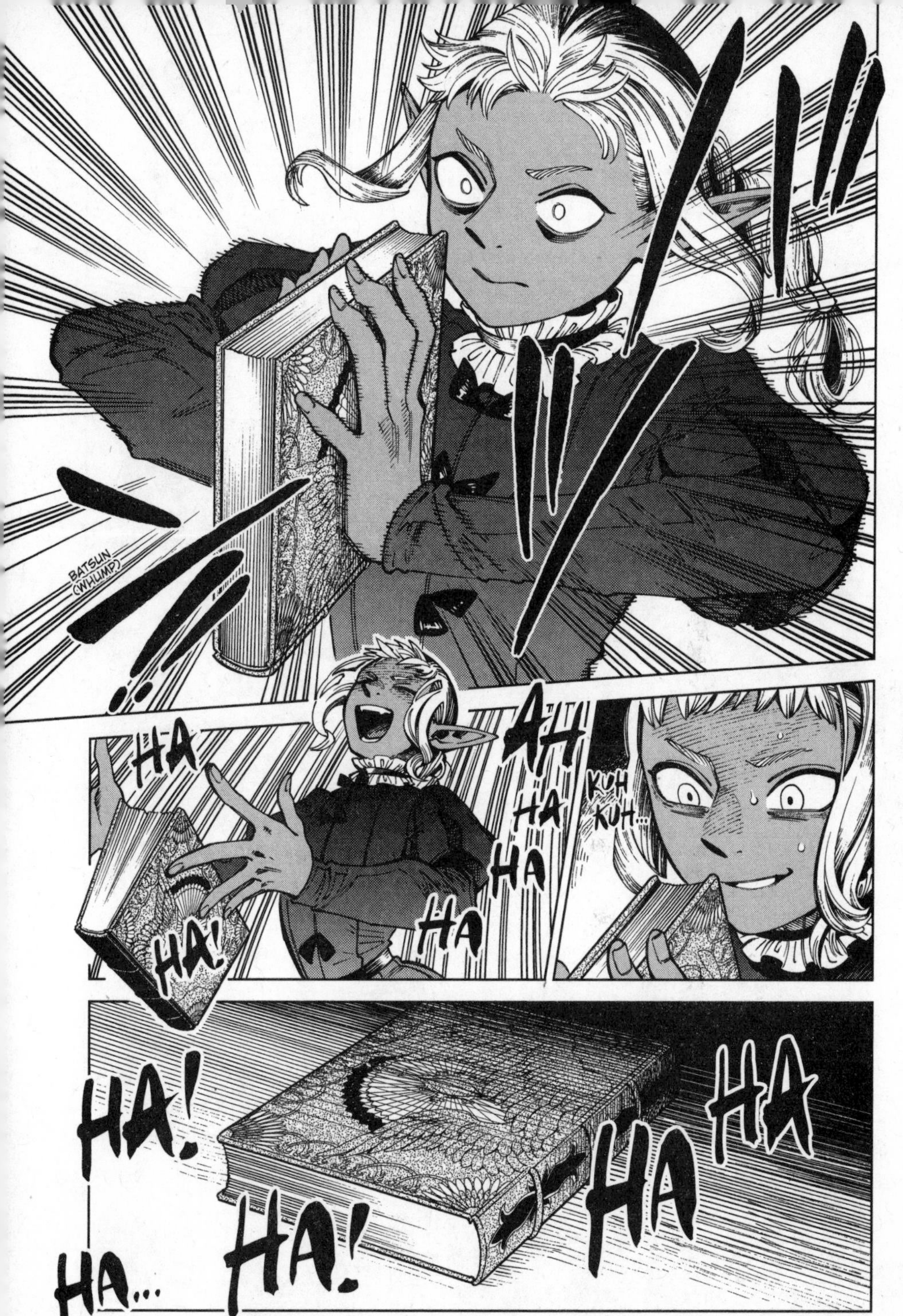
BATSUN
(WHUMP)
KUH
KUH...
AH
HA
HA
HA
HA
HA!
HA
HA
HA
HA!
HA!
HA...

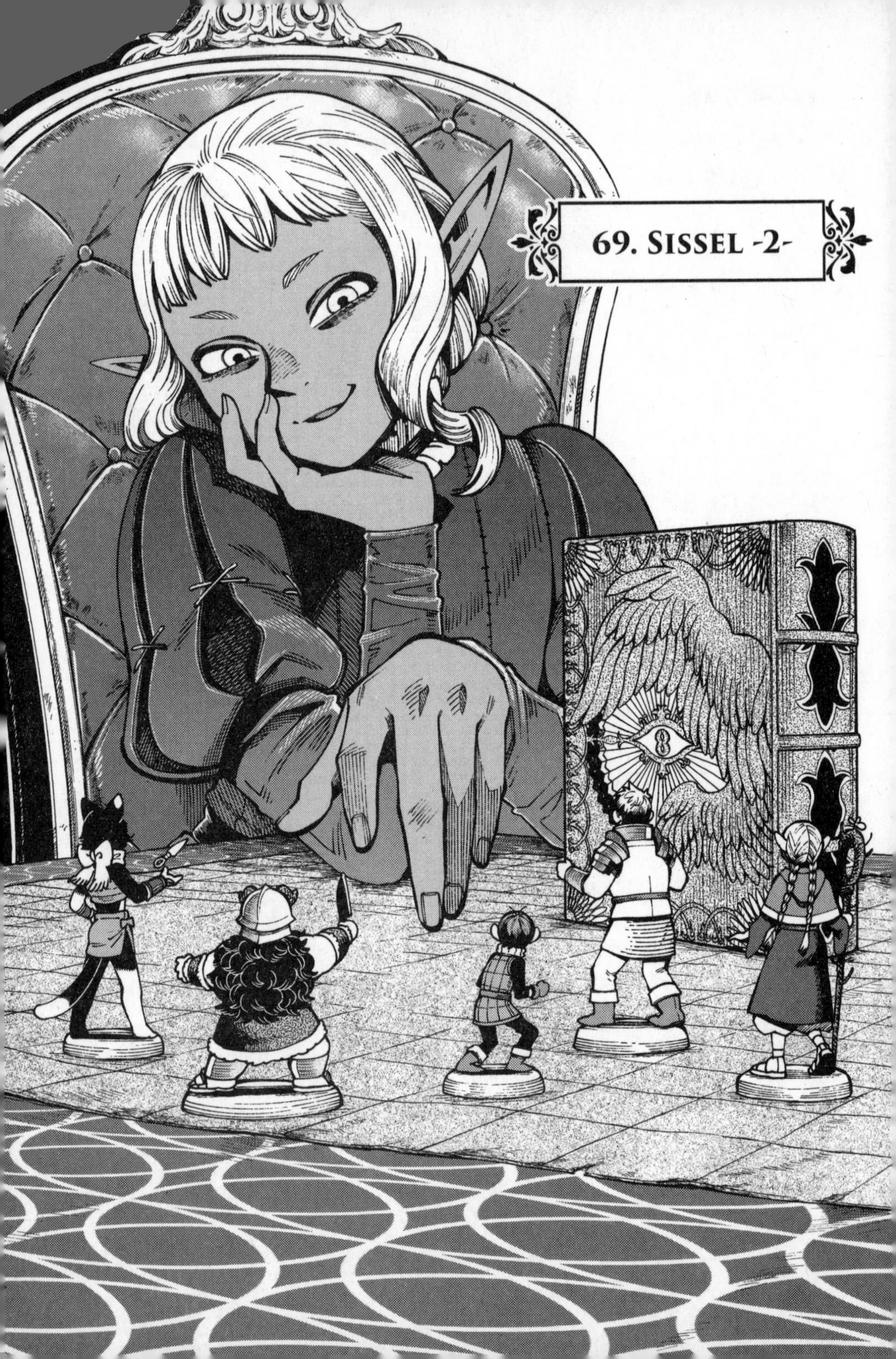
69. SISSEL -2-

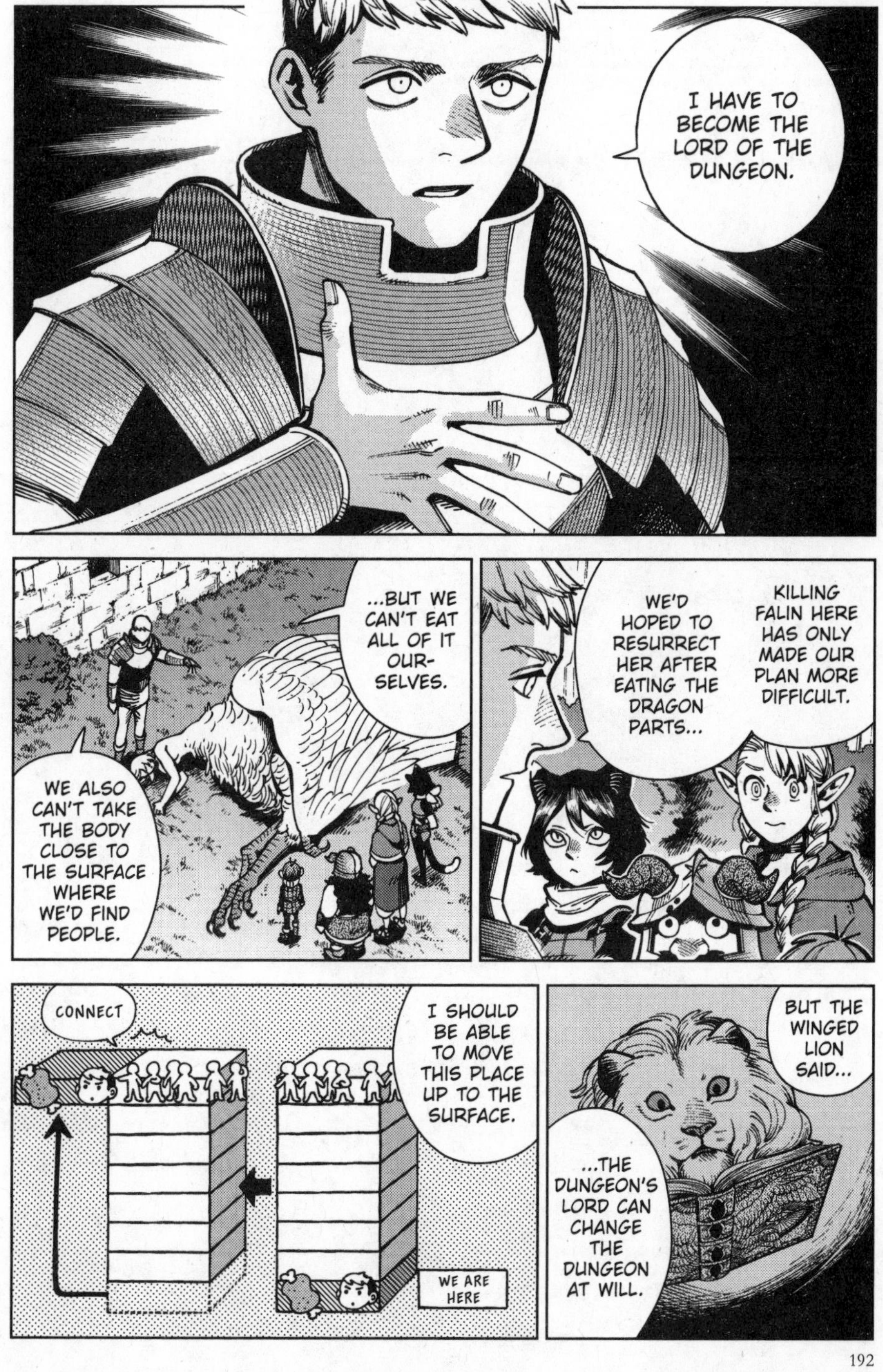
I HAVE TO BECOME THE LORD OF THE DUNGEON.
KILLING FALIN HERE HAS ONLY MADE OUR PLAN MORE DIFFICULT.
WE'D HOPED TO RESURRECT HER AFTER EATING THE DRAGON PARTS...
...BUT WE CAN'T EAT ALL OF IT OUR-SELVES.
WE ALSO CAN'T TAKE THE BODY CLOSE TO THE SURFACE WHERE WE'D FIND PEOPLE.
BUT THE WINGED LION SAID...
...THE DUNGEON'S LORD CAN CHANGE THE DUNGEON AT WILL.
I SHOULD BE ABLE TO MOVE THIS PLACE UP TO THE SURFACE.
CONNECT
WE ARE HERE

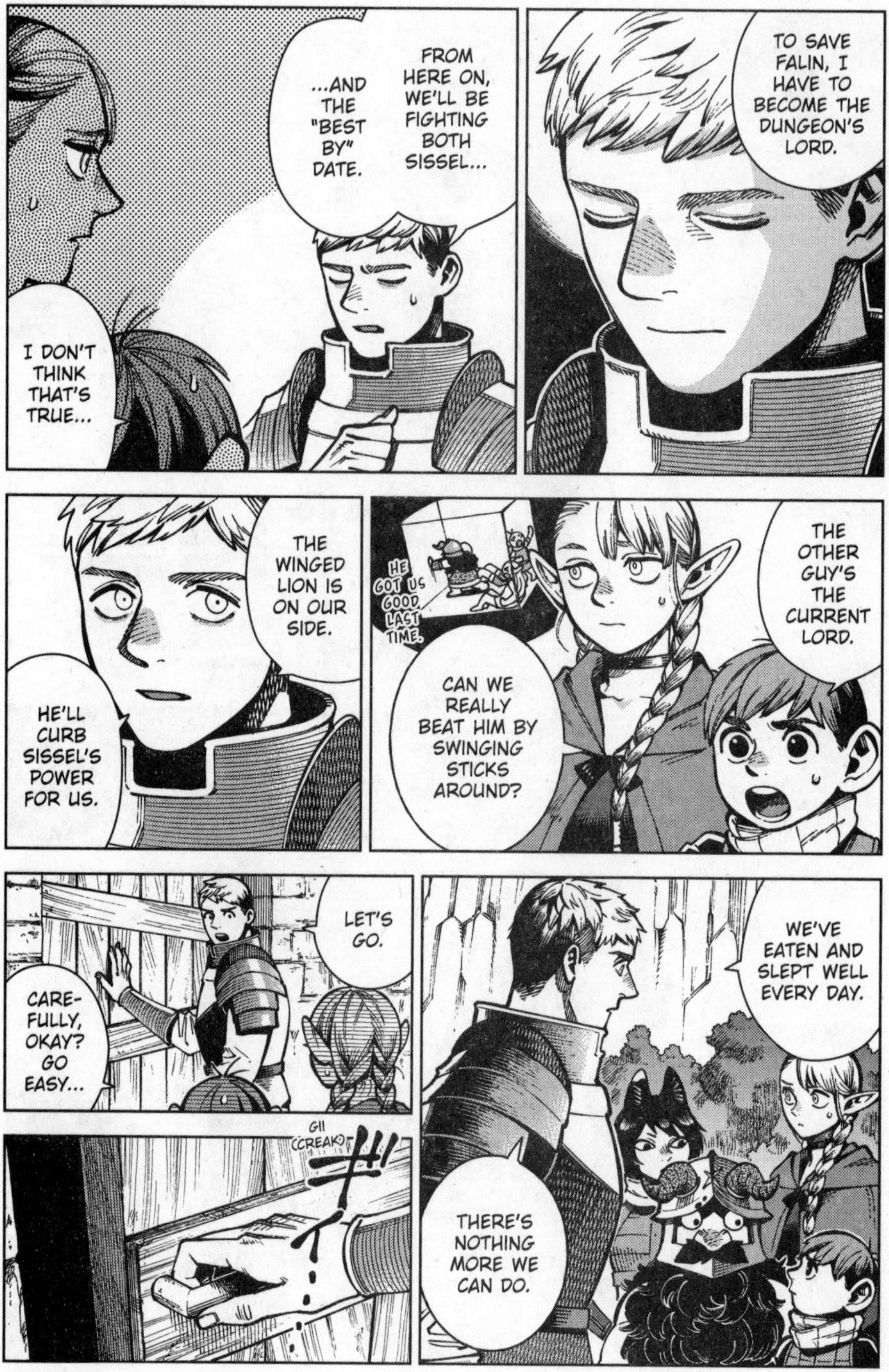
TO SAVE FALIN, I HAVE TO BECOME THE DUNGEON'S LORD.
FROM HERE ON, WE'LL BE FIGHTING BOTH SISSEL...
...AND THE "BEST BY" DATE.
I DON'T THINK THAT'S TRUE...
THE OTHER GUY'S THE CURRENT LORD.
CAN WE REALLY BEAT HIM BY SWINGING STICKS AROUND?
HE GOT US GOOD LAST TIME.
THE WINGED LION IS ON OUR SIDE.
HE'LL CURB SISSEL'S POWER FOR US.
WE'VE EATEN AND SLEPT WELL EVERY DAY.
THERE'S NOTHING MORE WE CAN DO.
LET'S GO.
CAREFULLY, OKAY? GO EASY...
GII (CREAK)

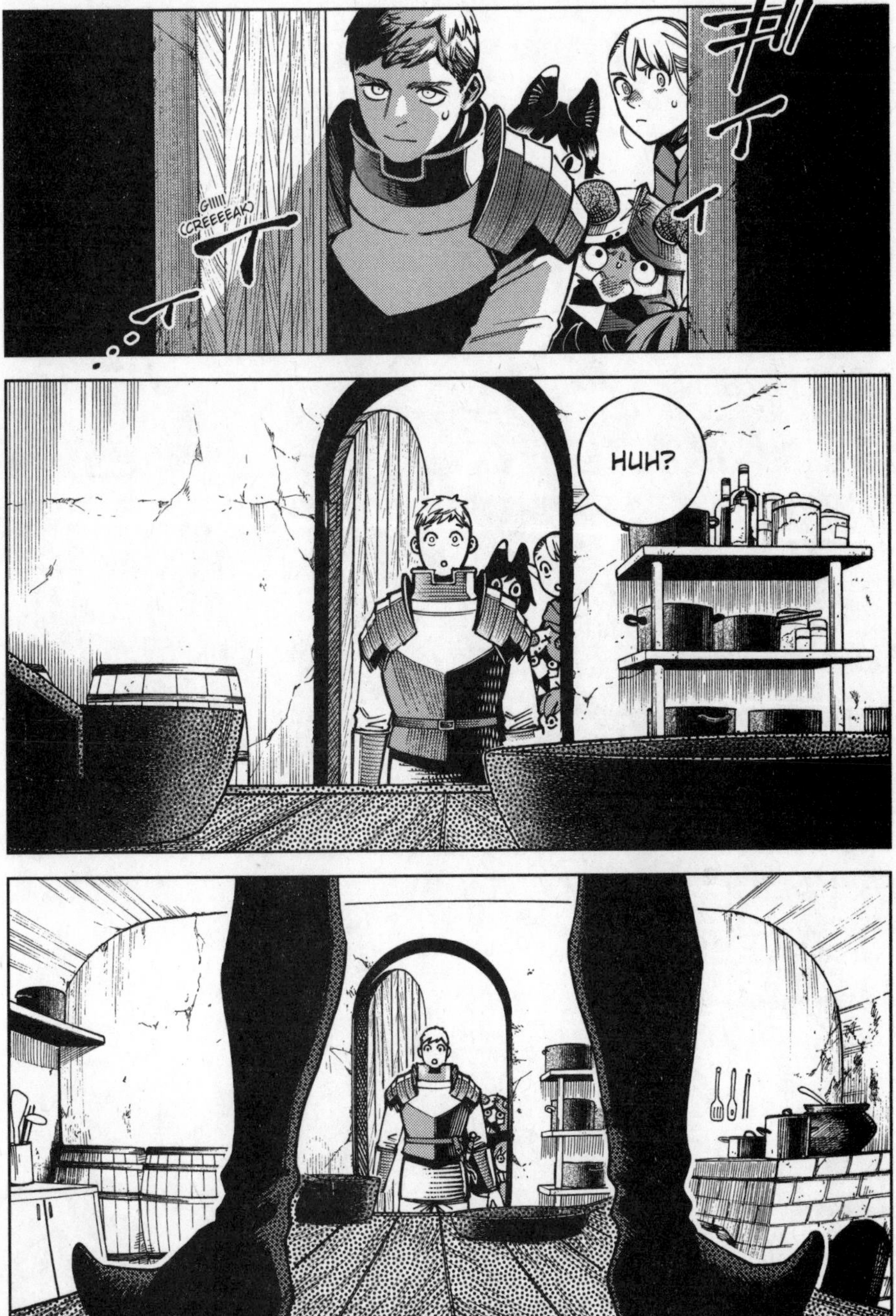
GIIII (CREEEEAK)
HUH?

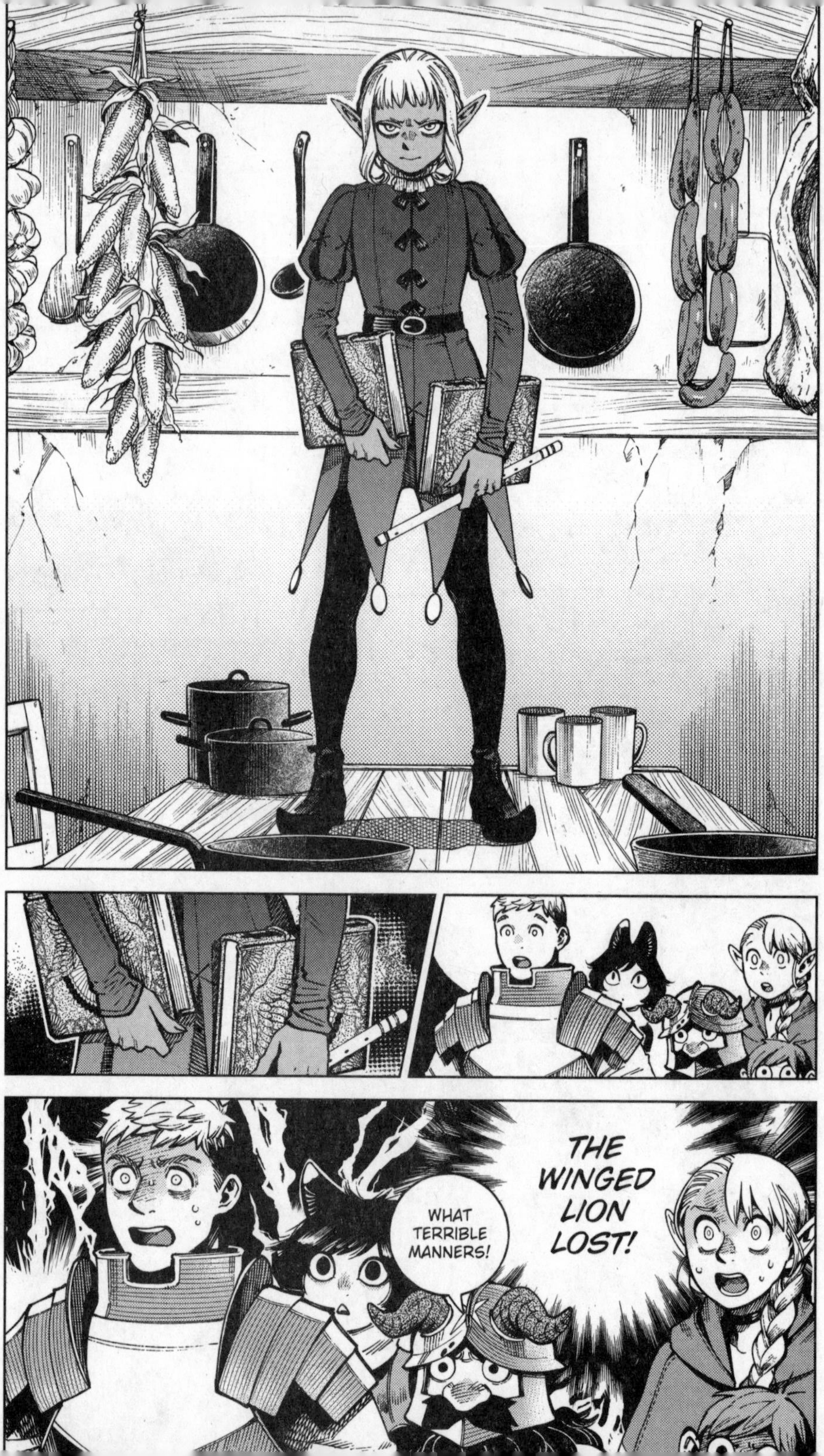
THE WINGED LION LOST!
WHAT TERRIBLE MANNERS!

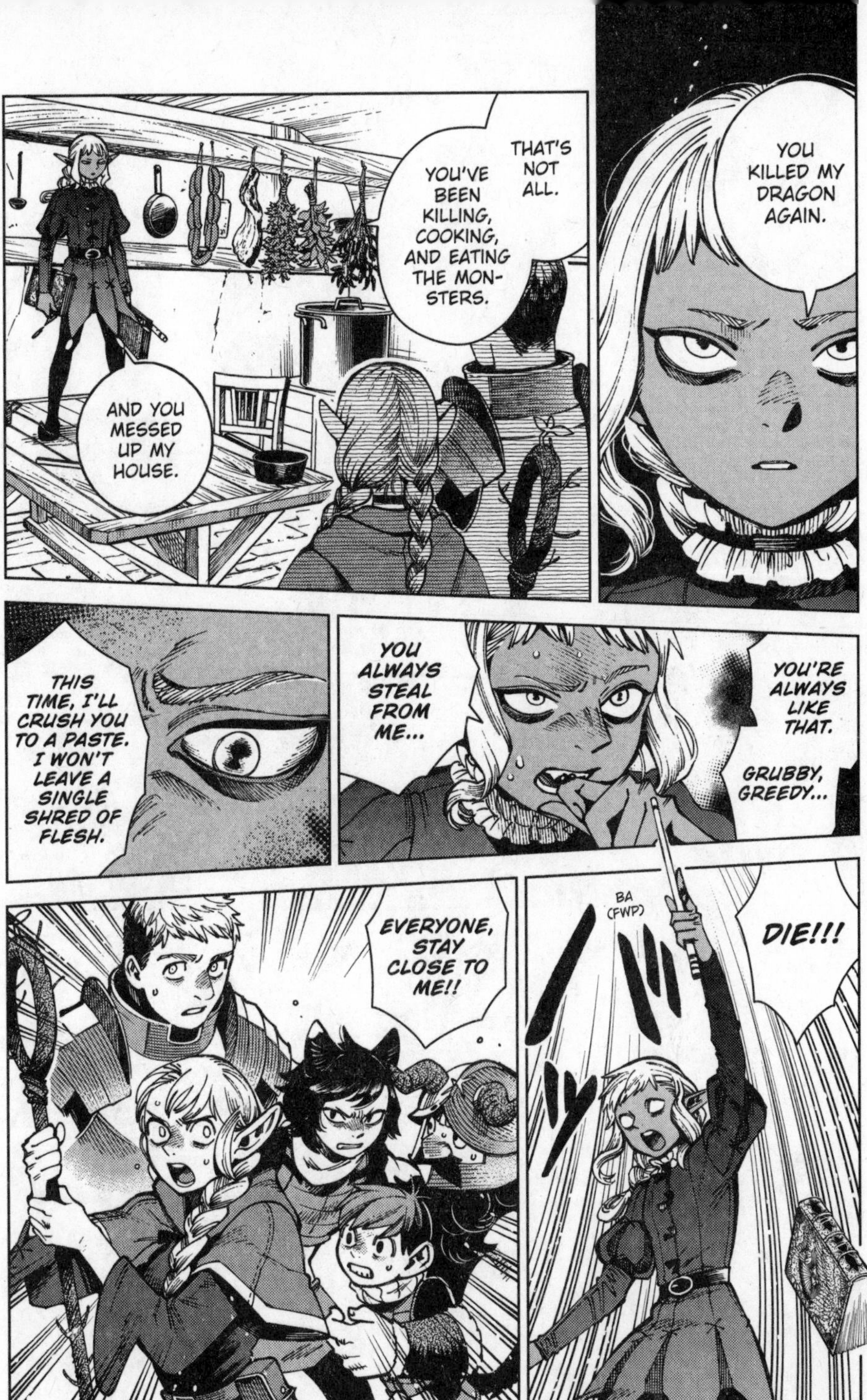
YOU KILLED MY DRAGON AGAIN.
THAT'S NOT ALL.
YOU'VE BEEN KILLING, COOKING, AND EATING THE MON-STERS.
AND YOU MESSED UP MY HOUSE.
YOU'RE ALWAYS LIKE THAT.
GRUBBY, GREEDY...
YOU ALWAYS STEAL FROM ME...
THIS TIME, I'LL CRUSH YOU TO A PASTE. I WON'T LEAVE A SINGLE SHRED OF FLESH.
DIE!!!
BA (FWP)
EVERYONE, STAY CLOSE TO ME!!

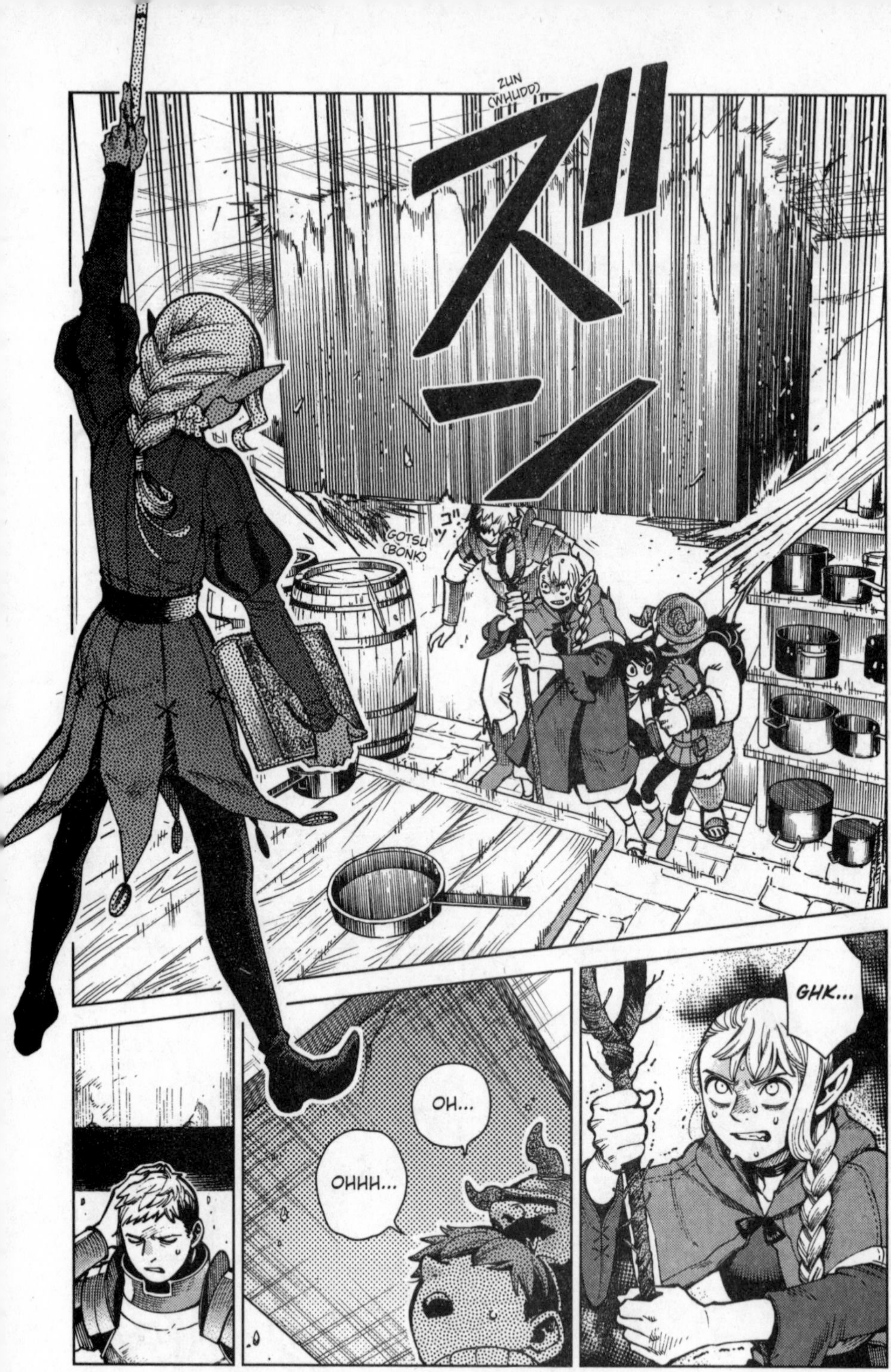
ZUN (WHUDD)
ズン
GOTSU (BONK)
GHK...
OH...
OHHH...

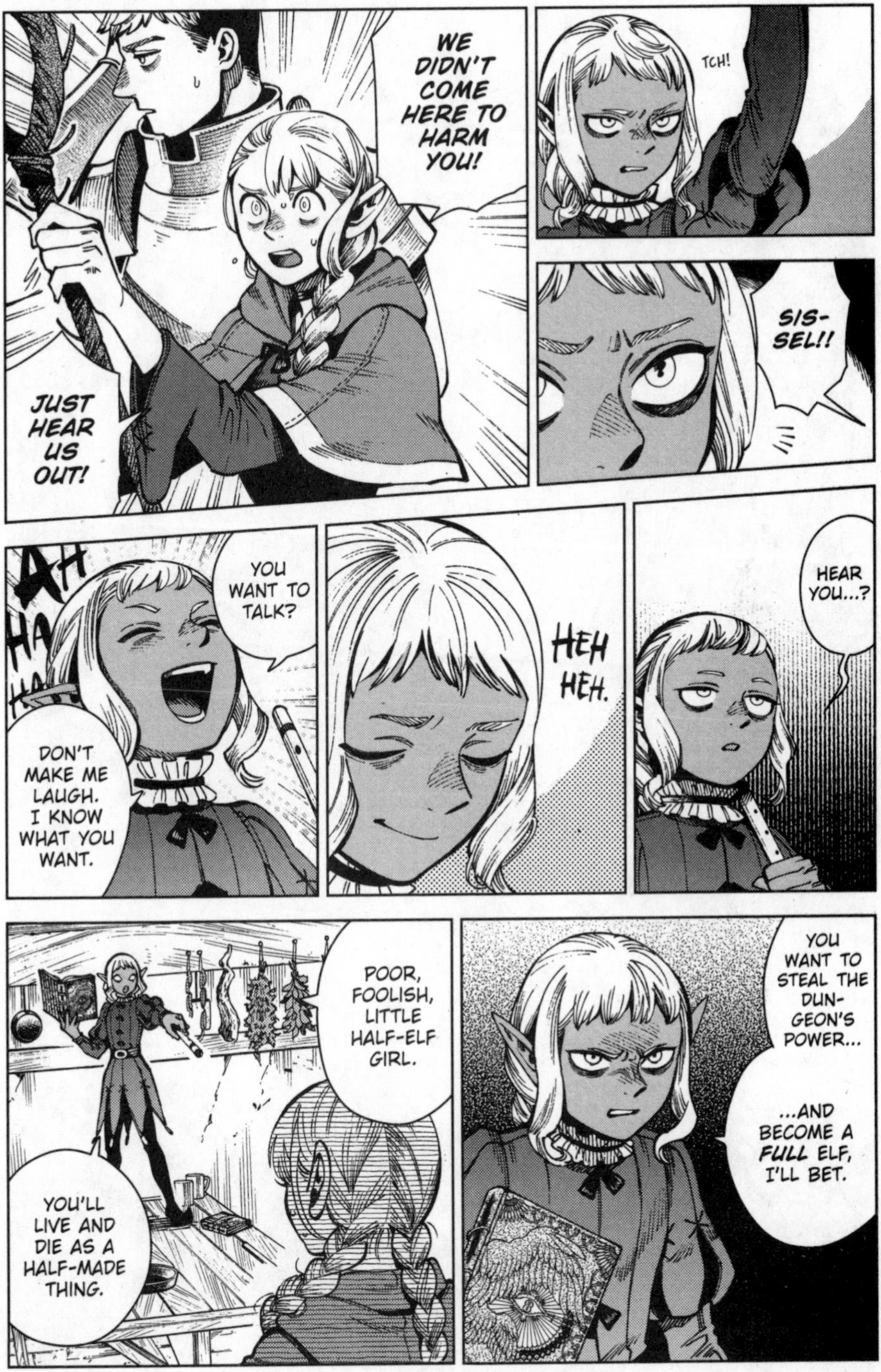
TCH!
SIS-SEL!!
WE DIDN'T COME HERE TO HARM YOU!
JUST HEAR US OUT!
HEAR YOU...?
HEH HEH.
AH HA HA
YOU WANT TO TALK?
DON'T MAKE ME LAUGH. I KNOW WHAT YOU WANT.
YOU WANT TO STEAL THE DUN-GEON'S POWER...
...AND BECOME A ***FULL*** ELF, I'LL BET.
POOR, FOOLISH, LITTLE HALF-ELF GIRL.
YOU'LL LIVE AND DIE AS A HALF-MADE THING.

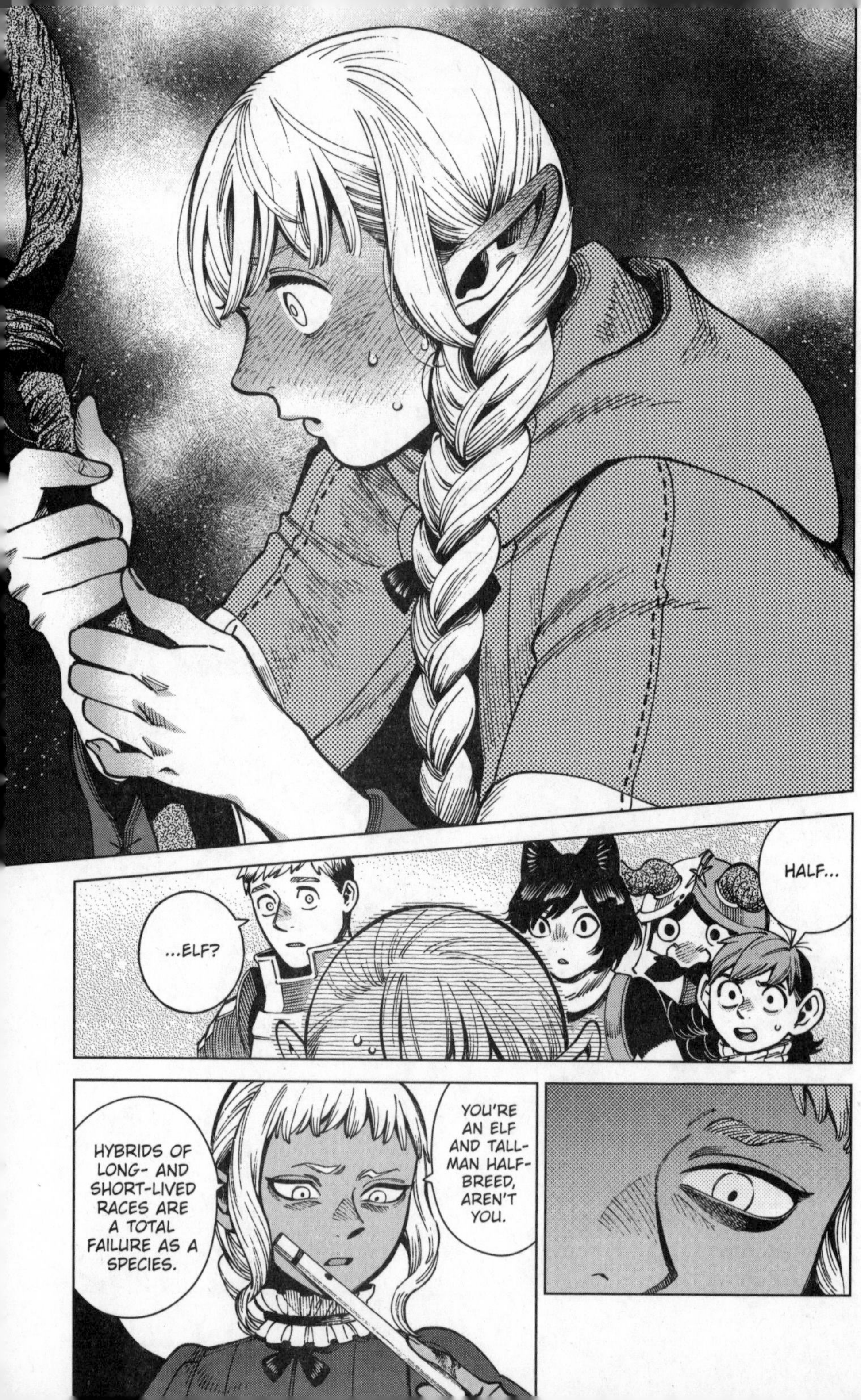
HALF...
...ELF?
YOU'RE AN ELF AND TALL-MAN HALF-BREED, AREN'T YOU.
HYBRIDS OF LONG- AND SHORT-LIVED RACES ARE A TOTAL FAILURE AS A SPECIES.

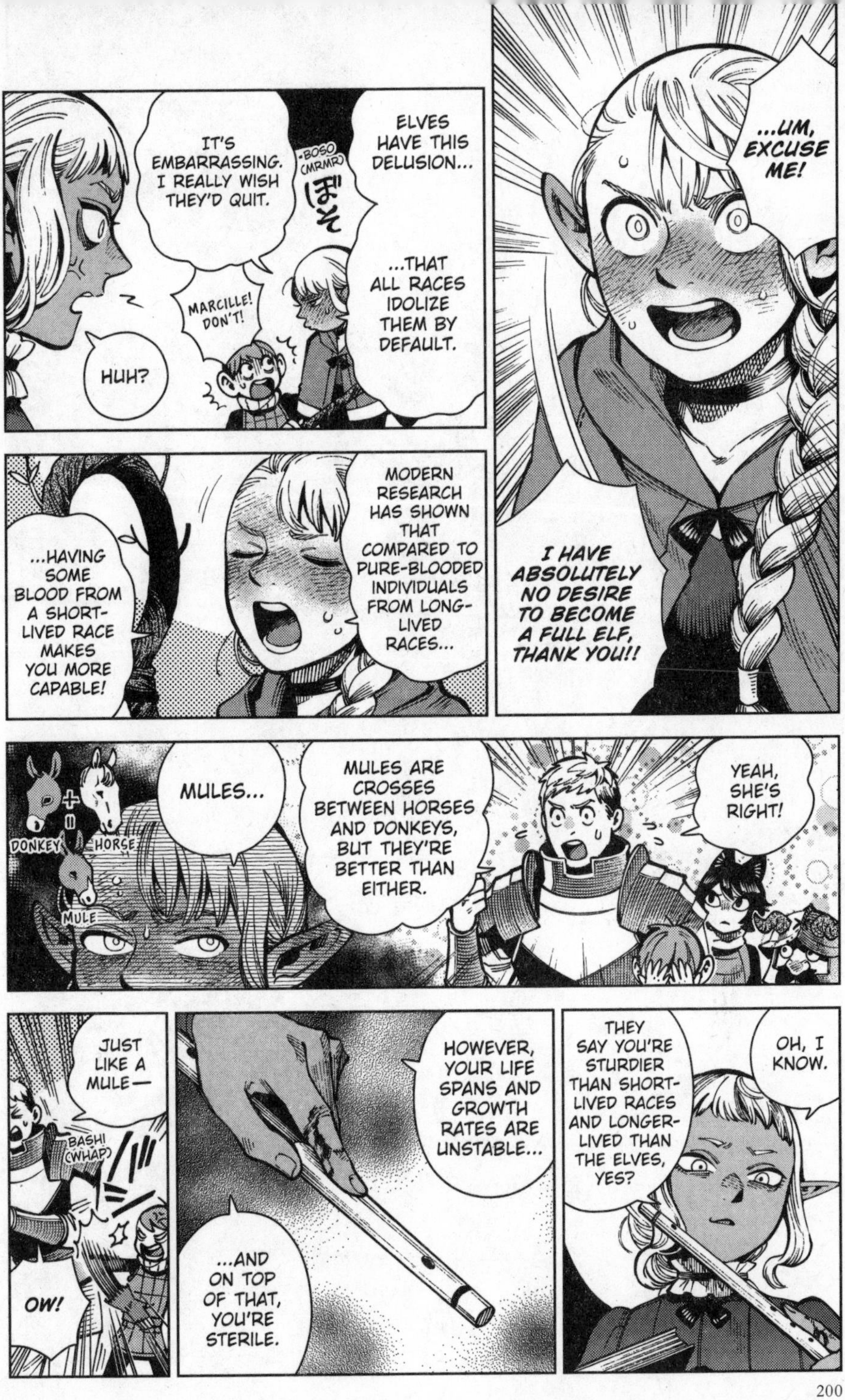
...UM, EXCUSE ME!
I HAVE ABSOLUTELY NO DESIRE TO BECOME A FULL ELF, THANK YOU!!
ELVES HAVE THIS DELUSION...
BOSO (MRMR)
ぼそ
...THAT ALL RACES IDOLIZE THEM BY DEFAULT.
IT'S EMBARRASSING. I REALLY WISH THEY'D QUIT.
MARCILLE! DON'T!
HUH?
MODERN RESEARCH HAS SHOWN THAT COMPARED TO PURE-BLOODED INDIVIDUALS FROM LONG-LIVED RACES...
...HAVING SOME BLOOD FROM A SHORT-LIVED RACE MAKES YOU MORE CAPABLE!
YEAH, SHE'S RIGHT!
MULES ARE CROSSES BETWEEN HORSES AND DONKEYS, BUT THEY'RE BETTER THAN EITHER.
MULES...
HORSE
DONKEY
MULE
OH, I KNOW.
THEY SAY YOU'RE STURDIER THAN SHORT-LIVED RACES AND LONGER-LIVED THAN THE ELVES, YES?
HOWEVER, YOUR LIFE SPANS AND GROWTH RATES ARE UNSTABLE...
...AND ON TOP OF THAT, YOU'RE STERILE.
JUST LIKE A MULE—
BASH! (WHAP)
OW!

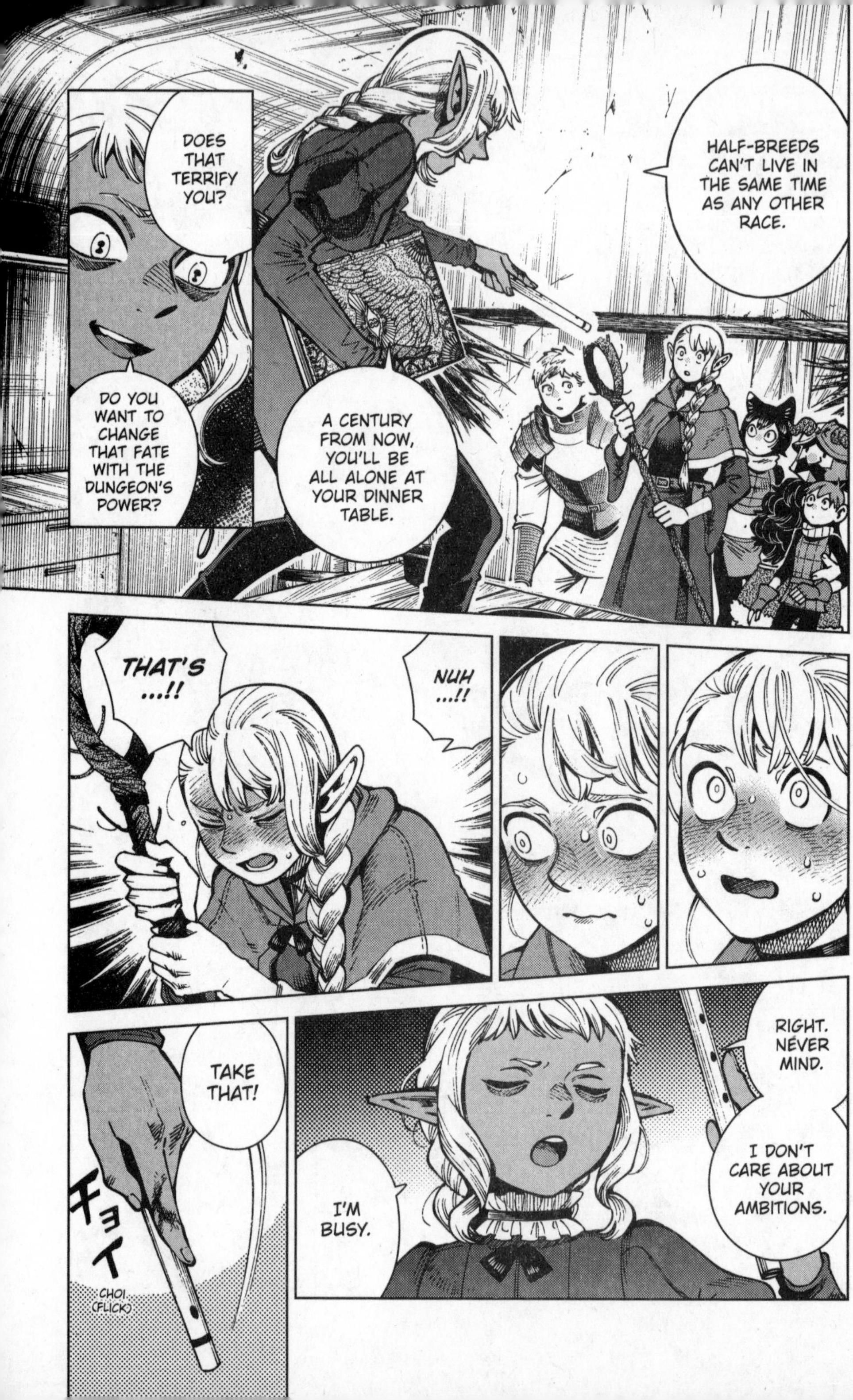
HALF-BREEDS CAN'T LIVE IN THE SAME TIME AS ANY OTHER RACE.
A CENTURY FROM NOW, YOU'LL BE ALL ALONE AT YOUR DINNER TABLE.
DOES THAT TERRIFY YOU?
DO YOU WANT TO CHANGE THAT FATE WITH THE DUNGEON'S POWER?
NUH ...!!
THAT'S ...!!
RIGHT. NEVER MIND.
I DON'T CARE ABOUT YOUR AMBITIONS.
I'M BUSY.
TAKE THAT!
チョイ
CHOI (FLICK)

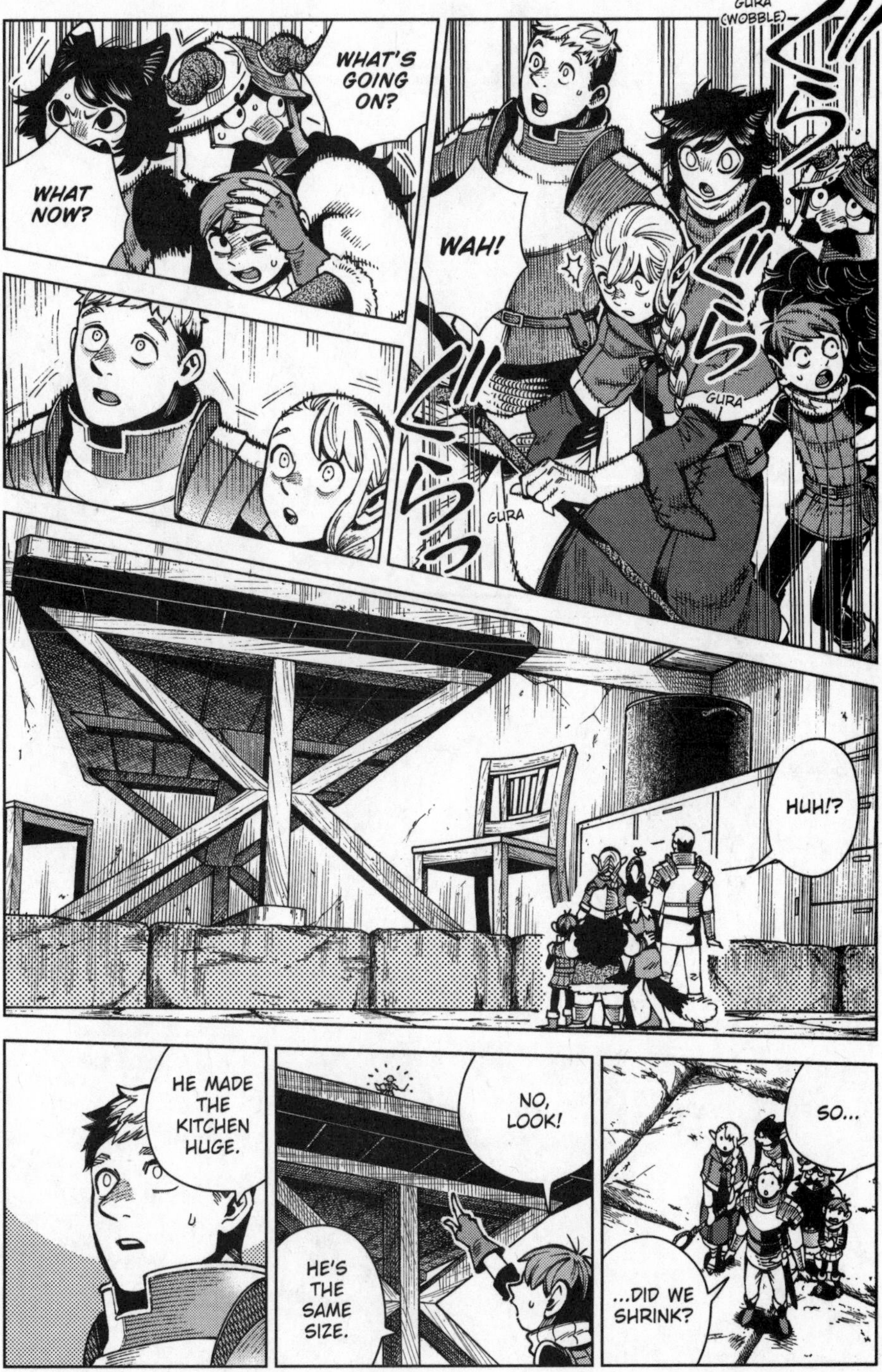
GURA (WOBBLE)
WAH!
GURA
GURA
WHAT'S GOING ON?
WHAT NOW?
HUH!?
SO...
...DID WE SHRINK?
NO, LOOK!
HE'S THE SAME SIZE.
HE MADE THE KITCHEN HUGE.

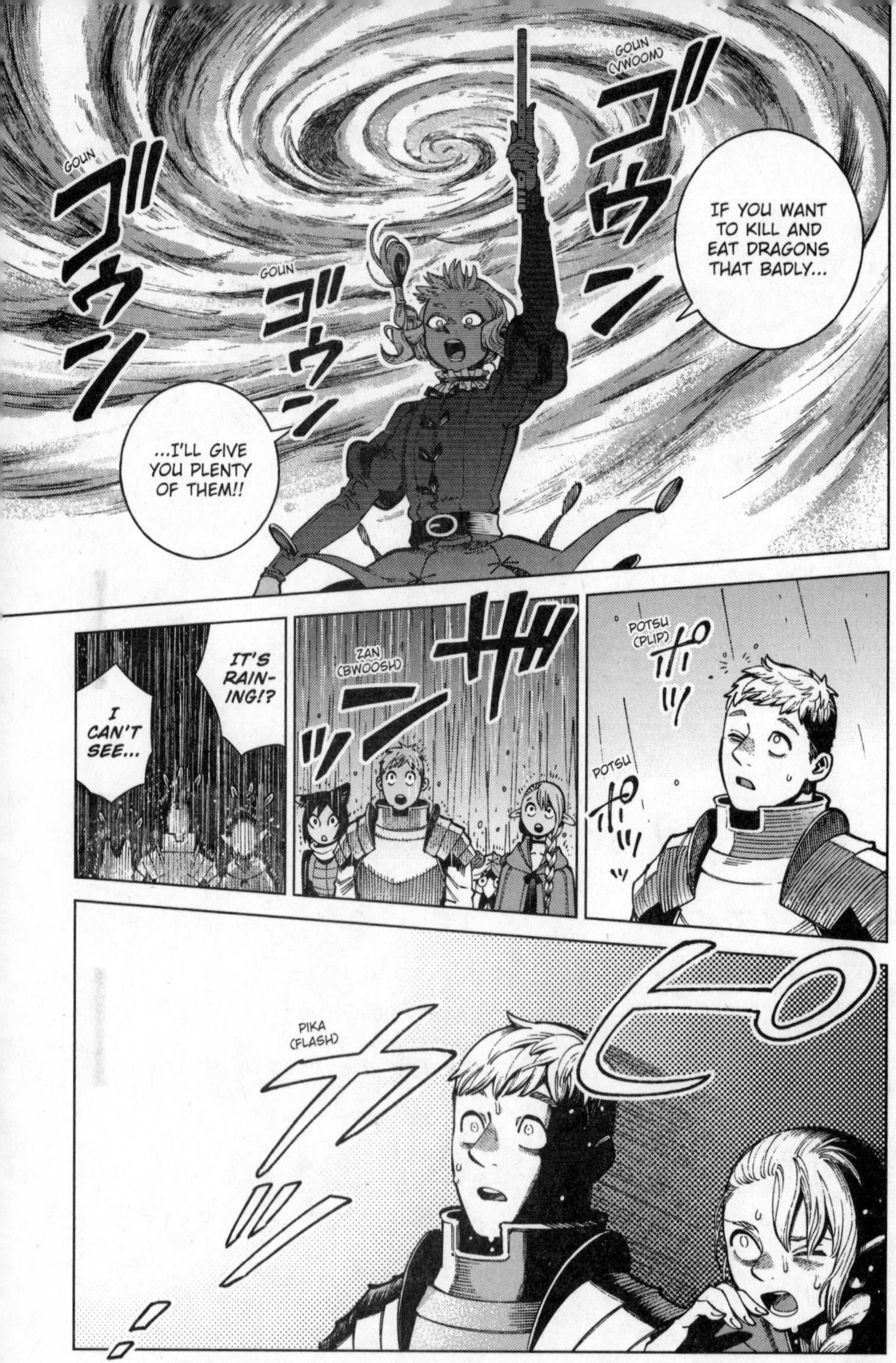
GOUN (VWOOM)
IF YOU WANT TO KILL AND EAT DRAGONS THAT BADLY...
GOUN
GOUN
...I'LL GIVE YOU PLENTY OF THEM!!
POTSU (PLIP)
POTSU
ZAN (BWOOSH)
IT'S RAINING!?
I CAN'T SEE...
PIKA (FLASH)

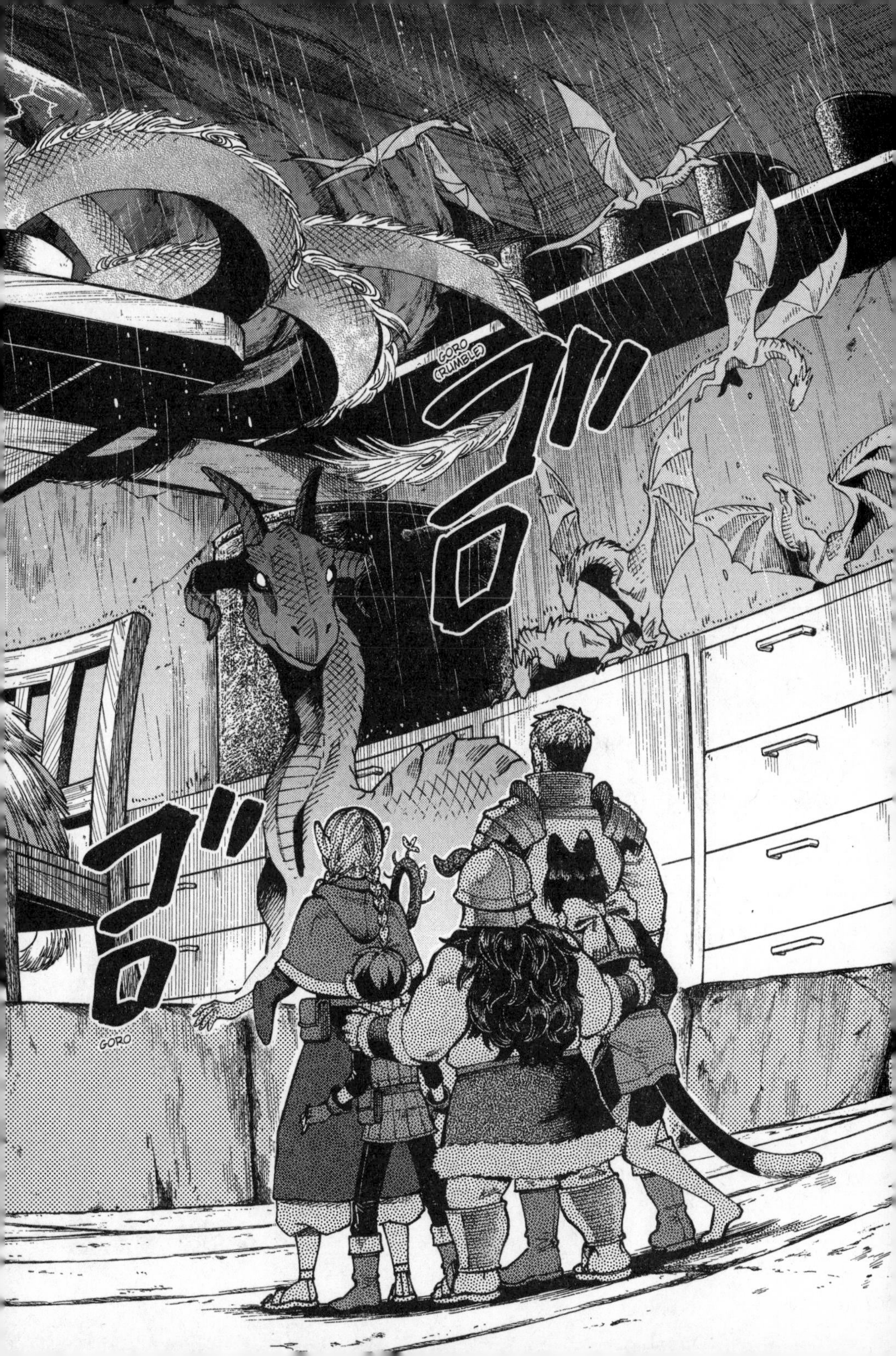
ゴロ
GORO (RUMBLE)
ゴロ
GORO

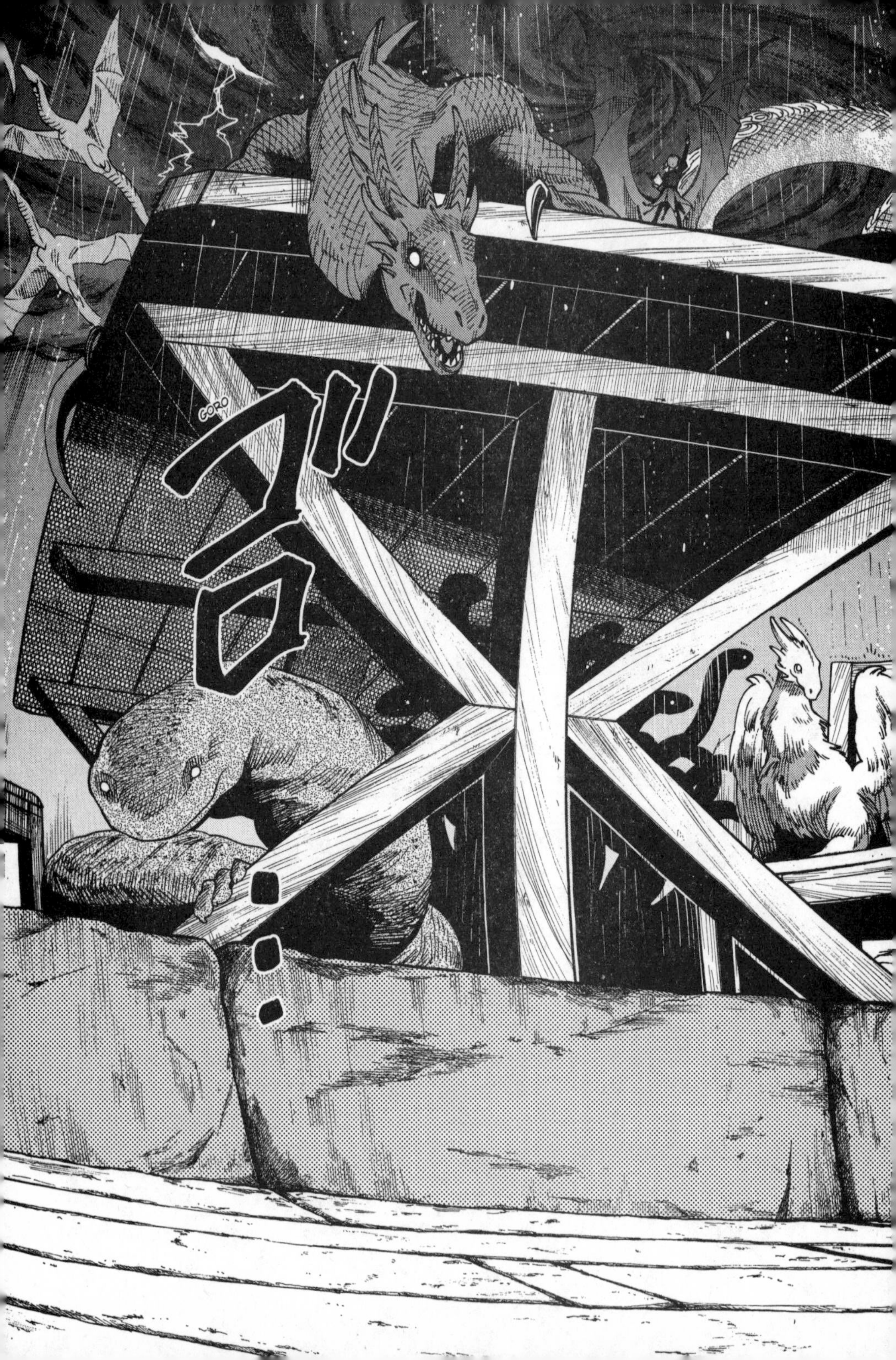
ゴロ
GORO
...

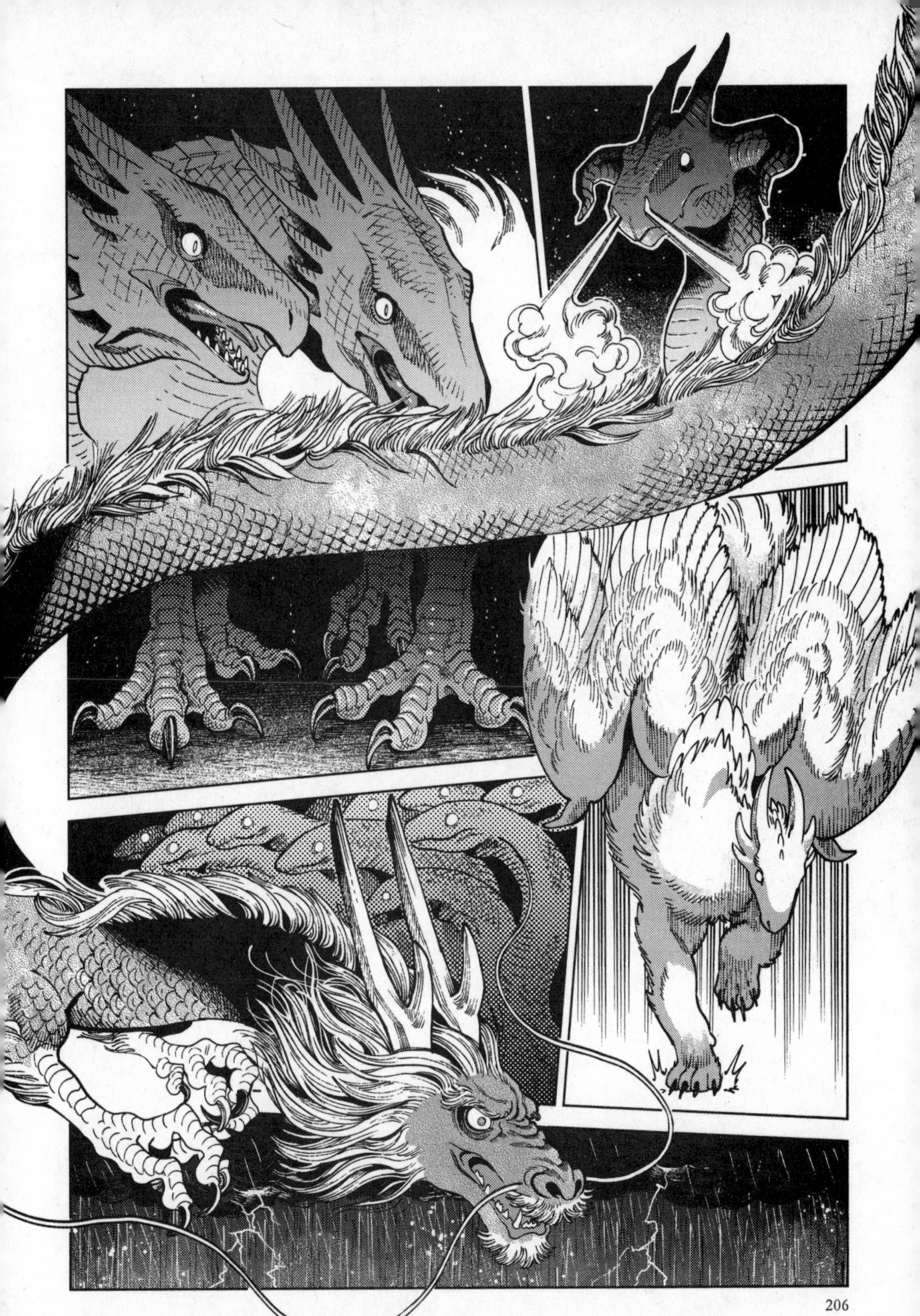

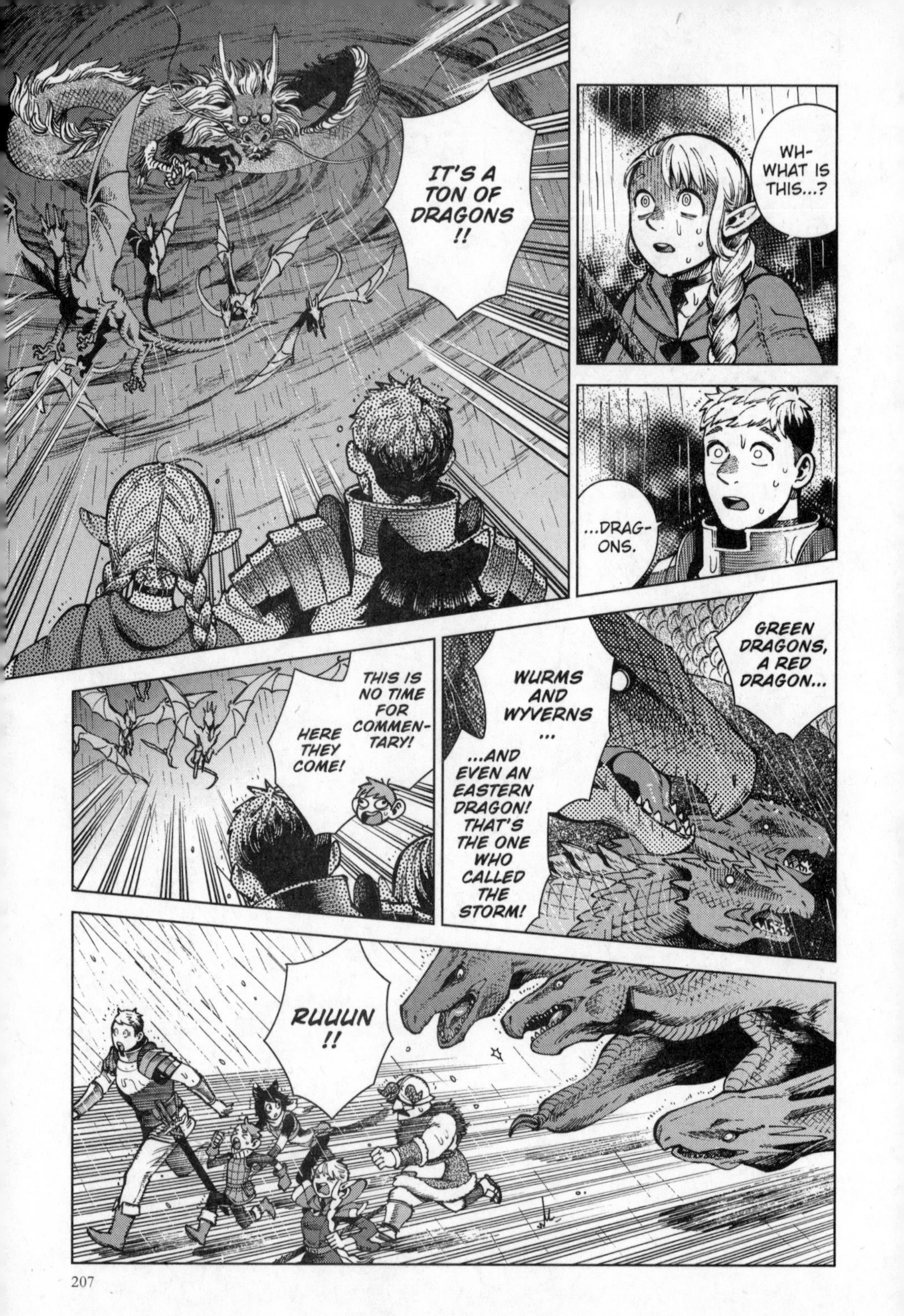
WH- WHAT IS THIS...?
...DRAG- ONS.
IT'S A TON OF DRAGONS !!
GREEN DRAGONS, A RED DRAGON...
WURMS AND WYVERNS ...
...AND EVEN AN EASTERN DRAGON! THAT'S THE ONE WHO CALLED THE STORM!
THIS IS NO TIME FOR COMMEN- TARY!
HERE THEY COME!
RUUUN !!

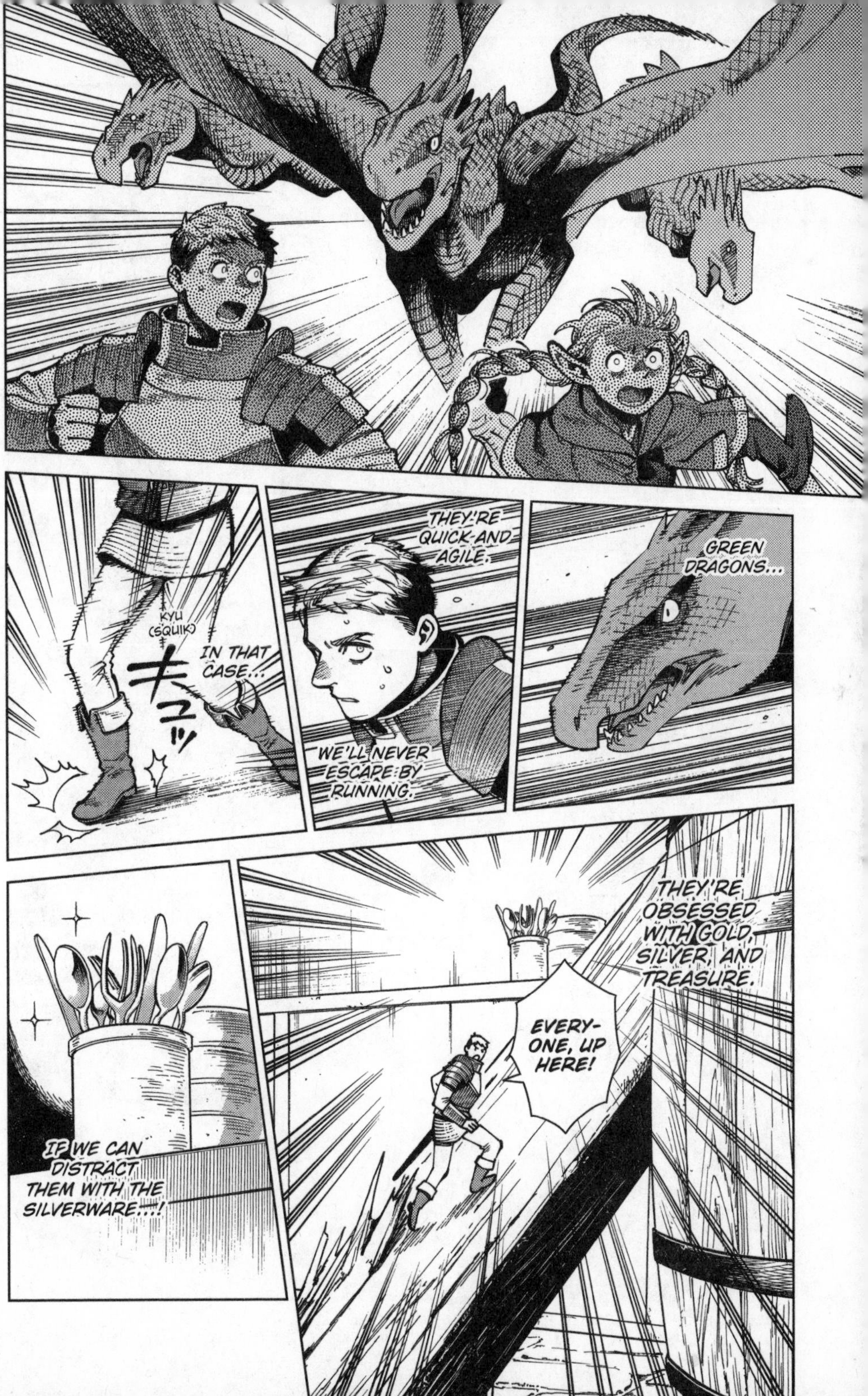
GREEN DRAGONS...
THEY'RE QUICK AND AGILE.
WE'LL NEVER ESCAPE BY RUNNING.
KYU (SQUIK)
IN THAT CASE...
THEY'RE OBSESSED WITH GOLD, SILVER, AND TREASURE.
EVERY-ONE, UP HERE!
IF WE CAN DISTRACT THEM WITH THE SILVERWARE...!

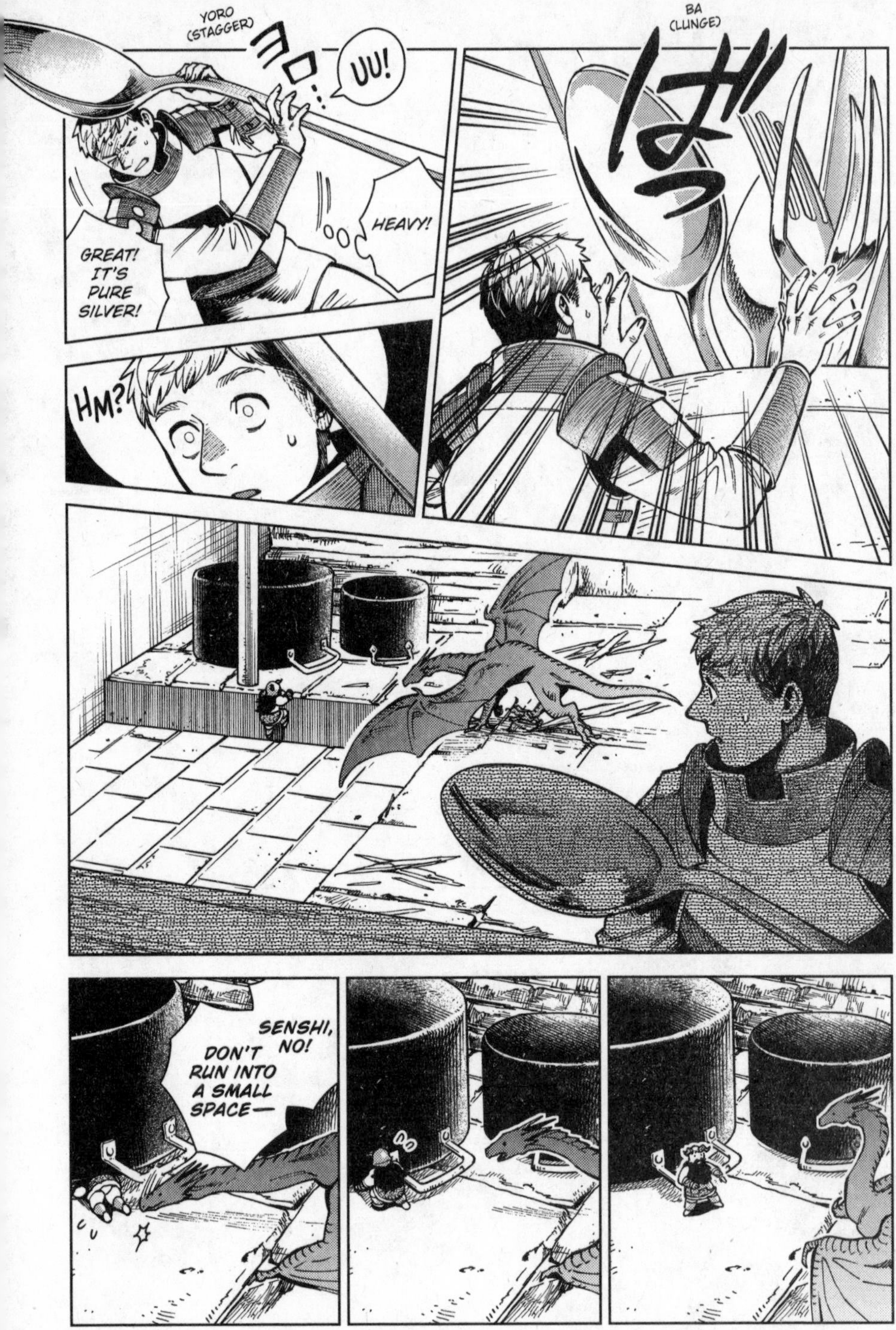
BA
(LUNGE)
ばっ
YORO
(STAGGER)
ヨロ…
UU!
HEAVY!
GREAT! IT'S PURE SILVER!
HM?
SENSHI, NO!
DON'T RUN INTO A SMALL SPACE—

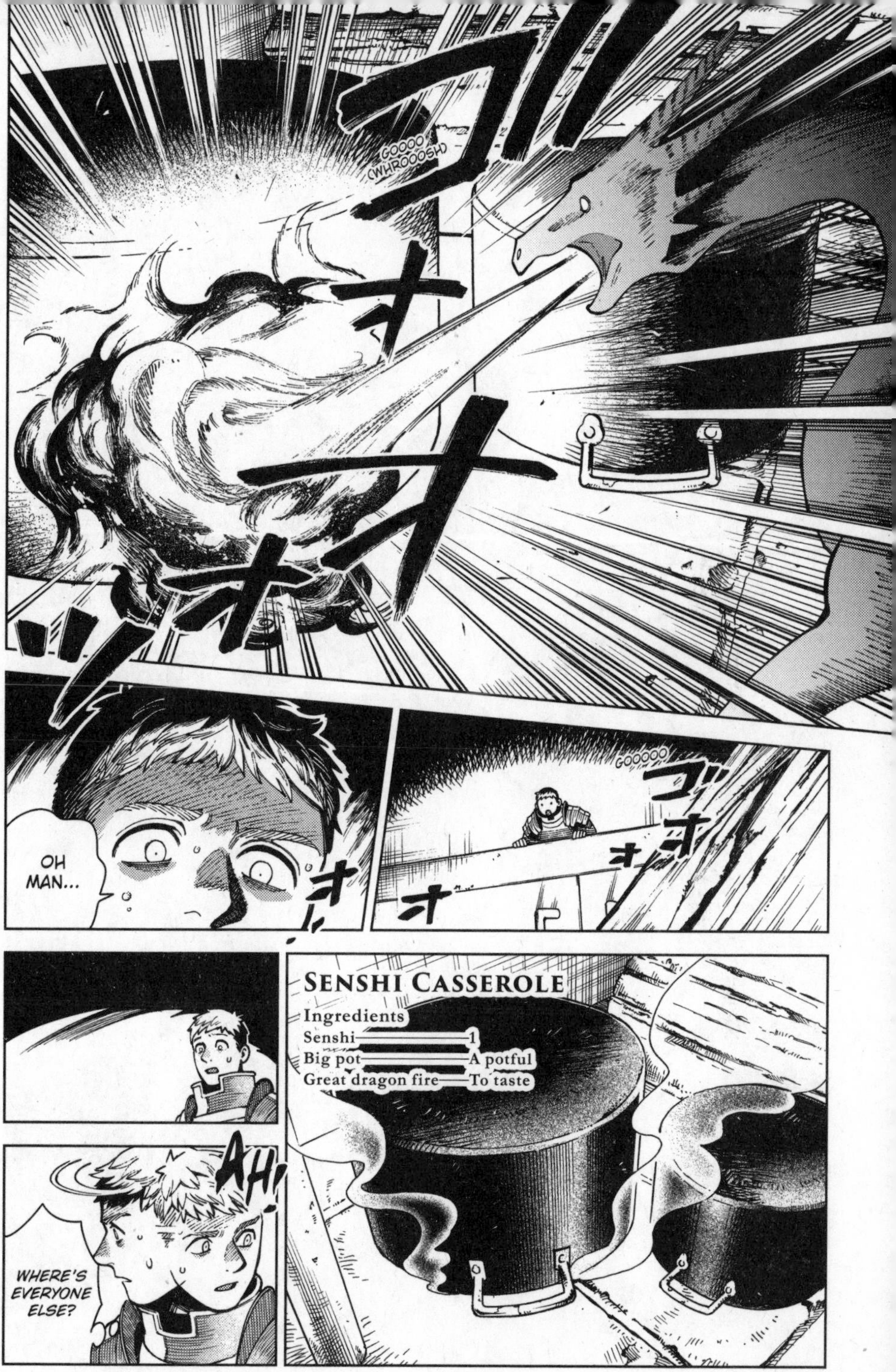
GOOOO (WHROOOSH)
GOOOOO
OH MAN...
SENSHI CASSEROLE
Ingredients
Senshi——1
Big pot——A potful
Great dragon fire——To taste
AH!
WHERE'S EVERYONE ELSE?

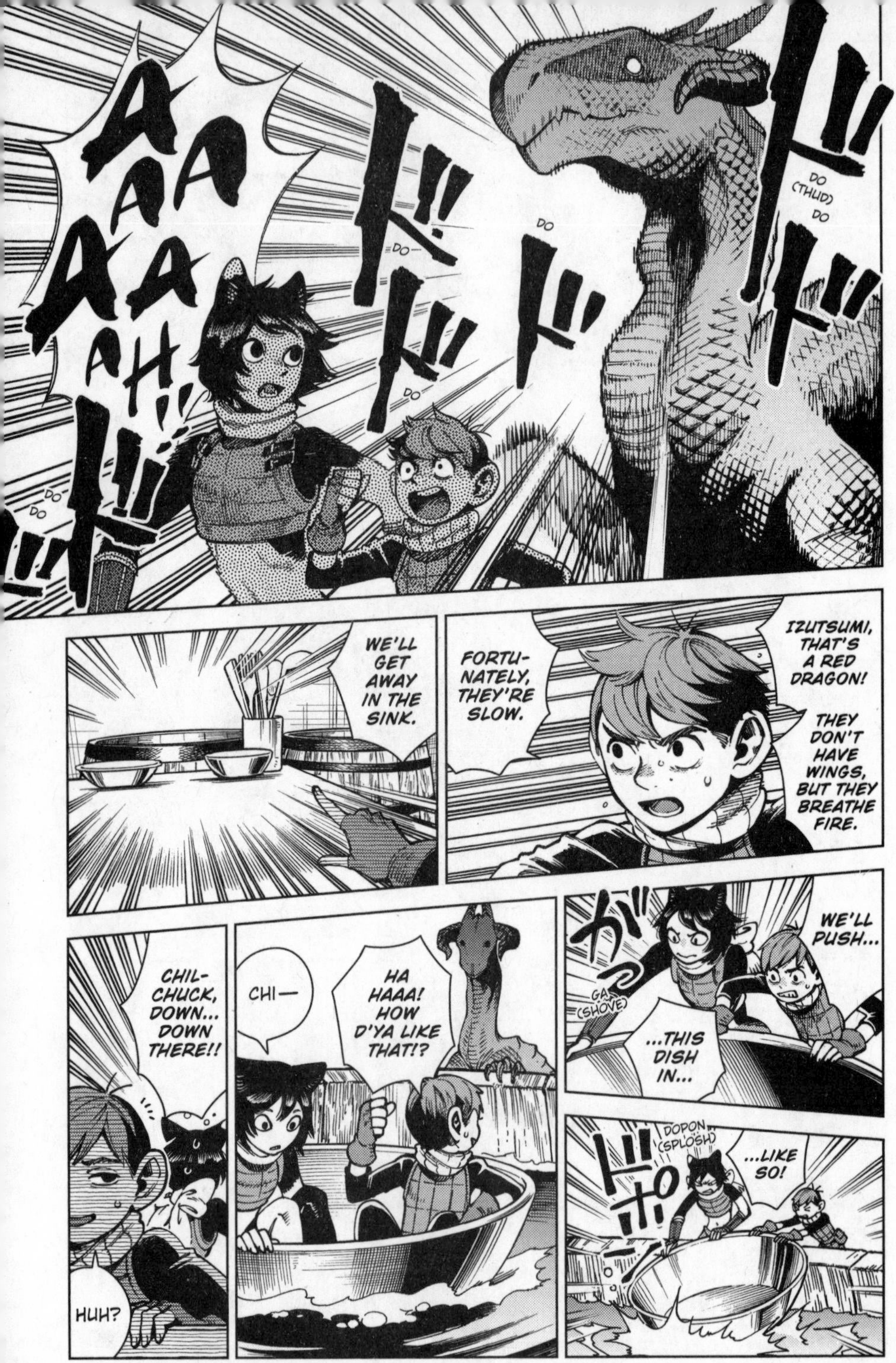
DO
(THUD)
DO
DO
DO
DO
AAAAAAH!!
DO
DO
IZUTSUMI, THAT'S A RED DRAGON!
THEY DON'T HAVE WINGS, BUT THEY BREATHE FIRE.
FORTUNATELY, THEY'RE SLOW.
WE'LL GET AWAY IN THE SINK.
WE'LL PUSH...
GA
(SHOVE)
...THIS DISH IN...
DOPON
(SPLOSH)
...LIKE SO!
HA HAAA! HOW D'YA LIKE THAT!?
CHI—
CHIL-CHUCK, DOWN... DOWN THERE!!
HUH?

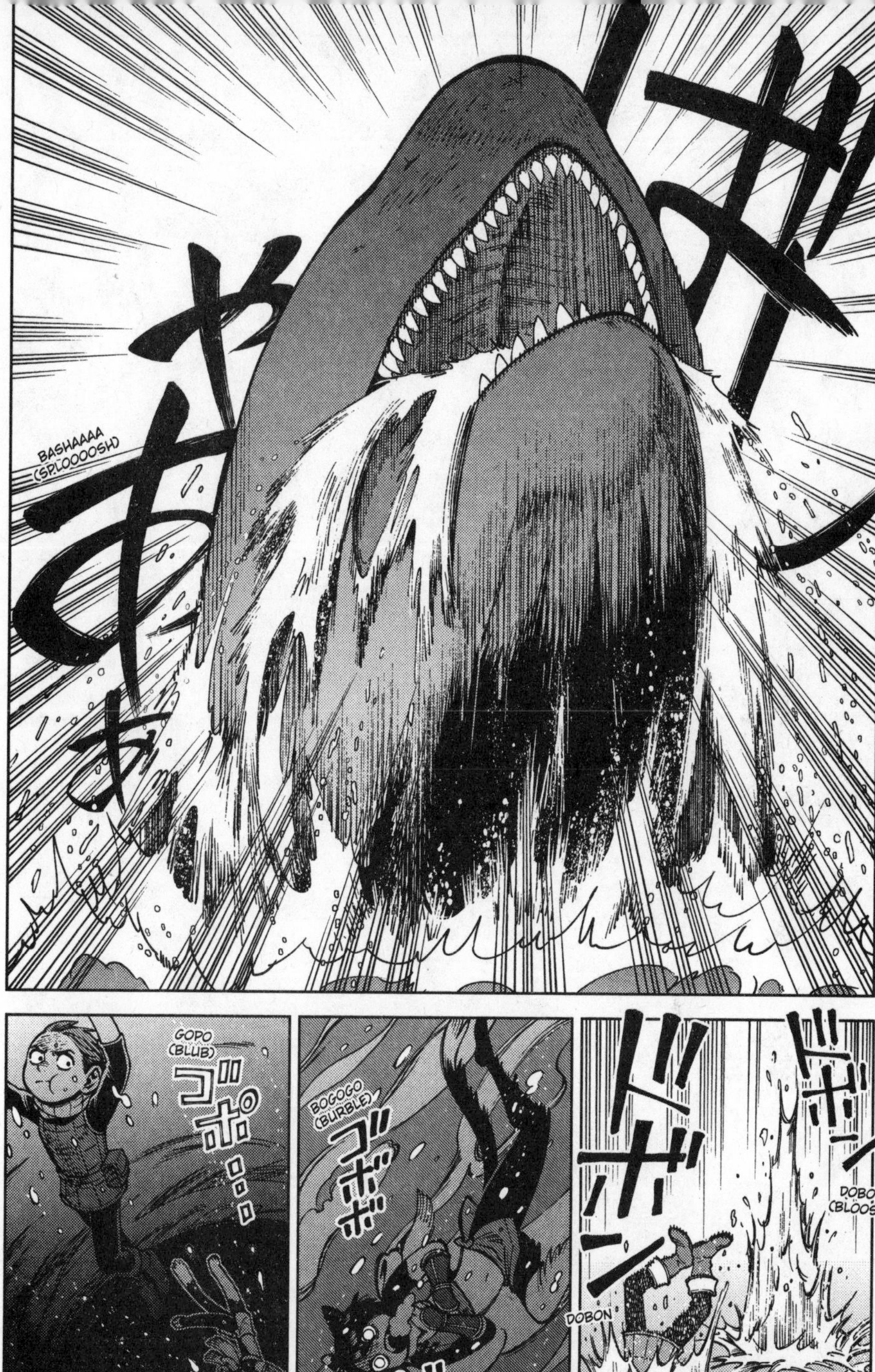
BASHAAAA (SPLOOOOSH)
ドボーン
DOBON (BLOOSH)
ドボン
DOBON
ゴボボ
BOGOGO (BURBLE)
ガボ
GABO (GLUB)
ゴポ
GOPO (BLUB)

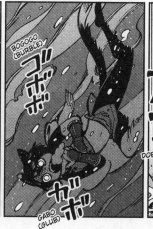

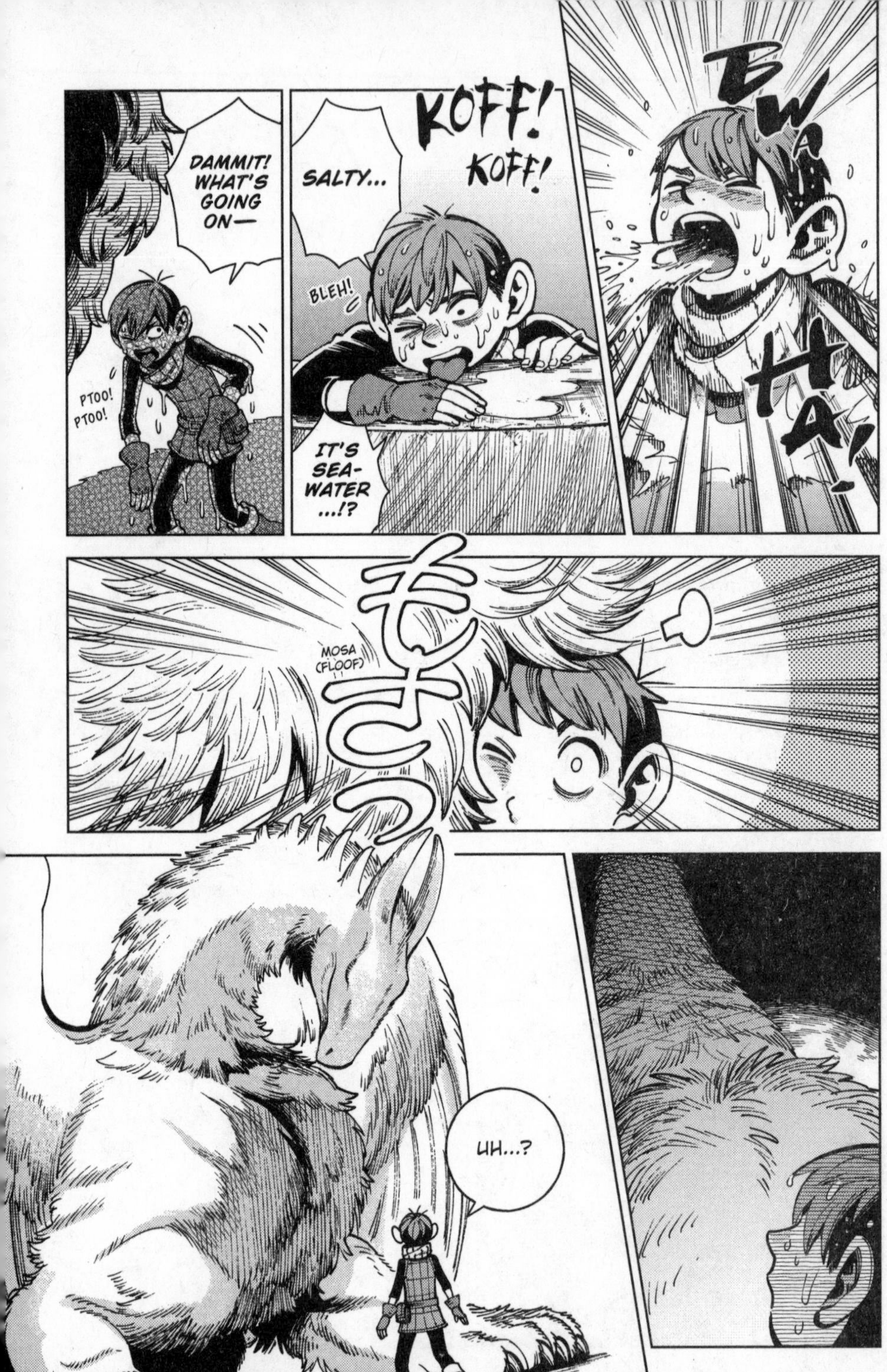
BWA HA!
KOFF! KOFF!
SALTY...
BLEH!
IT'S SEAWATER...!?
DAMMIT! WHAT'S GOING ON—
PTOO! PTOO!
もさっ
MOSA (FLOOF)
UH...?

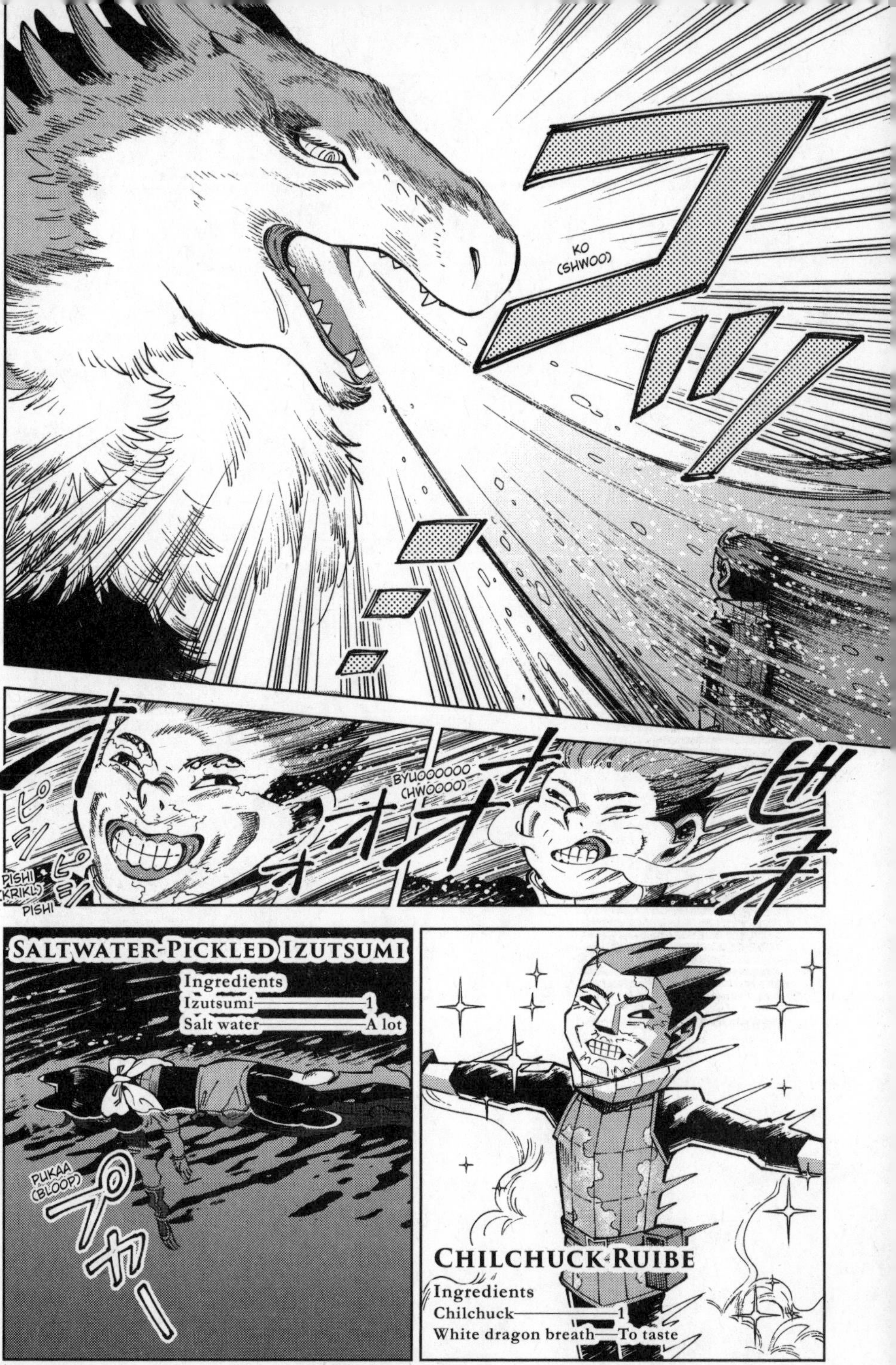
KO
(SHWOO)
BYUOOOOOO
(HWOOOO)
PISHI
(KRIKL)
PISHI
CHILCHUCK RUIBE
Ingredients
Chilchuck——1
White dragon breath——To taste
SALTWATER-PICKLED IZUTSUMI
Ingredients
Izutsumi——1
Salt water——A lot
PUKAA
(BLOOP)

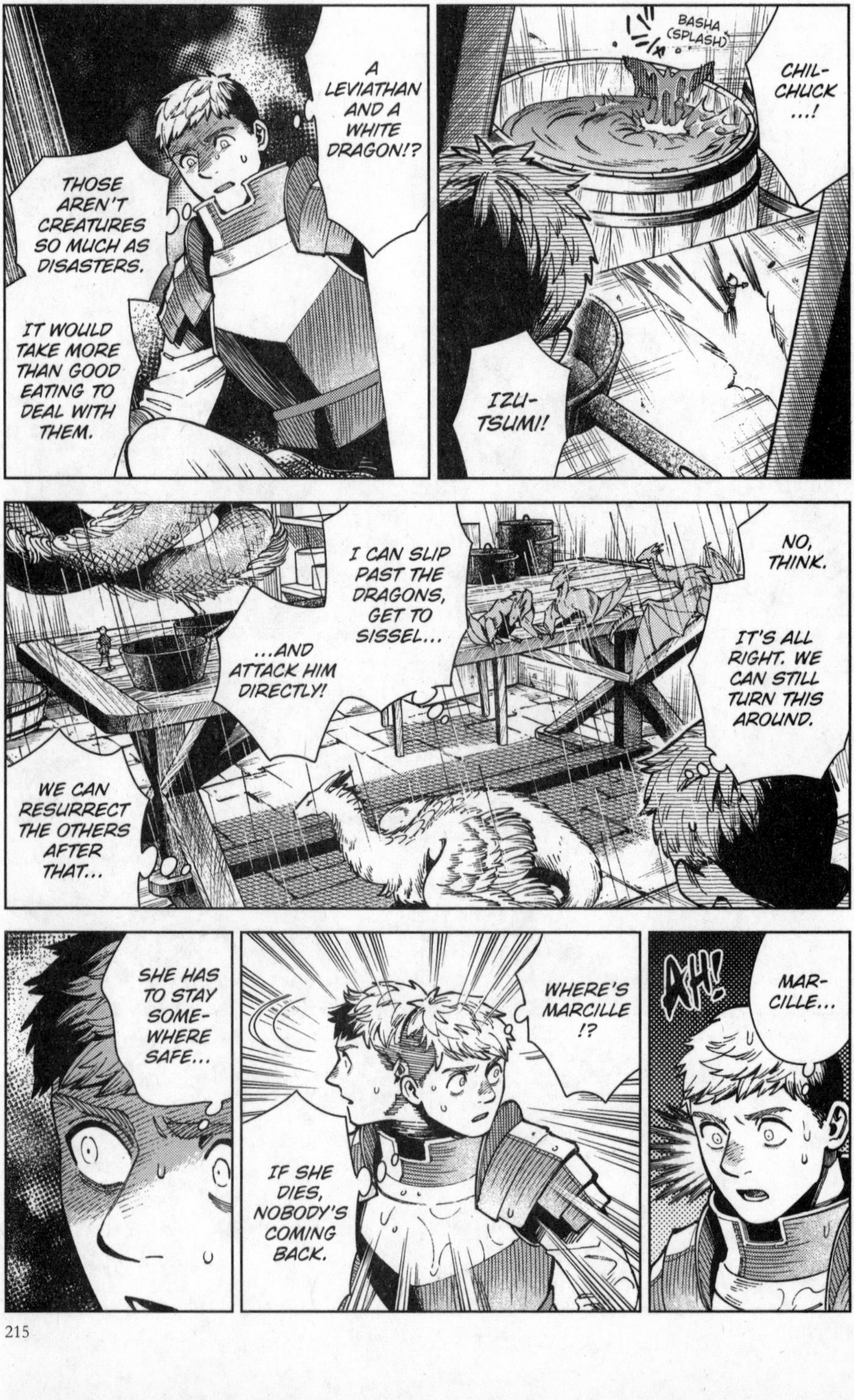
BASHA (SPLASH)
CHIL-CHUCK ...!
IZU-TSUMI!
A LEVIATHAN AND A WHITE DRAGON!?
THOSE AREN'T CREATURES SO MUCH AS DISASTERS.
IT WOULD TAKE MORE THAN GOOD EATING TO DEAL WITH THEM.
NO, THINK.
IT'S ALL RIGHT. WE CAN STILL TURN THIS AROUND.
I CAN SLIP PAST THE DRAGONS, GET TO SISSEL...
...AND ATTACK HIM DIRECTLY!
WE CAN RESURRECT THE OTHERS AFTER THAT...
AH!
MAR-CILLE...
WHERE'S MARCILLE !?
IF SHE DIES, NOBODY'S COMING BACK.
SHE HAS TO STAY SOME-WHERE SAFE...

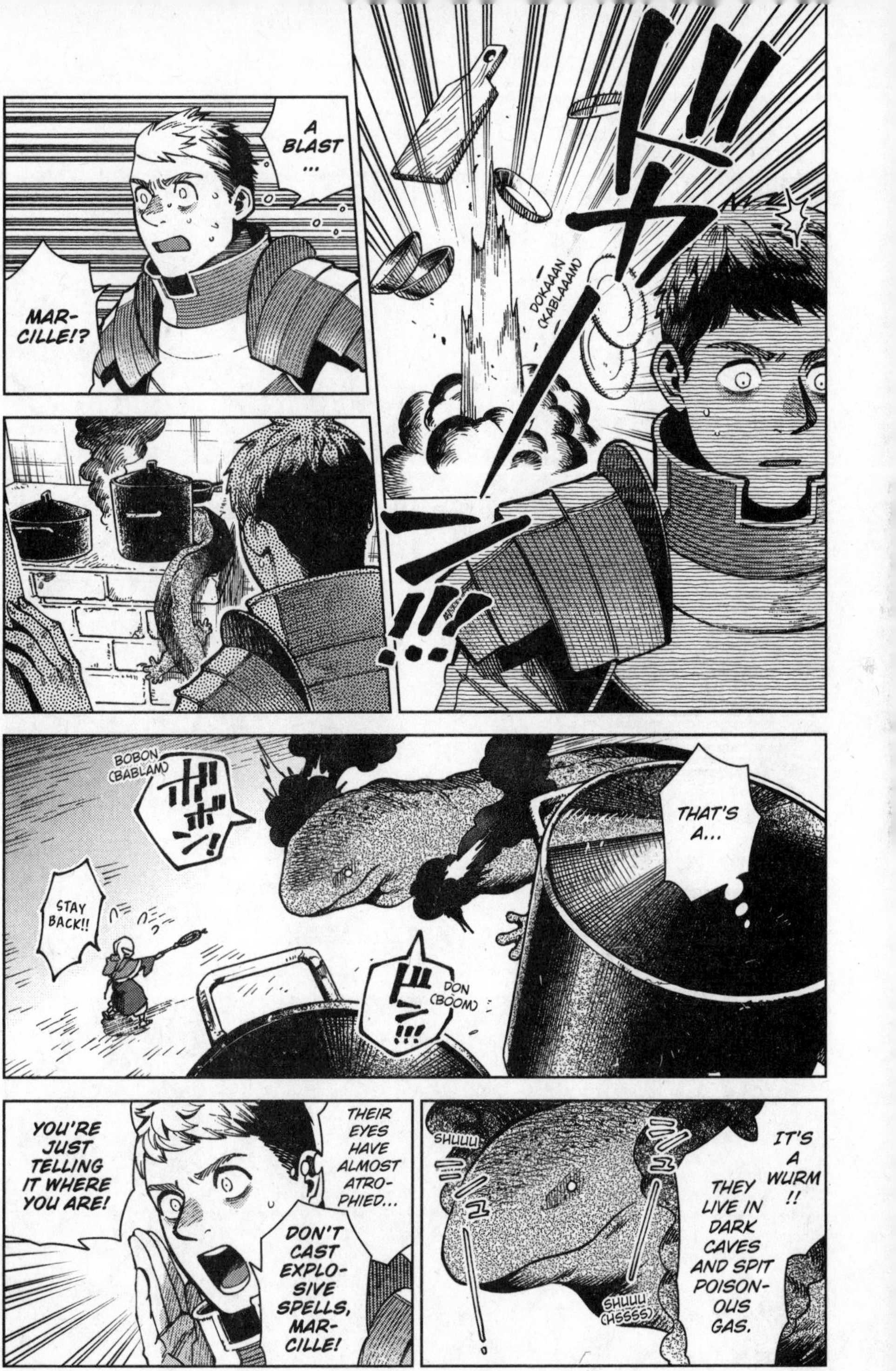
DOKAAAN (KABLAAAM)
A BLAST ...
MAR-CILLE!?
THAT'S A...
BOBON (BABLAM)
STAY BACK!!
DON (BOOM)
IT'S A WURM!!
THEY LIVE IN DARK CAVES AND SPIT POISON-OUS GAS.
SHUUU
SHUUU (HSSSS)
THEIR EYES HAVE ALMOST ATRO-PHIED...
DON'T CAST EXPLO-SIVE SPELLS, MAR-CILLE!
YOU'RE JUST TELLING IT WHERE YOU ARE!

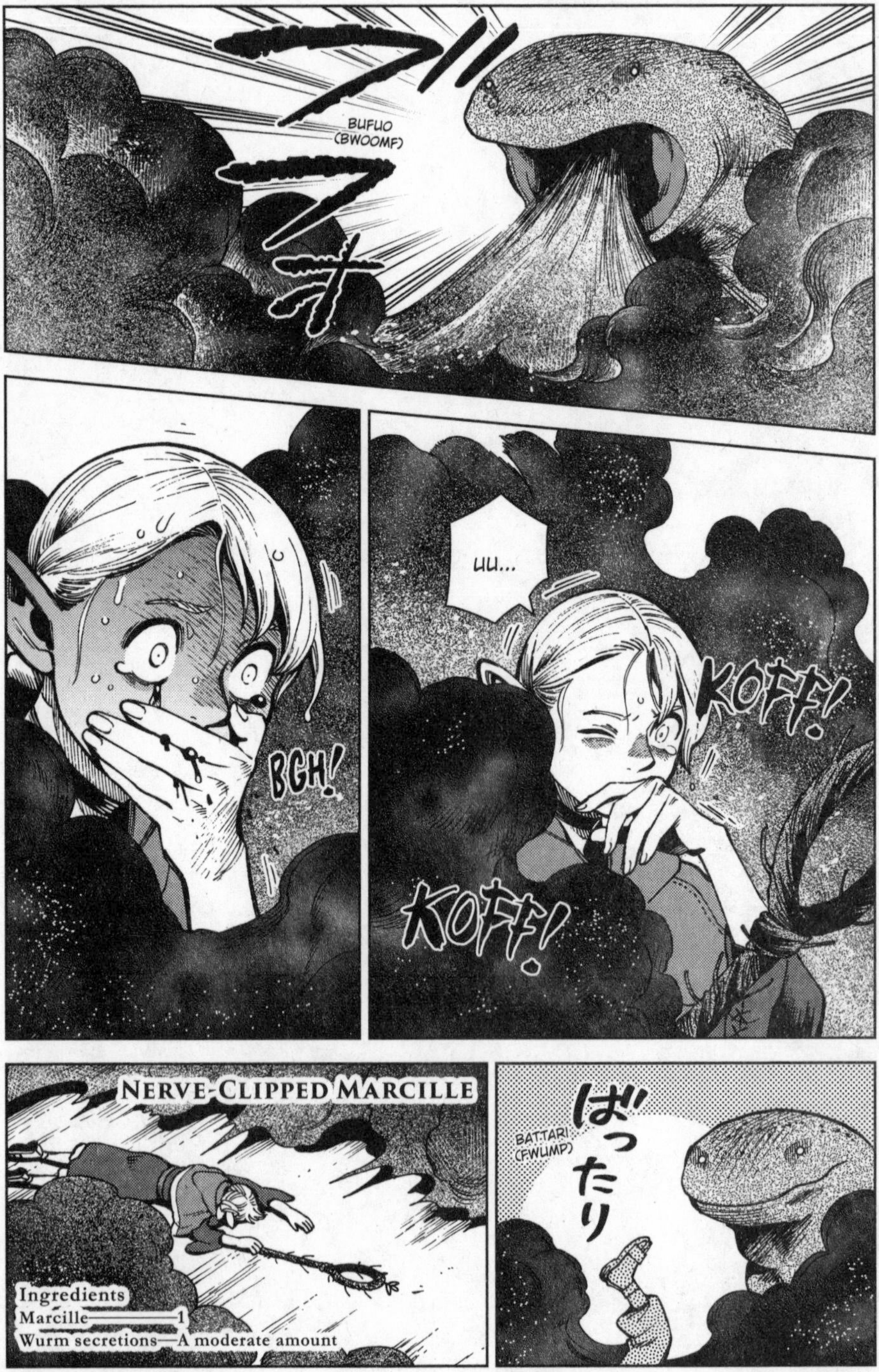
ブフォ
BUFUO (BWOOMF)
uu...
KOFF!
KOFF!
BGH!
ばったり
BATTARI (FWUMP)
Nerve-Clipped Marcille
Ingredients
Marcille——1
Wurm secretions—A moderate amount

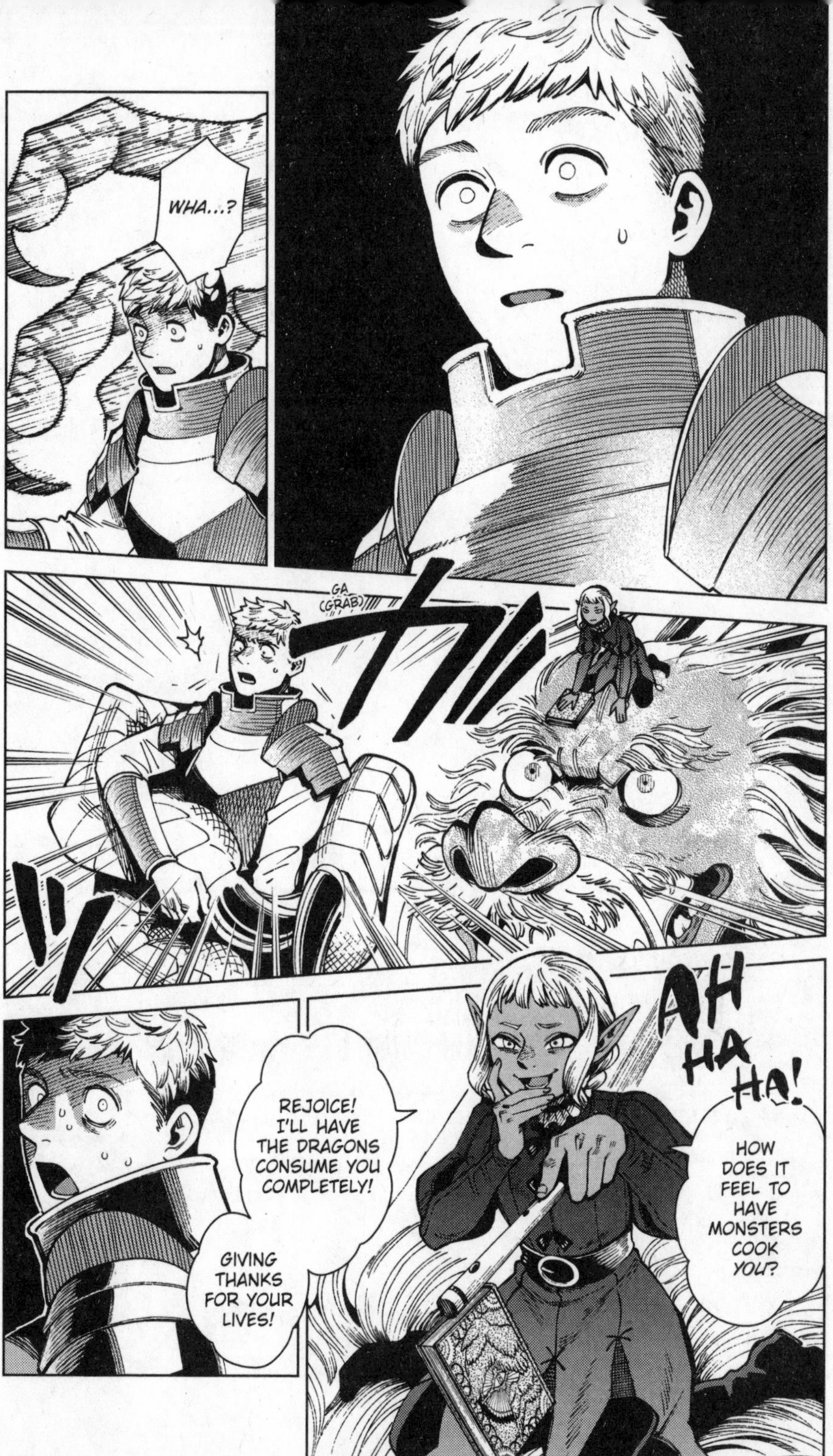
WHA...?
GA
(GRAB)
AH HA HA!
HOW DOES IT FEEL TO HAVE MONSTERS COOK YOU?
REJOICE! I'LL HAVE THE DRAGONS CONSUME YOU COMPLETELY!
GIVING THANKS FOR YOUR LIVES!

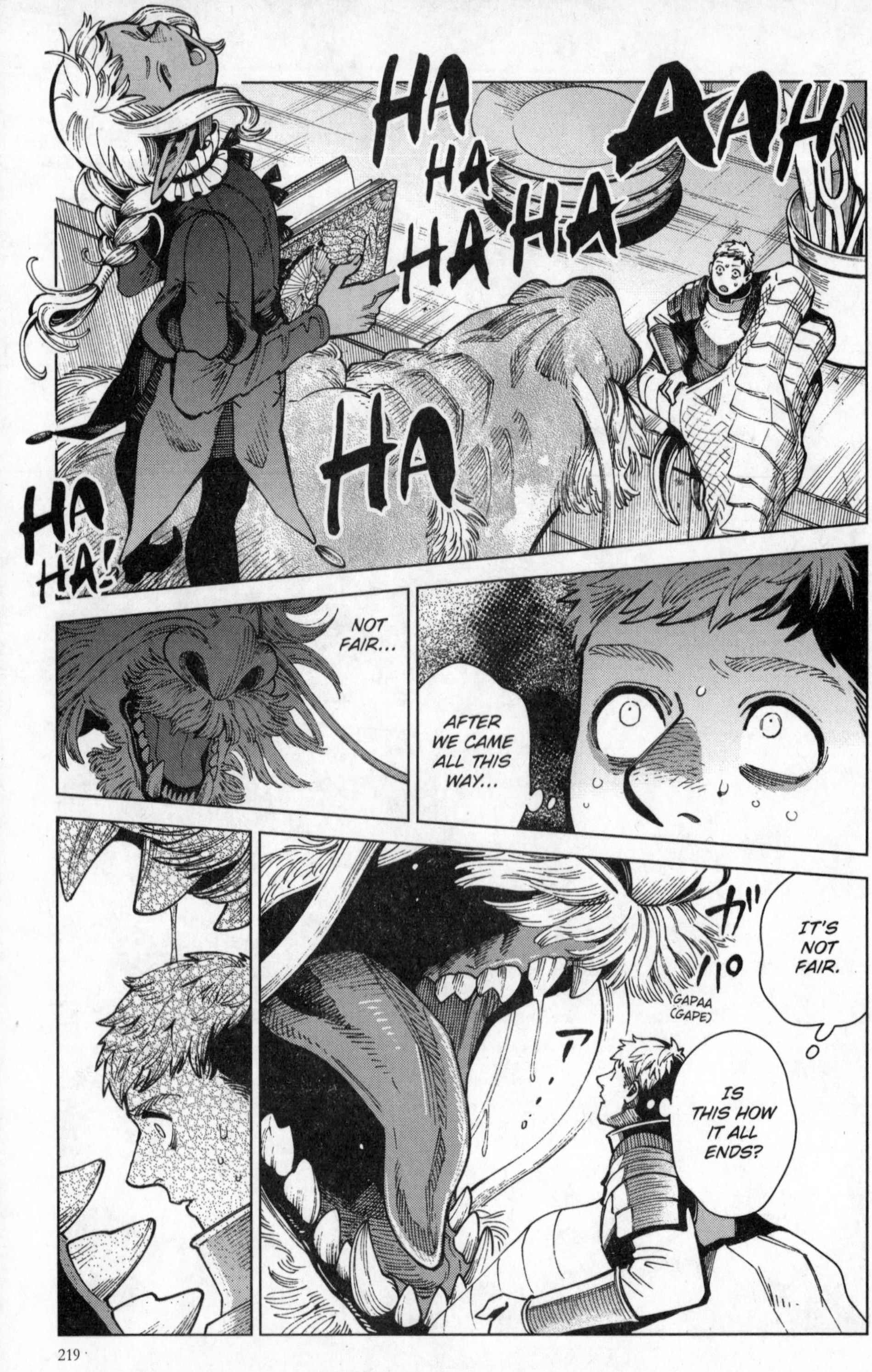
HA HA HA HA HAAAH
HA
HA HA!
AFTER WE CAME ALL THIS WAY...
NOT FAIR...
ガパ
GAPAA (GAPE)
IT'S NOT FAIR.
ア
IS THIS HOW IT ALL ENDS?

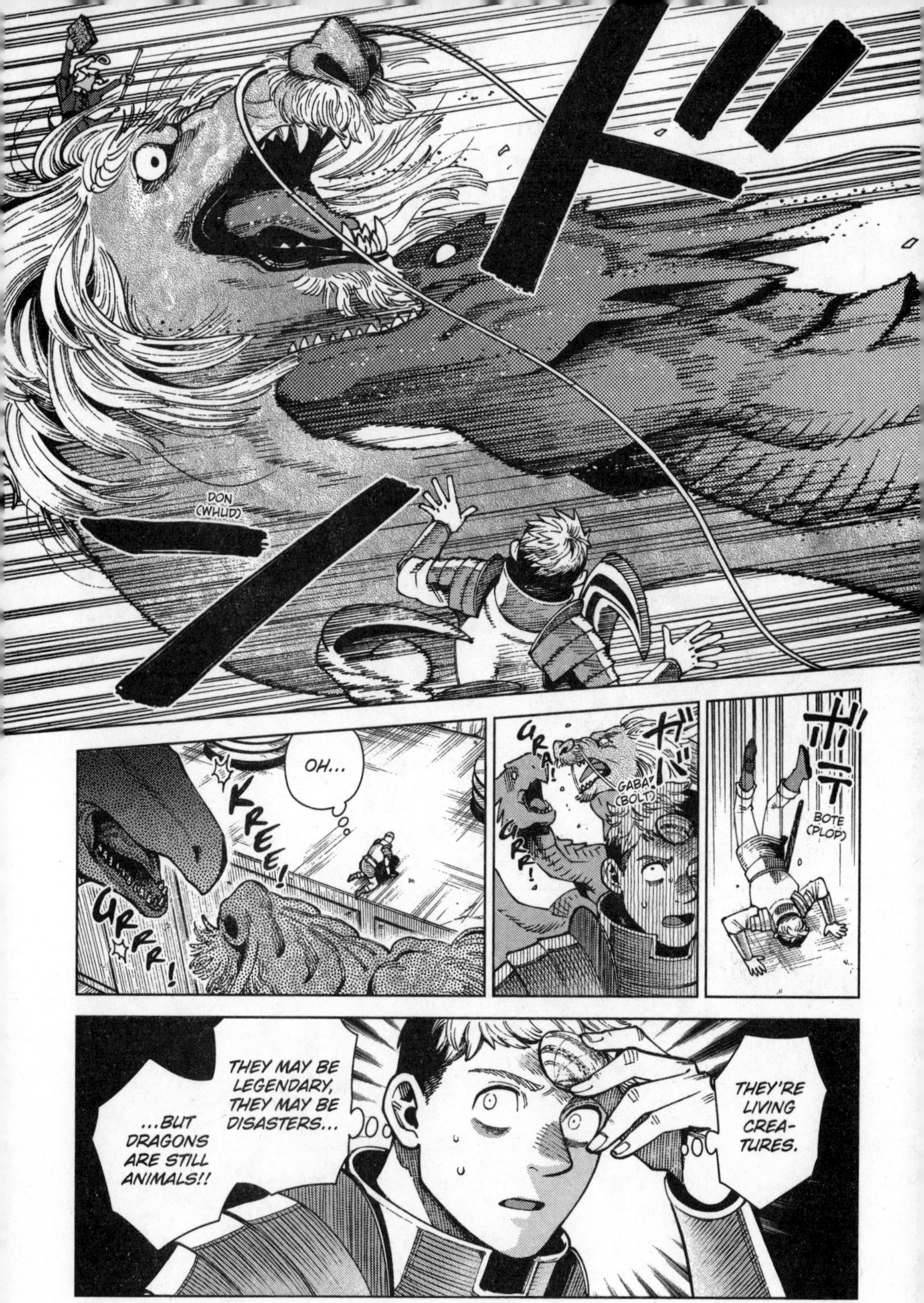
DON (WHUD)
BOTE (PLOP)
URAA!
GABA! (BOLT)
MURR!
OH...
KREEE!
URRR!
THEY'RE LIVING CREA-TURES.
THEY MAY BE LEGENDARY, THEY MAY BE DISASTERS...
...BUT DRAGONS ARE STILL ANIMALS!!

TRANSLATION NOTES

Page 5
Confit is a cooking method where food is cooked in grease, oil, or sugar water at a lower temperature and for a longer time than deep-frying would require.

Page 214
Ruibe is an Ainu dish made of raw seafood that's frozen outdoors, sliced like sashimi, and served with water peppers.

Page 217
Nerve-clipping is a method used to make caught fish taste fresher longer by destroying their brain and spinal cord soon after (or even before) death, which delays the onset of rigor mortis.

Page 223
Brood patches are spots of bare skin that develop on the belly of the females of most bird species during the nesting season. Feathers prevent the eggs from staying warm enough, so they are temporarily shed or plucked out by the birds to allow the skin to warm the eggs directly.

To be continued...

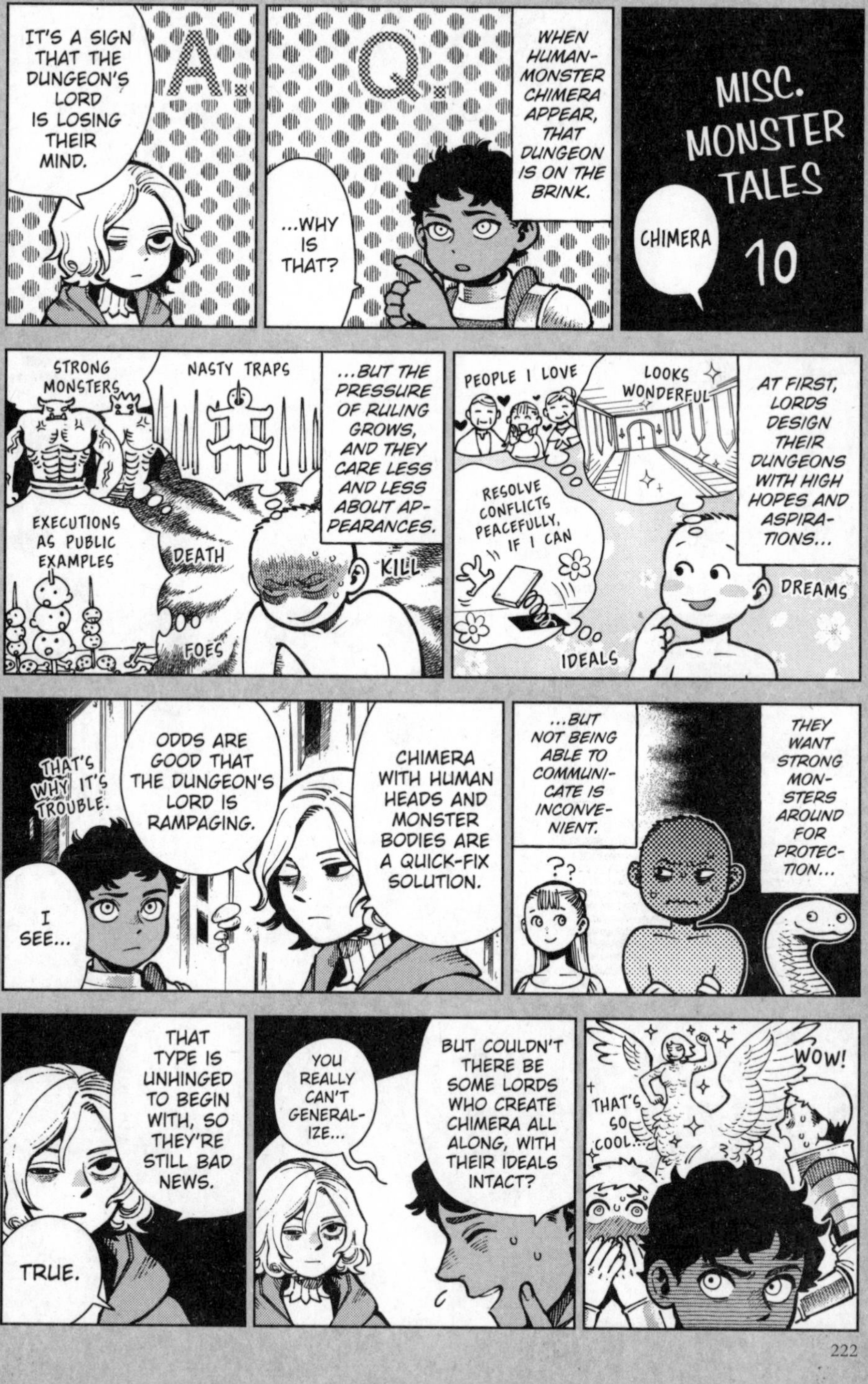
MISC. MONSTER TALES 10
CHIMERA
WHEN HUMAN-MONSTER CHIMERA APPEAR, THAT DUNGEON IS ON THE BRINK.
Q.
...WHY IS THAT?
A.
IT'S A SIGN THAT THE DUNGEON'S LORD IS LOSING THEIR MIND.
AT FIRST, LORDS DESIGN THEIR DUNGEONS WITH HIGH HOPES AND ASPIRATIONS...
PEOPLE I LOVE
LOOKS WONDERFUL
RESOLVE CONFLICTS PEACEFULLY, IF I CAN
DREAMS
IDEALS
...BUT THE PRESSURE OF RULING GROWS, AND THEY CARE LESS AND LESS ABOUT APPEARANCES.
NASTY TRAPS
STRONG MONSTERS
EXECUTIONS AS PUBLIC EXAMPLES
DEATH
KILL
FOES
THEY WANT STRONG MONSTERS AROUND FOR PROTECTION...
...BUT NOT BEING ABLE TO COMMUNICATE IS INCONVENIENT.
??
CHIMERA WITH HUMAN HEADS AND MONSTER BODIES ARE A QUICK-FIX SOLUTION.
ODDS ARE GOOD THAT THE DUNGEON'S LORD IS RAMPAGING.
THAT'S WHY IT'S TROUBLE.
I SEE...
WOW!
THAT'S SO COOL...
BUT COULDN'T THERE BE SOME LORDS WHO CREATE CHIMERA ALL ALONG, WITH THEIR IDEALS INTACT?
YOU REALLY CAN'T GENERALIZE...
THAT TYPE IS UNHINGED TO BEGIN WITH, SO THEY'RE STILL BAD NEWS.
TRUE.

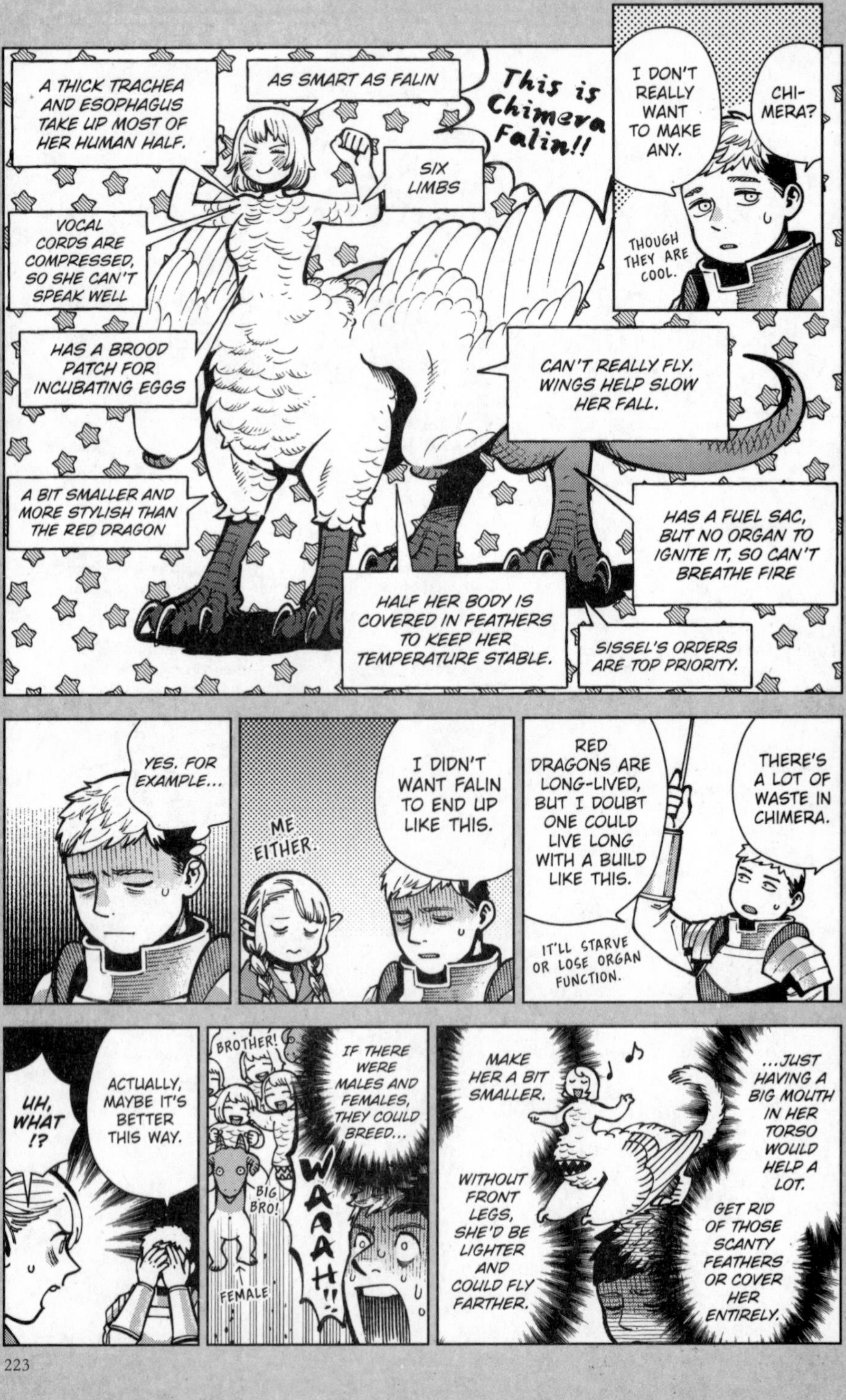

CHI-MERA?
I DON'T REALLY WANT TO MAKE ANY.
THOUGH THEY ARE COOL.
This is Chimera Falin!!
AS SMART AS FALIN
A THICK TRACHEA AND ESOPHAGUS TAKE UP MOST OF HER HUMAN HALF.
SIX LIMBS
VOCAL CORDS ARE COMPRESSED, SO SHE CAN'T SPEAK WELL
HAS A BROOD PATCH FOR INCUBATING EGGS
CAN'T REALLY FLY. WINGS HELP SLOW HER FALL.
A BIT SMALLER AND MORE STYLISH THAN THE RED DRAGON
HAS A FUEL SAC, BUT NO ORGAN TO IGNITE IT, SO CAN'T BREATHE FIRE
HALF HER BODY IS COVERED IN FEATHERS TO KEEP HER TEMPERATURE STABLE.
SISSEL'S ORDERS ARE TOP PRIORITY.
THERE'S A LOT OF WASTE IN CHIMERA.
RED DRAGONS ARE LONG-LIVED, BUT I DOUBT ONE COULD LIVE LONG WITH A BUILD LIKE THIS.
IT'LL STARVE OR LOSE ORGAN FUNCTION.
I DIDN'T WANT FALIN TO END UP LIKE THIS.
ME EITHER.
YES. FOR EXAMPLE...
...JUST HAVING A BIG MOUTH IN HER TORSO WOULD HELP A LOT.
MAKE HER A BIT SMALLER.
GET RID OF THOSE SCANTY FEATHERS OR COVER HER ENTIRELY.
WITHOUT FRONT LEGS, SHE'D BE LIGHTER AND COULD FLY FARTHER.
IF THERE WERE MALES AND FEMALES, THEY COULD BREED...
BROTHER!
BIG BRO!
WAAAH!!
FEMALE
ACTUALLY, MAYBE IT'S BETTER THIS WAY.
UH, WHAT!?

10

DELICIOUS IN DUNGEON

RYOKO KUI

Translation: Taylor Engel   Lettering: Abigail Blackman

DUNGEON MESHI Volume 10 ©Ryoko Kui 2021
First published in Japan in 2021 by KADOKAWA CORPORATION, Tokyo. English translation rights arranged with KADOKAWA CORPORATION, Tokyo through TUTTLE-MORI AGENCY, INC., Tokyo.

English translation © 2022 by Yen Press, LLC

Yen Press
150 West 30th Street, 19th Floor
New York, NY 10001

Visit us at yenpress.com
facebook.com/yenpress
twitter.com/yenpress
yenpress.tumblr.com
instagram.com/yenpress

First Yen Press Edition: February 2022

Yen Press is an imprint of Yen Press, LLC.
The Yen Press name and logo are trademarks of Yen Press, LLC.

Library of Congress Control Number: 2017932141

ISBNs: 978-1-9753-3558-8 (paperback)
          978-1-9753-3559-5 (ebook)

10 9 8 7 6 5 4 3 2 1

WOR

Printed in the United States of America